ONE TITTLE SHALL IN NO WISE PASS:

Destroying the Scholarly Myth
that God Did Not Inspire
the Vowels of the Old Testament

By Dr. Chester W. Kulus

Copyright ©2009 by Chester W. Kulus
All rights reserved
Printed in the United States of America

Library of Congress Control Number: 200690737
REL006410: Religion: Biblical Reference – Language Study
REL006210: Religion: Biblical Studies – Old Testament
REL006270 Religion: Bibles – Hebrew

ISBN 978-0-9820608-7-2

Address all inquiries to:
THE OLD PATHS PUBLICATIONS, Inc.
142 Gold Flume Way
Cleveland, Georgia, U.S.A.

Web: www.theoldpathspublications.com
E-mail: TOP@theoldpathspublications.com

Emmanuel Baptist Theological Press
296 New Britain Avenue
Newington, Connecticut 06111

1.0

About the cover: The background of the cover is the pointed and accented Hebrew Text from Jeremiah 36:1-7, wherein God told Jeremiah to write the words that He had spoken.

TO THE READER

I thank you for purchasing this book. It is my desire that it will aid in your understanding of God's Words. If you should find any typographical errors, I would appreciate it if you would bring them to my attention.

This book sets forth the complete reliability and trustworthiness of the Words of God. The Bible is so trustworthy that you can trust your soul's destiny to what the Scriptures teach. Dear Reader, have you trusted what the Bible teaches about salvation? Would you please consider the following points from the Word of God?

1. The Bible says, "For all have sinned, and come short of the glory of God" (Romans 3:23). According to the Word of God, you have sinned.

2. The Bible says, "For the wages of sin *is* death" (Romans 6:23a). Your sin results in death: physical death, spiritual death, and the second death. Concerning the second death, the Bible says, "And death and hell were cast into the lake of fire. This is the second death. And whosoever was not found written in the book of life was cast into the lake of fire" (Revelation 20:14,15). Your sin will ultimately take you to the lake of fire.

3. The Bible says, "But God commendeth his love toward us, in that, while we were yet sinners, Christ died for us" (Romans 5:8). Jesus died for your sins. As He died on the cross, Jesus shed His blood. He was then buried. And on the third day, He rose again. He is the only One ever to have done these things; therefore, He is the only One Who can save you. The Bible says of Jesus, "Neither is there salvation in any other: for there is none other name under heaven given among men, whereby we must be saved" (Acts 4:12).

4. The Bible says, "For by grace are ye saved through faith; and that not of yourselves: *it is* the gift of God: not of works, lest any man should boast" (Ephesians 2:8,9). You cannot possibly save yourself. No amount of good works, sacraments, or prayers to Mary will save your lost soul from hell and the second death. Only Jesus can save you. You must put all of your faith and trust in Him.

5. The Bible says, "Repent ye therefore, and be converted, that your sins may be blotted out" (Acts 3:19a). Would you repent and receive Christ as your Saviour? The Bible says, "For whosoever shall call upon the name of the Lord shall be saved" (Romans 10:13). Pray to Him and ask Him to save you.

If you have received Christ as your Saviour or would like to find out more about this all-important decision, please contact me.

Chet Kulus
873 NH Rt 4A
Enfield, NH 03748
chetkulus@netzero.net
January, 2009

ACKNOWLEDGEMENTS

I thank various ones who assisted in this project. First, I thank the Lord Jesus Christ for (1) saving me; (2) giving me the Bible, a wonderful Book which captivates my mind; and (3) giving me good health over the bulk of this work. "Blessing, and glory, and wisdom, and thanksgiving, and honour, and power, and might, *be* unto our God for ever and ever. Amen" (Revelation 7:12).

I thank both Pastor Richard Anderson and Dr. Thomas Strouse for encouraging me in this project. Both of these men also thoroughly proofread the text when it was in its dissertation format and provided valuable insights on its content. Also, I thank Calvary Independent Baptist Church in Lebanon, NH for their financial and spiritual support during this endeavor. Furthermore, I thank the Calvary Independent Baptist Churches of Tilton and Plymouth, NH for their encouragement and enthusiasm in getting this book into print.

And I thank various others: (1) David Bohn for his moral and financial support for this work; (2) Tom Kennedy for the use of some of his books as well as for gathering information from the internet; (3) Marjorie Carr and the rest of the staff at the Enfield Public Library for obtaining books through inter-library loan; (4) Dartmouth College Rauner Rare Book Collection for the use of *A New Greek and English and English and Greek Lexicon with An Appendix, Explanatory of Scientific Terms, &c.* by George Dunbar and *The Greek Lexicon of Schrevelius Translated into English with Many Additions* by Schrevelius; (5) Caspari Library of the University of Pennsylvania for the use of *Thesaurus Grammaticus Linguae Sanctae Bebraeae* by John Buxtorf; (6) Dr. Donald Waite for taking time out of his busy schedule to consult with me on several matters; (7) my wife, Nancy, for her prayers and support; (8) my son, Chester Haddon Kulus, for his work on the cover; (9) Mike Rucker for proofreading the entire document, as well as assisting on computer matters; and (10) those past and present who have defended or are defending the inspiration of the vowels of the Traditional Hebrew Old Testament Text.

TABLE OF CONTENTS

TO THE READER IV

ACKNOWLEDGEMENTS VI

TABLE OF CONTENTS VIII

CHAPTER ONE - INTRODUCTION 1
  PRELIMINARY 1
    What Is a Tittle? 1
    Why Write on the Tittle? 2
    Do Not Old Testament Words Have Vowels? 6
    Who Denies that Old Testament Words Have Vowels and Why Do They Deny It? 9
  PROBLEM 11
    Autographa Position 13
      The Position 13
      The Proponents 13
        Simon ben-Jochai or Moses de Leon – 120 AD or 13th century 14
        Levi ben-Joseph – 11th century or earlier 16
        Moses the Punctuator – 13th century and 1524-1525 17
        David Kimḥi – 13th century and 1540, 1545, 1550 20
        Johannes Isaac Levita – 1559 20
        Antoine Rudolphe Chevalier – 1560 21
        Azariah De' Rossi – 1574-1575 22
        William Fulke – 1583 23
        Guilielmus Eyrius – 1607 24
        Johannes Buxtorf, Sr. – 1609 25
        Valentin Schindler – 1612 26
        Amandus Polanus Von Polandsdorf – 1617 26
        Johannes Buxtorf, Sr. – 1620 27
        John Weemes – 1623 and 1630 28
        John Lightfoot – 1629 29
        Johannes Buxtorf, Jr. – 1648 30
        Gisbert Voetius – 1648–1699 30
        James Ussher – 1652 31
        John Owen – 1659 32

>   Matthias Wasmuth – 1664, 1669 32
>   Joseph Cooper – 1673 33
>   Formula Consensus Helvetica – 1675 33
>   Francois Turretin - 1696 34
>   Samuel Clark –1698, 1699 35
>   Johann Gottlob Carpzov – 1721, 1723 36
>   Pierre Guarin – 1724 36
>   Peter Whitfield - 1748 37
>   John Gill – 1767 37
>   James Robertson – 1770 39
>   Adam Benedict Spitzner – 1791 41
>   John Moncrieff - 1833 41
>   George Sayles Bishop - 1919 42
>   Kent Brandenburg – 2003 43
>   The Author – 2003 43
>   Gary Webb – 2003 43
>   Thomas Strouse – 2005 44
>   Various Others 45
>   Conclusion 46
>   The Problems 47
>   Historical Problems 47
>   Difficulty in Writing Points 48
>   Spelling Variations between the Hebrew and Other Languages 48
>   Unpointed Documents 51
>   Newspapers 51
>   Dead Sea Scrolls 52
>   Synagogue Scrolls 53
>   Other Languages and Inscriptions 53
>   Conclusion 54
>   Supposed Silence about the Points 54
>   Story about Joab 56
>   Vowel Point Names Are not in the Hebrew Language 57
>   Accents 58
>   Kethib / Keri 60
>   Matres Lectionis 61
>   Biblical Problems 63
>   Spelling of David's Name 63
>   New Testament Spelling of Old Testament Names 65
>   Matthew 5:18 69
>   Acts 15:17 69
>   Hebrews 11:21 70
>   Consonants with No Vowels 72
>   Conclusion 74
>   Summary 75
> *Accommodation Position* 75
>   The Position 76
>   The Proponents 77
>   Elias Levita – 1538 77

John Calvin – 1550 78
Louis Cappellus – 1624 79
Brian Walton – 1657 and 1659 80
Homer A. Kent – 1972 81
Randy Jaeggli and the Coalition – 1998 82
Larry Oats – 2003 83
David Sorenson – 2004 84
The Problems... 85
  Relying on Oral Tradition... 85
  Adding to the Words of God.. 86
  Neglecting Written Words 87
    Genesis 22:16.. 88
    Exodus 24:4 88
    Exodus 34:27 89
    Deuteronomy 11:18-20 89
    Deuteronomy 27:8.. 89
    Judges 12:6 90
    Nehemiah 8:8.. 90
    Jeremiah 36:1,2 90
    Habakkuk 2:2.. 90
    Matthew 22:31 90
    I Corinthians 9:10... 91
    II Timothy 3:16,17 91
    II Peter 1:21 91
    Summary 92
  Conclusion.. 92
Summary.. 92
Non-Authoritative Position... 93
  The Position.. 93
  The Proponents... 94
    Natronai II ben-Hilai – 9th Century... 94
    Louis Cappellus – 1650 94
    Albert Barnes – 1832... 96
    Most Modern-Day Scholars 96
  The Problems.. 97
    Psalm 12:6,7 97
    Psalm 19:7 97
    Psalm 93:5 98
    Psalm 111:7 98
    Psalm 119:89 98
    Psalm 119:105 98
    Psalm 119:138 98
    Psalm 119:152 99
    Psalm 119:160 99
    Psalm 138:2 99
    Proverbs 6:23 99
    Proverbs 22:20,21 100
    Isaiah 30:8 100

Isaiah 40:8	100
Matthew 4:4	100
Matthew 24:35	100
Luke 16:17	101
John 10:35	101
Acts 7:38	101
Romans 9:29	101
II Timothy 3:16,17	102
I Peter 1:23-25	102
II Peter 1:19	102
II Peter 3:2	102
Conclusion	103
Summary	103
PREVIEW	104

CHAPTER TWO – THE BIBLE IS THE ONLY AUTHORITY ... 113

DELINEATION OF THE DOCTRINE ... 115
Scripture Is the Authority for Salvation ... *115*
    Romans 10:17 ... 115
    II Timothy 3:15 ... 116
    I Peter 1:23-25 ... 117
    Conclusion ... 118
Scripture Is the Authority for Judging ... *118*
    Genesis 2:17 ... 118
    Exodus 5:1 ... 119
    Leviticus 10:1,2 ... 120
    Deuteronomy 4:1; 7:11; 27:26 ... 120
    I Samuel 15:3,22 ... 121
    Isaiah 8:20 ... 121
    John 5:39 ... 122
    John 12:48 ... 123
    Acts 17:11 ... 123
    Hebrews 8:5 ... 124
    Saith the Lord ... 125
    Conclusion ... 126
Scripture Is the Authority for Local Churches ... *127*
    New Testament Scripture Is for Local Churches ... 127
        Matthew 28:20 ... 128
        I Corinthians 14:37 ... 129
        I Timothy 3:14,15 ... 130
        II Peter 3:2 ... 131
        Jude 3 ... 132
        Conclusion ... 133
    Old Testament Scripture Is for Local Churches ... 134
        Acts 7:38 ... 134
        Romans 15:4 ... 135
        I Corinthians 10:11 ... 135

- Conclusion ... 136
- All of Word of God Is for Local Churches ... 136
  - II Timothy 3:16,17 ... 137
  - II Timothy 4:2 ... 137
  - Conclusion ... 138
- Local Churches Must Reject False Authorities ... 138
  - Colossians 2:8 ... 139
  - Titus 1:14 ... 141
  - Conclusion ... 143
- Summary ... 143

Scripture Is the Authority for Jesus' Life ... *143*
- Positively ... 144
  - Psalm 138:2 ... 144
  - Matthew 2:23 ... 144
  - Matthew 4:4,7,10 ... 145
  - Matthew 4:12-15 ... 146
  - Matthew 5:17 ... 146
  - Matthew 8:16,17 ... 146
  - Matthew 12:15-21 ... 147
  - Matthew 13:34,35 ... 147
  - Matthew 21:1-5 ... 147
  - Matthew 26:53,54 ... 148
  - Luke 22:37 ... 148
  - Luke 24:44 ... 149
  - John 13:18 ... 149
  - John 15:25 ... 150
  - John 19:28 ... 150
  - Hebrews 10:7 ... 150
  - Conclusion ... 151
- Negatively ... 151
  - Matthew 12:1-8 (Mark 2:23-28; Luke 6:1-5) ... 152
  - Matthew 12:9-13 (Mark 3:1-6; Luke 6:6-11) ... 154
  - Matthew 15:1-6 (Mark 7:1-9) ... 156
  - Luke 11:37,38 ... 158
  - Luke 13:10-17 ... 158
  - Luke 14:1-6 ... 159
  - John 5:5-12,16,18; 7:22,23 ... 159
  - John 9:14-16 ... 160
  - Conclusion ... 161

Scripture Is the Authority for All of Faith and Practice ... *162*
- Scripture ... 162
- Inspiration ... 163
- Profitable ... 163
- Purpose ... 165
- Conclusion ... 166

Summary ... *166*

DEVIATION FROM THE DOCTRINE ... 169
In Non-Baptist Groups ... *169*

- Eastern Orthodox ... 169
- Catholics ... 170
- Lutherans ... 171
- Others ... 171
- Conclusion ... 171
- *Amongst Fundamentalist Baptists* ... *172*
  - In the Matter of Preservation ... 172
  - In the Matter of the Text ... 174
  - In the Matter of the Vowel Points ... 178
    - Proponents ... 178
    - Problems ... 179
      - Reliance on Extra-Biblical Authority ... 179
      - Reliance on Oral Tradition ... 180
      - Reliance on Additions to the Bible ... 181
      - Reliance on Fables ... 182
    - Conclusion ... 183
- *Summary* ... *183*
- CONCLUSION ... 184

CHAPTER THREE – UNCERTAINTY ... **187**

- THE COMMENTS OF THE COMMENTATORS ... 189
  - *Genesis 10:6* ... *189*
  - *Genesis 47:31* ... *190*
  - *Genesis 49:10* ... *190*
  - *Exodus 2:25* ... *191*
  - *Leviticus 24:11* ... *191*
  - *Deuteronomy 33:27* ... *191*
  - *Joshua 4:24* ... *192*
  - *I Samuel 1:7* ... *192*
  - *I Samuel 18:11* ... *193*
  - *I Samuel 20:14,15* ... *193*
  - *I Samuel 20:17* ... *193*
  - *II Samuel 24:9* ... *194*
  - *I Kings 13:12* ... *194*
  - *I Kings 17:1* ... *195*
  - *I Kings 17:4* ... *195*
  - *I Kings 20:29* ... *196*
  - *I Kings 20:30* ... *197*
  - *I Chronicles 4:10* ... *197*
  - *I Chronicles 7:4* ... *197*
  - *II Chronicles 17:14-18* ... *198*
  - *Ezra 8:26* ... *198*
  - *Job 3:5* ... *198*
  - *Job 5:15* ... *199*
  - *Job 6:18* ... *200*

Job 15:23	200
Job 21:23	200
Job 21:24	200
Job 24:12	201
Job 27:19	201
Job 31:18	202
Job 36:33	202
Job 37:23	202
Job 39:16	202
Psalm 2:9	203
Psalm 7:11	203
Psalm 29:9	204
Psalm 33:7	204
Psalm 42:2	204
Psalm 52:5	204
Psalm 58:1	205
Psalm 59:10	205
Psalm 60:8	205
Psalm 69:22	206
Psalm 109:17	206
Psalm 110:3	206
Psalm 119:118	207
Psalm 147:17	207
Proverbs 1:7	207
Proverbs 6:24	208
Proverbs 10:4	208
Proverbs 11:23	208
Proverbs 12:19	208
Proverbs 14:1	208
Proverbs 21:4	209
Proverbs 23:7	209
Proverbs 25:27	209
Proverbs 26:23	209
Proverbs 29:14	210
Proverbs 30:1	210
Proverbs 30:1 & 31:1	210
Ecclesiastes 3:21	211
Song of Solomon 1:2	211
Song of Solomon 7:9	212
Isaiah 1:2	212
Isaiah 1:8	212
Isaiah 16:4	212
Isaiah 19:10	213

Isaiah 21:13 .... *213*
Isaiah 27:7 .... *214*
Isaiah 30:8 .... *214*
Isaiah 40:6 .... *214*
Isaiah 62:5 .... *215*
Jeremiah 2:16 .... *216*
Jeremiah 8:13 .... *216*
Jeremiah 10:18 .... *216*
Jeremiah 15:19 .... *216*
Jeremiah 23:17 .... *217*
Jeremiah 25:24 .... *217*
Jeremiah 48:4 .... *217*
Jeremiah 48:15 .... *218*
Jeremiah 48:18 .... *218*
Jeremiah 49:1 .... *219*
Jeremiah 50:38 .... *219*
Jeremiah 51:3 .... *219*
Ezekiel 8:2 .... *220*
Ezekiel 16:30 .... *220*
Ezekiel 23:4 .... *220*
Ezekiel 31:14 .... *220*
Ezekiel 34:3 .... *221*
Ezekiel 36:5 .... *221*
Ezekiel 39:26 .... *222*
Daniel 7:4 .... *222*
Daniel 9:27 .... *222*
Daniel 11:6 .... *223*
Hosea 13:7 .... *223*
Joel 1:18,19 .... *224*
Obadiah 3 .... *224*
Micah 2:7 .... *224*
Micah 6:9 .... *224*
Micah 6:11 .... *225*
Nahum 3:8 .... *225*
Habakkuk 1:8 .... *225*
Zephaniah 3:8 .... *226*
Haggai 1:11 .... *226*
Zechariah 9:8 .... *226*
Malachi 2:3 .... *226*
Conclusion *227*
THE COMMENTS OF THE AUTHOR *228*
Uncertainty *228*
Ambiguity *229*

- *Malignancy* 229
  - Permeates 230
  - Perpetuates 230
    - To Other Verses 230
      - LORD 230
      - Thousand 231
      - Milk or Fat 232
      - Summary 233
    - To Other Verbs 233
    - To Consonants 237
    - To Translations 238
  - Summary 238
- *Rationalism* 239
  - Concerning Miracles 239
  - Concerning Numbers 240
  - Concerning Grammar 240
  - Summary 241
- *Unbelief* 242
- *Summary* 242
- CONCLUSION 243

CHAPTER FOUR – BIBLICAL CONSIDERATIONS 245

- OLD TESTAMENT VERSES 246
  - *Exodus 4:22* 246
  - *Exodus 24:4* 247
  - *Exodus 34:1* 249
  - *Exodus 34:27* 249
  - *Deuteronomy 6:6-9; 11:18,19; & 30:13,14* 249
  - *Deuteronomy 27:8* 250
  - *Deuteronomy 31:24* 251
  - *Joshua 1:8* 251
  - *Judges 12:6* 252
  - *Nehemiah 8:8* 255
  - *Psalm 12:6,7* 255
  - *Psalm 19:7* 256
  - *Psalm 93:5* 259
  - *Psalm 111:7* 259
  - *Psalm 119:86* 260
  - *Psalm 119:89* 260
    - Thy Word 261
    - Is Settled 261
    - For Ever 262
    - In Heaven 262
      - Only in Heaven 262
      - On Earth Also 263

Conclusion	265
Psalm 119:105	*265*
Psalm 119:138	*266*
Psalm 119:152	*267*
Psalm 119:160	*268*
Psalm 138:2	*269*
Thou Hast Magnified	270
Thy Word	271
Above	271
All	271
Thy Name	272
Conclusion	273
Proverbs 22:20,21	*274*
Isaiah 30:8	*275*
Isaiah 40:8	*277*
Isaiah 59:21	*277*
Jeremiah 30:2	*278*
Jeremiah 36:1-4,6	*278*
Habakkuk 2:2	*279*
Summary	*279*
NEW TESTAMENT VERSES	280
Matthew 4:4	*280*
Matthew 22:31	*281*
Matthew 24:35	*285*
John 10:35	*288*
Acts 7:38	*289*
II Timothy 3:16,17	*290*
Hebrews 4:12	*291*
I Peter 1:23	*291*
II Peter 1:19	*292*
II Peter 1:21	*295*
Summary	*295*
NEW TESTAMENT WORDS	296
Gill's Illustrations	*296*
Eli, Eli	297
Names of Persons	298
Dagesh Forte	301
Dagesh Lene	305
Pathach Genubah	306
Strouse's Illustration	*306*
Summary	*307*
CONCLUSION	308
CHAPTER FIVE – ONE TITTLE	**310**

LEXICAL CONSIDERATIONS 310
   Pasor – 1621 .... *310*
   Schrevelius – 1812 .... *311*
   Donnegan - 1837 .... *312*
   Fradersdorff – 1860 .... *312*
   Thayer – 1901 .... *313*
   Arndt and Gingrich – 1979 .... *314*
   Perschbacher – 1990 .... *315*
   Conclusion *316*
CONTEXTUAL CONSIDERATIONS 317
   One Jot or One Tittle *317*
      Jot Refers to Consonants 318
      Tittle Refers to Non-Consonants 319
      Various Commentators 320
         Piscator 321
         Broughton 321
         Prideaux 321
         Lightfoot 322
         Owen 322
         Gill 322
         Whitfield 322
         Bengel 323
         Van Doren 323
         Yeager 324
         Franklin 324
      Summary 325
   Till All Be Fulfilled *326*
   One of These Least Commandments *328*
   Conclusion *330*
ETYMOLOGICAL CONSIDERATIONS 330
   Ch in Hebrew Equal to K in Greek *333*
   I in Hebrew Equal to E in Greek *335*
   R in Hebrew Equal to R in Greek *336*
   E in Hebrew Equal to Ai in Greek *336*
   Q in Hebrew Equal to A in Greek *336*
   Conclusion *338*
SCRIPTURAL CONSIDERATIONS 339
TRANSLATIONAL CONSIDERATIONS 341
   Tyndale – 1525 .... *341*
   Polyglot Testament – 1600 .... *342*
   Revised Standard Version – 1952 .... *342*
   New International Version – 1984 .... *342*
   English Standard Version – 2001 .... *343*
   Summary *343*
CONCLUSION 343

CHAPTER SIX – FURTHER OBJECTIONS 347

HISTORICAL OBJECTIONS 347
Unpointed Documents 347
Newspapers 348
Dead Sea Scrolls 351
Synagogue Scrolls 354
Other Languages and Inscriptions 359
Summary 361
Story about Joab 361
The Story 361
The Problems 362
Summary 364
Conclusion 365
BIBLICAL OBJECTIONS 365
Consonants without Vowels 366
Method of Conveying This Notation 366
At the Time of the Vision 366
At the Time of Writing 367
Conclusion 368
Purpose of This Notation 368
A Test 368
Punctuation Marks 369
Emphasis 370
Conclusion 371
Vowels without Consonants 372
Lone Vowels 373
Summary 373
CONCLUSION 375

CHAPTER SEVEN – CONCLUSION 377
ARGUMENT SUMMARY 377
EVIDENCE SUMMARY 383

DEFINITIONS AND DELIMITATIONS 394
DEFINITIONS 394
DELIMITATIONS 399

BIBLIOGRAPHY 402
BOOKS 402
ARTICLES, SERMONS, AND VIDEOS 422

BIOGRAPHICAL SKETCH 431

CHAPTER ONE - INTRODUCTION

As the reader picks up this book, a couple of immediate questions may come to his mind such as (1) what is a *tittle*; (2) why write a book about the *tittle*; (3) why is the *tittle* important; (4) why should a person read such a book as this; and more. The next section, subtitled "Preliminary," addresses these questions. The section following, "Problem," details three positions concerning the *tittle* and the problems connected with these positions. The last section of this chapter, "Preview," presents an overview and summary of the entire work.

PRELIMINARY

What Is a Tittle?

As the reader looks at the title of this book, he may be asking himself, "Just what is a *tittle*?" Chapter Five, "One Tittle," gives an in-depth analysis concerning the meaning of *tittle* as it exegetes Matthew 5:18 where Jesus states: "For verily I say unto you, Till heaven and earth pass, one jot or one tittle shall in no wise pass from the law, till all be fulfilled." Lexical, contextual, etymological, Scriptural, and translational considerations demonstrate that *tittle* in Matthew 5:18 refers to the smallest Hebrew vowel point known as *chirek*, which is as small as the dot atop the *i*. The reader should understand that the vowels of Old Testament Hebrew are dots and dashes that writers inserted amongst the consonants. It is for this reason that some refer to these vowels as vowel points.[1] When using the expression *vowel points*, one should not think that these points are somehow not actual vowels. In-

---

[1] For more about vowel points, see "Definition of Terms" in the back of the book.

deed, just as *a, e, i, o, u,* and sometimes *y* are actual vowels in English, so the vowel points are actual vowels in Hebrew and Aramaic.

For a complete treatment on why *tittle* in Matthew 5:18 is the Hebrew vowel point *chirek*, one should consult Chapter Five, but a brief presentation of the argument is fitting here. Lexically, *tittle* can mean a vowel point. Contextually, the word *jot* referring to the least of the Hebrew consonants, adequately guarantees the preservation of all the consonants (see Luke 16:10); therefore, *tittle* need not refer to consonants. Also, the phrase *one jot or one tittle* with the use of the disjunctive conjunction (ἤ *or*) makes it clear that *tittle* is different from the *jot*, which further establishes that *tittle* is referring to something other than consonants or something connected to consonants. Etymologically, the Greek word for *tittle* (κεραία) is a transliteration into Greek of the Hebrew חִירֶק[2] (*chirek*). Scripturally, the Bible teaches the inspiration and preservation of the vowels of the Old Testament (see the rest of this chapter as well as Chapter Four), which teaching is in exact agreement with understanding *tittle* to be a vowel point in Matthew 5:18. Translationally, many translations of the Bible understand the Greek word for *tittle* to be a dot, which describes exactly the *chirek*.

Why Write on the Tittle?

As to why write a book on the *tittle*, this subject is important theologically and practically. The fact that Jesus in two verses spoke of the *tittle* (Matthew 5:18; Luke 16:17) gives theological importance to this subject. These verses are the Words of God and, therefore, are "profitable for doctrine, for reproof, for correction, for instruction in

---

[2] The Hebrew and Greek fonts that the author uses in this work are BWHEBB, BWHEBL [Hebrew]; BWGRKL, BWGRKN, and BWGRKI [Greek] Postscript® Type 1 and TrueTypeT fonts Copyright © 1994-2002 BibleWorks, LLC. All rights reserved. These Biblical Greek and Hebrew fonts are used with permission from BibleWorks, software for Biblical exegesis and research.

righteousness: that the man of God may be perfect, throughly furnished unto all good works" (II Timothy 3:16,17).

Some may think that the subject of the *tittle* is merely an academic one, but this is not true since God's Word speaks of the *tittle* and all of the Words of God are designed to make the man of God throughly furnished unto all good works. In other words, the subject of the *tittle* has a practical importance to one's own spiritual growth. The practicality of this subject, however, reaches far beyond the two verses in which the word *tittle* occurs, for it is a subject that can affect the interpretation and understanding of thousands of Old Testament verses.[3] This may seem like an astounding claim, but a little two-part demonstration will help to prove the point. In the first part of this demonstration, consider the English word *cat*. It has just one vowel. If one were to remove that one vowel and substitute other vowels, then he could make several other words such as *cut, cot, coat, cute, acute, cite, cote,* and possibly more. Now consider the sentence: The girl loved her black cat. If *cat* has no vowels, then the sentence could be that the girl loved her black coat, cot, cote, or some other thing; and in certain contexts, it may be very difficult to determine what should be the exact word.

In the second part of this demonstration, consider some verses in the Bible. Genesis 49:10 in the *King James Version*, an accurate translation of the Traditional Hebrew Text, states: "The sceptre shall not depart from Judah, nor a lawgiver from between his feet, until Shiloh come, and unto him *shall* the gathering of the people *be*." Genesis 49:10 is a Messianic prophecy concerning the Lord Jesus Christ, for Jesus is from the tribe of Judah (Revelation 5:5)[4] and the

---

[3] In Chapter Three the author presents over five thousand (5,000) verses that are affected or infected by tampering with the vowels of the words. These five thousand cases may be just scratching the service.

[4] Leupold indicates that Genesis 49:10 uses the word *until* not in the exclusive sense, but in the inclusive sense "even as it is found in [Genesis] 26:13; 28:15; Ps.

people shall be gathered together unto Him in the Millennial Kingdom (Isaiah 11:1,10). But if one were to adjust the vowels in the word *Shiloh*, then he could dramatically change the teaching of Genesis 49:10 and remove its Messianic nature. Such is what the *English Standard Version* has done, for it reads: "Until tribute comes to him," instead of "until Shiloh comes." The *English Standard Version* removes the clear Messianic nature of Genesis 49:10. According to the *English Standard Version* there is no person named *Shiloh* who came from Judah in Genesis 49:10 and, therefore, the gathering of the people is not to Shiloh but to Judah. How did the *English Standard Version* arrive at its non-Messianic translation? A footnote gives the answer when it states that it arrived at *until tribute comes to him* "by a slight revocalization."[5] *A slight revocalization* means that the translators of the *English Standard Version* changed the Hebrew vowels in Genesis 49:10 to get different words. It should be clear to the reader that if God did not inspire the vowels of the Old Testament, then there would be no way to determine the exact words and teaching of Genesis 49:10, for either rendering fits the context. If it is impossible to determine the exact wording of Genesis 49:10, then how can it be "profitable for doctrine, reproof, correction, and instruction in righteousness" (II Timothy 3:16)? Indeed it could not be. Changing vowels has the result of making the Word of God of none effect (cf. Mark 7:13).

A couple more examples that are Biblical should suffice to prove the importance of the *tittle*. In a familiar verse in Deuteronomy the *King James Version* accurately reads: "The eternal God *is thy* refuge, and underneath *are* the everlasting arms: and he shall thrust out

---

112:8; Ps. 110:1. For if the dominion were to endure only up to a certain point, the word as such would constitute a threat rather than a blessing" (H. C. Leupold, *Exposition of Genesis* (Grand Rapids: Baker Book House, 1942), II:1181). Judah would continue to reign in the Person of Shiloh, therefore, Shiloh is from Judah.

[5] *The Holy Bible, English Standard Version* (Wheaton, IL: Crossway Bibles, a division of Good News Publishers, 2001), 42.

the enemy from before thee; and shall say, Destroy *them*" (Deuteronomy 33:27). The *New Revised Standard Version* through a change of the vowels reads: "He subdues the ancient gods, shatters the forces of old; he drove out the enemy before you, and said, 'Destroy!' "[6] Such a reading completely changes the meaning of the verse. Indeed, the changing of the vowels removes the wonderful personal promise at the beginning of the verse. If God did not inspire the vowels, then how would any one know for sure what Deuteronomy 33:27 should say?

Over in Ecclesiastes 3:21, the *King James Version* accurately states: "Who knoweth the spirit of man that goeth upward, and the spirit of the beast that goeth downward to the earth?" Through a change of the vowels the *New International Version* has: "Who knows if the spirit of man rises upward and if the spirit of the animal goes down into the earth?"; the *New Revised Standard Version* reads: "Who knows whether the human spirit goes upward and the spirit of animals goes downward to the earth?"; and the *English Standard Version* has: "Who knows whether the spirit of man goes upward and the spirit of the beast goes down into the earth?"[7] Does the spirit of man go upward, or does it not? Does the spirit of an animal go downward, or does it not? The *King James Version* makes it clear that the spirit of man does go upward and that the spirit of the beast does go downward; but the other versions are ambiguous here. The point is this: if God did not inspire the vowels, then there is no way of knowing for certain from Ecclesiastes 3:21 whether the spirit of man goes upward and the spirit of the beast downward.

To anyone who loves the Bible, tampering with the Words of God by changing the vowels should be alarming. Jesus said: "Man

---

[6] For more on this change see the discussion concerning the verse in Chapter Three.

[7] For more on this change see the discussion concerning the verse in Chapter Three.

shall not live by bread alone, but by every word that proceedeth out of the mouth of God" (Matthew 4:4). Without every Word of God, a child of God cannot properly live the Christian life. Without inspired vowels, much of the Old Testament is uncertain and one would have to say about many verses in the Old Testament, "Yea, hath God said?" Uncertainty about what God has said is exactly the place in which the devil would want God's Words (cf. Genesis 3:1). On the other hand, with inspired vowels the Old Testament provides a sure, certain, and solid foundation for the believer. Such a foundation is vital to the Christian life for "if the foundations be destroyed, what can the righteous do?" (Psalm 11:3).

Do Not Old Testament Words Have Vowels?

Now, the question may arise: is it not obvious that Old Testament words have vowels? It should be obvious that Old Testament words have vowels, for how could something be a word without vowels? For instance, is *dg* a word? No, but by inserting an *o* between the consonants, one gets the word *dog*. Consonants without vowels are not words. The Bible teaches in many verses that words must have vowels. At this time, may the reader briefly consider Exodus 34:27; Jeremiah 36:1,2; I Corinthians 9:10; and Matthew 4:4.

In Exodus 34:27 the Lord said to Moses: "Write thou these words: for after the tenor of these words I have made a covenant with thee and with Israel." *Tenor* (פִּי masculine singular construct noun from פֶּה) refers to the mouth. Ainsworth, commenting on *tenor of these words*, states that in Hebrew it means *"the mouth of these words*; which the Chaldee expounds, *the speech of these words."*[8] Mouthing

---

[8] Henry Ainsworth, *Annotation upon the Second Book of Moses Called Exodus: wherein, by Conferring the Holy Scriptures, Comparing the Chaldee and Greek Versions, and Other Records of the Hebrewes: Moses His Wordes, Lawes and Ordinances Are Explained* (London: n. p., 1617), comment on Exodus 34:27. There are no page numbers in this edition.

and speaking of words involves the use of vowels to vocalize the words. Exodus 34:27, then, defines these words as something that was mouthed, therefore vocalized, therefore having vowels. Indeed, it is impossible for one to mouth consonants. For example, how would one pronounce *cttl*? If one were to attempt to pronounce it, he would have to insert half-vowels to accomplish the task, but using half-vowels would be cheating since there are no half-vowels amongst the consonants. But what God gave to Moses were mouthed words, not just unpronounceable consonants and God wanted Moses to write (כְּתָב Qal masculine singular imperative from כָּתַב) according to the mouthing or the speaking of His Own Words; therefore, the words Moses wrote must have also had vowels.

Jeremiah 36:1,2 presents the same teaching as Exodus 34:27. Jeremiah 36:1,2 states: "And it came to pass in the fourth year of Je-

---

Tenor of these words occurs in Genesis 43:7 where the sons of Jacob say, "The man asked us straitly of our state, and of our kindred, saying, *Is* your father yet alive? Have ye *another* brother? And we told him according to the tenor of these words," that is, they gave answers suitable to Joseph's "questions, or such as his words required" (Matthew Poole, *A Commentary on the Holy Bible* (McLean, VA: MacDonald Publishing Company, n. d.), I: 96). They "answered him in conformity (עַל פִּי as in Ex. 34:27, etc.) with these words (i.e., with his questions)" (C. F. Keil, *Pentateuch*, vol. 1 in *Commentary on the Old Testament* (Edinburgh: T & T Clark, 1866-91, reprinted Peabody, MA: Hendrikson Publishers, 2001), 231). Though not related in Genesis 42, Joseph specifically asked them about their father and their brother (Genesis 44:19) and phrased his question on at least one occasion according to the exact words of Genesis 43:7. In the brother's answer, they took into account the mouthing of Joseph's words.

In English, *tenor* can mean "the general drift of thought" (F. Sturges Allen, ed., *Webster's New International Dictionary of the English Language* (Springfield, MA: G. & C. Merriam Company, 1923), 2128). However, for anyone to suggest that in the Bible *tenor* means according to the general idea, would be for him to suggest that Moses in Exodus 34:27 only wrote according to the general idea of what God said, which would suggest conceptual inspiration, rather than verbal inspiration – a most dangerous suggestion, indeed. If one desires to limit himself to the English definition of *tenor*, he should choose the legal definition, that is, "an exact copy of a writing, set forth in the words and figures of it. Setting forth a document to its *tenor* necessitates giving an exact copy of it, as distinguished from setting it forth according to its purport and effect" (Ibid.).

hoiakim the son of Josiah king of Judah, *that* this word came unto Jeremiah from the LORD, saying, Take thee a roll of a book, and write therein all the words that I have spoken unto thee against Israel, and against Judah, and against all the nations, from the day I spake unto thee, from the days of Josiah, even unto this day." Here the Lord instructed Jeremiah to write all the words that He had spoken. Again, since the speaking of words involves vocalizing with the use of vowels, and since Jeremiah was to write the spoken Words of the Lord, then the words Jeremiah wrote had to have vowels. Scripture defines the written words as having vowels.

I Corinthians 9:10, referring to a statement in Deuteronomy 25:4, presents the same truth when it states (in part): "Or saith he *it* altogether for our sakes? For our sakes, no doubt, *this* is written." I Corinthians 9:10 teaches that what the Lord said in the Old Testament is the same as what is written in the Old Testament. The Old Testament writers were not merely stenographers using some sort of shorthand notation to convey what the Lord said, but they were like human tape-recorders, so that what they wrote is the same as what God saith. And since speech involves vocalization with the use of vowels, then the written words of the Old Testament must have vowels.

Jesus also defined words as including vowels when He stated: "It is written, Man shall not live by bread alone, but by every word that proceedeth out of the mouth of God" (Matthew 4:4). According To Jesus, every Word of God proceeded out of the mouth of God. Since mouthing of words involves the use of vowels, then the Words of God must also have vowels. And since the Words of God are written, then the written Words of God must also have vowels. From Exodus 34:27; Jeremiah 36:1,2; I Corinthians 9:10; and Matthew 4:4 it is clear that according to Scripture the words of the Bible have vowels. These are not the only verses that teach that Bible words have vowels. In subsequent sections of this chapter and in Chapter Four this book presents many other verses that substantiates this view.

Who Denies that Old Testament Words Have Vowels and Why Do They Deny It?

It should be clear that Old Testament words have vowels, but are there those who think that Old Testament Hebrew as originally given by God had no vowels and, if so, why would they think such a thing? Yes, some think that when God inspired the Old Testament that He did so without the use of vowels. The next sections of this chapter detail some of those who think such a thing. As to why some would believe that there are no inspired vowels in the Hebrew Old Testament, a multitude of reasons surface. Subsequent sections of this chapter as well as Chapter Six present these reasons. Many of the reasons for thinking that God did not give inspired vowels involve a person walking by sight in the teachings of the scholars, instead of walking by faith in God's promises. One of God's promises concerning Hebrew vowels is Luke 16:17 where Jesus declares: "And it is easier for heaven and earth to pass, than one tittle of the law to fail." The middle part of Luke 16:17 speaks of the *tittle*. The writer, basing his position upon the sound principles of exegesis, understands *tittle* to refer to the smallest vowel point of the Hebrew Old Testament, the *chirek*, which is as small as the dot atop the *i* (see Chapter Five for more information). The *chirek* is the smallest little bit of the Hebrew Old Testament. Luke 16:17 presents powerful teaching concerning the Old Testament.

The first part of Luke 16:17 states, "It is easier for heaven and earth to pass." Lenski states that *pass* refers to heaven and earth passing "away in one sweep (παρελθεῖν, aorist)."[9] Only the power of God Almighty will bring about the passing away of heaven and earth in one sweep (Isaiah 65:17). No one else is able to make heaven and earth pass away in one sweep. Now since it is easier for heaven and earth to

---

[9] R. C. H. Lenski, *The Interpretation of St. Luke's Gospel* (Minneapolis: Augsburg Publishing House, 1963), 841.

pass, than for one tittle of the law to fail; and since only the power of God can make heaven and earth pass away; and since no one else has such power; then this means that no man, no fallen angel, or even Satan himself can cause a single tittle of the Old Testament to fail. Some believe that over time some things have been lost from the Old Testament, but not according to Jesus. The complete Old Testament will continue to stand in spite of all attacks or mishandlings from created beings!

The last part of Luke 16:17 uses the word *fail*. *Fail*, πεσεῖν, is a second aorist active infinitive from πίπτω. Here the Bible uses it metaphorically, "meaning to fall to the ground, to fail, become void."[10] In Luke 16:17, Jesus is, therefore, teaching that no human or demonic power is able to cause even the smallest bit of the Hebrew Old Testament to fail. If all anti-God power were concentrated on one small vowel, that is, on one small *chirek* or dot, it would be impossible for that power to cause that one small vowel point to fail! What a wonderful promise this is!

The promise of Luke 16:17 asserts a couple of truths about the Old Testament. First, Jesus' mentioning of the smallest of the Hebrew vowel points is further evidence that in His day, the words of the Old Testament had vowel points. Second, Jesus' words in Luke 16:17 assert that the entire Old Testament is perfectly preserved, for if God promises that the least aspect of the law will not fail, then the greater aspects will not fail either, for "he that is faithful in that which is least is faithful also in much" (Luke 16:10). Third, since one tittle shall not fail or become void, then Jesus' promise asserts that every tittle of the law is completely authoritative; therefore, one need not wonder if a particular word in the Old Testament is pointed correctly or if the

---

[10] Spiros Zodhiates, "4098. πίπτω" in *The Complete Word Study Bible & Reference CD* [CD-ROM] (Chattanooga, TN: AMG Publishers, 1997).

vowel points are of human origin. And fourth, since one tittle shall not fail, then to repoint or revocalize words in the Old Testament is to fly in the face of Jesus' Words, a very dangerous thing to do (see John 12:48).

For anyone who will believe it, the Words of Jesus in Luke 16:17 settle the matters of the vowel points, the perfect preservation, and the complete authority of the Traditional Hebrew Old Testament text; thereby showing the dangerous futility of trying to correct the Traditional Old Testament Text. If men would simply believe Luke 16:17, then there would be no need for this book. It is because men fail to comprehend and to believe the promise of Jesus that there is a serious problem – a problem that this book addresses.

PROBLEM

Beginning in the Garden of Eden to the present day, the devil has questioned God's Words. In Genesis 3:1 he said, "Yea, hath God said, Ye shall not eat of every tree of the garden?" With this question, Satan cast doubt upon the very Words of God. The Bible mentions others who "corrupt the word of God" (II Corinthians 2:17), handle "the word of God deceitfully" (II Corinthians 4:2), and wrest the Scriptures (II Peter 3:16). Furthermore, the Bible repeatedly warns about not adding to or diminishing from the Words of God (Deuteronomy 4:2; 12:32; Proverbs 30:6; and Revelation 22:18,19), indicating that it is distinctly possible that men would attempt to tamper with the Words of God.

These attacks upon the Words of God have taken various forms through the ages. One such attack, which is the subject of this book, is upon the vowel points of the Hebrew Old Testament text. Did God inspire the vowels? Did Ezra add the vowels to the text? Did the exilic prophets add the vowels? Did scribes after the time of Christ add them? Are the vowel points authoritative? The way in which some answer these questions poses real Biblical problems. In presenting these problems, it is necessary to present three positions that various writers espouse concerning the vowel points and about each position present the problems that arise. The author has grouped writers according to one of three positions: (1) the *autographa* position, that is, that God inspired the points; (2) the accommodation position, that is, that the points were passed down via oral tradition to the Masoretes of the sixth to ninth century after Christ and that these points reflect the correct vocalization of the text; and (3) the non-authoritative position, that is, that the points are merely the invention of men and are of no authority. Just so the reader knows that these positions are not merely arbitrary assessments by the author consider the following statement by Moncrieff in which he, too, categorizes the opinions on the points with the same three positions:

> There are three opinions respecting the Hebrew Vowel-Points. One or other of these have been maintained by men possessing an extensive knowledge of this sacred language.
>
> By one class it has been most strenuously maintained, that these Vowel-Points, as to their forms, names, and pronunciation, are wholly an arbitrary invention of a school of Rabbis, who lived at Tiberias in Palestine, about the beginning of the sixth century of the Christian Era.
>
> The opinion of a second class coincides to a certain extent, with that which has now been now stated. They hold that the Vowel-Points were invented by the Jewish doctors of Tiberias, but they, at the same time, maintain, that they were not intended by these Rabbis to point out any sounds of their own invention, but to fix down in all their variety of application, the vowel sounds which were in constant use in reading the scriptures, when the Hebrew was a living language, and which are understood by this class, to have been accurately preserved, by oral tradition, among the learned men of the Jewish nation, down to the late period in which those learned Rabbis are said to have flourished at Tiberias.
>
> A third opinion is, that since the time of Moses, and, at all events, since the days of Ezra, and the Great Synagogue, there were distinct Vowel-Points, which, if not the same in form, were, at least, signs for

the very same vowel sounds, which these points, now in common use in our Hebrew Bibles, were intended to express.[11]

Autographa Position

In discussing the *autographa* position, this section presents the position itself, the proponents of the position, and some problems that may arise from the position.

The Position

The first position in regard to the vowel points is, what the writer calls, the *autographa* position. The *autographa* position states that God gave the vowel points when He inspired His Words so that the vowel points were inscripturated at the same time as the consonants and are, therefore, part of the *autographa* and are fully authoritative.

The Proponents

The *autographa* position is the position that this book espouses and defends. Over the years, others have also espoused the *autographa* position and this section lists some of them. The reader will notice that the list of proponents is somewhat longer and more complete than the lists of proponents for the other positions. The author desires to give as exhaustive a list as he can so as to aid others in their research and to demonstrate that the *autographa* position is not merely a privately held interpretation. This is not to suggest that the writer arrived at a position by seeing which position has the largest number of proponents and then adopting it as his own. If that were the case, he would not hold the *autographa* view since it is a minority view.[12] The

---

[11] John Moncrieff, *An Essay on the Antiquity and Utility of the Hebrew Vowel-Points* (London: Whittaker, Treacher, and Arnot, 1833), 19,20.

[12] Pick writes: "Modern research and criticism have confirmed the arguments urged by Levita against the antiquity of the present vowel signs" (B. Pick, "The Vowel-Points Controversy in the XIV, XVII, and XVIII Centuries" in *The Princeton*

author has arrived at adopting the *autographa* position because he is convinced that the *autographa* position is the position that the Bible teaches. Indeed, if no one else held to the *autographa* position, but if he were convinced that the Bible teaches the inspiration of the vowel points, then, by God's grace, he would hold it. However, such is not the case with the *autographa* position, for a number of men have espoused and are espousing it, and their writings and insights can be a help to those seeking to better understand what the Word of God teaches on the subject.

Simon ben-Jochai or Moses de Leon – 120 AD or 13th century

This first entry concerns the *Zohar*, a Jewish cabalistic commentary on portions of the Old Testament, a work that argues for the inspiration of the vowel points. John Lightfoot and John Gill[13] believe that R. Simon ben-Jochai is its real author with Gill placing its date at

---

Review 6 (January 1877), 168). McClintock and Strong write that Cappellus believed that the points "were invented by the Jews of Tiberias some six hundred years subsequently to the death of Christ; whereas Buxtorf held them to be coeval with the language. The opinion of Cappellus has since been generally received" ("Cappel (Cappellus), Louis" in *Cyclopedia of Biblical, Theological, and Ecclesiastical Literature*, eds. John McClintock and James Strong (Grand Rapids: Baker Book House, 1981), II:106). Ginsburg notes that Walton's *Prolegomena* and *The Considerator Considered* "decided the battle in England in favour of the anti-vowelists. Henceforth all Biblical critics, with very few exceptions, regarded the points as modern, useless, and of no authority, though Walton himself . . . maintained that they, as a rule, represented the ancient and genuine reading" (Christian D. Ginsburg, *The Massoreth Ha-Massoreth of Elias Levita, Being an Exposition of the Massoretic Notes on the Hebrew Bible, or the Ancient Critical Apparatus of the Old Testament in Hebrew, with an English Translation, and Critical and Explanatory Notes, by Christian D. Ginsburg* (NY: KTAV Publishing House, Inc., 1968), 59). Keil writes, "The violent controversy as to the age of the Hebrew vowel points, set in motion two hundred years ago, was terminated in the second half of [the] last century by the general acknowledgement that they were of comparatively recent origin" (C. F. Keil, *Introduction to the Old Testament*, trans. G. C. M. Douglas (Edinburgh: T & T Clark, 1869, reprinted Peabody, MA: Hendrikson Publishers, Inc, 1991), II:190).

[13] "Zohar" in *Cyclopedia of Biblical, Theological, and Ecclesiastical Literature*, eds. John McClintock and James Strong (Grand Rapids: Baker Book House, 1981), XII:1028.

120 AD.[14] On the other hand, Christian Ginsburg and a host of others believe that "it is not the production of R. Simon, but of the 13th century, by Moses de Leon."[15] It is beyond the scope of this work to settle the exact authorship and date of the *Zohar*, nor are these matters germane to the main argument of this book. The fact remains, however, that the *Zohar* teaches a belief in the inspiration of the vowel points. For instance, the *Zohar* on the Song of Solomon states:

> The vowel-points proceeded from the same Holy Spirit which indited the sacred Scriptures, and that far be the thought to say that the scribes made the points, since even if all the prophets had been as great as Moses, who received the law direct from Sinai, they could not have had the authority to alter the smallest point in a single letter, though it be the most insignificant in the whole Bible.[16]

Elsewhere the *Zohar* declares: " 'The letters are the body and the vowel-points the soul, they move with the motion and stand still with the resting of the vowel-points, just as an army moves after its sovereign.' "[17] These statements from the *Zohar* are clear assertions concerning the importance, inspiration, and antiquity of the vowel points.

---

[14] John Gill, *A Dissertation concerning the Antiquity of the Hebrew Language, Letters, Vowel Points, and Accents* (London: G. Keith, 1767), 212.

[15] "Zohar" in *Cyclopedia*, XII: 1028. Ginsburg presents his own work on establishing the author of the *Zohar* in his book, *The Kabbalah* (London: Longmans, 1865), 85-93. Also, see the article in *Cyclopedia* for a list of reasons for the late date for the *Zohar*.

[16] Christian D. Ginsburg, *The Massoreth Ha-Massoreth of Elias Levita, Being an Exposition of the Massoretic Notes on the Hebrew Bible, or the Ancient Critical Apparatus of the Old Testament in Hebrew, with an English Translation, and Critical and Explanatory Notes, by Christian D. Ginsburg*, in The Library of Biblical Studies, ed. Harry M. Orlinsky (NY:KTAV Publishing House, Inc., 1968), 48. Ginsburg cites the *Zohar* on the Song of Solomon, Amsterdam edition, 57 b.

[17] Ibid. Ginsburg cites i., 15, *b* from the *Zohar*.

Levi ben-Joseph – 11th century or earlier

The author does not have a specific date for Levi ben-Joseph because he knows of no sources that give a specific date. However, in McClintock and Strong's chronological discussion of the debate over vowel points, they place him before an 11th century work. McClintock and Strong state: "Levi ben-Joseph, author of the book, *Semadar*, quotes, in favor of the antiquity of the vowel-points, the passage in Deut. xxvii, 8, 'And thou shalt write upon the stones all the words of this law *very plainly*'."[18] Burnett adds to the discussion of Levi ben-Joseph by saying that the elders having to write the words very plainly implies the use of vowel points, "since, for example, the root שלמה could mean 'wherefore, retribution, Solomon, garment or perfect',"[19] that is, without the vowel points there is the possibility that the Words of God would not be very plain. Elias Levita quotes Joseph:

> If any should ask, Whence do we know that the points and accents were dictates by the mouth of the Omnipotent? The reply is, It is to be found in the Scriptures, for it is written, "And thou shalt write upon the stones all the words of this law *very plainly*" (Deut. xxvii.8).[20]

---

[18] "Vowel-points" in *Cyclopedia*, X:820.

[19] Stephen G. Burnett, *From Christian Hebraism to Jewish Studies Johannes Buxtorf (1564-1629) and Hebrew Learning in the Seventeenth Century* (NY: E. J. Brill, 1996), 213.

[20] Elias Levita, *The Massoreth Ha-Massoreth of Elias Levita, Being an Exposition of the Massoretic Notes on the Hebrew Bible, or the Ancient Critical Apparatus of the Old Testament in Hebrew, with an English Translation, and Critical and Explanatory Notes, by Christian D. Ginsburg*, in *The Library of Biblical Studies*, ed. Harry M. Orlinsky (NY:KTAV Publishing House, Inc., 1968), 122. Though Levita quotes Joseph, one should not assume that Levita is in favor of the inspiration of the vowel points, for, indeed, he is not. See discussion under the accommodation position, which is the next major section.

Moses the Punctuator – 13th century and 1524-1525

Moses the Punctuator was a "Jewish exegetist, [who] lived in London about the middle of the 13th century."[21] He "suggested in his *Treatise on the Vowel Points and Accents* that the vowel points were given on Mount Sinai."[22] McClintock and Strong give the title of this work as *Treatise embodying the rules about the points of the Hebrew Scriptures.*[23] "Excerpts of this treatise, made by Jacob ben-Chayim, were first printed with the Massora in *the Rabbinic Bible* (Venice, 1524-25), and since in all the editions of the Rabbinic Bible."[24] It was in the second appendix in the fourth volume of 1524-1525 Rabbinic Bible.[25] According to McClintock and Strong, "Those who recognize the real importance of the Hebrew vowel-points and accents will find in this unpretentious treatise a useful guide."[26] While McClintock and Strong list several editions of this work,[27] the author failed to find a copy of it when doing a search for it in the World Catalog of Libraries.

Concerning the position of Moses the Punctuator, the author must make a comment. According to Burnett, while Moses the Punctuator advocated that the points were given to Moses on Mount Sinai, yet he believed that they "were forgotten until Ezra revealed them

---

[21] "Moses the Punctuator" in *Cyclopedia*, VI:690.

[22] Burnett, 213, 214.

[23] "Moses the Punctuator" in *Cyclopedia*, VI:690.

[24] Ibid.

[25] Christian D. Ginsburg, "Jacob Ben Chajim Ibn Adonijah" in *Jacob Ben Chajim Ibn Adonijah's Introduction to The Rabbinic Bible, Hebrew and English; with Explanatory Notes*, 2nd edition, in *The Library of Biblical Studies*, ed. Harry M. Orlinsky (NY: KTAV Publishing House, Inc., 1968), 7.

[26] "Moses the Punctuator" in *Cyclopedia*, VI:690.

[27] In addition to the edition published with *the Rabbinic Bible*, McClintock and Strong list an edition by Zebi ben-Menachem (Wilma, 1822) and one by Frensdorf (Hanover, 1847) (Ibid.).

again."[28] Johannes Buxtorf, Sr. and John Owen held similar views (see further). However, the belief that Ezra added the vowels is not the view of this treatise, for Exodus 34:27 speaks of Moses writing God's mouthed words, which would necessitate Moses writing the vowels along with the consonants. Further, Deuteronomy 27:8 teaches that the elders of the Jews were to write the words of the law very plainly, which necessitates the use of vowels so as to avoid confusion, for without the vowels some misunderstanding of the words could occur. If the vowels were present, as Exodus 34:27 and Deuteronomy 27:8 teach, and then later lost and then restored by Ezra, this would have a serious impact on the promises of preservation. For instance, in Psalm 12, which is a Psalm of David and, therefore, predates Ezra by over five hundred years, is this promise: "The words of the LORD *are* pure words: *as* silver tried in a furnace of earth, purified seven times. Thou shalt keep them, O LORD, thou shalt preserve them from this generation for ever" (Psalm 12:6,7[29]). However, what becomes of the prom-

---

[28] Burnett, 214.

[29] The author is aware of the controversy surrounding Psalm 12:6-7 and its application to the perfect preservation of God's Words. He realizes that some believe that both occurrences of *them* in vs. 7 refer to the poor and needy in vs. 5, rather than to *words* in vs. 6. The main argument in favor of *them* referring to *poor* and *needy* is that both of these words are masculine, whereas *words* is feminine. However, it is not out of the ordinary for a masculine pronoun to refer to a feminine noun, especially in the matter of a masculine pronoun referring back to a feminine noun that speaks of the Words of God as Psalm 119:111,129,152, and 167 demonstrate.

In Psalm 119:111, the masculine plural pronoun *them* refers back to *testimonies*, a feminine plural noun. In Psalm 119:129, the masculine plural pronoun *them* attached as a suffix to the verb *keep* refers back to *testimonies*, a feminine plural noun. In Psalm 119:152, the masculine plural suffix pronoun *them* attached to the verb *founded* refers to *testimonies*, a feminine plural noun. In Psalm 119:167, the masculine plural pronoun *them* attached as a suffix to the verb *love* refers to *testimonies*, a feminine plural noun.

In light of the above, the author asserts that both occurrences of *them* in Psalm 12:7 refer to *words* in Psalm 12:6 and that, therefore, the passage teaches the perfect preservation of God's Words. For a more complete treatment of Psalm 12:6,7, see the author's *Those So-Called Errors: Debunking the Liberal, New Evangelical, and Fundamentalist Myth that You Should Not Hear, Receive, and Believe All the Numbers of*

ise in Psalm 12:6-7, if the vowels were originally part of the text and then dropped out? Why, it would seem that God was not able to keep His promise!

Walton seized upon the supposed Ezra origin of the written points as a strong reason for the novelty of the points. Walton writes:

> The most of those that stand for the antiquity of the points, ascribe the first beginning of them to Esdras [Ezra], as Buxtorf and others. Now if the text might be read certainly, and without ambiguity, though without points, from the time of Moses to Esdras [Ezra], why might it not likewise be continued and preserved as well after Esdras [Ezra] his time as it was before?[30]

Walton makes a good observation here. The argument runs thusly: if there were no points before Ezra and people could understand the Bible, then why could not they continue to read it without the points? However, taking into account Deuteronomy 27:8 and other verses (Exodus 4:22; 24:4; 34:27; Deuteronomy 11:18-20; Judges 12:6; Psalm 19:7; 93:5; 111:7; 119:89, 105, 152, 160; 138:2; Proverbs 6:23; 22:20,21; Isaiah 30:8; 40:8; Jeremiah 36:1,2; Habakkuk 2:2)[31], it is evident that the points were not first written by Ezra, but by the writers of Scripture themselves.

Though Moses the Punctuator, Johannes Buxtorf, Sr. (see later), and John Owen (see later), all held to the view that Ezra wrote the points and inserted them in the text; the author, nonetheless, lists these men under the *autographa* position because it seems that they

---

Scripture (Newington, CT: Emmanuel Baptist Theological Press, 2003), 142-145. Also, see Strouse's article "The Permanent Preservation of God's Words" in *Emmanuel Baptist Theological Journal* 2 (Fall/Winter 2006): 27-36.

[30] Brian Walton, *The Considerator Considered: or, a brief view of certain Considerations upon the Biblia Polyglotta, the Prolegomena and Appendix thereof* (London: Roycroft, 1659), 216.

[31] For an exposition on these and other verses and how they prove that God inspired the vowels, see Chapter Four, "Biblical Considerations."

held to the inspiration of the points, which is something that is lacking in the other two positions.

David Kimḥi – 13th century and 1540, 1545, 1550

Kimḥi was "one of the most distinguished Jewish writers of the Middle Ages" and was a "great exponent of Hebrew grammar and lexicography."[32] He was born in 1160 and died about 1240,[33] therefore, his writings date back to the late twelfth or early thirteenth century. According to Burnett, Kimḥi in his book *Miklol* stated: "The vowel points had been given on Mount Sinai."[34] The above dates of 1540, 1545, and 1550 reflect when his work was published at various times and in various places, but as he was born in 1160 and died about 1240,[35] his view existed some three hundred years prior to 1550.

Johannes Isaac Levita – 1559

In 1559, Levita wrote Defensio Veritatis Hebraicae Sacrarum Scripturarum, adversus Libros tres Reveren. D. Wilhelmi Lindani S. T. Doctoris, quos de optimo Scripturas interpretandi genere inscripsit,[36] that is, "The Defense of the Truth of the Sacred Scriptures of the Hebrew, against three Books of the Reverend D. Wilhelmus Lindanus S. T. Doctor, in which he wrote concerning an honest method of interpreting the Scriptures." Lindanus, "a Roman Catholic prelate,"[37] wrote

---

[32] "Kimchi, David" in *Cyclopedia*, V:80.

[33] Ibid.

[34] Burnett, 213, citing David Kimḥi, מכלול (Venice, n. p., 1550), f. 25b. Burnett gives the date for this book as 1550, but McClintock and Strong give the date for a Venice edition as 1545 and a Latin Paris edition published by Guidacier in 1540 ("Kimchi, David" in *Cyclopedia*, V:80,81).

[35] "Kimchi, David" in *Cyclopedia*, V:80.

[36] Burnett, 207. Burnett gives the place of publishing as Cologne and the publisher as Jacob Soterem.

[37] "Linda or Lindanus" in *Cyclopedia*, V:437.

his work in 1558, in which he attacked the Hebrew text of the Bible[38] and in which he made use of Elias Levita's arguments,[39] a proponent of the novelty of the vowel points.[40]

Isaac Levita was a Jew who converted to Catholicism[41] and his book was "a blistering response to Lindanus" wherein "he stressed that the vowel points were essential to understanding the meaning of the Hebrew Bible text, noting that, 'He that reads the Scriptures without the points is like a man that rides a horse *achalinos*, without a bridle'."[42]

Antoine Rudolphe Chevalier – 1560

In 1560, Chevalier, a French theologian and professor of Hebrew,[43] published *Rudimenta Hebr. Ling. Accurata Methodo Conscripta*, that is, "Early Lessons of the Hebrew Language by a Carefully Written Method," where in chapter 4, according to John Owen's translation of the Latin, he wrote:

> As for the antiquity of the vowels and accents, I am of their opinion who maintain the Hebrew language, as the exact pattern of all others, to have been plainly written with them from the beginning; seeing that they who are otherwise minded do not only make doubtful the authority of the Scriptures, but, in my judgment, wholly pluck it up by the

---

[38] "Isaac Levita" in *Cyclopedia*, IV:673.

[39] Burnett, 206, citing Wilhelmus Lindanus, *De optimo Scripturas genere* (Cologne: Maternum Cholinum, 1558)..

[40] "Levita challenged the traditional Jewish view that the consonantal text and its vocalization were given by God to Moses when he received the Law on Mount Sinai" (Ibid., 205).

[41] "Isaac Levita" in *Cyclopedia*, IV:673.

[42] Burnett, 207, quoting "Eum, qui sine punctis et accentibus Scripturam legit, similem esse homini equitanti equum *achalinoton* effrenem," from Johann Gerhard, *Loci Theologici*, 10 vols. (Leipzig: J. C. Hinrichs, 1885), 1:146 (book 1, chap. 15).

[43] "Chevalier, Antoine Rudolphe" in *Cyclopedia*, XI:923.

roots, for without the vowels and notes of distinction it hath nothing firm and certain.[44]

Chevalier gives an excellent argument, an argument that receives further treatment in Chapters Two, Three, and Four of this book.

Azariah De' Rossi – 1574-1575

De' Rossi was a Jewish scholar who wrote *The Light of the Eyes* in 1574-1575.[45] Chapter fifty-nine of section four is "on the antiquity of the vowel points and the accents of the holy tongue."[46] De' Rossi wrote chapter fifty-nine as a response to the earlier Jewish scholar Elias Levita's contention that the Masoretes, that is, the Tiberian Jews[47] at about 600 A.D., instituted and formalized the vowels. De' Rossi gives historical evidence for the existence of the points before 600 A.D. Concerning the antiquity of the vowel points, De' Rossi writes:

> The opinion of those who claim that the vowels of the letters of our holy tongue, namely, the Hebrew script, were invented at Sinai or in the days of Ezra but did not exist prior to that time, according to my limited understanding, appears to be nonsensical. This view is corroborated by a comparative study. For when we examine all other known languages, we find that the letters have notations of sound and

---

[44] John Owen, "Of the Integrity and Purity of the Hebrew and Greek Text of the Scripture; with Considerations on the Prolegomena and Appendix to the Late 'Biblia Polyglotta' " in vol. 16 of *The Works of John Owen*, ed. William H. Goold (Carlisle, PA: The Banner of Truth Trust, 1968), 371. Owen refers to Chevalier by the name of Radulphus Cevallerius.

[45] "Rossi, Azariah (Ben Moses) de," in *Cyclopedia*, IX:137.

[46] Azariah De' Rossi, *The Light of the Eyes: Translated from the Hebrew with an introduction and annotations by Joanna Weinberg* (New Haven, CT: Yale University Press, 2000), 699. Buxtorf, Jr. in 1648 translated into Latin Chapter 59 along with chapters 9 and 42 and included them in his *Tractatus de Antiquitate Punctorum*, that is, "Discussion concerning Ancient Points" ("Rossi, Azariah (Ben Moses) de," in *Cyclopedia*, IX:138).

[47] De' Rossi, 700. The author presents a more detailed look at Elias Levita later in this introductory chapter in the section on the accommodation position

pronunciation. These are either indicated by actual letters as is the case with Italian, Latin, Greek used in our countries, and also in Armenian and Persian. . ... Alternatively, there are points, lines, markers which are put above, below, and in the middle, as in Hebrew, which was the first language to have this system.[48]

In a discussion of Deuteronomy 27:8, "And thou shalt write upon the stones all the words of this law very plainly," De' Rossi argues that if the words on the stones had "not been vocalized, the reader would have been unable to understand them and who could have explained them to him as he stood there at the river's side?"[49] Clearly, De' Rossi believed the points to be ancient and part of the law that Moses gave to Israel.

William Fulke – 1583

According to McClintock and Strong, Fulke, a Puritan theologian,[50] rebutted the view that the Hebrew vowels are of recent origin. He did so in his 1583 work entitled *Defence of the Sincere and True Translations of the Holy Scriptures into the English Tongue, against the Manifold Cavils, Frivolous Quarrels, and Impudent Slanders of Gregory Martin, one of the Readers of Popish Divinity in the Traitorous Seminary of Rheims*. Gregory Martin, a Roman Catholic, in *A Discovery of the Manifold Corruptions of the Holy Scriptures by the Heretics of our Days* charged that the Protestant Bibles followed the comparatively recent invention of the Hebrew vowel points. Fulke refuted Martin's view by writing that since

> our Saviour hath promised that never a particle of the law shall perish, we may understand the same also of the prophets, who have not received the vowels of the latter Jews, but even of the prophets them-

---

[48] Ibid., 703.

[49] Ibid., 704.

[50] "Fulke, William, D. D." in *Cyclopedia*, III:690.

selves, howsoever, that heathenish opinion pleaseth you and other papists.[51]

Fulke indicates that the prophets themselves supplied their own vowels to their own writings and that the Jews at a later date did not supply them. He also seems to indicate that it is his belief that the Mosaic Law also had the vowels from the start.

Guilielmus Eyrius – 1607

In 1652, James Ussher wrote a short book to which he appended a letter from Eyrius. Eyrius had written the letter to Ussher some forty-five years earlier; therefore, the date of his letter is 1607. The full title of Ussher's book is *De Textus Hebraici Veteris Testamenti Variantibus Lectionibus Ad Ludovicum Cappellum Epistola: Cui addita est et Consimilis Argumenti altera, ante annos XLV à Guilielmo Eyrio ad eundem Jacobum data, Epistola*,[52] that is, "Concerning the writing variations of the text of the Hebrew Old Testament in reply to Louis Capellus' Epistle: to which is added also of a similar argument another epistle from Guilemus Eyrius 45 years before the same Jacobus [James Ussher] presented his." From page 25 where Eyrius' epistle begins, it is clear that he was a close friend of Ussher's when Ussher was the theology professor at Dublin.[53]

---

[51] "Vowel-Points" in *Cyclopedia*, X:821,822, citing Fulke, *Defence of the Sincere and True Translations of the Holy Scriptures into the English Tongue, against the Manifold Cavils, Frivolous Quarrels, and Impudent Slanders of Gregory Martin, one of the Readers of Popish Divinity in the Traitorous Seminary of Rheims* (London: n.p., 1583, reprinted Cambridge: Parker Society, 1843), 578.

[52] James Ussher, *De Textus Hebraici Veteris Testamenti Variantibus Lectionibus Ad Ludovicum Cappellum Epistola: Cui addita est et Consimilis Argumenti altera, ante annos XLV à Guilielmo Eyrio ad eundem Jacobum data, Epistola* (London: J. Flesher, 1652), title page.

[53] "Spectatissimo viro ac amico suo singulari, M. Jacobo Ussherio Theologiae Professori apud Dublinienses" (Ibid., 25).

In Eyrius' letter he gives a series of propositions, one of which is: "Hebraica veteris Insturmenti scriptura iisdem vocalium & accentuum notis, quibus hodie utimur, antiquitus tradita,"[54] which roughly translates as, "The old Hebrew Scripture document is with the same marks of vowels and accents, which today we are using, is from of old an item of traditional knowledge." In other words, Eyrius espouses the view that the vowels and accents of the Hebrew were not a recent invention. The fact that according to the title of the book Eyrius' argument is similar to Ussher's argument means that Ussher was of the same opinion.

Johannes Buxtorf, Sr. – 1609

In 1609, Buxtorf, a Hebrew professor, wrote *Thesaurus Grammaticus Linguae Sanctae Hebraeae*, that is, "A Grammatical Collection of the Sacred Hebrew Language." In the 1609 edition of this work, he provided "a defense of the age and integrity of the vowel points."[55] He gave "a long excursus" wherein

> he provided a summary of [Elias] Levita's arguments for a post-talmudic dating of the vowel points, offered arguments for the antiquity of the vowel points drawn from Jewish tradition and Amandus Polanus' *Syntagma Theologiae Christianae*[56] [see below] together with his own reflections on the necessity for inspired vowel points, and then gave a point by point rebuttal of Levita's arguments.[57]

Subsequent editions of *Thesaurus Grammaticus* did not contain the excursus; however, many of the arguments in the first edition of *Thesaurus Grammaticus* reappear in *Tiberias sive Commentarius Ma-*

---

[54] Ibid., 29.

[55] Burnett, 210.

[56] The author dates Polanus' work at 1617, but from this quote, it seems that an earlier edition of the work existed, however, the author has not been able to find a date for it.

[57] Burnett, 212.

sorethicus[58] (see further). Buxtorf's 1609 edition of *Thesaurus Grammaticus* is a very rare Latin work. Only two libraries in the United States (Brown University and University of Pennsylvania) have it. The author was able to secure photocopies of certain pages from the University of Pennsylvania.

Valentin Schindler – 1612

Schindler died in 1604, but his *Lexicon Pentaglott* was not published until 1612, with a fourth edition appearing in 1695.[59] John Gill citing column 1792 of this work concerning the word *shibboleth* in Judges 12:6 writes: "Schindler is of the opinion that from hence it appears, that the point on the right and left hand of ש, was then in use and so by consequence the other points also."[60]

Amandus Polanus Von Polandsdorf – 1617

He wrote *Syntagma theologiae Christianae*, that is, "Writings of Christian Theology," in which he espoused:

> The points belonged to the original revelation of the Word to Moses and the Prophets and were produced simultaneously with the consonants of the Law, summing up the argument with the rabbinic maxim, "puncta vocalia sunt animae syllabarum et vocum atque adeo vivae pronunciationis."[61]

---

[58] Ibid.

[59] "Schindler, Valentin" in *Cyclopedia*, IX:410.

[60] Gill, *Dissertation*, 253.

[61] Richard A. Muller, "The debate over the vowel points and the crisis in orthodox theology" in *The Journal of Medieval and Renaissance Studies* 10 (Spring 1980): 58, quoting "Illa Elias Levitae narratio, hisoriae verae fidem non meretur. Nam evidentibus argumentis constat, puncta vocalis et puncta distinguentia quae accentus vocantur, in libris Veteris Testamenti non esse demum a Judaeis Tyberiadis excogitata, sed ab ipso Mose et Prophetis adscripta. . . . puncta vocalia sunt animae syllabarum et vocum atque adeo vivae pronunciationis" from Amandus Polanus von Polansdorf, *Syntagma theologiae Christianae* (Geneva, 1617), Lxxxvii (p. 75, col. 2).

The Latin rabbinic maxim roughly translates as "the vowel points are the souls of the syllables and of the words and so are the lives of the pronunciations." According to Burnett,

> At the heart of Polanus' position is the notion that "adequate written representation of words required some sort of vowel symbol." He made heavy use of Johannes Isaac Levita's *Defensio*, reproducing in outline form many of his arguments. He also used Pierre Chevallier's notes in Antoine Chevallier's *Rudimenta*.[62]

Johannes Buxtorf, Sr. – 1620

In 1620, Buxtorf defended the antiquity and inspiration of the vowel points in *Tiberias sive Commentarius Masorethicus*[63], that is, "Tiberias or a Masoretic Commentary," wherein, according to Pick, Buxtorf "made use of De' Rossi's arguments."[64] Many of the arguments that Buxtorf made in his 1609 *Thesaurus Grammaticus Linguae Sanctae Hebraeae* in favor of the antiquity and inspiration of the vowel points appear in *Tiberias*.[65] Burnett states:

> *Tiberias* was written not only to serve as a textbook on the Masora, but also to refute [Elias] Levita's position on the age of the vowel points. Buxtorf devoted six chapters (3-9) in the first part to describing Levita's arguments, supplying relevant historical description and offering elaborate rebuttals. Then in the next two chapters (10-11) he explained his own position, that the men of the Great Synagogue were responsible for adding the accents and vowel points.[66]

---

[62] Burnett, 209, citing Robert D. Preus, *The Theology of the Lutheran Reormers: A Study of Theological Prolegomena* (St. Louis: Concordia Publishing House, 1970), 308, and Amandus Polanus von Polandsdorf, *Syntagma Theologiae Christianae* (Geneva: Jacob Stoer, 1617) Lxxvii..

[63] B. Pick, "The Vowel-Points Controversy in the XVI, XVII, and XVIII Centuries" in *The Princeton Review* 6 (January 1877), 166.

[64] Ibid.

[65] Burnett, 212.

[66] Ibid., 219.

Again, the author in the discussion under Moses the Punctuator presented information on some difficulties with saying that Ezra and the men of the Great Synagogue provided the points,[67] as opposed to saying that each writer gave his own points. But Buxtorf did hold to the inspiration of the points and for that reason, the author lists him here. Indeed, in the last two chapters of *Tiberias*, Buxtorf argued "for the religious necessity of divinely inspired vowel points." Buxtorf reasoned: "If the vocalization of the Hebrew were solely a work of human intellect rather than an intrinsic part of the inspired biblical text then the result would be a plethora of questions about individual verses which together could undermine the authority of the Word of God."[68] Concerning "a plethora of questions about individual verses which together could undermine the authority of the Word of God," the reader should see Chapter Three of this work, wherein the author demonstrates that without inspired vowel points almost every verse of the Old Testament would be unreliable and, therefore, lack authority.

John Weemes – 1623 and 1630

In 1623 and 1630, Weemes published his first and second editions of The Christian Synagogue, Wherein is contained the diverse Reading, The right Pointing, Translation, and Collation of Scripture with Scripture.[69] In this book, he wrote: "The points and accents are naturally bred with the Scriptures, delivered by God to Moyses out of Mount Sinai, and so on to posteritie."[70] In his third edition, issued in

---

[67] Burnett states: "The Men of the Great Synagogue were, according to Jewish tradition, a group of scholars and prophets led by Ezra the Scribe in the early years after the Jews' return from the Babylonian Captivity" (Burnett, 223).

[68] Ibid., 222.

[69] Muller, 64.

[70] John Weemes, *The Christian Synagogue: Wherein is contained the diverse Reading, The right Pointing, Translation, and Collation of Scripture with Scripture* (London: T. and B. Gates, 1630), 37.

1636, he changed his view to say that Moses gave the vowels at Sinai, but that they were added to the text by the Masoretes.[71] For problems associated with the view that the Masoretes added the vowels, see the discussion on the accommodation position.

John Lightfoot – 1629[72]

Lightfoot in refuting the idea that the Tiberian Jews, that is, the Masoretes, developed the points, said, " 'The pointing of the Bible savours of the work of the Holy Spirit, not the work of lost, blinded besotted men.' "[73] Lightfoot also stated:

> Some there be, that think the vowels of the Hebrew were not invented for many years after Christ. Which to me seemeth to be all one, as to deny sinews to a body: or to keep an infant unswaddled, and to suffer him to turn and bend any way, till he grow out of fashion. For mine own satisfaction I am fully resolved, that the letters and the vowels of the Hebrew were, -as the soul and body of a child, - knit together at their conception and beginning; and that they had both one another.[74]

McClintock and Strong, quoting Chambers, relate: " 'Lightfoot was a very learned Hebraist for his time, but he was not free from the unscientific crotchets of the period, holding, for example, the inspiration of the vowel-points.' "[75] Such is the ridicule that some heap upon those who hold to the inspiration of the vowel points and ridicule such

---

[71] Muller, 65, quoting "the letters in the Scripture have two sorts of points, either in valor or in figure; the points in valor were from the beginning delivered by Moses in mount Sinai, but the figures of them were found out afterwards by the Mazarites, and no consonant can bee pronounced without them" from John Weemes, *The Christian Synagogue* in *The Workes of Mr. J. Weemes*, 3 vols. (London: n. p., 1636), I:48.

[72] John Lightfoot, "The Epistle Dedicatory" in vol. 4 of *The Whole Works of the Rev. John Lightfoot, D. D.* (London: J. F. Dove, 1822), iv.

[73] Ginsburg, *The Massoreth Ha-Massoreth*, 58. Ginsburg footnotes this quote of Lightfoot as coming from page 73 of volume 2 of the 1684 edition of Lightfoot's Works.

[74] Lightfoot, iv:50.

[75] "Lightfoot, John (1)" in *Cyclopedia*, V:426.

as this may deter others from holding to the *autographa* position. Such criticism, in the case of Lightfoot, is unfair and unfounded. Lightfoot would have had access to the arguments of Elias Levita, Cappellus, and Walton, all of whom advocated a position of the Masoretic writing of the points. Lightfoot, however, rejected their arguments and held to an *autographa* position for the points.

Johannes Buxtorf, Jr. – 1648

Buxtorf, Jr. published in 1648 Tractatus de punctorum vocalium, et accentuum, in libris Veteris Testamenti Hebraicis, origine, antiquate, et authoritate: oppositus arcano punctationis revelato, Ludovici Cappelli, that is, "Treatise on the origin, antiquity, and authority of the vowel points and accents in the Hebrew Scripture of the Old Testament: opposed to the mystery of the points unveiled, by Louis Cappellus."[76] The last words reveal that Buxtorf wrote this in opposition to The Mystery of the Points Unveiled of Louis Cappellus, who published it anonymously in 1624[77] and who took the opposite view in the debate on the points. Buxtorf's work is available worldwide in only twelve libraries.

Gisbert Voetius – 1648–1699

From 1648 to 1699 Voetius published parts I-V of *Selectarum disputationum theologicarum*, that is, "Disputation of Theological Selections." In part I, page 33 according to Muller, he espoused the view that the inspiration and the divine authority of Scripture went "beyond the sense of the scripture to the individual words, indeed to their letters and even to the tiny 'jots and tittles' of the system of vocalization."[78]

---

[76] Pick, 167. Pick gives an English title to Buxtorf's work, but it seems to be his translation of the Latin title. The author has failed to locate any English translation of this work.

[77] Muller, 59.

[78] Muller, 62,63.

Heppe referring to the same page from Voetius writes: "Even the *puncta vocalia* [vowel points] in the OT are inspired. On the other hand the 'marginal readings' (τὸ κέρι) are not to be regarded as authentic."[79] While Muller seems to question Voetius' view, does not the divine authority of Scripture depend upon the very jots and tittles, for is this not what Jesus taught in Matthew 5:18? And is not the Bible verbally (II Peter 1:21) and plenarily inspired (II Timothy 3:16)? Indeed, the inspiration and authority of Scripture does rest upon the very words, right down to the jots and tittles.

James Ussher – 1652

According to Muller, Ussher held to the Mosaic origin of the vowel points.[80] In light of this, he may also have believed that they were inscripturated at the same time that Moses wrote. Ussher wrote *De Textus Hebraici Veteris Testamenti Variantibus Lectionibus Ad Ludovicum Cappellum Epistola*,[81] that is, "Concerning the writing variations of the text of the Hebrew Old Testament in reply to Louis Capellus' Epistle." According to Muller, Louis Capellus took the view that the Masoretes added the points.[82] In Ussher's book is a letter from Eyrius, which takes the same position as Ussher (see earlier). In the letter, Eyrius espouses the position that the points that were then in use in his day, were the same points that were in the Hebrew Scripture of old.

---

[79] Heinrich Heppe, *Reformed Dogmatics: Set Out and Illustrated from Sources*, revised and edited Ernst Bizer, trans. G. T. Thomson (London: George Allen & Unwin Ltd., 1950), 27.

[80] Muller, 56.

[81] James Ussher, *De Textus Hebraici Veteris Testamenti Variantibus Lectionibus Ad Ludovicum Cappellum Epistola* (London: J. Flesher, 1652), title page.

[82] Muller, 56.

John Owen – 1659

John Owen believed that the vowels were completed by "the men of the great synagogue, Ezra and his companions, guided therein by the infallible direction of the Spirit of God."[83] Owen intimates that these men were moved by the Spirit of God (II Peter 1:21) to add the vowels and, therefore, these vowels were inspired and fully authoritative. See earlier under Buxtorf, Sr. and Moses the Punctuator for some weaknesses of Owen's position.

Matthias Wasmuth – 1664, 1669

Matthias Wasmuth was "a German doctor and professor of theology."[84] With the publication of *Vindiciae Hebr. Script.* in 1664, that is, "A Vindication of the Hebrew Scripture," he supported the views of Buxtorf.[85] In addition to this book, in 1669 he published *Pro Sanct. Hebr. Texta Vindiciarum Anti-Cappell-Walton; Pars i, qua Originalis Authentia Divina tam Accentuum et Vocalium quam at Ipsorum Literarum . . . Asseritur; Pars ii, qua Necessarius Accentuum Usus, etc., Demonstratur,*[86] that is, "Of Vindications in behalf of the Holy Hebrew Text against Cappell-Walton; part 1, that the original divine authenticity is preserved to the extent of accents and of vowels as much as of the letters themselves; part 2, that the necessary use of accents, etc. is demonstrated." Herein Wasmuth was arguing for the preservation of the original accents, vowels, and letters, indicating his belief that the accents, vowels, and letters that were present in his time were the very vowels, accents, and letters of the *autographa.* Furthermore, he was arguing against the views of Cappell, that is, Cappellus,

---

[83] Owen, 371.

[84] "Wasmuth" in *Cyclopedia*, XII:885.

[85] "Vowel-Points" in *Cyclopedia*, X:822.

[86] "Wasmuth" in *Cyclopedia*, XII:885.

and Walton, both of whom advocated the novelty of the vowel points (see later under the accommodation position).

Joseph Cooper – 1673

Joseph Cooper, an English nonconformist minister,[87] in 1673 published a book in favor of the antiquity of the vowel points, לתורה מפתח בית משה או סינ *Hoc est Domus Mosaicae Clavis, sive Legis Sepimentum: In quo punctorum Hebraicorum adstruitur antiquitas: Eaque omnia, cum accentualia tum vocalia, ipsis literis fuisse coaeva, argumentis, undique petitis, demonstratur,*[88] that is, "The Key of the House of Moses or The Hedge of the Law, here is The Key of Moses' House, or the Law's Hedge: wherein the antiquity of the points of the Hebrew is built: and this all collectively, not only the accents but also the vowels, with the letters themselves to have existed at the same time, with arguments, and from every point of view with the goal of moving toward the specified point, is demonstrated." Clearly, he believed that the points existed at the same time as the letters.

Formula Consensus Helvetica – 1675

The *Formula Consensus* is the last doctrinal confession of the Reformed Church of Switzerland. Concerning the vowel points, it states:

> In particular, do we accept the Hebrew codex of the Old Testament, which comes to us from the hands of the Jewish Church, to which were formerly committed the "Oracles of God"; and we firmly maintain it, not only as to the consonants, but also as to the vowels, *sive ipsa puncta*, the very points; the words as well as the things, as *theo-*

---

[87] "Cooper, Joseph (1)" in *Cyclopedia*, XII: 103.

[88] Joseph Cooper, מפתח בית משה או סינ לתורה *Hoc est Domus Mosaicae Clavis, sive Legis Sepimentum: In quo punctorum Hebraicorum adstruitur antiquitas: Eaque omnia, cum accentualia tum vocalia, ipsis literis fuisse coaeva, argumentis, undique petitis, demonstratur. Quae vero in contrarium ab Elia Levita Primipilo, Ludovia Capelli, D. Doctore Waltone* . . . (London: T. R., 1673), title page.

pneutos—God-breathed—part of our faith, not only, but our very life.[89]

Certainly, the words of the Bible are a Christian's very life, for "man shall not live by bread alone, but by every word that proceedeth out of the mouth of God" (Matthew 4:4) and to know the words for certain, the vowels are essential.

Francois Turretin - 1696

In 1696, Turretin, who was "one of the originators of the *Helvetic Consensus* [that is, *Formula Consensus Helvetica*],"[90] wrote *Institutes of Elenctic Theology* wherein he makes several statements about the points. In one place he writes:

> In order to weaken the authenticity (*authentian*) of the Hebrew edition, our opponents have recourse to the "newness of the points" (in vain, as if the punctuation was only a human invention devised by the Masoretes and therefore founded upon human authority, not upon divine and infallible authority; and that it can be changed at pleasure without risk and so always leave the meaning of a passage uncertain and doubtful).[91]

Turretin makes an excellent point. It is a point that the author will repeat in more detail later in Chapter Three.

In another statement, Turretin writes:

> Suffer us briefly to say that we have always thought the truer and safer way to keep the authenticity (*authentian*) of the original text safe and sound against the cavils of all profane persons and heretics whatever

---

[89] George Sayles Bishop, "The Inspiration of the Hebrew Letters and Vowel Points" in *Plains Baptist Challenger* L (July 1991), 47.

[90] "Turretini" in *Cyclopedia*, X:599.

[91] Francis Turretin, *Institutes of Elentic Theology*, 3 vols., trans. George Musgrave Giger, ed. James T. Dennison, Jr. (Phillipsburg, NJ: P & R Publishing, 1992), I:115.

and to put the principle of faith upon a sure and immovable basis, is that which holds the points to be of divine origin.[92]

This is another excellent observation by Turretin. Indeed, the Lord has given to saints a sure foundation for their faith (Psalm 93:5; 111:7), but without the points it is anything but sure.

Samuel Clark –1698, 1699

Samuel Clark defended the antiquity and the inspiration of the vowel points in An Exercitation Concerning the Original of the Chapters and Verses in the Bible.[93] In 1699, Clark wrote The Divine Authority of the Holy Scriptures Asserted in Two Discourses: The former shewing The Nature and Extent of the Inspiration vouchsafed by the Holy Ghost to the Penmen of the Scriptures, and the distinct share of each therein. The latter shewing the Divine Authority of the Vowels and Accents in the Hebrew Text; by new and intrinsic Arguments: in a Discourse concerning the Division of the Bible into Chapters and Verses.[94] The writer has been able to examine only the preface of this work in which Clark wrote:

> Besides this late debate [about inspiration], there has been another controversy of longer standing, which has been hotly canvast [that is, debated] and contested pro and con between the most learned pens on both sides, which has a great influence upon the divine authority of the holy Scriptures also, viz. about the original of the vowels and accents in the Hebrew Text of the Old Testament.[95]

Clark's statement indicates that as of 1699 the debate about the vowels had been long-standing and seemingly still on going. Clark also cor-

---

[92] Ibid., 116.

[93] Pick, 167.

[94] Samuel Clark, *The Divine Authority of the Holy Scriptures Asserted in Two Discourses* (London: St. Paul's Church-yard, 1699), title page.

[95] Ibid., preface.

rectly recognizes the impact that the vowels have on the authority of the Scriptures.

Johann Gottlob Carpzov – 1721, 1723

Carpzov was from "a family which was one of the most distinguished of the 17th century for theological learning."[96] Johann "was the most eminent of the family" and from 1719 to 1730, he was the "professor of Oriental literature at Leipzig."[97] During these years he wrote *Introductio ad libros canonicos bibliorum V. T. omnes*" (1721), that is, "An Introduction to All the Canonical Books of the Biblical Old Testament" and *Critica Sacra V. T.* (1723), that is, "Old Testament Sacred Criticism." According to Noordtzy, in these books, Carpzov "declares the accents and vowel points to be just as old as the text itself, denies textual errors, and declares that the writers of the Bible owe all their knowledge to verbal inspiration."[98]

Pierre Guarin – 1724

Guarin was a French Hebraist who had a lively controversy with Masclef.[99] Masclef's chief work was "the *Grammatica Hebraica, a punctis aliisque inventis Massorethicis libera*, still considered one of the best works of the kind; it embodies an elaborate argument against the use of the vowelpoints."[100] The tittle of the work indicates that Masclef believed that the Masoretes invented the points. In response

---

[96] "Carpzov, Johann Gottlob" in *Cyclopedia*, II:129.

[97] Ibid., II:130.

[98] A. Noordtzy, "The Old Testament Problem: Part 1" trans. Miner B. Stearm, in *Bibliotheca Sacra* 97 (Oct. 1940), 463.

[99] "Guarin" in *Cyclopedia*, III:1025.

[100] "Masclef," in *Cyclopedia*, V:857.

to Masclef's work, Guarin wrote "a defense of the points"[101] in 1724 when he "wrote *Grammatica Hebraica et Chaldaeobiblicum*."[102]

Peter Whitfield - 1748

In *A dissertation on the Hebrew vowel-points. Shewing that they are an original and essential part of the language*, Peter Whitfield presents nine arguments for the inspiration and authority of the vowel points. Whitfield's work is a fine book. Whitfield, however, allows for scribal errors in the Traditional Text when he states of irregularities in punctation, that is, irregularities in the vowel pointing: "They do, indeed, appear to me, to be nothing more than errors of the transcribers," which he suggests might have been corrected "by changing the points in the text."[103] In other words, Whitfield believes that the vowels are inspired, but not perfectly preserved. Such a position is incongruent with the teaching that the Lord has perfectly preserved His Words (Psalm 12:6,7). Despite Whitfield not holding to perfect preservation, he does offer some solid support along original arguments to show that the vowel points are inspired, and, therefore, it is a valuable book and one from which the author will quote at length.

John Gill – 1767

Gill in *A Dissertation concerning the Antiquity of the Hebrew Language, Letters, Vowel Points, and Accents* writes: "Others believe that they [i.e., the vowels] were *ab origine* [from the beginning], and were invented by *Adam* together with the letters, or however that they were coeval with the letters, and in use as soon as they were: which

---

[101] Ibid.

[102] "Guarin" in *Cyclopedia*, III:1025.

[103] Peter Whitfield, *A dissertation on the Hebrew vowel-points. Shewing that they are an original and essential part of the language* (Liverpoole: Peter Whitfield, 1748), 122.

account is most probable."[104] While Gill presents many fine arguments for the antiquity of the vowels, he, however, allows for scribal errors in the Traditional Hebrew Text when he writes: "I am not so great an enthusiast, for the integrity of the present printed *Hebrew* copy, as to imagine, that it is entirely clear of the mistakes of transcribers in all places."[105] However, such is not the position that Jesus took in regard to His copy of the Old Testament, for He regarded it as the truth (John 17:17). Again, despite not holding to perfect preservation, Gill's work is a valuable contribution to the subject at hand.

In a memoir about Gill are these comments concerning Gill's work:

> This masterly effort of profound research, which would have shewn our author to be a prodigy of reading and literature, had he never published a syllable on any other subject, "was written" by him "at his leisure hours, for his own amusement, not with any design, at first, to publish it to the world; but by way of essay to try how far back the antiquity of the things treated of in it could be carried." But the confidence which, about this time, some writers had expressed, "as if the victory was proclaimed on their side," prevailed on him to send it into the world.[106]

The memoir continues by saying, "When this elaborate work came before the public it was treated with candour and ingenuity by the *Critical Reviewers*; who, though they could not agree with every thing in it, particularly concerning the authority of the points, yet allowed the work was executed with great industry, sagacity, and learning."[107] The

---

[104] Gill, *Dissertation*, 137.

[105] Ibid., xxx, xxxi.

[106] John Rippon, "A Brief Memoir of The Life and Writings of the Reverend and Learned John Gill, D. D." in vol. 1 of *An Exposition of the Old Testament* by John Gill, (London: Mathews and Leigh, 1810, reprinted Paris, Arkansas: The Baptist Standard Bearer, Inc., 1989), lxi.

[107] Ibid.

Monthly Reviewers, however, took a different approach toward Gill's work, as Rippon notes:

> In the notice which the *Monthly Reviewers* took of this Dissertation, the Doctor [Gill] perceived so clearly their *ignorance* of the subject, and such a vein of dulness, and ill nature, running through the whole of what they say, that he thought their remarks too low for his attention, and acted according to the spirit of his resolution in the *Preface* to the work – "Should any truly learned gentleman do me the honour to animadvert upon what I have written, I am sure of being treated with candour and decency; but should I be attacked by sciolists [pretentious scholars], I expect nothing but petulance, supercilious airs, and opprobrious language—such will be righteously treated with neglect and contempt."[108]

The last comment indicates the contempt and ridicule that comes from some quarters if one announces his position in favor of the inspiration and antiquity of the points.

James Robertson – 1770

In 1770, Robertson, Professor of Oriental languages at University of Edinburgh,[109] wrote Clavis Pentateuchi, sive Analysis omnium vocum hebraicarum suo ordine in Pentateucho Moseos occurrentium: una cum versione latina et anglica: notis criticus et philologicus adjectis; in quibus, ex lingua arabica, Judaeorum moribus, et doctorum iteneraiis, plurium locorum S. S. sensus eruitur, novaque versione illustratur. In usum juventutis academicae edinburgenae. Cui praemittuntur dissertationes duae; I. De antiquitate linguae arabicae, ejusque convenientia cum lingua hebraea, etc. II. De genuina punctorum vocalium antiquitate, contra clariss. Capellum, Waltonum, Masclefum, Hutchinsonium,[110] that is, "The key of the Pentateuch of

---

[108] Ibid., lxii.

[109] Ibid.

[110] James Robertson, *Clavis Pentateuchi, sive Analysis omnium vocum hebraicarum suo ordine in Pentateucho Moseos occurrentium: una cum versione latina et anglica: notis criticus et philologicus adjectis; in quibus, ex lingua arabica,*

the analysis of every Hebrew word in its order of occurrence in the Mosaic Pentateuch: one with a Latin and an English version, with critical notes and with literary insertions in which, out of the Arabic language, customs of the Jews, and journeys of doctors, the sense of more places S. S. is brought to light, and a new version is illustrated. For the use of the youth of the academy of Edinburgh. To which are set forward two dissertations: I. Concerning the antiquity of the Arabic language, and of its agreement with the Hebrew language, etc. II. Concerning the genuine antiquity of the vowel points contrary to the honorable Capellus, Walton, Masclef, Hutchinson." Of particular interest is the second dissertation wherein Robertson discusses the antiquity of the vowel points. In the second dissertation he espouses a view that is contrary to that of Capellus, Walton, Masclef, and Hutchinson, all of whom advanced the view of the novelty of the points.[111] The 1770 edition of Robertson's work contains these dissertations, but some subsequent editions do not contain them.

In his book, Robertson refers to the work of Gill and writes: " 'Vir Doctissimus Joannes Gill, et qui in Rabbinicis scriptis versatissimus esse videtur, in Dissertatione suâ de punctorum vocalium antiquitate, summâ cum industriâ et doctrinâ, ne vestigium quoddam masoretharum, ut pote punctorum vocalium auctorum, in totâ historiâ Ju-

---

Judaeorum moribus, et doctorum iteneraiis, plurium locorum S. S. sensus eruitur, novaque versione illustratur. In usum juventutis academicae edinburgenae. Cui praemittuntur dissertationes duae; I. De antiquitate linguae arabicae, ejusque convenientia cum lingua hebraea, etc. II. De genuina punctorum vocalium antiquitate, contra clariss. Capellum, Waltonum, Masclefum, Hutchinsonium (Edinburg: R. Fleming and P. and A. Neill, 1770), title page.

[111] For more information on Cappellus and Walton, see the next section on the accommodation position. Concerning Masclef, see earlier in this section under Guarin. The Hutchinson to whom Robertson refers may have been John Hutchinson (1674-1737) who "laid great stress on the evidence of Hebrew etymology, and asserted that the Scriptures are not to be understood and interpreted in a literal, but in a typical sense, and according to the radical import of the Hebrew expressions" ("Hutchinson, John 2" in *Cyclopedia*, IV:425,426).

daicâ, a nata Christo ad annum 1037, addesse affirmat, probatque,' "[112] which roughly translates as, "The most learned man John Gill, and who in Rabbinic writings is the most versatile to be seen, in his Dissertation concerning the antiquity of the vowel points, foremost of its kind with diligence and learning, they [i.e., the vowel points] are not just an imprint of the Masoretes, it is possible they are vowel points of the authors, in all Jewish history, before Christ was born up to the year 1037, he affirms, and he proves." Robertson's agreed with Gill's *Dissertation*.

Adam Benedict Spitzner – 1791

Spitzner was "a Protestant clergyman of Germany," who in 1791 wrote *Vindiciae Originis et Auctoritatis Divinae Punctorum Vocalium et Accentuum in Libris Sacris Veteris Testamenti*,[113] that is, "Vindications of the origin and of the authority of the Divine Vowel Points and Accents in the Sacred Books of the Old Testament." The subtitle indicates that these vindications oppose Elias Levita and Louis Capellus.[114]

John Moncrieff - 1833

In 1833, Moncrieff published An Essay on the Antiquity and Utility of the Hebrew Vowel-Points; with an Introduction Stating the Importance of the Question, and the Proper Manner of Discussing it – Likewise showing the Principal Advantages of Reading with the Points, and that the Difficulties have been Improperly Magnified. An Appendix is Added, Giving a Concise View of the Vowel-Points,

---

[112] Rippon, lxii. The Memoir indicates that Robertson's treatment of Gill's *Dissertation* was different from that of the *Monthly Reviewers* (see discussion under Gill above).

[113] "Spitzner, Adam Benedict" in *Cyclopedia*, IX: 960.

[114] "Ubi Imprimis ea Diluuntur quae post Eliam Levitam Ludovicus Capellus in Arcano Punctationis eiusque Vindiciis Opposuit" (Ibid.).

Their Grammatical Changes, and Their Great use in Determining the Precise Meaning of Words.[115] In this work Moncrieff writes:

> Years ago, after inquiring into this subject with all the assistance I could command, and all the impartiality I could exercise, I felt convinced, that these Points are not, as they have been represented, "a modern Jewish device, and a gross imposition deserving to be totally rejected," but that they were of an early date, and have been of great use in ascertaining the proper meaning of the Sacred Scriptures.[116]

Elsewhere Moncrieff writes: "Distinct Vowel-Points are not only useful, but necessary, for ascertaining the ideas which the inspired holy men intended to convey to our minds in their writings, and we may further be guided to the conclusion, that the origin of the Hebrew Vowel-Points is not of a modern but of an ancient date."[117]

George Sayles Bishop - 1919[118]

Bishop wrote an article entitled "The Inspiration of the Hebrew Letters and Vowel-Points." Concerning Deuteronomy 27:8, which speaks of writing the words of the law very plainly, Bishop states: "This must include the vowel-marks, as well as consonants, for on them, most of all, the plainness must depend."[119] Elsewhere he writes: "The Bible asserts the inspiration of the very vowel-points."[120]

---

[115] Moncrieff, title page.

[116] Ibid., 14.

[117] Ibid., 20.

[118] Bishop lived from 1836-1914 (George Sayles Bishop, "The Inspiration of the Hebrew Letters and Vowel-Points" in *Plains Baptist Challenger* L (July 1991), 47). But his view was published in 1919 by Gospel Publishing House of New York in *The Doctrine of Grace and Kindred Theme* (Kent Brandenburg, "It Is Not Hidden, Neither Is It Far Off: Deuteronomy 30:11-14" in *Thou Shalt Keep Them: A Biblical Theology of the Perfect Preservation of Scripture*, ed. Kent Brandenburg (El Sobrante, CA: Pillar & Ground Publishing, 2003), 88).

[119] George Sayles Bishop, "The Inspiration of the Hebrew Letters and Vowel-Points" in *Plains Baptist Challenger* L (July 1991), 48.

[120] Ibid.

Kent Brandenburg – 2003

Brandenburg writes: "In addition to Matthew 5:18 several other verses relate to the originality and inspiration of the vowel points."[121] Brandenburg then lists a number of verses; many of which and even more, the writer presents later.

The Author – 2003

The author in 2003 wrote:

> It is a common belief that the Masoretes invented vowel points and added them to a consonantal Hebrew text. However, inasmuch as Moses and others wrote the words of the Lord (Exodus 24:4; Deuteronomy 31:24) and inasmuch as words presuppose vowels and consonants, then vowels were present in the *autographa*. Jesus guarantees that the vowels of the *autographa* were present in His day and will be preserved for future generations.[122]

There was a time when the author repeated the assertion that the Masoretes added the vowel points to a Hebrew consonantal text, for this is what he was taught through much of his schooling. However, upon further reflection on what the Bible teaches, the writer has come to the position that God inspired the Hebrew vowels.

Gary Webb – 2003

Gary Webb writes:

> The Hebrew words depend (like English words) upon both consonants and vowels. However, modern scholarship has excluded the vowels of the Hebrew text from the operation of Divine inspiration, stating that

---

[121] Kent Brandenburg, "It Is Not Hidden, Neither Is It Far Off: Deuteronomy 30:11-14" in *Thou Shalt Keep Them: A Biblical Theology of the Perfect Preservation of Scripture*, ed. Kent Brandenburg (El Sobrante, CA: Pillar & Ground Publishing, 2003), 88.

[122] Chester Kulus, *Those So-Called Errors: Debunking the Liberal, New Evangelical, and Fundamentalist Myth that You Should Not Hear, Receive, and Believe All the Numbers of Scripture* (Newington, CT: Emmanuel Baptist Theological Press, 2003), 68,69.

inspiration only gave the Hebrew consonants. This position which denies that "tittle" [see Matthew 5:18] also refers to the vowel pointing of the Hebrew text completely undermines the Divine authority of the Hebrew Scriptures.[123]

Thomas Strouse – 2005

Concerning the vocalization of the Lord's Old Testament name Strouse writes:

> The Lord has promised to preserve all of His inspired, canonical Words through His ordained institutions for all generations subsequent to the inscripturation of these Words. Therefore, He has preserved His OT Words, consonants and vowels, jots and tittles, including the inspired vocalization of His name, the *tetragrammaton*.[124]

Herein Strouse advocates the position that the vowels were inspired and, therefore, given at the same time as the consonants. In two other recent articles, Strouse also espouses that the vowels of the Hebrew Old Testament are inspired of God.[125]

In an earlier work, Strouse expressed a different view when he wrote: "The Masoretic Text of the OT derives its name from the Masoretic Scribes (AD 6-10th centuries) who added vowel pointings to the tri-consonantal *apographa* [copies of Scripture]."[126] At one time, Strouse believed that the Masoretes added the vowel points, but upon further study he changed his assessment and now believes that God

---

[123] Gary Webb, "Not One Jot or One Tittle Matthew 5:17,18" in *Thou Shalt Keep Them: A Biblical Theology of the Perfect Preservation of Scripture*, ed. Kent Brandenburg (El Sobrante, CA: Pillar & Ground Publishing, 2003), 43,44.

[124] Thomas M. Strouse, "Who is this Deity named Yahweh," *The Biblical Astronomer* 15 (Winter, 2005): 17.

[125] The two articles are (1) "Luke 16:17 – One Tittle," *Emmanuel Baptist Theological Journal* 2 (Spring, 2006): 7-23; and (2) "Scholarly Myths Perpetuated on Rejecting the Masoretic Text of the OT," *Emmanuel Baptist Theological Journal* 1 (Spring, 2005): 37-64.

[126] Thomas M. Strouse, *THE LORD GOD HATH SPOKEN: A Guide To Bibliology*, revised (Newington, CT: Emmanuel Baptist Theological Press, 2001), 16.

gave the vowels under inspiration. The hope of the author is that others will do likewise.

Various Others

According to Muller,[127] some others who held to the Mosaic origin of the vowel points were Gerardus,[128] Junius (possibly Franciscus Junius, an eminent Protestant French theologian, 1545-1602),[129] Gomarus (Francis Gomar, 1563-1641),[130] William Whitaker,[131] John Rainolds,[132] Deodatus, and Heidegger.[133] The fact that they held to Mosaic origin of the vowel points may indicate that they also believed the points to be inspired and part of the written Words of God. John

---

[127] Richard A. Muller, "The debate over the vowel points and the crisis in orthodox hermeneutics" in *The Journal of Medieval and Renaissance Studies* 10 (Spring 1980): 56.

[128] *Gerardus* is probably *Gerard* Latinized. John Owen mentions a Gerard who wrote *De Sacrae Script.*, that is, *Of the Sacred Scripture* and who held to the antiquity of the points (Owen, *Works*, XVI:372), which was Johann Gerard, who published his work in 1610 ("Gerhard, Johann" in *Cyclopedia*, III:818). Burnett mentions that Buxtorf Sr.'s "position on the vowel points also became part of the Lutheran dogmatice tradition through Johann Gerhard's *Loci Theologici*" (Burnett, 228).

[129] "Junius, Franciscus" in *Cyclopedia*, IV:1097.

[130] "Gomar, Francis" in *Cyclopedia*, III:920. He "attended at Oxford the divinity lectures of Dr. John Rainolds, and at Cambridge those of Dr. William Whittaker" (Ibid.). Muller also lists Rainolds and Whitaker as adherents of the Mosaic origin of the vowel points.

[131] He lived from 1548 to 1595 and was "a powerful champion of Protestantism against the attacks of popery" ("Whitaker, William" in *Cyclopedia*, X:981).

[132] He lived from 1549 to 1607. "It is thus that we owe to Rainolds the *King James Version* of the Scriptures, for it is well known that Rainolds urged the king to the undertaking, and demonstrated its necessity" ("Rainold(e)s" in *Cyclopedia*, VIII:888).

[133] "He was the compiler of the famous *Formula Consensus*, adopted by the Synod of Zurich in 1675" ("Heidegger, Johann Heinrich" in *Cyclopedia*, IV:159). See discussion on the *Consensus* earlier.

Owen[134] also indicates that Glassius, Flacius Illyricus (he wrote his work in 1567[135]), Hassret, and Wolthius held to the antiquity of the vowel points. Furthermore, Keil notes: "*Loescher* and almost all the orthodox divines of the seventeenth and eighteenth centuries defend the primitive antiquity or the divine origin (whether by Moses or by Ezra) of the vowel points."[136]

Conclusion

The above survey lists forty-seven (57) men who, during a period of nearly a thousand years, or nineteen hundred years if one accepts an early date for the *Zohar*, have written in defense of the antiquity or of the inspiration of the vowel points. From this survey, a couple of conclusions come to the surface. First, the belief concerning the antiquity and inspiration of the vowel points is not something that only a few isolated individuals believed.

A second conclusion arises from the fact that various writers mention the names of Elias Levita, Walton, and Cappellus, who were men that espoused the view of the novelty of the points. These three men were primarily responsible for persuading many to abandon the position of the antiquity of the points.

A third conclusion is that even after Levita, Walton, and Cappellus published their works, there were men who were not persuaded by their arguments and continued to advocate the antiquity and inspiration of the points.

---

[134] Owen, *Works*, XVI:372. Owen cites Glassius' *De Text. Heb. Puri.*; Illyricus' work entitled *Clavis Scripturae Sacrae*, p.2, trac. 6; Hassret's *De Templ. Ezec.*; and Wolthius' *Disputat. Jenae*.

[135] "Flacius" in *Cyclopedia*, III:585.

[136] Keil, *Introduction to the Old Testament*, II:190,191.

The Problems

Various writers suppose that there are a couple of problems with the *autographa* position. The author groups these problems under the headings of historical and Biblical and confronts many of these problems in this section. The problems that need a further treatment receive that treatment in Chapter Six, "Further Objections."

Historical Problems

There are several historical problems that some pose against the *autographa* position. The historical problems concern (1) difficulty in writing the points; (2) spelling variations between the Hebrew and various translations of the Hebrew; (3) various unpointed documents; (4) supposed silence about the points; (5) an extrabiblical story about Joab; (6) vowel point names not being in the Hebrew language; (7) accents; (8) *kethib* and *keri* readings; and (9) *matres lectionis*. None of these historical problems relies on an exegesis of the Scripture, as such, they are powerless to decide the issue of the points, since the Bible is the sole authority for faith and practice, and not history. Regardless of the evidence of history, if the Bible teaches otherwise, one should follow the Bible. "Let God be true, but every man a liar" (Romans 3:4). But these historical arguments tend to convince many of the supposed novelty of the points; therefore, it is necessary to mention them. Another reason for listing these arguments is to demonstrate that this treatise is neither ignorant nor unaware of these arguments. Before getting into the historical problems, may the writer draw the reader's attention to how often various writers assert that these historical arguments are their strongest reasons for holding to the novelty of the points. Reliance on historical arguments demonstrates the precedence that people give to history instead of to the Bible. Sadly, it seems that most walk by sight, rather than by faith (see II Corinthians 5:7).

Difficulty in Writing Points

Green expresses one of his reasons for the novelty of the points when he writes: "The cumbrous minuteness of their notation renders it extremely improbable that they were in use so long as the Hebrew was a living tongue."[137] Granted that pointed Hebrew is more difficult to write than unpointed Hebrew; however, such a difficulty can hardly be a reason for the Bible, the most important of all books, being unpointed. Indeed, many verses not only suggest but also teach that the Old Testament had points (e.g., Exodus 34:27; Deuteronomy 27:8; 31:24; Nehemiah 8:8; Habakkuk 2:2; Matthew 5:18; etc.). Just because something is difficult is no reason for it not happening. If one were to use the same reasoning as Green's, then he could argue that the substitutionary atonement of Christ did not happen because of all things ever done that was the most difficult and burdensome. Such reasoning would be absurd. When determining a matter, it is best to rely on the Bible, rather than to rely on one's own reasoning.

Spelling Variations between the Hebrew and Other Languages

Whitfield writes:

> One great objection against the antiquity of the Hebrew points, is the very great difference betwixt the proper names in the Old Testament, as they are read in the pointed Hebrew, and as they are in the Greek version ascribed to the *Septuagint*, and in the *Vulgate Latin*, called St. *Jerome's* Version. As for instance, in Gen. 10 for גֹּמֶר *Gomer*, the *Septuagint* hath γαμέρ *Gamer*. . . For חֲוִילָה *Hhavilah*, the Greek hath ἐυιλὰ, St. Jerome *Hevila* . . . . Those who maintain the *novelty* of the points, take this to be no less than a demonstration, that they were not in being, when those versions were made: for they say, it is not to be imagined, that the *Septuagint* and St. Jerome would have wrote the proper names so widely different from the Hebrew had they had the vowel-points to direct them; but that they surely would have expressed them, as near the true Hebrew reading, as the languages they translated

---

[137] William Henry Green, *General Introduction to the Old Testament: the Text* (NY: Charles Scribner's Sons, 1899), 65.

> into, would allow; which, it is very plain, they have not done. . . . This is one of the strongest arguments brought in support of the novelty of the points; and this Capellus says is so clear; that to go about to prove, that the *Septuagint* and St. Jerome had not pointed copies of the Hebrew Scriptures, is the same thing as to attempt to prove that the sun gives light at noonday.[138]

Green writes, "The present vowel system could not have been in existence when the Septuagint version was made; for it deviates from it considerably in its manner of transliterating proper names, and repeatedly translates words as the letters would admit, but the vowels would not."[139] Green also states, "Origen in the third century A.D. in his Hexapla gives a pronunciation of the Hebrew words in Greek letters, which does not agree with the vowel points."[140] Green furthermore observes:

> It has been a disputed question whether Jerome in the fourth century was acquainted with the present vowel system; but it is now well established that he was not. He generally adheres to that pronunciation and understanding of the text which is yielded by the vowels; but he often speaks of the ambiguity of words, which are only ambiguous when written without the points.[141]

Green, who is not an advocate for the inspiration of the points, makes an interesting admission here when he acknowledges that in writing with no points, the Hebrew words become ambiguous. That is, an unpointed Old Testament would make the Old Testament very unsure, something that cannot be true according to Psalm 93:5 which states: "Thy testimonies are very sure." When the statements of scholars conflict with the Bible, one should reject the scholar and side with Scripture. In light of the fact that Green admits that unpointed Hebrew is ambiguous and in light of the fact that Psalm 93:5 states that God's

---

[138] Whitfield, 222,223.

[139] William Henry Green, 65, 66.

[140] Ibid., 66.

[141] Ibid.

testimonies are very sure, it is clear that Green, in denying that the points are inspired, cannot be right.

Now whether or not the so-called Seventy of the LXX or Jerome had pointed copies of the Hebrew Old Testament is a matter that one will have a difficult time to decide conclusively. Arguments abound on both sides of this question. Maybe they did not have pointed copies of the Old Testament, which could account for the differences in their translations of the Hebrew. Or, maybe they did have pointed copies, but because of poor translation technique, or theological bias they produced a poor translation in places. Turretin writes: "The variance of the Septuagint from the original text does not imply that the text is corrupt, but rather the version is at fault."[142] Whitfield provides another reason for differences in spelling between the Hebrew and the Greek when he states:

> These differences in proper names might proceed from an endeavour in the authors to accommodate the pronunciation to the idiom of the Greek language: and so the before mentioned St. Jerome writes: "Graeci, plerunq; per circuitus transferunt et verba Hebraica non interpretationis fide, sed linguae suae proprietatibus nitumtur exprimere," i.e. "The Greeks paraphrase, instead of translating; and render the Hebrew words, not by a true version; but in conformity to the idiom of their own language."[143]

Many appeal to the LXX and to other ancient translations of the Old Testament. Why do they make such an appeal? McClintock and Strong's *Cyclopedia* provides an answer when it opines: "Being made from MSS. far older than the Masoretic recension, the Sept. [LXX] often indicates readings more ancient and more correct than those of our present Hebrew MSS. and editions, and often speaks decisively between the conflicting readings of the present MSS."[144] Some

---

[142] Turretin, 109.

[143] Whitfield, 225. Quotation of Jerome is from *Epist. Ad Sun. & Fratell.*

[144] "Septuagint" in *Cyclopedia*, IX:545.

critics believe that the LXX is older than the Masoretic Text and that the LXX reflects an older Hebrew text. Therefore, these critics will use the LXX to correct the Masoretic Text. The correction of the Masoretic Text by the LXX is nothing more than the-oldest-is-the-best rule of New Testament textual criticism applied to the Old Testament. But it is not valid to use a translation of the Hebrew Old Testament, no matter how old, to determine the true nature of the underlying Hebrew Text, for God's promise of Old Testament preservation concerns the Hebrew and Aramaic words of the Old Testament, not a translation of the Old Testament. Jesus spoke of not one jot or tittle passing from the law (Matthew 5:18), which concerns the Hebrew and Aramaic of the Old Testament, not the Greek and Latin of various translations. In light of this, the believer should not be concerned with the fact that various ancient versions exhibit spelling variations between themselves and the Hebrew. The spelling variations between the ancient versions and the Hebrew have no authority or bearing to decide the vowel point issue.

Unpointed Documents

Those who argue for the novelty of the points often refer to various unpointed documents such as newspapers, the Dead Sea Scrolls, the Samaritan Pentateuch, synagogue copies of the Law, as well as to unpointed languages. Along with the argument that there are unpointed documents is the reasoning that if people can read these documents and languages without points, then it was possible for people to read unpointed Hebrew Bibles.

Newspapers

David Sorenson, a proponent for the novelty of the points, writes: "If you care to check out *HaEretz* [sic] online in their Hebrew edition (one of two major newspapers in Israel today), you will notice again that there are no vowel points."[145] Larry Oats, who also holds to the novelty of the points, in a review of *Thou Shalt Keep Them*, argues:

> A person can take unpointed Hebrew (just the consonants) and without changing or even moving a consonant add all the vowels. Gary Webb declares that without the vowels, the Old Testament would have been "an unintelligible grouping of consonants" (44). Obviously, Webb has never been to Israel and looked at their daily newspapers. There are no vowels – and no one complains that they cannot read their papers.
>
> This argument has almost been lost in this generation, primarily because of the discovery of the Dead Sea Scrolls. These manuscripts were copied near the time of Christ by radical Jews, who had meticulous requirements for accuracy in copying, but whose manuscripts have no vowel points.[146]

Dead Sea Scrolls

In the above quote, Oats mentions the Dead Sea Scrolls. David Sorenson also writes: "Modern Israeli society in its entirety operates with a language (i.e., Hebrew) with no vowel points. The fact that neither synagogue copies of the Scripture nor the DSS [Dead Sea Scrolls] have pointing is troubling to me. Is not Israel the custodian of the Old Testament? Were not the Jews scrupulously careful in the copying of their own Scriptures?"[147] Sorenson seems to neglect the fact that at the time of the New Testament, God committed the keeping of the Scriptures (both Old and New Testaments) to local churches (Matthew 28:19,20; Jude 3; Revelation 3:8,10), and not to the Jews.

---

[145] David Sorenson, personal letter to the author dated January 31, 2004. The correct spelling for the newspaper is *Ha Aretz*.

[146] Larry Oats, *Thou Shalt Keep Them: A Review by Larry Oats* (Watertown, WI: Maranatha Baptist Bible College, n. d.), 6. Oats' *Review* has no date, but obviously, Oats wrote it after the publication of *Thou Shalt Keep Them*, which was published in August of 2003.

[147] David Sorenson, personal letter to the author dated March 1, 2004.

Synagogue Scrolls

Sorenson in the above quote refers to unpointed synagogue scrolls. Walton also states that the Jews in the Synagogue "use one special book of the Law unpointed; for this end and purpose, that it may represent the Original Copy written by Moses, and laid up in the Ark, which they acknowledge was written without points; and that this book, if it be pointed, is thereby profaned, and not fit for that use."[148] Walton goes on to state that he had heard that the argument about unpointed synagogue scrolls "was a great motive to draw" Ussher to the opinion of the novelty of the points.[149] Earlier in 1652, Ussher wrote in defence of the antiquity of the points, but, if Walton's account is true, then apparently sometime after 1652, Ussher changed his mind and it was the historical argument about synagogue scrolls that seemed to hold great weight with him. Green observes: "The synagogue rolls, to which special sacredness is attached, never have the vowel points; this can only be accounted for, if the points are not an original constituent of the sacred text, but a subsequent innovation."[150]

Other Languages and Inscriptions

Green appeals to the lack of vowel points in other languages as a reason for the novelty of the points. He writes, "Syriac and Arabic were originally written without vowel signs; these are a later invention. The Samaritan uses substantially the old form of the Hebrew letters, but has no vowel signs; neither have the ancient Hebrew inscriptions,

---

[148] Walton, *The Considerator Considered*, 241.

[149] Ibid., 242.

[150] William Henry Green, 65.

nor the Phoenician monuments."[151] Keil argues that the lack of vowels on Jewish coins is a proof for the novelty of the points.[152]

Conclusion

While the topic of unpointed documents receives further treatment in Chapter Six, may the writer insert an observation at this juncture: synagogue practice, Samaritan practice, Dead Sea scroll practice, modern-day practice, inscription practice, or the custom of other languages are not what determines faith and practice for local churches. Paul wrote inspired words to Timothy saying, "These things write I unto thee, hoping to come unto thee shortly: But if I tarry long, that thou mayest know how thou oughtest to behave thyself in the house of God, which is the church of the living God, the pillar and ground of the truth" (I Timothy 3:14,15). What Paul wrote to Timothy, that is, God's inspired Words, determined faith and practice in local churches at that time, and it should be so today as well.

Supposed Silence about the Points

Walton argues that the silence of Origen, Eusebius, Epiphanius, and Josephus, who were skilled in Hebrew antiquities, concerning the points and accents "though they had often occasion to mention them" is a proof that they did not exist at that time. Furthermore, Walton asserts that the Talmud speaks "not one word or tittle of any pointed vowel or accent, . . . though there was occasion, yea a necessity to have mentioned them in some places."[153] This, too, he proffers as proof that there were no points at that time. Walton also states: "The ancient Cabalists draw all their allegories and mysteries from the letters (as they are called) not one from the points, which if they had

---

[151] Ibid.

[152] Keil, *Introduction to the Old Testament*, II:190.

[153] Walton, 245, 246.

been known in their times, would have yielded them matter enough, yea more than the letters, for their mystical expositions, as we see in the later Cabalists which have been since the invention of points."[154]

Concerning the Talmud, Green writes, "It is more difficult to determine whether the Talmud contains any allusion to the vowel points, but a thorough examination of the case has shown that it does not." He further states that where the Talmud says, " 'Do not read so, but so,' where the word in question is capable of different senses, that are only distinguishable by the vowels, the sense intended in each case is indicated, however, not by inserting written signs for the vowels, but by the connection [i.e., the context], or else it is supplied by the teacher, as this was primarily designed for oral instruction."[155]

According to De' Rossi, Elias Levita's strongest proof for the novelty of the points "is that in all the statements of the rabbis of blessed memory in the Gemara, Aggadot, and Midrashim there is no reference or allusion to any vowel point or accent."[156] De' Rossi's contention that Rabbinic silence about the points is Levita's strongest proof seems justified in that Levita gives this as his first argument for the novelty of the points.[157]

In answer to these statements about the silence of the Talmud, Whitfield writes:

> The argument from the Talmud has been represented by Elias Levita and others, from him, thus: the Talmud makes no mention of the Hebrew-points in long tracts where their mention would very properly have come in and much facilitated the explication of the subject treated on; therefore, the authors of those tracts had no knowledge of the points. In answer to which, I say, the principle upon which alone this reasoning depends, and which is here not expressed, is false. The ar-

---

[154] Walton, 246.

[155] William Henry Green, 68, 69.

[156] De' Rossi, *The Light of the Eyes*, 700.

[157] Levita, *Massoreth Ha-Massoreth*, 127.

gument, in full, would stand thus: every person, who writes upon any subject, always mentions every thing, which he knows necessary to elucidate his subject, but the authors of those Talmudic tracts, where the mention of the Hebrew points would have helped to explain their subject, have not made mention of such points; therefore, they did not know them, i.e., they did not exist. It is manifest the major proposition is false, and consequently the conclusion null.[158]

That is, just because a writer does not mention something, it does not mean that it does not exist.

The proponents of the novelty of the points, while partially basing their argument on the silence of various men, are neglecting the clear statements of Scripture itself, which argue for the presence of the points. In contrast to these men, Moses said, "I will hear what the LORD will command" (Numbers 9:8). Jesus repeatedly said, "He that hath an ear, let him what the Spirit saith unto the churches" (Revelation 2:7, 11, 17, 29; 3:6, 13, 22). What God says is the standard, not what man has left unsaid.

Story about Joab

Elias Levita relates an extra-Biblical story about Joab, in which he places great confidence because he believes that it demonstrates that there were no points in the days of Joab. The story about Joab concerns a supposed conversation between David and Joab wherein David questioned Joab as to why he only killed the Edomite males, as opposed to everybody. Joab responded by saying that his teacher had taught him to read Deuteronomy 25:19 with the word *male*, instead of *remembrance*. Levita says of the story,

> What is still greater proof [that is, greater proof than the supposed silence of the Rabbins concerning vowel-points, see above], is the following remark in the Talmud (*Baba Bathra*, 21 *b*), "Joab slew his teacher because he had performed the work of the Lord deceitfully, in reading to him זָכָר [male] instead of זֵכֶר [remembrance] (Deut. xxv.

---

[158] Whitfield, 260,261.

19)." Now is it credible that he would have attempted to read זָכָר with two *Kametz*, if they had had the points, and the word in question had been pointed זֵכֶר with six points?[159]

The problem with the story is that it has no Biblical basis and, therefore, lacks any authority whatsoever to decide the issue about the points. It also suffers from a multitude of other problems, which this work presents in Chapter Six.

Vowel Point Names Are not in the Hebrew Language

Levita argues: "Almost all the names of both the vowel-points and the accents are not Hebrew, but Aramean and Babylonian."[160] He then asks, "What is the meaning of Aramean names at Mount Sinai? Were not all the commandments given on Sinai in Hebrew?"[161] He then states: "It is perfectly evident to me that the vowel-points neither existed nor obtained in the days of the Talmudic sages, and much less in the time of the men of the Great Synagogue."[162] In response to Levita's argument, De' Rossi states:

> Now naming that is not divinely inspired is arbitrary, and as the wise Galen states in many passages of his works, one should not be concerned about names but only about the matters which they denote. I do not find it problematic, therefore, that according to the region or teacher, a vowel may be designated a *ḥireq* by one sage and *shever* by another, and *melofum*, *ḥolem*, and so on.[163]

De' Rossi makes an excellent observation. No where in the Bible does God give the names of the Hebrew vowels, therefore, different regions

---

[159] Levita, 128.

[160] Ibid., 129.

[161] Ibid.

[162] Ibid.

[163] De' Rossi, *The Light of the Eyes*, 707, 708.

and teachers could have different designations for the vowels. Such a situation is not at all a problem.

Accents

Another argument that Levita uses to try to prove his contention that the points are new is to say that there were not only no vowels, but also no accents. Before proceeding with Levita's statement, it is necessary to state that some of the vowels and accents of Hebrew are interconnected. For example, Kelley observes:

> A word marked by either 'átnāḥ or sillûq (as well as certain other strong disjunctive accents) is said to be "in pause." This means that there is a break in the recitation at this point. (Compare this to the pause that follows commas, semi-colons, and periods in modern languages.) A word in pause must have a long vowel in its accented or tone syllable. If the vowel of the tone syllable is regularly short, it must be lengthened when placed in pause.[164]

An example of that to which Kelley refers is in Jeremiah 17:18 where the Hebrew word for the second use of *I* is אָֽנִי. Normally, the unaccented word for *I* is אֲנִי; however, in Jeremiah 17:18 it has a long first vowel as opposed to its normally short vowel. The *'átnāḥ* ( ) accent under א indicates that such a change has occurred. One can see that in this case the accent and the vowel are connected. Kelley teaches that it is the accent that caused the change in the vowel, but if this is the case then there is a lost short vowel in Jeremiah 17:18, which someone replaced with a long vowel. But such an explanation is an impossibility according to Jesus' statement in Matthew 5:18, where Jesus taught that not even one tittle, that is, a vowel, will pass from the Old Testament till all be fulfilled. Two other explanations remain for the long vowel in Jeremiah 17:18: either (1) God inspired the long vowel and men noticing the difference in spelling placed an

---

[164] Page H. Kelley, *Biblical Hebrew: An Introductory Grammar* (Grand Rapids: Eerdmans, 1992), 17.

accent at this place, so that it was the vowel that led to the accent; or (2) both vowels and accents are inspired. It is beyond the scope of this work to delve into the issue of the Hebrew accents (see under Delimitations in the back of the book). In the Hebrew language, accents and vowels are interconnected; therefore, Levita's contention that there are no accents also affects the presence of vowels in the text.

Now concerning accents Levita writes:

> In *Chagiga*, where the passage "they brought burnt offerings and killed sacrifices," &c., (Exod. xxiv. 5) is discussed, Mar Sutra remarks, this discussion is necessary, in order to know where to place the dividing accent (*Chagiga* 6 *b*). From this, too, it is evident that they had no accents.[165]

Levita's argument concerns Exodus 24:5 and the dividing accent or *'átnāḥ* at the word for *burnt offerings*. *Burnt offerings* is from the Hebrew word עֹלָה, but in Exodus 24:5 it is pointed עֹלָה, with the *'átnāḥ* indicating a change from the normal vocalization of the word. In this case, the accent and the vowel are interconnected; therefore, Levita's argument against the accent is indirectly an argument against the vowel as well. Levita's understanding of the citation from *Chagiga* 6 *b* is debatable. Gill, in referring to the very same citation says, "And so in other places [that is, in the Talmud] mention is made of the distinctions of the accents."[166] And these accent marks would indicate that the vowels were already there. Gill uses the citation as evidence for the antiquity of the accents and by extension of the vowels as well, whereas Levita uses it as an evidence for the novelty of the points. Who is right? Gill further writes: "The marks and figures of them [the accents], they say in the *Talmud, Solomon* {T. B. Eruvim, fol. 21.2.} instructed the people in; for so those words are paraphrased in it, *he taught the people knowledge*, for he instructed them בסימני טעמים *in*

---

[165] Levita, 128, 129.

[166] Gill, *Dissertation*, 159.

the signs, marks, figures, or characters *of the accents.*"[167] In other words, the *Talmud* teaches that the accents are of old, which would point to the vowels already being in place, and would, therefore, indicate that Levita's understanding of the discussion concerning the accent in Exodus 24:5 is incorrect.

Kethib / Keri

Kethib refers to the word written in the text. *Keri* refers to a note in the margin that instructs the reader to read the text differently from what is written in the text. The *keri* note only has consonants; the reader is to supply the vowels from the *kethib* reading in the text to the consonants in the keri note to get the full-vocalized word. Walton expresses the view that the *keri* readings prove that the points are not part of the text when he writes:

> The *Keri* and *Ketib* which are confessed by all to be for the most part various readings gathered out of ancient Hebrew copies, are all about the letters only, not about the points, which yet if the points had then been in use, had been more subject to mistakes of the scribes then the letters, and so more various readings might have been gathered out of them, then from the difference of the letters.[168]

Whitfield, holding the opposite view, writes that most of the *keri's* show "a manifest and immediate relation to the points, and, without them, are, for the most part, without meaning, groundless and absurd; and thence it seems highly probable, that the points must, at that time, have been with the text."[169]

Be this as it may, the fact is that God's Words are pure and not in need of marginal readings, known as the *keri*. "The words of the LORD *are* pure words: *as* silver tried in a furnace of earth, purified seven times" (Psalm 12:6). God promises to keep these words and to

---

[167] Ibid., 160.

[168] Walton, 246, 247.

[169] Whitfield, 273.

"preserve them from this generation for ever" (Psalm 12:7). To try to determine a matter of faith and practice on marginal notes is to ignore the fact that God has perfectly preserved His pure, inspired words.

Matres Lectionis

Walton asserts: "The ancient Hebrew vowels were the same before the invention of points, which are in all other Eastern tongues, as the Chaldee, Syriac, Arabic, etc., viz. י ו א which are yet commonly called *matres lectionis*, because they direct the reading in books not pointed, to which some add ה and St. Jerome ע."[170] *Matres lectionis* means mothers of reading because some scholars think that these letters assisted in the reading of the language. Gill observes: "In Rabbinical books, the *matres lectionis*, as י ו א are called, are used to supply the want of vowels; whereas in the Bible they are most frequently omitted, and even in places where they might be expected, and least of all should be omitted."[171] In other words, Biblical words often lack the *matres lectionis*, and instead the Bible represents vowels by points, which means that if Walton's assertion is correct that at one time, the *matres lectionis* served as vowels in Hebrew, then at some later time someone replaced the *matres lectionis* with points. Indeed, Walton seems to suggest that a replacement occurred when he writes, "*Aleph, Vau,* and *Jod,* were the vowels before the points were invented."[172] According to Ginsburg, Cappellus believed that "in adding the points, the *matres lectiones* were eliminated,"[173] which would mean that in some cases, someone replaced a *yodh* (י), as well as other letters, with points.

---

[170] Walton, 202.

[171] Gill, *Dissertation*, 273,274.

[172] Walton, 200.

[173] Ginsburg, 56.

Compare, for instance, the spelling of David's name. In some places it is דָּוִד (I Kings 2:24), but in another place it is דָּוִיד (I Kings 3:14). Both of these words have the same accent, but notice that in one case there is no *yodh*, whereas in the other spelling there is a *yodh*. Do the variations in the spelling of David's name mean that at one time the *yodh* had existed, but someone removed it and allowed a point to replace it, so that a *yodh* has passed from the law? Perish the thought, for Jesus promised that one jot, that is, a *yodh*, shall in no wise pass from the law (Matthew 5:18). For one to suggest that Hebrew originally had *matres lectionis*, which were later replaced by points, is for such a one to ignore the Bibliology of Jesus and is for him to build his theological house upon sand, rather than on the firm foundation of the Words of God.

Whitfield makes an interesting observation about the supposed adding of points when he writes about the *dagesh forte*, which is a dot in a consonant so as to double the consonant. For instance, he observes that in Genesis 1:2 is the word הַמַּיִם, which has the *dagesh forte* in the מ, which is a point inside the letter. Before the supposed introduction of points, Moses should have written הַמַּיִם as המםים and such a practice should have held true for the other Old Testament writers. Whitfield then asks a couple of questions: "Can anyone produce an ancient copy in which these words are so writ? . . . Or, can anyone produce an authentic account from any author that those words were ever so writ?"[174] The answer to both of these questions is that no one has produced such things. It seems to be pure fancy on the part of those who suggest that points were added later and that the points replaced consonants.

---

[174] Whitfield, 19,20.

Biblical Problems

There are several Biblical problems that some propose against the *autographa* position concerning the points. These problems involve the spelling of David's name in the Old Testament, the spelling of various Old Testament names in the New Testament, Matthew 5:18, Acts 15:17, Hebrews 11:21, and consonants in the Hebrew Old Testament that have no vowels. The author answers most of these problems in this section. However, Matthew 5:18 receives a full treatment in Chapter Five, and the question about consonants without vowels receives a fuller treatment in Chapter Six.

Spelling of David's Name

Oats contends that a problem with the *autographa* position of the vowel points concerns the spelling of David's name. Oats observes:

> David's name in the OT is spelled DWD in some places and DWYD in others. If the Hebrew had vowels, this change would not have been needed. If there were no vowels, however, and if David's name was being mispronounced, the addition of the "Y" would have assured the pronunciation of "David."[175]

In the case of David's name, it is דָּוִד and דָּוִיד. In both cases, the vowels are the same, but the consonants differ. Oats concludes that since the Bible spells David's name with different consonants, that perhaps it indicates that originally there were no vowels and that the insertion of the *yodh* helped to insure the correct pronunciation of David's name.

However, there are a few problems with Oats' observation. First, it is not extraordinary to spell the same name in different ways, either with different vowels or with different consonants. For instance, Proverbs spells *Lemuel* two different ways in the space of four verses, לְמוּאֵל in Proverbs 31:1 and לְמוֹאֵל in Proverbs 31:4. An interesting

---

[175] Oats, *Thou Shalt Keep Them: A Review*, 7.

thing about the two different spellings for *Lemuel* is that if someone added the points later, why did he not point the two words the same way? Nehemiah also gives two different spellings for the same individual: Geshem, that is, וְגֶ֫שֶׁם (*and Geshem*) in Nehemiah 2:19; and Gashmu, that is, וְגַשְׁמ֫וּ (*and Gashmu*) in Nehemiah 6:6. In this case, the consonants and the vowels are different. What the above examples demonstrate is that sometimes writers operating under inspiration give different spellings for the same name, could not this have happened with David's name? A second problem with Oats' thinking arises when one realizes that Solomon used the longer spelling of David's name (דָּוִיד) in Song of Solomon 4:4. Surely, he was not in danger of mispronouncing his father's own name. Indeed, in I Kings 2:24 Solomon used the shorter spelling of his father's name (דָּוִד). It seems that these were just two different ways of spelling David's name. The same phenomenon occurs in Ezekiel where in Ezekiel 34:23 is the long spelling and then in the next verse is the short spelling. A third potential problem with Oats' thinking is that he states that a *yodh* was inserted into David's name, which seems to suggest that someone altered the spelling, that is, that someone added to the Words of God and that somehow the addition became affixed in the Traditional Text. At this point, a number of questions arise. Could there be other additions? How would one know if there are other additions? If there are other additions, then what of the promise of God concerning perfect preservation (Psalm 12:6,7)?

    The best course of action is to believe that God has perfectly preserved His Words (Psalm 12:6,7), that is, both vowels and consonants; and understand that one can spell names and words differently just as he could today. In fact, might the spelling changes be a test from the Lord, to see if a man will simply walk by faith and believe God's promises of perfect preservation, instead of walking by sight and questioning God's Words? It is likely that the spelling variations are a test, but many are flunking the test and are teaching their students to flunk the test as well (cf. Luke 24:25).

New Testament Spelling of Old Testament Names

Keil, in arguing for the novelty of the points, bases one of his arguments upon the non-authoritative Greek Alexandrian translation of the Old Testament, which is a version of the LXX.[176] Keil's argument finds a parallel in the New Testament. Before showing that parallel, may the reader note that earlier comments about the LXX in the "Historical Problems" section apply here. The LXX has no authority to decide the issue concerning the vowel points because God has not promised to preserve a Greek translation of the Old Testament, but rather to preserve the Hebrew and Aramaic words of the Old Testament (Matthew 5:18). Now to Keil's argument and how it finds a parallel in the New Testament: Keil states that in the Alexandrian translation various names do not fully follow the vowels present in the Hebrew text. For example, *Midian* (מִדְיָן) appears as Μαδιαν; *Samson* (שִׁמְשׁוֹן) as Σαμψων; *Samuel* (שְׁמוּאֵל) as Σαμουηλ; *Zebulun* (זְבֻלוּן) as Ζαβουλων; and *Kidron* (קִדְרוֹן) as Κεδρων.[177] In each of these cases the first vowels in the Greek are different from the first vowels of the Hebrew. In *Midian* and *Samson*, Hebrew has an *i*, whereas the Greek has an *a*; in *Samuel* and *Zebulun*, the Hebrew has a vocal shewa (an half *e* sound), whereas the Greek has an *a*; and in *Kidron*, the Hebrew has an *i*, whereas the Greek has an *e*. While Keil speaks of the LXX, yet these same spelling variations also appear in the New Testament. Μαδιάμ[178] is in Acts 7:29; Σαμψών and Σαμουήλ in Hebrews 11:32;

---

[176] "Alexandrian" in *Cyclopedia*, I:155.

[177] Keil, *Introduction to the Old Testament*, II:192, 193.

[178] The last consonant in the New Testament spelling (an *m*) differs from the last consonant in the Old Testament spelling (an *n*). In light of this difference, could not someone, using the same argumentation for lack of vowels, argue that the Hebrew consonants were also not available at the time of the writing of the New Testament? However, such an argument would lead to the ridiculous conclusion that the Old Testament was written after the New Testament! Such is where the novelty-of-the-points advocates find themselves? To suggest that the Masoretes or some other group added vowels to the Old Testament hundreds of years after the completion of the New Testament means that the words of the Old Testament were completed after the writing of

Ζαβουλών in Matthew 4:13; and Κεδρών in John 18:1. Other names may manifest a difference in spelling and the answers in this section would apply to them as well.

Some might think that since several of the names that Keil lists in the LXX have parallels in the New Testament that this would bolster his argument for the novelty of the points. However, this is not the case, for there are legitimate answers for why the New Testament Greek words do not follow the first vowel of the Hebrew names. Before getting to these answers, one should, first of all, notice that in each of the above examples, the Greek follows the Hebrew vowels in the rest of the words, which indicates that the writers of the New Testament were not totally ignorant of the Hebrew vowels. Therefore, one cannot use these examples to say that the New Testament writers did not have any vowels in their Hebrew Old Testament. But the question remains as to why did not the New Testament writers follow the first vowels of the Hebrew names? A couple of answers are possible. First, Whitfield in speaking of Greek translations of the Old Testament states: "Differences in the proper names might proceed from an endeavour in the authors to accommodate the pronunciation to the idiom of the Greek language."[179] The same could be true with the New Testament, except that the New Testament writers were under the influence of the inspiration of the Holy Spirit and, therefore, did their work exactly as God wanted. In looking at the names *Samson* (שִׁמְשׁוֹן) and *Samuel* (שְׁמוּאֵל), the first letter in each is שׁ, which has an *sh* sound, but Greek has no *sh* letter, therefore, in Greek the first letter of these names is Σ, that is, *s*. Certainly, there is some Helenization of the

---

the New Testament! The variation in the last consonant between the Greek (*Madiam*) and the Hebrew (*Midian*) lends further credence to the Helenization of the word *Midian* with the result that in Greek it is *Madiam*. See further discussion in the text about Helenization.

[179] Whitfield, 225.

names as the names go from the Hebrew language into Greek, which could be a reason for the difference in the first vowels of these names.

Another answer as to why there is a difference in spelling lies in the fact that names often have alternate spellings and it could be that the New Testament writers were simply using a different spelling. May the reader note that even with the different spelling there is no doubt as to whom the New Testament writers are referring. The Words of God remain sure and certain, which is very different compared to the examples presented in the beginning of this book from Genesis 49:10; Deuteronomy 33:27; and Ecclesiastes 3:21. But now to the case at hand, in *Midian* and *Samson*, Hebrew has an *i*, whereas the Greek has an *a*. Sometimes writers of Scripture exchange *i* and *a* in referring to the same place. For example, II Kings 17:24 speaks of Ava (עַוָּא) where the first vowel is an *a*; whereas II Kings 18:34, referring to the same place, gives its name as Ivah (עִוָּה) where the first vowel is *i*.[180] Therefore, for the writers of the New Testament Scripture to have an *a*, instead of an *i* is not as unusual as it might first seem. Concerning *Samuel* and *Zebulun*, the Hebrew has a vocal shewa, whereas the Greek has an *a*. At times the writers of the Old Testament Scripture exchange an *a* with a vocal shewa. For instance, in Genesis 14:7 is the expression *in Hazazontamar* (בְּחַצְצֹן תָּמָר), whereas II Chronicles 20:2 has *in Hazezontamar* (בְּחַצְצוֹן תָּמָר). The writers of the New Testament follow the same pattern concerning *Samuel* and *Zebulun*. Concerning *Kidron*, the Hebrew has an *i*, whereas the Greek has an *e*. Again, the writers of the Old Testament exchange an *i* for an *e*. Isaiah 8:6 has הַשִּׁלֹחַ (translated as *Shiloah*), which transliterates as *hashshilach*; whereas Nehemiah 3:15 has הַשֶּׁלַח (translated as *Siloah*), which transliterates as *hashshelach*. The writers of the New Testament follow the same pattern concerning *Kidron*. In each of these examples,

---

[180] The example concerning *Ava / Ivah* presents other differences in spelling, but the main point concerns the exchange of *a* and *i*.

the New Testament writers follow a pattern that God had already established in the Old Testament, that is, that names for people and places can have different spellings. From the viewpoint of the writer, just as God inspired different spellings of the same Old Testament name, so He inspired the New Testament writers also to give alternate spellings on occasion. The fact of these different spellings is not sufficient ground to overthrow the *autographa* position about the points.

As an interesting aside, the alternate spellings of some names in the Old Testament argue against the novelty of the points. If the points were of a recent invention, then one would expect a consistency and uniformity in spelling, but such is not the case. Arguing in a similar fashion, Whitfield presents a multitude of examples of unusual pointing and reasons that such cases prove the antiquity of the points. Three examples will serve to illustrate Whitfield's line of thinking. First, concerning יֻלַּד (*were born*) in Genesis 46:22, Whitfield observes that if the Masoretes "made the points, the word יֻלַּד would have been pointed יָלַד, and so the translation would be *which she bare unto Jacob*. . . . This instance proves the antiquity of the points, almost beyond question."[181] Second, in regard to וַיָּבוֹא (*then came*, a Qal masculine singular verb) in Ezekiel 14:1, Whitfield writes: "Here appears a very great impropriety: a verb singular with a nominative case plural [subject]. Had the points been lately added, their authors would have put a *kibbuts* under א thus, יָבֹאוּ."[182] Third, Whitfield states:

> In Ps. 71.15 the word סְפֹרוֹת *numbers*; is a singularity not occurring again in the whole Old Testament; and is an irregular feminine plural of סֵפֶר which sometimes signifies *number*. Had the points lately been added; as the former *Hbolem* is without the ו, the authors would certainly have made it סְפָרוֹת the regular plural feminine.[183]

---

[181] Whitfield, 126.

[182] Ibid., 131.

[183] Ibid., 124.

One could find many other examples of irregularity in the pointing, all of which serve to prove the antiquity of the points.

Matthew 5:18

Matthew 5:18 states: "For verily I say unto you, Till heaven and earth pass, one jot or one tittle shall in no wise pass from the law, till all be fulfilled." Concerning this verse, Oats writes:

> The "jot" is the "yodh," the smallest of the Hebrew consonants. While most view "tittle" as a part of a consonant, this book [*Thou Shalt Keep Them*] argues that the word refers to vowels. It is inconsistent, however, for Jesus to use the actual name of a consonant, but not the actual name of a vowel.[184]

Chapter Five presents a detailed exegesis of Matthew 5:18 in wherein the author shows that *tittle* is not part of a consonant, but rather is referring to the vowel point *chirek*, thereby removing Oats' alleged inconsistency.

Acts 15:17

In Acts 15:17 is a quotation of Amos 9:12. Of particular interest is that Amos has the word *Edom* ("the remnant of Edom"), whereas Acts has *men* ("the residue of men"). Concerning the difference between Acts 15:17 and Amos 9:12, Oats writes, "The NT and the LXX (the OT translated into Greek by the Jews) read the Hebrew 'DM as *adam* (man) and the MT reads these same consonants as *edom* (Edom)." Oats concludes: "The NT writers either quoted from the LXX or they did not have the vowel points in the Hebrew text and were uncertain which way to translate the consonants."[185] There is a big problem with Oats' contention here and the problem is that the consonantal text in Amos 9:12 for *Edom* has אדום, that is, 'DWM, whereas the consonants for *Adam* are אדם, that is, 'DM. For Oats

---

[184] Oats, *Thou Shalt Keep Them: A Review*, 6.

[185] Ibid., 6, 7.

contention to have even a slimmer of validity *Edom* would have to be missing the ו, but it is not missing the ו, and never will for Jesus promised that not even one jot will pass from the law (Matthew 5:18). The *jot* is the least of the letters and since the least of the letters will not pass, then the greater letters will not pass either (Luke 16:10). In light of this, Oats' reasoning behind his suggestion that the New Testament writers did not have the vowel points in the Hebrew text is incorrect. As to why Acts 15:17 has *men*, instead of *Edom*, the Holy Spirit is giving an inspired commentary upon the words of Amos as He does in other places (compare, for instance, Hebrews 10:5 with Psalm 40:6).[186]

Hebrews 11:21

Hebrews 11:21 says, "By faith Jacob, when he was a dying, blessed both the sons of Joseph; and worshipped, *leaning* upon the top of his staff." Some believe that Hebrews 11:21 is supposed to be a quote or a direct reference to Genesis 47:31, which reads, "And Israel bowed himself upon the bed's head." Concerning Hebrews 11:21, Calvin writes:

> This is one of those places from which we may conclude that the points were not formerly used by the Hebrews; for the Greek translators could not have made such a mistake as to put staff here for a bed, if the mode of writing was then the same as now. No doubt Moses spoke of the head of his couch, when he said על ראש המטה but the Greek translators rendered the words, "On the top of his staff" as though the last word was written, *mathaeh*.[187]

Along the same course of thinking, Homer Kent writes:

---

[186] That the writers of the New Testament did not use the LXX, see the author's *Those So-Called Errors* (Newington, CT: Emmanuel Baptist Press, 2003), 170-174.

[187] John Calvin, *Commentaries on the Epistle of Paul to the Hebrews* in vol. 22 of *Calvin's Commentaries*, trans. and ed. John Owen (Grand Rapids: Baker Book House), 290.

The statement that Jacob worshipped upon the top of his staff is drawn from Genesis 47:31, but employs the wording of the Septuagint, rather than the Massoretic Hebrew text which reads "bed" instead of "staff." The problem arose from the fact that the ancient Hebrew Scriptures were written in a consonantal text, and the addition of vowels to indicate pronunciation (i.e., vowel pointing), such as are found in the present text, was not done until by the Massoretic scholars between the sixth and ninth centuries A.D. It so happens that the consonants for "bed" and "staff" are exactly the same in Hebrew.[188]

But there is another explanation as to the difference between Genesis 47:31 and Hebrews 11:21. For instance, Bengel supposes that Jacob "might on the *bed* itself support his side or arm with a *staff*,"[189] that is, both are true. As both are in the Bible, it is the best course of action to believe that both are true, rather to think that one or the other of these passages is in error, as does Calvin and Kent. Indeed, Jesus stated, "Thy word is truth" (John 17:17), therefore, what is in the Old Testament is true, as well as what is in the New Testament.

Concerning the supposed use of the Septuagint by the Apostle Paul in Hebrews, Owen writes:

> I suppose I may conclude that it is more probable, at least, that the apostle's interpretations of the testimonies used by him, all agreeably unto the mind of the Holy Ghost, were by some of old inserted into the vulgar copies of the Greek translation of the Old Testament, and therein prevailed unto *common acceptation*, than that he himself followed, in the citation of them, a translation departing without reason from the original text, and diverting unto such senses as its authors knew not to be contained in them, which must needs give offence unto them with whom he had to do.[190]

---

[188] Homer A. Kent, *The Epistle to the Hebrews: A Commentary* (Grand Rapids: Baker Book House, 1981), 233.

[189] John A. Bengel, *New Testament Word Studies*, trans. Charlton T. Lewis and Marvin R. Vincent (Grand Rapids: Kregel Publications, 1971), II: 661, 662.

[190] John Owen, *An Exposition of the Epistle to the Hebrews with Preliminary Exercitations*, ed. W. H. Goold (Edinburgh: Johnstone and Hunter, 1854, reprinted Carlisle, PA: Banner of Truth Trust, 1991), I: 117.

In other words, it was the LXX that followed Paul, and not Paul who followed the LXX.

Consonants with No Vowels

The Traditional Hebrew text has eight places where consonants are unpointed (אם in Ruth 3:12; II Samuel 13:33; 15:21; Jeremiah 39:12; נא in II Kings 5:18; את in Jeremiah 38:16; ידרך in Jeremiah 51:3; and חמם in Ezekiel 48:16). The author has not found anyone who uses unpointed consonants as proof for an unpointed text. Perhaps someone might claim that the lack of points with these consonants shows that the text was originally unpointed and that the Masoretes happened to have missed these places when they supposedly pointed the text. Again, the author has found no one who makes such an argument. But if anyone were to pose such an argument, then by the same reasoning one could argue that the text originally had no consonants because there are places where only points occur, for example, ֻ in Judges 20:13 and ֻ in Ruth 3:15,17 (see also II Samuel 8:3; 16:23; 18:20; II Kings 19:31,37; Jeremiah 31:38; 50:29). Furthermore, the Traditional Hebrew text has places where just a point serves to indicate the article, as opposed to a ה with the point (I Samuel 14:32; II Samuel 23:9; I Kings 4:7; 7:20; 15:18; II Kings 11:20; 15:25; Isaiah 32:15; Jeremiah 10:13; 17:19; 40:3; 52:32; Lamentations 1:18; Ezekiel 18:20). What is one to make of these instances?

First, because verses such as Psalm 12:6,7 teach a perfect preservation, then one must conclude that verses in the Traditional Text that have consonants with no vowels are not errors. Second, since Jesus promised that one jot and one tittle shall in no wise pass from the Old Testament (Matthew 5:18), then one must also conclude that not a single vowel or consonant has been lost in these instances. Third, these difficulties are an opportunity for a person to manifest faith and thereby please God (Hebrews 11:6). Fourth, God may have purposely placed these things in the text to see if a Bible student would savour the things of God or the things of men (Matthew 16:23). The bottom line is this: one must choose either to walk by faith and trust that the consonants without vowels in the Traditional Text are exactly how God inspired and preserved His Words, or to walk by sight and adopt some unbelieving, rationalistic explanation for the consonants with no vowels. Just as God purposely inspired and preserved His Words with apparent contradictions (cf., for instance, II Kings 8:26 with II Chronicles 22:2), so He has inspired and preserved His Words with what appear to be apparent textual difficulties to see if man will really walk by faith. Will a man simply believe God's Words, although he may not be able to explain it?

The fact is that none of the places where there are unpointed consonants, vowels without consonants, and a single point for the article results in the text being unclear. In the case of the unpointed consonants, it seems that the consonants are inspired notations highlighting some teaching in the verse. For instance, on Ezekiel 48:16, Hengstenberg believes that החמש emphasizes "that the south side *equally* with the north side has 4500 cubits."[191] Whether one accepts Hengstenberg's opinion is immaterial, what is more important is that one believe that God's Words are correct in Ezekiel 48:16 and all other verses.

If one should argue that since these unpointed consonants cause no difficulty in understanding the text, then would it not be possible to have a completely unpointed text with it causing no difficulty? The answer is no. To have eight instances of unpointed consonants is one thing, to have the entire Old Testament text unpointed is quite another. Chapter Three presents many examples of the confusion that would reign if the entire text were unpointed. But also if the entire text were unpointed what would one do in the cases where just the point indicates the article, or where there are points with no consonants? A

---

[191] E. W. Hengstenberg, *The Prophecies of the Prophet Ezekiel Elucidated*, trans. A. C. Murphy and J. G. Murphy (Edinburgh: T & T Clark, 1869, reprinted Eugene, OR: Wipf and Stock Publishers, n. d.), 489.

pointless text would eliminate the places where a point or points indicate a word causing the omission of nearly two dozen words, which, in light of God's promises of perfect preservation, is unacceptable. Chapter Six, "Further Objections," presents more information about the places where consonants are without vowels, vowels are without consonants, and a lone vowel indicates the article.

Conclusion

Some raise historical problems with the *autographa* position such as difficulty in writing the points, spelling variations, unpointed documents, silence about points, a story about Joab, vowel point names not in Hebrew, the *kethib* and *keri* readings, and the *matres lectionis*. But none of these historical arguments carries any weight since it is not history that is the rule for faith and practice, but it is the Bible (see Chapter Two). These historical problems, then, cannot overthrow the *autographa* position.

Some raise biblical problems with the *autographa* position such as the spelling of David's name, New Testament spelling of Old Testament names, *tittle* supposedly not being the name of a vowel point, the word *men* in Acts 15:17, the words *top of his staff* in Hebrews 11:21, and consonants with no vowels. David's name could have different spellings just as other names do. New Testament writers through the process of inspiration could spell Old Testament names differently. *Tittle* is the name of the Hebrew vowel point *chirek*. In Acts 15:17 the Spirit of God is giving an inspired commentary upon an Old Testament word. Concerning Hebrews 11:21 Jacob both leaned upon the top of his staff and bowed himself upon the bed's head as Genesis 47:31 says. Concerning consonants with no vowels one should believe by faith that God has perfectly preserved His Words (Psalm 12:6,7). The Biblical problems some pose against the *autographa* position have answers and are not sufficient to overthrow the position.

Summary

In summary, the *autographa* position believes that God gave the points by inspiration and are, therefore, fully authoritative. Many have held the *autographa* position among them being Simon ben-Jochai, Levi ben-Joseph, Moses the Punctuator, David Kimḥi, Johannes Isaac Levita, Antoine Rudolphe Chevalier, Azariah De' Rossi, William Fulke, Guilielmus Eyrius, Johannes Buxtorf, Sr., Valentin Schindler, Amandus Polanus Von Polandsdorf, John Weemes, John Lightfoot, Johannes Buxtorf, Jr., Gisbert Voetius, James Ussher, John Owen, Matthias Wasmuth, Joseph Cooper, Francois Turretin, Samuel Clark, Johann Gottlob Carpzov, Pierre Guarin, Peter Whitfield, John Gill, James Robertson, Adam Benedict Spitzner, John Moncrieff, George Sayles Bishop, Kent Brandenburg, Gary Webb, Thomas Strouse, Gerardus, Junius, Gomarus, William Whitaker, John Rainolds, Deodatus, Heidegger, Glassius, Flacius Illyricus, Hassret, Wolthius, and Loescher. For over a period of a thousand years men have held to the inspiration of the vowel points.

Some pose problems with the *autographa* position, but the historical and Biblical problems that opponents of the *autographa* position pose all have answers. What is clear as one examines the problems is that the advocates of these arguments, generally have a low view of either inspiration or of preservation. But this is not all, they also have a low view of the absolute authority of Scripture, as this book presents in the next sections. A low view of the inspiration, preservation, and authority of the Scriptures should cause some concern for those who might align themselves with the advocates of arguments against the *autographa* position.

Accommodation Position

The second position about the vowel points is, what the writer calls, the accommodation position. In discussing the accommodation position, this section presents the position itself, the proponents of the position, and some problems that may arise from the position.

The Position

The accommodation position seeks, on the one hand, to say that the vowel points are fully or partially authoritative, but, on the other hand, to say that they are not inspired. Since, according to the accommodation position, the vowel points are not inspired, then they were added by men who were not moved by the Spirit of God. For many of the accommodationists, the men who added the vowel points were the Masoretes. In reality, however, it does not matter who these men were. The fact is, according to the accommodation position, the ones who added the vowel points did not get them from God, but, rather, either invented the vowel points on their own, or passed them down from others. Such a situation presents a real difficulty for the advocates of the accommodation position. In saying that the points are either fully or partially authoritative, the accommodationists are relying on an uninspired addition to the Bible as an authority (see later for more information).

The author chooses the word *accommodation* because it seems to him that the proponents of the accommodation position are trying to accommodate two different groups. They seem to want the recognition of a certain group of scholars, who say that the vowel points are not inspired. At the same time, the accommodationists do not want to appear to alienate another group that holds to the authority of the vowel points. Another term for the accommodation position might be middle-of-the-road. The accommodation position wants to sound scholarly, while at the same time sounding Scriptural. And herein belies its weakness for "no man can serve two masters" (Matthew 6:24). Who or what will be the sole authority for faith and practice, the Bible, so-called uninspired additions to the Bible, or the scholars? The accommodation position seeks to hold to the scholarly tradition of the novelty of the points, while sounding Scriptural by claiming that the points are authoritative. However, in so doing they actually make the Words "of God on none effect by" their tradition (Matthew 15:6), for they are elevating a scholarly tradition above the sole authority of Scripture. Chapter Two to discusses the issue of authority in detail.

That the novelty of the points is the prevailing, scholarly, traditional view is evident from several sources. Pick writes: "Modern research and criticism have confirmed the arguments urged by Levita against the antiquity of the present vowel signs."[192] McClintock and Strong write that Cappellus believed that the points "were invented by the Jews of Tiberias some six hundred years subsequently to the death of Christ; whereas Buxtorf held them to be coeval with the language. The opinion of Cappellus has since been generally received."[193] Keil writes, "The violent controversy as to the age of the Hebrew vowel points, set in motion two hundred years ago, was terminated in the second half of [the] last century [18th century] by the general acknowledgement that they were of comparatively recent origin."[194]

The Proponents

Since the novelty of the points is the prevailing view, it has many proponents. This section will limit itself to listing some of the important historical proponents of the accommodation position as well some present-day Fundamentalists.

Elias Levita – 1538

Levita published *Masoreth ha-Masoreth* wherein he writes: "The vowel-points and the accents did not exist either before Ezra, or

---

[192] Pick, "The Vowel-Points Controversy in the XIV, XVII, and XVIII Centuries," 168.

[193] "Cappel (Cappellus), Louis" in *Cyclopedia*, II:106.

[194] Keil, *Introduction to the Old Testament*, II:190.

in the time of Ezra, or after Ezra until the close of the Talmud."[195] He claims: "I have made it evident that the vowel-points and the accents were neither given on Sinai, nor were they invented by the men of the Great Synagogue, but that they are the work of the Massorites, who flourished at a later period."[196] While holding to the novelty of the points, he nonetheless believed that they were authoritative. Ginsburg writes:

> Levita, though maintaining the novelty of the vowel-points, firmly believed that the very same pronunciation and sounds, which are now denoted by the vowels and accents, were perfectly known and used by the Jews from the remotest antiquity, long before these arbitrary signs were invented, and that they represent the true and genuine reading as it came from the inspired writers of the respective books; and, consequently, the reading which these points have fixed is as much of divine authority as the letters.[197]

John Calvin – 1550

Earlier, this chapter quoted Calvin on Hebrews 11:21 wherein he wrote, "This is one of those places from which we may conclude that the points were not formerly used by the Hebrews."[198] Commenting on Zechariah 11:7, Calvin writes:

> Zechariah did not set down the points, for they were not then in use. I indeed know with how much care the old scribes contrived the points, when the language had already ceased to be in common use. They then who neglect, or wholly reject the points, are certainly void of all

---

[195] Levita, *The Massoreth Ha-Massoreth*, 127.

[196] Ibid., 133.

[197] Ginsburg, *The Massoreth Ha-Massoreth of Elias Levita, Being an Exposition of the Massoretic Notes on the Hebrew Bible, or the Ancient Critical Apparatus of the Old Testament in Hebrew, with an English Translation, and Critical and Explanatory Notes, by Christian D. Ginsburg*, 55,56.

[198] Calvin, *The Commentaries on the Epistle of Paul to the Hebrews*, 290.

judgment and reason; but yet some discrimination ought to be exercised.[199]

While Calvin held to the novelty of the points, it appears that he thought they had some authority, though not absolute authority in all cases.

Louis Cappellus – 1624

In 1624, Cappellus published *Arcanum punctionis revelatum*, that is, "The Mystery of the Points Unveiled" in which he expressed the view that the "points were invented by the Jews of Tiberias some six hundred years subsequently to the death of Christ."[200] According to Ginsburg, Cappellus' book with "its immense erudition, conclusive reasoning, and overpowering arguments soon convinced the most learned Biblical scholars that the vowel-points were centuries later than the Christian era."[201] Ginsburg also states that Cappellus' book "created quite as great a revolution among scholars in the seventeenth century as the *Massoreth Ha-Massoreth*, of which it was an exposition."[202] In spite of Ginsburg's assessment, the author was only able to find one library worldwide that has Cappellus' book with that library being in Europe. In his work, Cappellus, while arguing for the novelty of the points, nevertheless upheld their authority. Cappellus wrote:

> When I say that the points were invented and added to the consonants by the Massorites of Tiberias, I do not mean, as I have stated before, that the reading of the sacred text was invented by them out of their own brain, and that they fixed, according to their own will and fancy, what these points denote and express; but what I mean is, that they express by these marks of their own invention the reading of the sacred text which obtained everywhere among the Jews, which they them-

---

[199] John Calvin, *Commentaries on the Twelve Minor Prophets*, in vol. 15 of *Calvin's Commentaries*, trans. John Owen (Grand Rapids: Baker Books, 2003), 313, 314.

[200] "Cappel (Cappellus), Louis" in *Cyclopedia*, II:106.

[201] Ginsburg, 54, 55.

[202] Ibid., 57.

selves had been taught by their masters in the scholastic institutions, which they had received by oral tradition from the Fathers, and which reading the Jews believed to be the same ancient and authentic reading of Moses and the prophets.[203]

In the above quote, Cappellus says that the Jews conveyed the vowels via an oral tradition, which the Masoretes subsequently wrote down. At this time in Cappellus' life, he was willing to consider Jewish oral tradition authoritative. Later, he would reject putting any authority in the points (see further under the non-authoritative position).

Brian Walton – 1657 and 1659

In 1659, Walton wrote *The Considerator Considered* in which he states:

> For we neither affirm that the vowels and accents were invented by the Masorites, but that the Hebrew tongue did always consist of vowels and consonants. *Aleph, Vau,* and *Jod,* were the vowels before the points were invented, as they were also in the Syriac, Arabic, and other Eastern tongues: nor that these points which are now used for vowels and accents, were the arbitrary invention of the Masorites, but that they pointed the text according to the true and received reading, and not as they pleased; nor that it is lawful for any to reject their reading at pleasure, but that all are tied to it, unless some error, or better reading can be clearly proved; nor that the authority of the reading depends upon the Masorites, but that they pointed it according to the received reading, which expressed the true sense of the Holy Ghost; so that the

---

[203] Ibid., 56. Ginsburg refers to "cum dico a Masorethis Tiberiensibus excogitata esse puncta et consonis addita, non hoc volo, uit jam monui, ab iis excogitatam, atque de proprio cerebo pro eorum libitu et arbitrio confictam esse lectionem sacri textus, quam punctis illis signarunt, atque expresserunt; sed hoc duntaxat volo, expressam esse ab iis, notulis a se excogitatis, lectionem sacri textus, quae tum ubique inter Judaeos obtinebat, quamque ipsi edocti fuerant a suis magistris scholastica institione, atque orali, et πατροπαραδότῳ traditione ab iis acceperant, quam lectionem credebant Judaei antiquae Mosaicae et Propheticae authenticae conformem esse" from Louis Cappellus, *Arcanum punctationis revelatum* (Amsterdam, 1689), lib. ii,. cap. xvii. 5 & 6, p. 775.

controversy is only about the present points, in regard of their forms, not or their force and signification.[204]

While Walton holds to the novelty of the points, he, nevertheless, mostly holds to their authority. But his position is not without major problems for he (1) rejects perfect preservation (Psalm 12:6,7), when he says that there may be better readings; (2) seems to suggest that the Masoretes removed *yodhs* and replaced them with points contrary to Matthew 5:18, resulting in replacing that which was inspired and preserved with that which was not inspired; (3) places his confidence in the uninspired vowel points of the Masoretes, instead of in what was written; and (4) contradicts himself in first saying that the Masoretes pointed the text according to the true reading so that they "expressed the true sense of the Holy Ghost," and then saying that there may be better readings.

In 1657, Walton published the *London Polyglot*. Volume One of the *Polyglot* contains the *Prolegomena*.[205] Ginsburg notes that Walton's *Prolegomena* and *The Considerator Considered* "decided the battle in England in favour of the anti-vowelists. Henceforth all Biblical critics, with very few exceptions, regarded the points as modern, useless, and of no authority, though Walton himself . . . maintained that they, as a rule, represented the ancient and genuine reading."[206] Clearly, Walton's works had quite an impact in persuading people to reject the antiquity and inspiration of the points.

Homer A. Kent – 1972

In 1972, Homer Kent wrote a commentary on Hebrews, in which he wrote: "The ancient Hebrew Scriptures were written in a consonantal text, and the addition of vowels to indicate pronunciation

---

[204] Walton, *The Considerator Considered*, 200.

[205] "Polyglot Bibles" in *Cyclopedia*, VI: 368.

[206] Ginsburg, 59.

(i.e., vowel pointing), such as are found in the present text, was not done until by the Massoretic scholars between the sixth and ninth centuries A.D."[207] The writer does not believe that Kent would be for the wholesale abandoning of the points, but in some cases Kent thinks that one can adjust the points (see earlier discussion under Biblical problems with the *autographa* position).

Randy Jaeggli and the Coalition – 1998

In 1998 Jaeggli of Bob Jones University stated:

> A group of Jewish scribes called the Masoretes who did their work from approximately five hundred A.D. to nine hundred A.D. are the ones who were the guardians of the text during that time period and they added in vowel points to a text that they had that originally had only consonants.[208]

Jaeggli made the above statement as a member of the Coalition for the Defense of the Scriptures and as such, it represents the position of the coalition. Other members of the coalition were Robert Delnay of Clearwater Christian College, Sam Horn of Northland Baptist Bible College, Larry Oats of Maranatha Baptist Bible College, William Combs and David Doran of Detroit Baptist Theological Seminary, Dave Burgraff of Calvary Baptist Theological Seminary, Kevin Bauder of Central Baptist Theological Seminary, and Thurman Wisdom of Bob Jones University. While the coalition expresses the view that the vowel points are not inspired, the author does not believe that the coalition would advocate a total rejection of the points; therefore, he places the members of the coalition in the accommodation position. May the reader be aware that the author graduated from two of the schools represented by the coalition, Bob Jones University and Calvary

---

[207] Homer A. Kent, *The Epistle to the Hebrews: A Commentary* (Grand Rapids: Baker Book House, 1972), 233.

[208] *Fundamentalism and the Word of God* (Allen Park, MI: Coalition for the Defense of the Scriptures, 1998), videocassette.

Baptist Theological Seminary, and he adopted the accommodation position about the points without considering the full and serious Biblical ramifications of such a view. Upon further reflection, however, the author changed his mind and he hopes that these men and others like them will do likewise.

Larry Oats – 2003

Oats of Maranatha Baptist Bible College, in a review of *Thou Shalt Keep Them*, writes:

> This book argues for the inspiration of the vowel points in the Hebrew text. Most scholars acknowledge that Hebrew had no vowels until the spoken language began to be lost after the destruction of Jerusalem. The Masoretes (Jewish scribes who were the preservers of the written Old Testament) developed vowels to preserve the pronunciation of the words.[209]

There are several things to note about Oats' quote. First, Oats refers to the assessment of "most scholars" as a reason for why he thinks the points are uninspired. And Oats aligns himself with these scholars. Second, Oats believes that the Masoretes were the preservers of the Old Testament partly by means of the vowel points. Therefore, it seems that Oats would place some authority in the points and, by so doing, would seem to be aligning himself with those who would regard these points as authoritative. But here Oats has a real problem, for if the points are not inspired, then in what way are they authoritative? If they are uninspired, then they are uninspired additions to the Words of God, and one should soundly reject them as such. Third, Oats believes that it was the Masoretes who were the preservers of the Old Testament. However, Jesus promised that the vowels would not pass away (Matthew 5:18; Luke 16:17). Further, Jesus commissioned His local church to keep the words of Scripture (Matthew 28:20), not the Masoretes.

---

[209] Larry Oats, *Thou Shalt Keep Them: A Review*, 6.

David Sorenson – 2004

In a letter to the author, David Sorenson writes: "I frankly believe the Masoretic vowel points (1) are not inspired and (2) were not part of the originals."[210] In another letter to the author, Sorenson writes:

> My *theory* regarding the vowel points since the second millennium AD is that God used Jewish scribes of his choosing, perhaps the Masoretes or some other unknown scribes, to invent the pointing to (1) help Jews in danger of losing their language and (2) to help gentile Christians such as you and I understand Hebrew better. (Perhaps the scribes and rabbis did not have that in mind, but I think that God did.) In distinction to what I wrote earlier, I am willing to entertain the possibility that God even superintended the insertion of the vowel points along the way. Call that whatever you may wish.[211]

While Sorenson soundly rejects the inspiration of the points, he is willing to place some authority in the vowel points. If the points are not inspired, and if they are not part of the originals, and if scribes inserted them some time after the closing of the canon, which is when the Masoretes thrived; then men who were not under the influence of the inspiration of God added the points to the Old Testament. Uninspired additions to the Old Testament raise some serious problems as the next section details.

May the author say that he appreciates the work that Sorenson has done in defending the Received Text of the New Testament in the book *Touch Not the Unclean Thing* and looks upon him as an ally. However, the author respectfully disagrees with Sorenson's position on the vowel points and hopes that Sorenson will reconsider.

---

[210] David Sorenson, letter to the author, January 31, 2004.

[211] David Sorenson, letter to the author, March 1, 2004. Emphasis is that of Sorenson's.

The Problems

Several major Biblical problems exist with the accommodation position, for the accommodation position relies on oral tradition, allows for additions to the Words of God, and neglects the written Words of God.

Relying on Oral Tradition

Many of the advocates of the accommodation position assert that the Jews conveyed the vowels of the Hebrew Old Testament by oral tradition and that some time after Christ the Masoretes or some other group added the oral tradition of the vowels to the written record of the consonants. Since the advocates of the accommodation position regard the vowels as either fully or partially authoritative, and since they believe that the vowels were passed along by oral tradition; then the accommodationists are relying, at least in part, on Jewish oral tradition for their authority. Jesus, however, vehemently spoke and acted against the esteeming of an oral tradition as authoritative in matters of faith and practice (Matthew 15:1-6). According to the actions and Words of Jesus, an oral tradition has no authority. While Walton does not rely on an oral tradition for the conveying of the vowels, instead saying that the *matres lectionis* conveyed the vowels and that the Masoretes later replaced the *matres lectionis* with vowel points, yet such a view puts him in the place of also relying on uninspired vowel points (see above under Walton and see further in the next section). However, it is the inspired and preserved written Words of God that are the sole authority for faith and practice (II Timothy 3:16,17), not Jewish oral tradition or an uninspired work from the Masoretes. Chapter Two of this work establishes that the Bible is the sole authority.

Those who believe that Jews passed down the vowels by oral tradition and that the Masoretes then later added them to the Bible and that these vowels are either fully or partially authoritative are acting out of step with the Lord Jesus Christ. They do not have a Bibliology that is consistent with the teaching and practice of Jesus. In fact, not only are they acting like the Pharisees, who added their oral tradition to the Bible, but they are also acting much like Catholics who think that the written Words of God are not the only rule for faith and practice. For instance,

> Bellarmine [a Roman Catholic of the late 1500's] recognized the Bible, the *verbum Dei scriptum* [the written word of God], to be "the true word of God and the certain and sure rule of faith," but he denied that Scripture could stand alone. It did not contain all necessary doctrine and its meaning was often unclear apart from the tradition of the Church, the *verbum Dei non scriptum* [the unwritten word of God].[212]

Likewise, the advocates of the accommodation position have the written Old Testament consonants to which they have added the oral tradition of the vowels, therefore, they seem to have a similar Bibliology as the Catholics.

Adding to the Words of God

In addition to the problem of following Jewish oral tradition, instead of solely following the Bible as the sole authority for faith and practice, the accommodation position allows for an adding to the Words of God, namely the adding of written vowels to an already existing written consonantal text. This creates a real dilemma for the accommodation position, for the Bible clearly forbids anyone from adding to it (Deuteronomy 4:2; 12:32; Proverbs 30:6; and Revelation 22:18). If the inspired Hebrew Old Testament only had consonants, then it should remain that way. Men who are not acting under the influence of the inspiration of God have no business adding to the Words of God. If the Old Testament only consisted of consonants, then the

---

[212] Richard A. Muller, "The debate over the vowel points and the crisis in orthodox hermeneutics" in *The Journal of Medieval and Renaissance Studies* 10 (Spring 1980): 56.

Masoretes or anyone else, therefore, lacked any authority to add written vowels to it.

If one follows Walton's idea that the Masoretes replaced so-called *matres lectionis* with vowel points, this does not alleviate the problem, for the Masoretes would have lacked authority to do this as well. This is evident since Jesus stated that one jot shall in no wise pass from the law (Matthew 5:18), and since the jot is one of the *matres lectionis* and if the Masoretes replaced it with a vowel point; then they were doing so in complete rebellion to the Lord Jesus Christ, and as such, one should reject their work in toto. But more than this, Jesus states that one jot shall in no wise pass from the law till all be fulfilled. Therefore, each and every jot of the Old Testament is inviolate. However, if the Masoretes were able to remove only one jot so that it passed from the law, then what of Jesus' promise? Indeed, if the Masoretes were able to cause a jot to pass from the law, then what does this say about Jesus Himself? When one contemplates the answers to these questions, he should be able to understand that Walton's position is not only anti-scriptural, but it is also anti-Christ! Consider, for example, the spelling of David's name: דָּוִד and דָּוִיד, the first spelling occurs five hundred ninety six times (596), whereas the second occurs two hundred fifty times (250). The spellings differ by a *yodh*. The first spelling has the *yodh*, but the second does not. If the *yodh* were originally in the first spelling, then five hundred ninety six (596) *yodhs* have disappeared from the Old Testament. Such a thing is impossible according to Jesus. Rather than accept the fanciful theory of Walton, one should adhere to the sure statement of Jesus in Matthew 5:18.

Neglecting Written Words

Many in the accommodation position teach that a Jewish oral tradition supplied vowels to the consonantal text to maintain the correct understanding of the Words of God. However, such teaching goes directly contrary to several statements in the Bible that teach that God had the writers write inspired words, not merely consonants. Following is a list of thirteen (13) passages, which in the opinion of the writer, present real problems for the accommodation position. The writer also presents another list of verses underneath the problems for the non-authoritative position. In all, the author presents thirty-seven (37) passages that pose real problems for anyone who teaches that the vowel points are not part of the *autographa*. Chapter Four presents exegesis of these and other passages.

Genesis 22:16

In Genesis 22:16 the Bible records the Lord saying, "By myself have I sworn, saith the LORD." This is the first of eight hundred fifty four (854) times where the Bible says, "Saith the LORD." When the Bible uses *saith the LORD*, it records what the Lord actually said. But if there are no vowels, then in what way did the writers of Scripture record what the Lord saith? If there are no vowels, it seems that such a system would truncate what the Lord saith, and not accurately record in writing what the Lord saith.

Exodus 24:4

Exodus 24:4 states, "And Moses wrote all the words of the LORD, and rose up early in the morning, and builded an altar under the hill, and twelve pillars, according to the twelve tribes of Israel." From Exodus 3:4-7, 12, 14, 15; 4:2-4, 6, 7, 11, 14, 19, 21; 6:1, 2, 26; 7:1, 14; 8:16, 20; 9:1, 8, 13, 22; 10:1, 12, 21; 11:1, 9; 12:43; 14:15, 26; 16:4, 28; 17:5, 14; 19:9, 10, 21, 24; 20:22; 23:13; 24:1, it is obvious that up to the point of Exodus 24:4 where the Bible states that Moses wrote all the Words of the Lord that the Lord regularly spoke with Moses and communicated His Words to Moses by speaking to him. Since speaking requires vocalization, which requires vowels, and since Moses wrote these vocalized words, then it would seem that he used vowels as well as consonants. He wrote words, not abbreviations of words. But if there were no vowels, then in what sense did Moses write all the Words of the Lord?

Exodus 34:27

In Exodus 34:27, the Lord said to Moses: "Write thou these words: for after the tenor of these words I have made a covenant with thee and with Israel." *Tenor* refers to the mouth. In other words, God wanted Moses to write according to the mouthing of His Words (see the beginning of this chapter). The mouthing of words involves vowels. However, if there were no written vowels, then in what way did Moses write these words so that they were "after the tenor"?

Deuteronomy 11:18-20

Deuteronomy 11:18-20 states: "Therefore shall ye lay up these my words in your heart and in your soul, and bind them for a sign upon your hand, that they may be as frontlets between your eyes. And ye shall teach them your children, speaking of them when thou sittest in thine house, and when thou walkest by the way, when thou liest down, and when thou risest up. And thou shalt write them upon the door posts of thine house, and upon thy gates." Whitfield states that some assert that none could attain to the reading of unpointed Biblical Hebrew, "but those, who by long study and familiar exercise, in the language, and in the Sacred Writings, had made themselves masters of most, or all of the words." Whitfield then asks: "But how does this agree with the command of the Almighty to all the people of *Israel*, in general; to be diligent in reading the Law, writing it upon the posts of their houses, and on their gates"?[213] An unpointed text does not seem to be conducive to executing such commands.

Deuteronomy 27:8

If there were no vowels, then what does it mean when the Lord commanded the children of Israel to write all the words of the law very

---

[213] Whitfield, 11.

plainly (Deuteronomy 27:8)? In what way did they write the words very plainly, if there were no vowels?

Judges 12:6

In Judges 12:6 the Gileadites demanded that the Ephraimites say *Shibboleth*, but the Ephraimites could not pronounce it right and, instead, said *Sibboleth*. Hebrew uses a dot to indicate the *h* in the *sh* in *Shibboleth*. However, if there were no points, then how did the writer of Judges convey the distinction between *Shibboleth* and *Shibboleth*?

Nehemiah 8:8

Nehemiah 8:8 states: "So they read in the book in the law of God distinctly, and gave the sense, and caused *them* to understand the reading." In what way did they read in the book of the law of God distinctly, if there were no vowel points?

Jeremiah 36:1,2

In Jeremiah 36:1,2 the Lord commanded Jeremiah to write all the words that he had spoken. Since speaking involves the use of vowels, then in what way did Jeremiah write the words that the Lord spoke, if he did not use vowels?

Habakkuk 2:2

In what way did Habakkuk "write the vision, and make it plain upon tables" (Habakkuk 2:2), if there were no vowels?

Matthew 22:31

In Matthew 22:31 the Lord Jesus Christ said to the Sadducees, "But as touching the resurrection of the dead, have ye not read that which was spoken unto you by God, saying." Herein Jesus equates what they could read, that is, what is written, with what God spoke and said. In other words, the written record duplicates what God actually spoke. But if there are no vowels in the written record, then in what way does the written record duplicate what God spoke?

I Corinthians 9:10

I Corinthians 9:10 states: "Or saith he *it* altogether for our sakes? For our sakes, no doubt, *this* is written: that he that ploweth should plow in hope; and that he that thresheth in hope should be partaker of his hope." I Corinthians 9:10 equates what the Lord saith with what is written. Since speaking involves the use of vowels, then in what way is the written record equal with what the Lord saith if the written record has no vowels?

II Timothy 3:16,17

II Timothy 3:16,17 teaches that the Bible is the sole authority for faith and practice, but if there are no vowels in the Old Testament, then how is the Bible the sole authority? If there are no vowels, then the Old Testament is an uncertain authority requiring an oral tradition about vowels to make it more certain. If this be so, then it seems that the authority becomes what is written, plus what is not written. However, such a system would be contrary to what the Bible says about it and it alone being the authority.

II Peter 1:21

II Peter 1:21 states: "Holy men of God spake *as they were* moved by the Holy Ghost." Also, I Corinthians 2:13 states, "Which things also we speak, not in the words which man's wisdom teacheth, but which the Holy Ghost teacheth; comparing spiritual things with spiritual." The Holy Ghost, as He moved in holy men of old, used words. But if the Hebrew Old Testament only has consonants, then in what sense did the Holy Ghost move these men to speak and to write words?

Summary

The thirteen (13) above passages pose real problems for the accommodation position. These thirteen passages are not the only passages the accommodation position seemingly neglects. Chapter Four presents forty passages and Chapter Five treats in detail Matthew 5:18 all of which pose great problems for the accommodation position. It should become clear just from this cursory treatment of these passages that the accommodation position has Scriptural difficulties.

Conclusion

The accommodation position suffers from several serious flaws in that it relies on oral tradition, allows for additions to the Words of God, and neglects the written Words of God. For anyone who loves the Bible this should be cause for great concern. The problem is that the accommodationist in seeking the approval of scholars may be fearful to abandon his position, but if one seeks to please men, he is not the servant of Christ (Galatians 1:10). Let the accommodationist go without the camp of scholars and bear the reproach of Christ (Hebrews 13:13).

Summary

To summarize: the accommodation position on the one hand, says that the vowel points are fully or partially authoritative, but, on the other hand, are not inspired. Some of the proponents of this position are Elias Levita, John Calvin, Louis Cappellus, Brian Walton, Homer A. Kent, Coalition for the Defense of the Scriptures, Larry Oats, and David Sorenson. The accommodation position suffers from serious Scriptural problems. First, it relies on oral tradition to convey the vowels through history to the Masoretes; but oral tradition has no authority (Matthew 15:1-6). Second, it relies on the additions of these vowels by the Masoretes to the Words of God; but the Bible forbids adding to it (Deuteronomy 4:2; 12:32; Proverbs 30:6; and Revelation 22:18). Third, it neglects the written words of the Bible in that it fails to recognize that (1) God's spoken and, therefore, vocalized words, are written (Exodus 34:27; Jeremiah 36:1,2; Matthew 22:31; I Corinthians 9:10); (2) the Bible is the sole authority for faith and practice (II Timothy 3:16,17); (3) the Spirit of God used words, which necessitates vocalization, which the prophets wrote (I Corinthians 2:13; II Peter 1:21); (4) God commanded that people write His Words very plainly, which seems to require the use of vowels (Deuteronomy 27:8; Habakkuk 2:2); and (5) the Words of God were for the common people, which would seem to require vowels to make it easier for one and all to understand (Deuteronomy 11:18-20). To the writer's knowledge, no one holding to the accommodation position has attempted an answer to these problems.

Non-Authoritative Position

The third position about the vowel points is, what the author calls, the non-authoritative position. In discussing the non-authoritative position, this work presents the position itself, the proponents of the position, and some problems that may arise from the position.

The Position

The non-authoritative position asserts that the vowel points are not inspired and that the Masoretes or some other group added the vowels some time after the inscripturation of the consonants. However, unlike the accommodation position, the non-authoritative position believes that these vowels have no authority. While some, who hold the non-authoritative position, may at times regard the vowels as a useful guide for determining the meaning of the text, similar to how one might regard a commentary or reference notes in a study Bible; however, they still do not view the vowels as authoritative.

The Proponents

The non-authoritative position is a popular view and, therefore, has many proponents, but this section limits itself to listing some of the important proponents.

Natronai II ben-Hilai – 9th Century

Natronai, according to McClintock and Strong,

> In reply to the question whether it is lawful to put the points to the synagogal scrolls of the Pentateuch, distinctly declared that "since the law, as given to Moses on Sinai, had no points, and the points are not Sinaitic (i.e. sacred), having been invented by the sages, and put down as signs for the reader; and, moreover, since it is prohibited to us to make any additions, on our own cogitations, lest we transgress the command: 'Ye shall not add,' etc. (Deut. iv, 2); hence we must not put the points to the scrolls of the law."[214]

Since Natronai states that the points are not sacred, were invented by the sages, and are unwarranted additions, then it would seem that he did not believe them to be authoritative. Natronai also forbade the pointing of the synagogue scrolls in his day. However, did every synagogue throughout history have unpointed scrolls? This is an important question. For more on this subject, see Chapter Six.

Louis Cappellus – 1650

Earlier, this chapter stated that in 1624, Cappellus published *Arcanum punctionis revelatum*, that is, "The Mystery of the Points Unveiled" wherein he presented the view of the novelty of the points, but, nonetheless, held to their authority. Later, however, he argued that the points were not authoritative. In 1650, he published *Critica Sacra*, that is, "Sacred Criticism." In this volume, according to Ginsburg, Cappellus "changed his mind [from what he previously espoused], or, perhaps, more boldly avowed, what he had hitherto kept back, that,

---

[214] "Vowel-Points" in *Cyclopedia*, X:820.

with the changing of the ancient letters in which the Hebrew was originally written, and in adding the points, the *matres lectiones* were eliminated and the Hebrew text was greatly corrupted."[215]

Muller writes: "Cappel's method, however, more and more assumed that the vowel points had been corrupted in the transmission and that the *textus receptus* needed to be altered on the basis of ancient translations like the Chaldee, the newly discovered Syriac, and the Septuagint."[216] Muller makes an interesting comment here. Many modern Bible translators and commentators give more credence to the Septuagint and other versions than they do to the Hebrew. Could it be that they, too, believe the vowel points are corrupt? Indeed, this seems to tbe case with the *Revised Standard Version*, which states:

> The vowel-signs, which were added by the Masoretes, are accepted also in the main, but where a more probable and convincing reading can be obtained by assuming different vowels, this has been done. No notes are given in such cases, because the vowel points are less ancient and reliable than the consonants.
>
> Departures from the consonantal text of the best manuscripts have been made only where it seems clear that errors in copying had been made before the text was standardized. Most of the corrections adopted are based on the ancient versions (translations into Greek, Aramaic, Syriac, and Latin), which were made before the time of the Masoretic revision and therefore reflect earlier forms of the text.[217]

The *Revised Standard Version* not only disparages the vowel points but also, at times, departs from the consonantal text. The above quote well illustrates the lack of respect for the Traditional Text of the Hebrew Old Testament, the very text upon which Jesus put His stamp of

---

[215] Ginsburg, 56.

[216] Muller, 62.

[217] *The Holy Bible Containing the Old and New Testaments: Revised Standard Version* (NY: Thomas Nelson & Sons, 1952), iv.

approval (Matthew 4:4; 5:18; 24:35; Luke 16:17; 24:25; John 10:35; 17:17).

Albert Barnes – 1832

In 1832, Barnes published his *Notes on the Bible*.[218] In commenting on Hebrews 11:21, Barnes states:

> The English version of that place is, "and Israel bowed himself upon the bed's head," which is a proper translation, in the main, of the word מטה—*mittĕh*. That word, however, with different vowel points — מטה *mattĕh*, means a branch, a bough, a rod, a staff, and the translators of the Septuagint have so rendered it. The Masoretic points are of no authority, and either translation, therefore, would be proper.[219]

Note that Barnes refers to the points as "Masoretic points," as if the Masoretes invented them. If the points were merely the invention of the Masoretes, then Barnes would have a valid observation. However, it is the contention of this work that the points are not the invention of the Masoretes, but that they are from God. The Masoretes merely conveyed them.

Most Modern-Day Scholars

Ginsburg notes that Walton's *Prolegomena* and *The Considerator Considered* "decided the battle in England in favour of the anti-vowelists. Henceforth all Biblical critics, with very few exceptions, regarded the points as modern, useless, and of no authority, though Walton himself . . . maintained that they, as a rule, represented the ancient and genuine reading."[220]

---

[218] "Barnes, Albert, D. D." in *Cyclopedia*, XI:348.

[219] Albert J. Barnes, *Hebrews* in vol. 13 of *Barnes' Notes on the Bible*, Heritage Edition (London: Blackie & Son, 1847, reprinted Grand Rapids: Baker Book House Company, 2005), 272.

[220] Ginsburg, *The Massoreth Ha-Massoreth of Elias Levita*, 59.

The Problems

Without the vowels, many words are ambiguous. Since without the vowels there is only an abbreviation for a word, then in some contexts it is impossible to determine the exact word to which the abbreviation refers. One example will suffice to show that this is the case. I Kings 17:4 speaks of the Lord having the ravens feed Elijah during the drought. Concerning the words *the ravens*, Cook writes: "This is the translation of most of the ancient versions; others, omitting the points, which are generally allowed to have no authority, read 'Arabians'."[221] The context cannot decide whether it should be *ravens* or *Arabians*. Chapter Three, quoting from various commentaries and other sources, presents over one hundred examples showing the uncertainty that arises in the Old Testament if the vowels are not authoritative. The uncertainty is inconsistent with many statements that the Bible makes about itself.

Psalm 12:6,7

If the vowels are not authoritative, then in what way has God preserved His Words "from this generation for ever" (Psalm 12:7)? It would seem that if there are no vowels, that some of God's Words are not perfectly preserved.

Psalm 19:7

Psalm 19:7 states: "The law of the LORD is perfect," but in what way is the Law perfect if there are no vowels? Without the vowels, it would seem that the Law is full of imperfections. Psalm 19:7 also states: "The testimony of the LORD is sure," but in what way is

---

[221] F. C. Cook, ed., *I Samuel to Esther*, abridged and edited by J. M. Fuller in vol. 2 of *Barnes' Notes*, Heritage Edition (London: Blackie & Son, 1847, reprinted Grand Rapids: Baker Book House Company, 2005), 201.

the testimony of the LORD sure, if there are no vowel points in the Old Testament?

Psalm 93:5

Psalm 93:5 states: "Thy testimonies are very sure." But if there are no vowels, then in what way are God's testimonies very sure? Indeed, without vowels, many of God's testimonies are unsure.

Psalm 111:7

The Bible states, "All his commandments *are* sure" (Psalm 111:7). In what way are God's commandments sure, if there are no vowel points in the Old Testament?

Psalm 119:89

Psalm 119:89 states: "For ever, O LORD, thy word is settled in heaven." God communicated part of the forever-settled-in-heaven Words of God to Daniel (Daniel 10:21; 11:2), which then became part of the book of Daniel. Therefore, the forever-settled-in-heaven Words of God are on earth. However, if there are no vowels, then in what way are the forever-settled Words of God here on earth?

Psalm 119:105

Psalm 119:105 states: "Thy word *is* a lamp unto my feet, and a light unto my path." But if the vowels are not authoritative, then in what way are God's Words a lamp and a light? Without the vowels, then it would seem that the light has been extinguished, or, at the very least, greatly dimmed.

Psalm 119:138

Psalm 119:138 states, "Thy testimonies *that* thou hast commanded *are* righteous and very faithful." *Faithful* means "firmness, fidelity, steadfastness, steadiness."[222] But in what way are God's testimonies firm and steadfast if there are no vowels?

Psalm 119:152

If the vowels are not authoritative, then in what way has God founded His testimonies for ever (Psalm 119:152)? It would seem that with no vowels, some of His testimonies are rather lost for ever.

Psalm 119:160

If the vowels are not authoritative, then in what way does every one of God's righteous judgments endure for ever (Psalm 119:160)?

Psalm 138:2

God has exalted His Word above all His name (Psalm 138:2). God's nature includes that of being perfect (II Samuel 22:31), therefore, the fact that He has exalted His Words above all His name would suggest that His Words are likewise perfect. But in what sense are the Words of God perfect, if they have no vowels? They would seem to be imperfect.

Proverbs 6:23

Proverbs 6:23 states: "For the commandment *is* a lamp; and the law *is* light; and reproofs of instruction *are* the way of life." But if there are no vowels, then many of the commandments are uncertain, therefore, in what way are they a light? Also, in what way is the law light? Furthermore, in what way are the reproofs of instruction the way of life?

---

[222] "0530 אמונה" in *Online Bible Hebrew Lexicon* in *Online Bible*, version 1.33 (Winterbourne, Ontario: Timnathserah Inc., 2003).

Proverbs 22:20,21

If there are no vowels, then in what sense has the Lord written "excellent things in counsels and knowledge" so as to make men "know the certainty of the words of truth" (Proverbs 22:20,21)? If there are no vowels, then many of God's Words are uncertain.

Isaiah 30:8

In Isaiah 30:8 God commanded Isaiah to write words "in a table, and note it in a book, that it may be for the time to come for ever and ever." But if there are no vowels, then in what way are God's Words preserved? Indeed, it seems that many of the words are not preserved, if there are no vowels.

Isaiah 40:8

If the vowels are not part of the *autographa*, then in what way do the Words of God stand for ever (Isaiah 40:8)? Without the vowels, it seems that some of the words have for ever fallen, rather than for ever standing.

Matthew 4:4

Jesus states, "Man shall not live by bread alone, but by every word that proceedeth out of the mouth of God" (Matthew 4:4). With no authoritative vowel points, does man know what every word is so that he is sure that he has every word?

Matthew 24:35

If the points are not fully authoritative, then the text itself, in many places, is uncertain. If the text is uncertain, then what of Christ's promise that His "words shall not pass away" (Matthew 24:35)? With so many words up for debate, it would seem according to the non-authoritative position that some of His Old Testament Words have passed away.

Luke 16:17

If the points are not authoritative, then why did Jesus speak of one tittle, that is, one vowel point (see Chapter Five) of the law not failing (Luke 16:17)? If the points are not authoritative, then many of the points have failed.

John 10:35

In what way is it true that "the Scripture cannot be broken" (John 10:35), if there are no vowels? With no vowels, it would seem that many passages are broken beyond repair, so that even the assistance of textual critics cannot determine with certainty the wording of many texts of the Old Testament.

Acts 7:38

In Acts 7:38, Stephen spoke of the "fathers: who received the lively oracles to give unto us." But if there are no vowels to the Old Testament words, then in what way are the Old Testament words lively oracles? Indeed, without vowels, it would seem that they are half-dead. Also, in what way are the Old Testament words for New Testament believers, because if there are no vowels, then many of the oracles are obscure and hidden?

Romans 9:29

Romans 9:29 says, "And as Esaias said before, Except the Lord of Sabaoth had left us a seed, we had been as Sodoma, and been made like unto Gomorrha." This refers to Isaiah 1:9. *Said before* (προείρηκεν from προλέγω) is a perfect active indicative, indicating that what Isaiah had said in the past still continued in the present. What Isaiah spoke continued, that is, even the vocalization continued. But if there are no vowels, then in what way does the speech of Isaiah continue?

II Timothy 3:16,17

II Timothy 3:16,17 teaches that the Bible is the sole authority for faith and practice, but if there are no vowels in the Old Testament, then how are the Old Testament Scriptures included in that sole authority? If there are no vowels, then Scripture is an uncertain authority requiring the comments of commentators, or the correction of the critics to make it more certain. And if such be the case, then it seems that the authority becomes the Bible plus the commentator, or the Bible plus the critic. Therefore, the Bible is no longer the sole authority.

I Peter 1:23-25

With all the uncertainty that arises over the lack of vowels, then in what way do the Words of the Lord endure forever (I Peter 1:23-25)? Indeed, without the vowels, it would seem that some of the Words of the Lord have not endured at all.

II Peter 1:19

If the vowels are not part of the text, then in what way could Peter say, "We have also a more sure word of prophecy" (II Peter 1:19)? If there are no vowels, then many of the words are unsure.

II Peter 3:2

In II Peter 3:2, Peter exhorts his readers to "be mindful of the words which were spoken before by the holy prophets, and of the commandment of us the apostles of the Lord and Saviour." *Spoken before* is a perfect passive participle, which indicates "permanence, the speaking still continues in Holy Writ."[223] "The perfect tense . . . underlines the permanence of these prophetic utterances; the speaking

---

[223] R. C. H. Lenski, *The Interpretation of I and II Epistles of Peter, the Three Epistles of John, and the Epistle of Jude* (Minneapolis: Augsburg Publishing House, 1966), 337.

still continues in the inspired Scriptures."²²⁴ In other words, *the words which were spoken before* were still speaking in Peter's day. Since the prophets vocalized the God-inspired words that they spoke, and since these spoken words continue, then the vowels must also continue. But if there are no vowels, then in what way do these spoken words continue?

Conclusion

The above list presents twenty-four (24) serious Biblical problems with the non-authoritative view. To anyone who is serious about the Words of God, these Biblical problems are indeed troubling. These Biblical considerations ought to carry far more weight than any historical evidence to the contrary. Having written such a statement, the author is not ignoring history, but he is seeking to honor the Words of God as the only authority for faith and practice. May others do likewise.

Summary

In summary, the non-authoritative position regards the vowel points as uninspired. However, with uninspired points, uncertainty would be present in just about every verse of the Old Testament (see Chapter Three). Therefore, one would have to rely on other authorities to decide what word or words should be in a verse. Some of the proponents of non-authoritative position are Natronai II ben-Hilai, Louis Cappellus, Albert Barnes, and most modern-day scholars. But the non-authoritative position suffers from serious Scriptural problems among which are that it fails to see that God's Words are preserved (Psalm 12:6,7; Isaiah 30:8; 40:8; Matthew 24:35; Luke 16:17); perfect (Psalm 19:7); sure (Psalm 93:5; 111:7; II Peter 1:19); settled (Psalm 119:89); a

---

[224] D. Edmond Hiebert, *Second Peter and Jude: An Expositional Commentary* (Greenville, SC: Unusual Publications, 1989), 139.

lamp and a light (Psalm 119:105; Proverbs 6:23); faithful (Psalm 119:138); founded (Psalm 119:152); enduring (Psalm 119:160; I Peter 1:23-25); exalted above all His name (Psalm 138:2); certain (Proverbs 22:20,21); necessary for life (Matthew 4:4); cannot be broken (John 10:35); lively oracles (Acts 7:38); continuing to speak (Romans 9:29; II Peter 3:2); and the sole authority (II Timothy 3:16,17). Again, to the writer's knowledge no one holding to the non-authoritative position has attempted an answer to these problems.

PREVIEW

The introductory chapter has presented three views on the vowel points: the *autographa* position, the accommodation position, and the non-authoritative position. The next chapter demonstrates that the accommodation and non-authoritative positions are Scripturally untenable because both fail to see that the Bible is the sole authority for faith and practice. Scripture is the sole authority when it comes to salvation (Romans 10:17; II Timothy 3:15; I Peter 1:23); to judging (Genesis 2:17; Exodus 5:1; Leviticus 10:1, 2; Deuteronomy 4:1; 7:11; 27:26; I Samuel 15:3, 22; Isaiah 8:20; John 5:39; 12:48; Acts 17:11; Hebrews 8:5); to local churches (Matthew 28:20; Acts 7:38; Romans 15:4; I Corinthians 10:11; 14:37; Colossians 2:8; I Timothy 3:14, 15; II Timothy 3:16, 17; 4:2; Titus 1:4; II Peter 3:2; Jude 3); and to Jesus' life, both negatively as He rejected the false authority of the oral tradition (Matthew 12:1-13; 15:1-6; Luke 11:37, 38; 13:10:17; 14:1-6; John 5:5-12, 16, 18; 7:22, 23; 9:14-16), and positively as He followed the written Words of God (Psalm 138:2; Matthew 2:23; 4:4, 7, 10, 12-15; 5:17; 8:16, 17; 12:15-21; 13:34, 35; 21:1-5; 26:53, 54; Luke 22:37; 24:44; John 13:18; 15:25; 19:28; Hebrews 10:7). The authority for faith and practice is not the Bible plus oral tradition, the Bible plus the Masoretes, the Bible plus the textual critics, the Bible plus history, or the Bible plus some other uninspired work. The teaching of the Bible being the sole authority for faith and practice is devastating to the accommodation and non-authoritative positions, for the advocates of these positions do not have a Bible that is the sole authority.

Chapter Three presents over one hundred (100) places in the Old Testament where uncertainty would reign if the vowels are not inspired. The following list presents a number of questions that would arise if the vowels are not inspired. The first group of words in the list is from the *King James Version*, which provides an accurate translation of the Hebrew of the Traditional Text. The second group of words reflect the changes in translation that would occur if one were to change the vowels. These suggested changes come from commentators as well as from translators. In other words, these are not changes that the author has fabricated, just for the sake of making a point, but these are actual changes that various writers suggest.

- In Genesis 47:31, is it "upon the bed's head," or "on the top of his staff"?
- In Genesis 49:10, is it "until Shiloh come," or "until tribute comes to him"?
- In Deuteronomy 33:27, is it "the eternal God is *thy* refuge, and underneath *are* the everlasting arms," or "He subdues the ancient gods, and shatters the forces of old"?
- In Joshua 4:24, is it "that ye might fear," or "that ye feared"?
- In I Samuel 1:7, is it "he did so year by year," or "so she did year by year"?
- In I Samuel 18:11, is it "Saul cast the javelin," or "Saul lifted the javelin"?
- In I Samuel 20:17, is it "Jonathan caused David to swear again," or "Jonathan sware again to David"?
- In II Samuel 24:9, is it "eight hundred thousand," or "eight hundred specially trained warriors"?
- Again, in II Samuel 24:9, is it "five hundred thousand," or "five hundred specially trained warriors"?
- In I Kings 13:12, is it "had seen," or "showed"?
- In I Kings 17:1, is it "Tishbite," or "stranger"?
- Again, in I Kings 17:1, is it "inhabitants," or "Tishbi"?

In I Kings 17:4, is it "ravens," or "Arabians"?

In I Kings 20:29, is it "an hundred thousand footmen," or "an hundred officers"?

In I Kings 20:30, is it "twenty and seven thousand," or "twenty and seven officers"?

In I Chronicles 4:10, is it "and that thou wouldest keep me from evil," or "to provide pasture"?

In I Chronicles 7:4, is it "six and thirty thousand," or is it "six and thirty chiefs"?

In I Chronicles 12:24-37, where *thousand* occurs thirteen times, is it "thousand," or "leaders"?

In I Chronicles 27:1-15, where *thousand* occurs thirteen times, is it "thousand," or "leaders"?

In II Chronicles 13:3, where *thousand* occurs twice, is it "thousand," or "leaders"?

In II Chronicles 13:7, is it "thousand," or "leaders"?

In II Chronicles 14:8-9, where *thousand* occurs thrice, is it "thousand," or "leaders"?

In II Chronicles 17:14-18, where *thousand* occurs six times, is it "thousand," or "leaders"?

In II Chronicles 25:5-6, where *thousand* occurs twice, is it "thousand," or "leaders"?

In II Chronicles 26:12-13, where *thousand* occurs thrice, is it "thousand," or "leaders"?

In II Chronicles 28:6, is it "thousand," or "leaders"?

In II Chronicles 28:8, is it "thousand," or "leaders"?

In Ezra 8:26, is it "and silver vessels an hundred talents," or "and silver vessels worth 200 talents"?

In Job 5:15, is it "from the sword," or "to make desolate"?

In Job 6:18, is it "paths," or "caravans"?

In Job 15:23, is it "he wandereth about for bread," or "he wanders abroad to be the food of vultures"?

In Job 21:24, is it "full of milk," or "full of fat"?

In Job 24:12, is it "men," or "mortals"?

Again, in Job 24:12, is it "folly," or "prayer"?

In Job 27:19, is it "but he shall not be gathered," or "is he not swept away"?

In Job 31:18, is it "he was brought with me," or "from my youth he honoured me as a father"?

In Job 36:33, is it "vapour," or "evil"?

In Job 37:23, is it "he will not afflict," or "he will not answer"?

In Psalm 2:9, is it "thou shalt break," or "thou shalt rule," or "thou shalt feed"?

In Psalm 7:11, is it "God," or "not"?

In Psalm 29:9, is it "maketh the hinds to calve," or "causes the oaks to whirl"?

In Psalm 33:7, is it "as an heap," or "as in a bottle"?

In Psalm 42:2, is it "and appear before God," or "and behold the face of God"?

In Psalm 52:5, is it "he shall take thee away," or "he will destroy you"?

In Psalm 58:1, is it "sons of men," or "mighty lords"?

In Psalm 59:10, is it "the God of my mercy shall prevent me," or "my God shall meet me with his lovingkindness"?

In Psalm 60:8, is it "a snare before them: and *that which should have been* for *their* welfare, *let it become* a trap," or "a snare, and retribution and a trap"?

In Psalm 109:17, is it "so let it come unto him," or "let curses come on him"?

In Psalm 119:118, is it "their deceit," or "their thought"?

In Psalm 147:17, is it "cold," or "hail"?

In Proverbs 1:7, and over five thousand five hundred (5,500) other verses is the Hebrew name for God "Jehovah," or "Yahweh"?

In Proverbs 6:24, is it "from the evil woman," or "from the wife of another"?

In Proverbs 10:4, is it "he becometh poor," or "poverty humbleth a man"?

In Proverbs 11:23, is it "wrath," or "shall perish"?

In Proverbs 12:19, is it "the lip of truth shall be established for ever," or "true lips establish testimony"?

In Proverbs 14:1, is it "wise," or "wisdom"?

In Proverbs 21:4, is it "the plowing," or "the fallow-field," or "the lamp"?

In Proverbs 23:7, is it "for as he thinketh in his heart, so is he," or "for as if one should swallow a hair, so he eats and drinks"?

In Proverbs 25:27, is it "so for men to search their own glory is not glory," or "but as an inquirer to enter on what is difficult is honor"?

In Proverbs 26:23, is it "silver dross," or "glaze"?

In Proverbs 29:14, is it "his throne shall be established for ever," or "his throne shall be established for a testimony"?

In Proverbs 30:1, is it "and Ucal," or "and I became dull"?

In Ecclesiastes 3:21, is it "who knoweth the spirit of man that goeth upward, and the spirit of the beast that goeth downward to the earth," or "who knows if the spirit of man rises upward and if the spirit of the animal goes down into the earth"?

In Song of Solomon 1:2, is it "let him kiss me," or "let him give me to drink"?

In Isaiah 1:2, is it "hath spoken," or "speaking"?

In Isaiah 1:8, is it "as a besieged city," or "so is the delivered city"?

In Isaiah 16:4, is it "let mine outcasts dwell with thee, Moab," or "let the outcasts of Moab sojourn with thee, O Zion"?

In Isaiah 19:10, is it "and they shall be broken in the purposes thereof, all that make sluices *and* ponds for fish," or "and all who make beer shall lament, and shall afflict their souls"?

In Isaiah 21:13, is it "Arabia," or "evening"?

In Isaiah 27:7, is it "them that are slain by him," or "them that slew him"?

In Isaiah 30:8, is it "for ever and ever," or "for a testimony forever"?

In Isaiah 40:6, is it "and he said," or "and I said"?

In Isaiah 62:5, is it "thy sons," or "they builder," or "thy restorer"?

In Jeremiah 2:16, is it "have broken," or "shall break," or "shall feed off"?

In Jeremiah 8:13, is it "and the things that I have given them shall pass away from them," or "and I will give them to those who shall pass over them"?

In Jeremiah 10:18, is it "that they may find it so," or "that they may be found," or "that thy stroke may be found"?

In Jeremiah 15:19, is it "then will I bring thee again," or "I will give thee a settled place"?

In Jeremiah 23:17, is it "unto them that despise me, The LORD hath said," or "unto those who despise the word of the Lord"?

In Jeremiah 25:24, is it "mingled people," or "Arabs"?

In Jeremiah 48:4, is it "her little ones," or "unto Zoar"?

In Jeremiah 48:15, is it "gone up," or "gone down"?

In Jeremiah 48:18, is it "sit in thirst," or "sit on the parched ground"?

In Jeremiah 49:1, is it "their king," or "Milcom"?

In Jeremiah 50:38, is it "a drought," or "a sword"?

In Jeremiah 51:3, is it "against him that bendeth let the archer bend his bow," or "let not him who bendeth his bow bend it"?

In Ezekiel 8:2, is it "the appearance of fire," or "the appearance of a man"?

In Ezekiel 16:30, is it "how weak is thine heart," or "how I am filled with anger against you"?

In Ezekiel 23:4, is it "Aholah," or "her tent"?

Again, in Ezekiel 23:4, is it "Aholibah," or "my tent in her"?

In Ezekiel 31:14, is it "neither their trees stand up in their height, all that drink water," or "and that no drinkers of water may stand upon their own greatness"?

In Ezekiel 34:3, is it "fat," or "milk"?

In Ezekiel 36:5, is it "to cast it out for a prey," or "in order to plunder its pasturage"?

In Ezekiel 39:26, is it "they have borne," or "they will forget"?

In Daniel 9:27, is it "and for the overspreading of abominations he shall make it desolate," or "and – upon the wing – the porch of the temple – abominations! And a desolator!"?

In Daniel 11:6, is it "and he that begat her," or "whom she brought forth"?

In Hosea 13:7, is it "will I observe," or "by the way of Assyria"?

In Obadiah 3, is it "hath deceived," or "carrying out"?

In Micah 2:7, is it "is the spirit of the LORD straitened," or "is the ear of the Lord shortened"?

In Micah 6:9, is it "shall see thy name," or "shall fear thy name"?

In Micah 6:11, is it "shall I count *them* pure," or "shall I acquit"?

In Habakkuk 1:8, is it "evening wolves," or "wolves of Arabia"?

In Zephaniah 3:8, is it "until the day that I rise up to the prey," or "until the day of my rising up for testimony"?

In Haggai 1:11, is it "I called for a drought," or "I called for a sword"?

In Zechariah 9:8, is it "because of the army," or "against the army," or "from the army," or "as a garrison," or "as a rampart"?

In Malachi 2:3, is it "I will corrupt your seed," or "I will rebuke your arm"?

The above one-hundred five (105) questions well illustrate the uncertainty and lack of authority that would reign throughout the Bible if one were to adopt the non-authoritative view of the vowels. This lack of authority is diametrically opposed to the teaching that the Bible is the sole authority for faith and practice and, therefore, cannot possibly be a correct view on the vowel points.

Chapters Two and Three destroy the accommodation and non-authoritative views showing that they are Biblically untenable. With the accommodation and non-authoritative views destroyed, this leaves only the *autographa* position. Chapter Four, "Biblical Considerations," presents Scriptural evidence from over fifty (50) passages for why the *autographa* position is the correct view. Chapter Four presents the Bible teaching that God inspired words (Genesis 22:16; Exodus 24:4; Jeremiah 36:1,2), which words proceeded out of His mouth (Exodus 4:22; 34:27; Jeremiah 30:2; 36:1-4; Matthew 4:4), and, therefore, included vowels (Matthew 22:31; I Corinthians 9:10; cf. Romans 9:29; II Peter 3:2). These words are fully preserved (Psalm 12:6,7; Isaiah 30:8; 40:8; 59:21; Matthew 5:18; 24:35; Luke 16:17), so that the words are pure (Psalm 12:6,7), perfect (Psalm 19:7), sure (Psalm 93:5; 111:7), faithful (Psalm 119:89,138), settled (Psalm 119:89), a lamp and a light (Psalm 119:105), founded for ever (Psalm 119:152), enduring for ever (Psalm 119:160), magnified above all of God's name (Psalm 138:2), certain (Proverbs 22:20,21), standing for ever (Isaiah 40:8), not passing away (Matthew 24:35), not broken (John 10:35), lively oracles (Acts 7:38), the sole authority (II Timothy 3:16,17), quick (Hebrews 4:12), liveth and abideth for ever (I Peter 1:23), and a more sure word of prophecy (II Peter 1:19). These verses demand the presence of the vowels. Furthermore, the New Testament asserts that the written words of the Old Testament are equivalent to spoken words (Matthew 22:31; Luke 24:25; John 1:23; 12:38; Acts 3:22; 7:48,49; 8:32-34; 28:25; Romans 9:29; 12:19; 14:11; I Corinthians 9:10; Hebrews 3:7; II

Peter 3:2). Since speaking requires the use of vowels, then these written words must also have vowels. The above Bible teaching further refutes the non-authoritative and the accommodation positions while at the same time establishes the *autographa* position.

Chapter Five, "One Tittle," gives an in-depth exegesis of Matthew 5:18, which further establishes the *autographa* position as the correct view. In Matthew 5:18, Jesus states: "For verily I say unto you, Till heaven and earth pass, one jot or one tittle shall in no wise pass from the law, till all be fulfilled." Lexical, contextual, etymological, Scriptural, and translational considerations demonstrate that *tittle* in Matthew 5:18 refers to the Hebrew vowel point known as *chirek*. Lexically, *tittle* can mean a vowel point. Contextually, *jot*, the least of the Hebrew consonants, adequately guarantees the preservation of all the consonants (see Luke 16:10), therefore, *tittle* need not refer to consonants. Also, the phrase *one jot or one tittle* with the use of the disjunctive conjunction (ἤ *or*) makes it clear that *tittle* is different from the *jot*, which further establishes that *tittle* is referring to something other than consonants or something connected to consonants. Furthermore, the expression *till all be fulfilled* refers to the fulfillment of prophecy, the exact fulfillment of which depends on the vowels.[225] In addition to this, *one of these least commandments* in the next verse, Matthew 5:19, depends on the vowels.[226] The context of Matthew 5:18

---

[225] Please consider Genesis 49:10; I Kings 17:4; Job 24:12; 37:23; Psalm 2:9; Proverbs 12:19; 29:14; Isaiah 19:10; 21:13; Jeremiah 8:13; 15:19; 25:24; 48:4; 50:38; Daniel 9:27; Hosea 13:7; Micah 6:9; Zephaniah 3:8; and Malachi 2:3. These verses are all prophecies that some would like to repoint, but repointing would affect the fulfillment, making it impossible to know if they are fulfilled.

[226] In Exodus 23:19, is the prohibition against seething a kid in his mother's milk. Some might classify this command as one the least of the commandments. Since one could repoint the word *milk* (חָלָב) to *fat* (חֵלֶב), then without the vowel pointing one, thinking that the word was *fat* instead of *milk*, could easily break this commandment and teach others also to break it. If one is not going to break one of the least of the commandments, he must have the vowel points so that he clearly knows the demands of the commandment.

points to one tittle referring to a vowel. Etymologically, the Greek word for *tittle* (κεραία) is a transliteration into Greek of the Hebrew חִירֶק (*chirek*), wherein *chirek* is the name of the smallest Hebrew vowel point. Scripturally, God spoke words involving the use of both vowels and consonants (Genesis 22:16; Exodus 4:22; 24:4; Jeremiah 30:2; 36:1-4; Matthew 4:4). These words God's prophets wrote necessitating their having used vowels (Exodus 34:27; Matthew 22:31; Luke 24:25; John 1:23; 12:38; Acts 3:22; 7:48,49; 8:32-34; 28:25; Romans 9:29; 12:19; 14:11; I Corinthians 9:10; Hebrews 3:7; II Peter 3:2). Jesus guaranteed the perfect preservation of God's Words (Matthew 24:35; John 10:35; 17:17). These Scriptural considerations, along with the fact that God's Words are sure (Chapter Four) and are the sole authority for faith and practice (Chapter Two) demand the presence of the vowels. In other words, Scripture teaches the inspiration and preservation of the vowels of the Old Testament, which teaching is in exact agreement with understanding *tittle* to be a vowel point in Matthew 5:18. Translationally, many translations of the Bible understand the Greek word for *tittle* to be a dot, which describes exactly the *chirek*.

Chapter Six, "Further Objections," presents more information and discussion on certain objections that scholars raise against the *autographa* position. These objections concern both historical and Biblical matters. The introduction has introduced all of the objections. Only objections needing further treatment are in Chapter Six.

Chapter Seven, "Conclusion," gives an overall summary of the book and is a good synopsis of the arguments contained herein.

Following Chapter Seven are sections entitled "Definitions and Delimitations" and "Bibliography." The definition section presents definitions of various terms and words that this book uses. The delimitation section explains the limits that the author has placed upon this book, thereby limiting and narrowing its focus. The bibliography section is an extensive list of books, articles, and other sources that the author consulted in writing this book.

CHAPTER TWO – THE BIBLE IS THE ONLY AUTHORITY

The advocates of both the accommodation and non-authoritative positions ultimately rely on uninspired authorities, that is, on works that were not inspired of God. For instance, the accommodation position relies on the Masoretes to insert the vowel points, with many of the accommodationists also relying on Jewish oral tradition to convey the sounds of the vowels to the Masoretes. Because the advocates of the non-authoritative position believe that the points are of no authority, then they must also rely on uninspired works to supply vowels in order to determine what they think is the correct word. But in so doing, both positions are neglecting the fact that the Bible teaches that Scripture is the sole authority for faith and practice. The authority is not the Bible plus oral tradition, the Bible plus the Masoretes, the Bible plus the textual critics, the Bible plus history, or the Bible plus some other uninspired work. On the contrary, the Bible and the Bible alone is the sole authority for faith and practice, and such a teaching devastates the non-authoritative and accommodation positions on the points, for it shows that these positions are unbiblical. And with these positions being unbiblical, this leaves only one position left standing, namely, the *autographa* position.

The Bible being the sole authority for faith and practice is the very first of the Baptist distinctives. *Baptist Doctrines* states:

> The book called the Bible is given by the inspiration of God, and is the only rule of Christian faith and practice. The consequence is, that we have no creeds, nor catechisms, nor decretals, which bind us by their authority. We think a creed worth nothing, unless it is supported by Scriptural authority, and if the creed is founded on the word of God, we do not see why we should not rest on that word which props up the creed; we prefer to go back directly to the foundation itself and rest there alone. . . . Our churches hold that Jesus Christ is the only Lawgiver, and the only King in Zion; that his law is laid down in the Scriptures, and it is perfect: and, therefore, they refuse to follow all

forms of tradition and ecclesiastical ordinations whatever, bowing only to the behests of inspired precept, and the recorded practices of the apostolic churches, as their record is found in the Scriptures.[227]

While the writer is a Baptist and while the very first of the Baptist distinctives is that the Bible is the sole authority for faith and practice, it is not for these reasons that he adheres to this principle. Rather he adheres to this vital principle because the Bible itself teaches it. This chapter presents a Biblical delineation of the doctrine of the Bible being the sole authority for faith and practice, followed by a presentation concerning an unbiblical deviation from this doctrine.

Before getting into the delineation of this teaching, the author must make a distinction. That distinction is this: the Bible is the sole or only authority for faith and practice, not just the final authority. What is the difference between a final authority and a sole authority? *Sole authority* means there is nothing else to which to appeal. On the other hand, *final authority* implies that there are lessor authorities. Take the judicial system as an example. If a person has a legal problem, he might go to a city court, then to a county court, then to the state court, then to a federal court, then to the Supreme Court. The Supreme Court is the final authority, but it is not the sole authority. However, the Bible is not simply the final authority, it is the sole authority. Therefore, the Bible and the Bible alone determines faith and practice. It is not a creed plus the Bible, it is not a commentary plus the Bible, it is not tradition plus the Bible; but it is only the Bible that decides faith and practice. With this distinction in mind, the author now presents a delineation of this doctrine.

---

[227] Thomas Armitage, "Baptist Faith and Practice" in *Baptist Doctrines: Being an Exposition, in a Series of Essays by Representative Baptist Ministers, of the Distinctive Points of Baptist Faith and Practice*, ed. Charles A. Jenkins (St. Louis: C. R. Barns Publishing Co., 1890, Reprint, Watertown, WI: Baptist Heritage Press, 1989), 34,35.

DELINEATION OF THE DOCTRINE

The author delineates the doctrine of the Bible being the sole authority for faith and practice by giving five points about the Bible: (1) Scripture is the authority for salvation; (2) Scripture is the authority for judging; (3) Scripture is the authority for local churches; (4) Scripture is the authority for Jesus' life; and (5) Scripture is the authority for all faith and practice.

Scripture Is the Authority for Salvation

Salvation is the start of the Christian life and right at the start of the Christian life, the Bible is the sole authority. The Bible presents the message, meaning, and the Messiah of the Gospel, which is all "according to the Scriptures" (I Corinthians 15:3,4). Consequently, the Bible is able to produce saving faith (Romans 10:17), make a person wise unto salvation (II Timothy 3:15), and is the means by which a person is born again (I Peter 1:23).

Romans 10:17

Paul states: "Whosoever shall call upon the name of the Lord shall be saved" (Romans 10:13). In Romans 10:14-19, Paul then asks a series of questions related to salvation (Romans 10:14-19). In the midst of Romans 10:14-19 are the words: "Faith *cometh* by hearing, and hearing by the word of God" (Romans 10:17). Earlier, Romans 10 uses *faith* (πίστις) to refer to "the righteousness which is of faith" (Romans 10:6), that is, to saving faith and that is its meaning here in Romans 10:17 as well. If one will have faith in the Lord for the saving of his soul, this faith comes by hearing, and the hearing by the Word of God. Men cannot be saved apart from the Word of God. For instance, Cornelius sent for Peter who told him words, whereby Cornelius and all his house were saved (Acts 11:14). In the words of Peter to Cornelius, Peter referred to the witness of the Old Testament prophets concerning forgiveness in Jesus (Acts 10:43). But more than this, the entire message of Peter to Cornelius is the Word of God, for it is recorded in the Bible in Acts 10:34-43. The Book of Acts manifests the same pattern throughout (Acts 2:14-36; 3:12-26; 7:2-53; 13:16-41; and 17:2,3). The preachers refer to the Old Testament and their messages, being recorded in the Bible, are themselves the Word of God. Also, I Corinthians 1:21 says, "It pleased God by the foolishness of preaching to save them that believe." What are preachers to preach? They are to preach the Word (II Timothy 4:2). Saving faith does not come from hearing the word of a man, not even the word of a man raised from the dead (cf. Luke 16:27-31); the word of an angel (cf. Galatians 1:8); or the word of tradition (cf. Colossians 2:8); but it comes from hearing the Word of God. There is no salvation apart from the Word of God. The Bible is the authority when it comes to saving faith.

II Timothy 3:15

In II Timothy 3:15, Paul observes that Timothy from a child had known the Holy Scriptures (that is, the Old Testament) and that the Scriptures were able to make him wise (σοφίσαι aorist active infinitive from σοφίζω and means to "enlighten in regard to divine things"[228]) unto salvation. Without these Scriptures, Timothy would not have known about salvation. Timothy did not know about salvation through creation. Nor did he know about salvation by looking inward to his own heart. The knowledge of salvation only comes through the Scriptures. Scripture is the authority when it comes to salvation. Gill writes:

> About the way of Salvation; if that is the affair the doubt is concerning, look up to the way-posts, look into the word of God, and read what that says; search the Scriptures, for therein is the way of eternal life; life and immortality, or the way to an immortal life, is brought to light by the gospel. The Scriptures, under a divine influence, and with a di-

---

[228] Zodhiates, "4679. σοφίζω."

vine blessing, are able to make a man wise unto salvation, and they do point unto men the way of it: it is not the light of nature[229]

The Scriptures are able to make a man wise unto salvation. It is not tradition, antiquity, or one's own intellect. The Scriptures are the authority when it comes to salvation.

I Peter 1:23-25

I Peter 1:23-25 states: "Being born again, not of corruptible seed, but of incorruptible, by the word of God, which liveth and abideth for ever. For all flesh *is* as grass, and all the glory of man as the flower of grass. The grass withereth, and the flower thereof falleth away: But the word of the Lord endureth for ever. And this is the word which by the gospel is preached unto you." The Word of God is the source and means by which a person is born again,[230] for it is through the Word of God that the Gospel is preached unto men. It is, therefore, the authority when it comes to salvation. Other verses attest to the fact that the Bible is the sole authority concerning salvation. James 1:18 states, "Of his own will begat he us with the word of truth." And Ephesians 1:13 declares, "In whom ye also *trusted*, after that ye heard the word of truth, the gospel of your salvation." Peter further asserts that the Word of the Lord will outlast even the best that man can produce on his own, for the Word of God is incorruptible, lives forever, abides forever, and endures forever. How ridiculous it is, then, for any to look to something other than the Word of God as an authority in matters of faith and practice.

---

[229] John Gill, *The Scriptures the Only Guide in Matters of Religion Jeremiah 6:16* in *The Collected Writings of John Gill*, Version 2.0 [CD-ROM] (Paris, Arkansas: The Baptist Standard Bearer, 1999), 6.

[230] The word *of* in *of corruptible seed* is from ἐκ and the word *by* in *by the word of God* is from διά. Lenski writes, " ἐκ states the source of spiritual life and names the seed; διά adds the thought that this seed is the means for our being begotten and adds the idea of what this seed really is: 'by means of God's living and abiding Word' " (Lenski, *The Interpretation of the Epistles of St. Peter, St. John and St. Jude*, 73).

Conclusion

Romans 10:17; II Timothy 3:15; and I Peter 1:23 along with other verses all teach that Scripture is the sole authority for salvation. No one can be saved apart from the Bible.

Scripture Is the Authority for Judging

Many passages demonstrate that the Bible is the rule by which a person should judge actions. Any time the Bible gives an instruction or a command then that command becomes the standard by which to judge. To list all of these commands and instructions would be a considerable undertaking. Instead, this section presents a representative sampling of those commands and instructions.

Genesis 2:17

In Genesis 2:17, the Lord gave a command for Adam not to eat of the tree of the knowledge of good and evil. God gave this command to govern Adam's actions. These spoken Words of God to Adam were the authority in his life. Genesis 2:17, however, was not written until some years later by Moses, long after Adam died, which demonstrates that what God speaks is authoritative, even before it is written. Much of the Word of God was spoken before it was written. For example, Jesus spoke His teachings decades before the Gospel writers inscripturated them. The teachings were immediately binding upon all those who heard them and then once inscripturated became binding on all men.[231] In this present time, since prophesy has failed (I Corinthians 13:8), then there is no audible authority, as in the days of Adam, but all authority is in the written Word of God. And it is the written Word of God that is the authority for judging.

---

[231] Of course, the above statement assumes that the original spoken instruction was intended for all men.

It is profitable to note that the first command that God gave to Adam, which was the authority in Adam and then Eve's lives, is the very thing that the devil attacked. Satan disputed the authority of God's Words (Genesis 3:1). Satan then denied the authority of God's Words (Genesis 3:4,5), which he did in order to get Eve to disobey the authority of God's Words (Genesis 3:6) and to displace God's authority with what she thought was best. Satan continues to work in the same manner today. For instance, despite God's authoritative and repetitive statements that His Words are pure and true (Psalm 12:6,7; John 17:17; etc.); Satan disputes the purity and verity of God's Words. He then denies the Bible's purity and verity. Satan operates thusly in order to get God's people to disobey God's command to keep, that is, to guard and to protect, His Words (Matthew 28:20, cf. II Timothy 4:7; Revelation 2:26; 3:8,10), and to then displace God's authority with what they think is best. For instance, some reject God's command to keep His Words so that they may keep[232] their own tradition (Mark 7:9); namely, scholarly, historical, and Jewish traditions about the Words of God. Such traditions dispute and deny the purity and verity of God's Words (see further in next section).

Exodus 5:1

Exodus 5:1 states: "And afterward Moses and Aaron went in, and told Pharaoh, Thus saith the LORD God of Israel, Let my people go, that they may hold a feast unto me in the wilderness." Concerning this verse, Spurgeon wrote:

> "Thus saith the Lord" is that *with which we must confront the Lord's enemies*. When Moses went in before Pharaoh, the words which he used were not, "The elders of Israel have consulted, and thus have they bidden me say," not "Our Father Abraham once said, and his words have been handed to us by long tradition"-such talk would have been

---

[232] Note that *keep* in Mark 7:9 and *observe* in Matthew 28:20 are both from the same Greek root word (τηρέω).

readily resisted-but he confronted the haughty monarch with "Thus saith the Lord, let my people go."[233]

All authority resided in what God said. God's Words were the standard by which one was to judge actions. And God's Words are still the standard for judging actions today.

Leviticus 10:1,2

Leviticus 10:1 relates the incident of Nadab and Abihu offering "strange fire before the LORD, which he commanded them not." Instead of allowing the authority of the Words of God to govern them, Nadab and Abihu acted independently. Because they did this, "there went fire out from the LORD, and devoured them" (Leviticus 10:2). Leviticus 10:1-2 is representative of many examples in the Bible, demonstrating that the commandment of God is the standard. Nadab and Abihu took a new and innovative approach to the work of the Lord, just as many are doing in the early twenty-first century by following rationalistic scholarship. However, it is best to "ask for the old paths, where is the good way, and walk therein" (Jeremiah 6:16).

Deuteronomy 4:1; 7:11; 27:26

God taught the children of Israel statutes and judgments so that they would do them (Deuteronomy 4:1; 7:11). They were not to add to or diminish from these commandments, so that they could carefully obey them (Deuteronomy 4:2). What God commanded is the authority and they were to honor that authority by not tampering with it in any way. Indeed, they were cursed if they did not confirm "*all* the words of this law to do them" (Deuteronomy 27:26). Scripture is the authority for judging and one must take this very seriously.

---

[233] Charles H. Spurgeon, " 'Thus Saith the Lord,' or the Book of Common Prayer Weighed in the Balances of the Sanctuary," in vol. 10 of *The Metropolitan Tabernacle Pulpit* (Pasadena, TX: Pilgrim Publications, 1969), 537.

I Samuel 15:3,22

God gave a clear command to King Saul to "go and smite Amalek, and utterly destroy all that they have, and spare them not; but slay both man and woman, infant and suckling, ox and sheep, camel and ass" (I Samuel 15:3). However, Saul did not fully obey the command. When the prophet Samuel confronted Saul, Samuel said, "Hath the LORD *as great* delight in burnt offerings and sacrifices, as in obeying the voice of the LORD? Behold, to obey *is* better than sacrifice, *and* to hearken than the fat of rams" (I Samuel 15:22). What God says is the absolute authority, and one has no right to alter it in any way. Saul thought that he had a better idea (I Samuel 15:21). However, the best plan of action is to follow what God says, for what God says is the authority, not what a man thinks, not even what a king thinks. Also, in this day, God's Words are the authority, not what a scholar says, or what a leading textual critic teaches.

Isaiah 8:20

Isaiah 8:20 says, "To the law and to the testimony: if they speak not according to this word, *it is* because *there is* no light in them." *Law* and *testimony* speak of God's "divine revelation, considered as a system of belief and as a rule of duty."[234] "The law . . . is the revelation of God expressing His will for man's obedience, and the testimony is His revelation expressing His will as a system to be believed. These are the standards by which all opinions and utterances are to be judged."[235] The Bible is the only authority. Isaiah does not say, "To the law and to the testimony and to the general opinion of the scholars." Nor, does he say, "To the law and to the testimony and to

---

[234] Joseph A. Alexander, *Commentary on Isaiah* (Grand Rapids: Kregel, 1992), 183.

[235] Edward J. Young, *The Book of Isaiah: the English Text, with Introduction, Exposition, and Notes* (Grand Rapids: Eerdmans, 1965), 319.

the Assyrian Chronicles." No, one is to judge a matter only by God's Words. The Bible is the sole authority for faith and practice.

John 5:39

In speaking to the Jews, Jesus said, "Search the scriptures; for in them ye think ye have eternal life: and they are they which testify of me" (John 5:39). Jesus commanded the Jews to search the Scriptures. *Search* (ἐρευνᾶτε a second person plural present active imperative[236] from ἐραυνάω) "means to *search diligently* or *anxiously*. It is applied to miners, who search for precious metals—who look anxiously for the *bed* of the ore with an intensity or anxiety proportionate to *their sense* of the value of the metal."[237] *Scriptures* refers to the Old Testament. Being that the Words of God are "more to be desired . . . than gold, yea, than much fine gold" (Psalm 19:10), then truly one should search the Scriptures very diligently.

Now Jesus did not tell the Jews to search the tradition of the elders, or the annals of history, or the edicts of the rabbis. Therefore, it is clear that Jesus regarded the Scriptures as the authority and desired that the Jews would let the Scriptures be the authority in their life by allowing the Scriptures to teach them of Jesus. Hutcheson, commenting on John 5:39, says that Jesus directs "them to the scriptures, or

---

[236] An alternate parsing of ἐρευνᾶτε is a second person plural present indicative verb, but from the context it seems that the imperative parsing is correct, for "our Lord had told the Jews that His Father had borne witness of Him, though not by audible voice, nor by visible apparition. How then had He borne witness? They would find it in His Word. 'Go and search your own Scriptures,' our Lord seems to say. 'Examine them, and become really acquainted with their contents; you will find that they testify clearly and distinctly of Me. If you wish to know God the Father's testimony to Me, search the Scriptures' " (J. C. Ryle, *Expository Thoughts on John* (Carlisle, PA: The Banner of Truth Trust, 1987), I:313,314).

[237] Albert Barnes, *Luke and John*, edited by Robert Frew in vol. 9 of *Barnes' Notes*, Heritage Edition (London: Blackie & Son, 1847, reprinted Grand Rapids: Baker Book House Company, 2005), 238.

written word, as to God's rule in this controversy."²³⁸ The Word of God is what rules. In John 5, the Jews did not consider Jesus to be the Messiah, but Jesus counsels them to surrender to the rule and authority of Scripture, which Scripture testifies of Him. By so doing, they would have come to receive Christ as the Messiah. Likewise today, a man needs to surrender to the rule and authority of Scripture regardless of what he has always thought, for Scripture is the sole authority for faith and practice.

John 12:48

In John 12:48, Jesus states: "He that rejecteth me, and receiveth not my words, hath one that judgeth him: the word that I have spoken, the same shall judge him in the last day." The Words of God will judge man. On this verse, Strouse writes: "His preserved Words are the standard for Christian living in every generation and will be the basis for His righteous judgment in the future."²³⁹

Acts 17:11

When Paul preached to the Bereans, what did they do? Acts 17:11 says, "They received the word with all readiness of mind, and searched the scriptures daily, whether those things were so." In other words, the Bereans regarded the Words of God as the authority and for this God commends them. *Searched* (ἀνακρίνοντες is a present active masculine singular nominative participle from ἀνακρίνω) means "to examine accurately or carefully."²⁴⁰ *Scriptures* (γραφάς feminine accusative plural noun from γραφή) refers to that which is written, in this

---

[238] George Hutcheson, *An Exposition of John's Gospel* (Grand Rapids: Sovereign Grace Publishers, 1971), 91.

[239] Thomas Strouse, "The Translation Model Predicted By Scripture" (Newington, CT: Emmanuel Baptist Theological Press, 2001), 9.

[240] Zodhiates, "350. ἀνακρίνω."

context, it refers to the Old Testament Scriptures. What was written was the standard and the authority by which the Bereans examined and judged all doctrine. It seems that Scripture was their only authority, for one does not read of their searching the oral tradition or Greek philosophy to see if these things were so. No, their standard was this: is it true to the Bible? The Bible was their authority for judging matters of faith. Nothing has happened since the time of the Bereans for anyone to dethrone the Bible from that exalted position – it is still the standard, even in this twenty-first century, the standard by which one ought to judge all doctrine.

Hebrews 8:5

When Moses was about to make the tabernacle, God admonished him with these words: "See that thou make all things according to the pattern shewed to thee in the mount" (Hebrews 8:5). Spurgeon, commenting on this incident, writes:

> "Thus saith the Lord" is the only authority in God's Church. When the tabernacle was pitched in the wilderness, what was the authority for its length and breadth? Why was the altar of incense to be placed here, and the brazen altar there? Why so many lambs or bullocks to be offered on a certain day? Why must the Passover be roasted whole and not sodden? Simply and only because God had shown all these things to Moses in the holy mount; and thus had Jehovah spoken, "Look that thou make them after their pattern, which was showed thee in the mount." It is even so in the Church at the present day; true servants of God demand to see for all Church ordinances and doctrines the express authority of the Church's only Teacher and Lord. They remember that the Lord Jesus bade the apostles to teach believers to observe all things whatsoever he had commanded them, but he neither gave to them nor to any men power to alter his own commands. The Holy Ghost revealed much of precious truth and holy precept by the apostles, and to his teaching we would give earnest heed; but when men cite the authority of fathers, and councils, and bishops, we give place for subjection, no, not for an hour. They may quote Irenaeus or Cyprian, Augustine or Chrysostom; they may remind us of the dogmas of Luther or Calvin; they may find authority in Simeon, or Wesley, or Gill - we will listen to the opinions of these great men with the respect which they deserve as men, but having so done, we deny that we have any-

thing to do with these men as authorities in the Church of God, for there nothing has any authority, but "Thus saith the Lord of hosts." Yea, if you shall bring us the concurrent consent of all tradition - if you shall quote precedents venerable with fifteen, sixteen, or seventeen centuries of antiquity, we burn the whole as so much worthless lumber, unless you put your finger upon the passage of Holy Writ which warrants the matter to be of God. You may further plead, in addition to all this venerable authority, the beauty of the ceremony and its usefulness to those who partake therein, but this is all foreign to the point, for to the true Church of God the only question is this, is there a "Thus saith the Lord" for it? And if divine authority be not forthcoming, faithful men thrust forth the intruder as the cunning craftiness of men.[241]

Spurgeon expresses this quite well. But, oh, how men are taken with antiquity. But does not the Bible student have in his possession something that is older than the oldest? Indeed, he does, for he has the very Words of God, whose Author is "from everlasting to everlasting" (Psalm 90:2). Let the Word of the Eternal and Living God be the authority, and not the word of some frail, mortal, and dead man. The Word of God is the authority for faith and practice.

Saith the Lord

In the above quote, Spurgeon refers to "thus saith the Lord" as the only authority in God's church. Throughout the Bible, one finds various expressions indicating that God's Words are from the Lord and are, therefore, binding upon men. Following is a list of some these expressions and the numbers of times in which they occur.

Expression	Number of Times
Said God	2
Spake the Lord	3
Saith God	4

---

[241] Spurgeon, " 'Thus Saith the Lord,' or the Book of Common Prayer Weighed in the Balances of the Sanctuary," 535,536.

God hath spoken	5
Lord saith	12
God spake	13
Said the Lord	16
Lord hath spoken	31
God said	46
Lord spake	144
Lord said	221
Word of the Lord	255
Saith the Lord	854

The above list accounts for one thousand six hundred six (1,606) expressions that indicate that God gave the Bible. Theissen states, "It is claimed that statements like these occur more than 3,800 times in the Old Testament."[242] It is obvious, then, that the Bible is a revelation from God wherein God gives instructions to men concerning their conduct. The Bible is the authority for judging right and wrong from God's perspective, for the Scriptures reveal the mind of God and what the Lord requires.

Conclusion

From the very start of the Bible it is clear that the Bible is the authority for judging as Genesis 2:17 demonstrates. This impression is not at all lessened as one continues through the pages of the Bible. In fact, repeatedly the Lord lets man know that the Bible is the authority for judging (Exodus 5:1; Leviticus 10:1,2; Deuteronomy 4:1; 7:11; 27:26; I Samuel 15:3,22; Isaiah 8:20; John 5:39; 12:48; Acts 17:11; Hebrews 8:5).

---

[242] Thiessen, Henry Clarence, *Introductory Lectures in Systematic Theology* (Grad Rapids: Wm. B. Eerdmans publishing Company, 1949), 90.

Scripture Is the Authority for Local Churches

Scripture is the authority in salvation, which specifically applies to local churches because a person must be saved in order to be part of a local church (Acts 2:47). Scripture is also the authority in judging. Since the Lord commands local churches to "prove all things" (I Thessalonians 5:21), which activity involves judging, then local churches must also appeal to the Scripture in order to judge correctly. Scripture, then, is the authority for local churches. Other factors also establish that Scripture is the authority for local churches: (1) New Testament Scripture is for local churches; (2) Old Testament Scripture is for local churches; (3) all of the Word of God is for local churches; and (4) false authorities must be rejected by local churches.

New Testament Scripture Is for Local Churches

In Matthew 28, Christ commanded His disciples (Matthew 28:16) to teach the saved "to observe all things whatsoever" He had commanded (Matthew 28:20). The things Jesus commanded are in the Gospels. As the book of Acts illustrates, the disciples carried out Jesus' instructions in the context of the local church, thus showing that the Gospels are for the local church. The book of Acts provides an inspired, historical account of the start of local churches in various places, and is certainly to the benefit of local churches. God directed Paul to write epistles to local churches, namely Romans (Romans 1:7; 12:5), I and II Corinthians (I Corinthians 1:2; II Corinthians 1:1), Galatians (Galatians 1:2), Ephesians (Ephesians 1:1,22; 3:10,21; cf. Acts 20:17,28), Philippians (Philippians 1:1; 4:15), Colossians (Colossians 1:2,18), I and II Thessalonians (I Thessalonians 1:1; II Thessalonians 1:1); Philemon (Philemon 2[243]); and Hebrews (Hebrews 10:25; 13:7,17,24). The Pastoral Epistles of I and II Timothy and Titus speak of pastoral matters and, therefore, are for local churches (cf. Acts

---

[243] Paul wrote Philemon to a man who had a church in his house.

20:28). James writes to those who were in a local church (James 5:14). Peter wrote his epistles to the saved who were scattered abroad (I Peter 1:1; II Peter 3:1), who had elders among them (I Peter 5:1,2), indicating that these saved Jews were in a local church. John addressed his epistles to believers and specifically mentions local church matters (I John 2:19[244]; III John 6, 9, 10). Jude addressed his epistle to the saints (Jude 1), who presumably assembled (Hebrews 10:25; Jude 4, 12). And in the book of Revelation, Jesus addresses the seven churches of Asia Minor (Revelation 1:4). All of the New Testament is for local churches and the New Testament Scripture is authoritative for local churches. In addition to the fact that all of the New Testament concerns local church matters, several passages clearly state that the New Testament is for local churches, among which are Matthew 28:20; I Corinthians 14:37; I Timothy 3:14,15; II Peter 3:2; and Jude 3.

Matthew 28:20

Matthew 28:20 is part of the Great Commission. "The Great Commission is the commission to establish local, New Testament, immersionist assemblies. Christ had a New Testament, immersionist assembly, and He commanded His followers to duplicate His efforts."[245] These instructions, then, concern local churches. The first part of Matthew 28:20 states, "Teaching them to observe all things whatsoever I have commanded you." Since Christ is God (I Timothy 3:16), then what Christ commanded is the Word of God. Furthermore, in His authoritative teaching Jesus exalted all the Words of God (Mat-

---

[244] Here John mentions antichrists leaving *us*, which seems to refer to them leaving a group. Since the New Testament pattern is for believers to assemble in a local church, the group that the antichrists left is presumably the local church (see also Acts 20:29,30).

[245] Thomas M. Strouse, *I Will Build My Church: The Doctrine and History of Baptists* (Newington, CT: Emmanuel Baptist Theological Press, 2001), 31. Strouse further observes: "That this is the proper interpretation of the Great Commission is validated by the actions of the early Apostles and disciples who obeyed their Lord."

thew 5:18; Luke 8:21; 11:28; John 5:39; 10:35), which serves as an example to local churches also to exalt all of the Words of God.

Matthew 28:20 reveals the "responsibility of churches."[246] Part of this responsibility involves "teaching them to observe all things whatsoever I have commanded you" (Matthew 28:20) which means that "local immersionist churches were given the divine responsibility to guard God's Word."[247] *Observe* (τηρεῖν a present active infinitive from τηρέω) means "to keep an eye on, watch, and hence to guard, keep, obey."[248] Local immersionist churches are to keep their eye on the commandments of Christ so that they can perfectly obey those commandments. Therefore, it is obvious that the Words of God are for the local church and that the Words of God must be the authority for faith and practice in the local church.

I Corinthians 14:37

In I Corinthians 14:37, Paul writes, "If any man think himself to be a prophet, or spiritual, let him acknowledge that the things that I write unto you are the commandments of the Lord." *Commandments* (ἐντολαί) is a feminine plural nominative noun from ἐντολή and in this context refers to "the precepts of Christ relative to the orderly management of affairs in religious assemblies."[249] Under inspiration, Paul wrote the commandments of the Lord, which became part of the New Testament, and these New Testaments commandments are binding upon the local church. I Corinthians 14:37 also teaches that those who think that they are spiritual (πνευματικός referring to "persons who are spiritual, enlightened by the Holy Spirit, enjoying the influences,

---

[246] Strouse, "The Translation Model Predicted by Scripture," 15.

[247] Ibid., 17.

[248] Zodhiates, 5083. τηρέω.

[249] Thayer, 218.

graces, gifts of the Holy Spirit"[250]) will acknowledge (ἐπιγινωσκέτω a third person singular present active imperative, meaning "let him continually take knowledge"[251]) that the inspired writings are the commandments of the Lord and will, therefore, submit to them. When a man ignores, disregards, or explains away what God's Words say, he is not being spiritual, but rather, he is being carnal. A man who is spiritual will hear what the Lord says, for "he that is of God heareth God's words" (John 8:47). When a Bible teacher, a preacher, or an expositor will not submit to the authority of the Words of God, he is acting just like the Pharisees who would not hear God's Words (John 8:13,47,48). To not submit to the Words of God is a most dangerous place in which to place one's self.

I Timothy 3:14,15

In I Timothy, Paul gives inspired instructions to Timothy concerning local church affairs. In the midst of this inspired instruction, Paul writes: "These things write I unto thee, hoping to come unto thee shortly: But if I tarry long, that thou mayest know how thou oughtest to behave thyself in the house of God, which is the church of the living God, the pillar and ground of the truth" (I Timothy 3:14,15). *House of God* refers to the local church, for the context speaks of the qualifications of a bishop who must take care of the church of God (I Timothy 3:5) and the qualifications of deacons (I Timothy 3:8-13), who also serve in a local church (Acts 2:47; 5:11; 6:1-7). *To behave thyself* is a present passive infinitive from ἀναστρέφω and means "to turn oneself

---

[250] Zodhiates, "4152. πνευματικός."

[251] Archibald Robertson and Alfred Plummer, *A Critical and Exegetical Commentary on the First Epistle of St. Paul to the Corinthians* in *The International Critical Commentary on the Holy Scriptures of the Old and New Testaments*, eds. Samuel Rolles Driver, Alfred Plummer, and Charles Augustus Briggs (Edinburgh: T & T Clark, 1978), 327.

around,"[252] that is, Timothy was to submit himself to the inspired New Testament instructions that came from Paul and allow these to turn him around so that his conduct would be right. Clearly, these inspired New Testament instructions from Paul are to be the authority for faith and practice in a local church. It is not the Word of God plus Hiscox's *The New Directory for Baptist Churches*. It is not the Word of God plus the rules of the convention. It is not the Word of God plus the statements of scholars. No, the Word of God alone is the authority.

II Peter 3:2

In II Peter 3:2, Peter exhorts his readers to "be mindful of the words which were spoken before by the holy prophets, and of the commandment of us the apostles of the Lord and Saviour." Peter writes "to them that have obtained like precious faith" (II Peter 1:1), that is, to the saved. II Peter is the second epistle that Peter had written to them (II Peter 3:1). In the first epistle, he mentioned that they had elders among them (I Peter 5:1) who were over the flock (I Peter 5:2), that is, the local church (Acts 20:17,28). Therefore, the saved to whom Peter writes are part of a local church and what Peter writes to them applies to the local church. Peter exhorts these saved local church members to be mindful. *Mindful* (μνησθῆναι an aorist middle infinitive from μνάομαι) means "to remember, to recollect"[253] and expresses "purpose and restates the actual result he hopes to achieve in giving his reminder."[254] Robertson states that the purpose use of this infinitive indicates an indirect command.[255]

---

[252] Zodhiates, "390. ἀναστρέφω."

[253] Zodhiates, "3415. μνάομαι."

[254] D. Edmond Hiebert, *Second Peter and Jude: An Expositional Commentary* (Greenville, SC: Unusual Publications, 1989), 139.

[255] Archibald Thomas Robertson, "The Second Epistle of Peter" in vol. 6 of *Word Pictures in the New Testament* (Nashville, TN: Broadman Press, 1930), 172.

Peter commands them to be mindful of two things: (1) "the words which were spoken before by the holy prophets," and (2) "the commandment of us the apostles of the Lord and Saviour." Both of these point to the Words of God. *The words spoken before*[256] *by the holy prophets* refers to Old Testament Scripture. *The commandment of us the apostles of the Lord and Saviour* refers to New Testament revelation. Peter wants them to be mindful of Old and New Testament Scripture. Adams writes:

> St. Peter refers us to the words of the prophets, and commandments of the apostles, . . . not human traditions, not the constitutions and impositions of usurpers, . . . , not the inventions of men, . . . , not the wisdom of the philosophers, not all the morality that dropped in verse from the pens of poets.[257]

The Bible, both Old and New Testaments, is the authority for local churches.

Jude 3

Jude 3 commands the saved to "earnestly contend for the faith which was once delivered unto the saints." Saints assembled in local churches (Acts 9:13 cf. with Philippians 3:6; I Corinthians 1:2; 14:33; II Corinthians 1:1; Philippians 1:1), therefore, Jude 3 affects local churches. Another thing that identifies the readers of Jude with a local church is that Jude mentions them as a group amongst whom certain had crept in unawares (Jude 4) something that Paul stated would happen to local churches (Acts 20:28,29). Furthermore, Jude mentions

---

[256] *Spoken before* is an interesting expression as it relates to the matter of preservation, for it is a perfect passive participle, which indicates "permanence, the speaking still continues in Holy Writ" (Lenski, *The Interpretation of I and II Epistles of Peter, the Three Epistles of John, and the Epistle of Jude*, 337). "The perfect tense . . . underlines the permanence of these prophetic utterances; the speaking still continues in the inspired Scriptures" (Hiebert, 139).

[257] Thomas Adams, *A Commentary on the Second Epistle General of St. Peter* (Ligonier, PA: Soli Deo Gloria Publications, 1990), 601, 602.

their feasts of charity (Jude 12), perhaps a reference to the Lord's Supper, a local church ordinance (I Corinthians 11:23).

David Cloud writing on Jude 3 states,

> "The faith" refers to the body of New Testament truth delivered by the Apostles through Holy Spirit inspiration. The term "once delivered" tells us that this body of truth was given during one particular period of time and was completed. It refers to the New Testament Scriptures.[258]

God has delivered the faith to the saints, clearly showing that the New Testament is for local churches. That this New Testament truth was delivered unto the saints

> implieth a leaving things in another's hand by way of trust, and so doth not only note the mercy of God, but the duty of the church, to whom "the oracles of God are committed" to be kept. Whence observe, that God hath delivered the doctrine and rule of faith to the church as a public trustee, that it may . . . keep it and preserve it for ages to come.[259]

Conclusion

All of the New Testament is for local churches, which is clear from the fact that all of the books of New Testament concern local church members and matters. Furthermore, in at least five passages (Matthew 28:20; I Corinthians 14:37; I Timothy 3:14,15; II Peter 3:2; and Jude 3), the Bible specifically teaches that New Testament instruction is the authority for faith and practice in local churches. To allow other things (history, text critics, tradition, etc.) to be the authority is to ignore God's instruction for the local church, which can only end in ruin (cf. Matthew 7:24-27).

---

[258] David W. Cloud, "The Sufficiency of the Bible" in *Fundamental Baptist CD-Rom Library* [CD-ROM] (Port Huron, MI: Way of Life Literature, 2000).

[259] Thomas Manton, *Am Exposition of the Epistle of Jude* (Minneapolis: Klock & Klock, 1978), 110.

Old Testament Scripture Is for Local Churches

Not only did the Lord specifically give New Testament Scripture to local churches, but He also makes clear that the Old Testament Scriptures are for local churches as well. Matthew 28:20 and II Peter 3:2, which this chapter previously presented, and other passages (Acts 7:38; Romans 15:4; and I Corinthians 10:11) all elucidate that the Old Testament Scriptures are for local churches.

Acts 7:38

In Acts 7, Stephen, a deacon of the local church in Jerusalem (Acts 6:1-6), is giving his answer to charges brought against him by the Jews (Acts 6:8-7:1). In the midst of his answer, he states that the fathers "received the lively oracles to give unto us" (Acts 7:38). The fathers, that is, the Old Testament Jews received the lively oracles (Romans 3:2). *Oracles* (λόγια an accusative neuter plural noun from λόγιον) refers to "the declarations of God."[260] *Lively* (ζῶντα a present active participle accusative neuter plural from ζάω) refers metaphorically in the participle to things that are "living, lively, active, also enduring, opposed to what is dead, inactive, and also transient."[261] The fact that *lively* is a present participle indicates that at the time Stephen spoke in Acts 7, these oracles were still lively. They had not lived in the past and then died, but were still alive. These declarations of God from the OT are living, they are not dead declarations, but they have a vitality about them. And Stephen says that these lively oracles are "unto us." Since Stephen was a deacon of the local church in Jerusalem then the *us* includes local church believers and indicates that the Old Testament Scriptures are for local churches.

---

[260] Zodhiates, "3051. λόγιον."

[261] Zodhiates, "2198. ζάω." That *lively* refers to something that is opposed to that which is transient indicates that these oracles will endure and argues for their preservation.

Romans 15:4

Romans 15:4 states, "For whatsoever things were written aforetime were written for our learning, that we through patience and comfort of the scriptures might have hope." Paul wrote Romans 15:4 "to all that be in Rome, beloved of God, called *to be* saints" (Romans 1:7), that is, to the saved, who were "one body in Christ" (Romans 12:5), indicating that they were a local church (Ephesians 1:22,23).[262] The *things written aforetime* refer to the Old Testament Scriptures. These Old Testament Scriptures "were written for our learning." *Learning* (διδασκαλίαν from διδασκαλία is a feminine singular accusative noun) refers to teaching or instruction. Barnes writes, "Not that this was the only purpose of the writings of the Old Testament, to instruct Christians; but that all of the Old Testament might be useful *now* in illustrating and enforcing the doctrines of piety towards God and man."[263] In others words, Old Testament Scripture is the authority for faith and practice.

I Corinthians 10:11

In I Corinthians 10, the Bible presents incidents that occurred during the wilderness wanderings of the Israelites. After presenting these, the Bible says, "Now all these things happened unto them for ensamples: and they are written for our admonition, upon whom the ends of the world are come" (I Corinthians 10:11). I Corinthians was written to the local church in Corinth (I Corinthians 1:2). The things that are written refer to incidents recorded in the Old Testament. This Old Testament Scripture is written for the admonition of New Testament local church believers. *Admonition* (νουθεσίαν a feminine singular accusative noun from νουθεσία) means "warning, exhortation . . .

---

[262] Paul uses "we" in Romans 12:5 indicating that his local church body of Antioch was united with their local church body in Rome (cf. I Corinthians 6:16; 12:13).

[263] Barnes, *Romans* in *Notes on the New Testament*, ed. Robert Frew, 314.

any word of encouragement or reproof which leads to correct behaviour."[264] Clearly, what was written in the Old Testament has authority for a local church believer's practice.

Conclusion

Matthew 28:20; Acts 7:38; Romans 15:4; I Corinthians 10:11; and II Peter 3:2 all teach that Old Testament Scripture is for local churches and as such is authoritative. Sadly, many question the authority of the Old Testament Scriptures by claiming that it has scribal errors and, or no vowels. To do so, is to mimic Satan who said of the Old Testament authority, "Yea, hath God said?" (Genesis 3:1). It behooves those who claim to believe the Bible not to mimic Satan, but to bend the knee to the authority of the Old Testament.

Also, since God states that the Old Testament is for local churches, then the Old Testament Scriptures will be preserved. Furthermore, since local churches are to have a part in preserving God's Words (Matthew 28:20; Jude 3), then let local churches believe God and work to the upholding of God's Words. It seems to the author that those who question the inspiration of the Old Testament Hebrew vowels are working against the preservation of the Old Testament Scriptures, rather than for it. May they repent.

All of Word of God Is for Local Churches

Since both the New Testament Scriptures and the Old Testament Scriptures are for local churches, then all of the Words of God are for local churches. Again, this is evident from Matthew 28:20 and II Peter 3:2 (see above). Other passages also speak of the entire Word of God being the rule for faith and practice in local churches, namely II Timothy 3:16,17 and II Timothy 4:2.

---

[264] Zodhiates, "3559. νουθεσία."

II Timothy 3:16,17

II Timothy 3:16,17 states: "All scripture *is* given by inspiration of God, and *is* profitable for doctrine, for reproof, for correction, for instruction in righteousness: that the man of God may be perfect, throughly furnished unto all good works." A fuller treatment of this passage comes later; however, a few comments are in order at this time. First, this passage is in one of the pastoral epistles and, as such, concerns local churches. Second, this passage speaks of the man of God being throughly furnished unto all good works, one of which has to be involvement in a local church according to Hebrews 10:25, which further connects this passage with local churches. And third, this passage speaks of all Scripture, which refers to both Old and New Testaments. In light of these comments, it is clear that all of the Word of God is for local churches.

II Timothy 4:2

II Timothy 4:2 states: "Preach the word; be instant in season, out of season; reprove, rebuke, exhort with all longsuffering and doctrine." This command is to Timothy, who was involved in local church work (II Timothy 3), and teaches that the Word, that is, the Word of God, is for local churches. *Preach* (κήρυξον a second person singular aorist active imperative from κηρύσσω) is a command. Wuest observes that *preach* would call to Timothy's mind "the Imperial Herald, spokesman of the Emperor proclaiming in a formal, grave, and authoritative manner which must be listened to, the message which the Emperor gave him to announce."[265] Such should be the manner of the preacher.

---

[265] Kenneth S. Wuest, *The Pastoral Epistles in the Greek New Testament* in vol. 2 of *Wuest's Word Studies from the Greek New Testament for the English Reader* (Grand Rapids: Wm. B. Eerdmans Publishing Company, 1973), 154.

What is the message of the preacher? He must preach the Word, that is, the Word of God.[266] From the words *reprove, rebuke,* and *exhort*, it is clear that the preacher is to preach the Word of God in such a way that he urges his listeners to submit to the Bible's authority. Lenski observes that these three words are akin to convict, chide, and admonish. He states:

> "Convict!" There is no need to say with what (the Word) or whom (sinners, who are always in season). "Chide!" or censure, blame. Again there is no need to say with what (the Word) or whom (Christians who get into sin or error). "Admonish!" or urge, encourage (here the meaning can scarcely be: comfort), once more with the Word, to stimulate slow and lagging Christians. Recall 3:16.[267]

Clearly, all of the Word of God is the standard by which a person is to live and the preacher is to hold people to that standard.

Conclusion

II Timothy 3:16 and 4:2 present the fact that all of the Word of God is local churches and is the sole authority for faith and practice.

Local Churches Must Reject False Authorities

Colossians 2:8 and Titus 1:14 teach that local churches must not only receive God's inspired Words, but they must also reject false authorities. Just as Jesus rejected false religious authorities (see further), so must local churches.

---

[266] Knight observes: "The background for Paul's charge that Timothy proclaim τὸν λόγον is found in 2:9, 15, which speak of 'God's word' and 'the word of truth,' i.e., the message and teachings from God. With this background Paul can use ὁ λόγος here for this 'word' without further specification" (George W. Knight III, *The Pastoral Epistles: A Commentary on the Greek Text* in *The New International Greek Testament Commentary*, eds. I. Howard Marshall and W. Ward Gasque (Grand Rapids: William B. Eerdmans Publishing Company, 1992), 453).

[267] R. C. H. Lenski, *The Interpretation of St. Paul's Epistles to the Colossians, to the Thessalonians, to Timothy, to Titus and to Philemon* (Minneapolis: Augsburg Publishing House, 1961), 853.

Colossians 2:8

Colossians 2:8 states, "Beware lest any man spoil you through philosophy and vain deceit, after the tradition of men, after the rudiments of the world, and not after Christ." God gave the book of Colossians to a local church (Colossians 1:1,18); therefore, Colossians 2:8 gives inspired instruction that commands the saints in local churches to beware of those who would try to persuade them to follow the tradition of men, rather than Christ. *Beware* (βλέπετε) is a second person plural present active imperative from βλέπω and means "look to it, take heed, be on the watch."[268] Since *beware* is a present active imperative, it further indicates that the Colossians were to be on constant watch. They were to constantly watch lest any man spoil them (that is, rob them from what they had in Christ) through philosophy (φιλοσοφίας, literally, love of wisdom, and "came to mean the doctrine or tenets of the heathen or Gentile philosophers"[269]) and vain deceit (that is, empty deceit or delusion), both of which are after the tradition of men (that is, according to the doctrine of men), and not after or according to Christ. In other words, these doctrines of men seek to take a believer away from following Christ. Sometimes these doctrines of men will sound very sophisticated, but the local church members must diligently resist them, or else the local church will depart from Christ.

According to the traditions of men, it is scholarly to deny perfect preservation, reject the Traditional Texts, and mock the inspiration of the vowel points. However, if one follows such traditions, he is departing from the teaching of Christ, wherein He taught perfect preservation (Matthew 24:35), upheld the Traditional Hebrew Text (John 10:35; 17:17), and spoke of the vowel points (Matthew 5:18; Luke 16:17). It is interesting to note that *tradition* here in Colossians 2:8 is the same word that occurs in the expression *tradition of the elders*

---

[268] Zodhiates, "991. βλέπω."

[269] Zodhiates, "5385. φιλοσοφία."

(Mark 7:3,5), something which Jesus soundly rejected (see further). The local church needs to follow the example of Christ.

In a sermon concerning the Scriptures being the only guide in matters of religion, John Gill writes:

> Nor are the traditions of men to be regarded; the Pharisees were very tenacious of the traditions of the elders, by which they transgressed the commandments of God, and made his word of no effect; and the apostle *Paul*, in his state of unregeneracy, was zealous of the same; but neither of them are to be imitated by us: it is right to observe the exhortation which the apostle gives, when a Christian; (Colossians 2:8) beware lest any man spoil you through philosophy and vain deceit, after the traditions of men, after the rudiments of the world, and not after Christ.
>
> Take care you are not imposed upon, under the notion and pretense of an *apostolical tradition;* unwritten traditions are not the rule, only the word of God is the rule of our faith and practice. Nor do the decrees of popes and councils demand our attention and regard; it matters not what such a pope has determined, or what canons such a council under his influence has made . . ..
>
> Nor are the examples of men, no not of the best of men, in all things to be copied after by us; we should indeed be followers of all good men as such, *of those who through faith and patience inherit the promises* [Hebrews 6:12]; and especially of such, who are or have been spiritual guides and governors in the church; who have made the scriptures their study, and have labored in the word and doctrine; their *faith* we should *follow, considering the end of their conversation* [Hebrews 13:7]; how that issues, and when it terminates in Christ, his person, truths and ordinances, the same to-day, yesterday and for ever (Hebrews 6:12, and 13:7): but then we are to follow them no further than they follow Christ; the apostle *Paul* desired no more than this of his *Corinthians* with respect to himself [I Corinthians 11:1]; and no more can be demanded of us; it should be no bias on our minds, that such and such a man of so much grace and excellent gifts thought and practiced so and so. We are to call no man father or master on earth [Matthew 23:9,10]; we have but one father in heaven, and one master, which is Christ, whose doctrines, rules, and ordinances we should receive and observe. We are not to be influenced by men of learning and wealth; though they should be on the other side of the question, it should be no stumbling to us; had this been a rule to be attended to, Christianity had never got footing in the world: "Have any of the rulers or of the Phari-

sees believed on him? But this people, who knoweth not the law, are cursed" (John 7:48, 49).

It pleased the Lord, in the first times of the gospel, to *hide* the things of it *from the wise and prudent,* and *reveal* them *unto babes;* and to call by his grace, "not many wise men after the flesh, not many mighty, not many noble; but the foolish, weak, and base things of the world, and things that are not, to confound the wise and mighty, and bring to nought things that are; that no flesh should glory in his presence" (Matthew 11:25, 26; 1 Corinthians 1:26-29) nor should it concern us that the greatest number is on the opposite side; we are *not* to *follow a multitude to do evil;* the whole world once wondered after the beast; Christ's flock is but a little flock.

The scriptures are the only external guide in matters of religion; they are the way-posts we should look up unto, and take our direction from, and should steer our course accordingly:[270]

Let local churches and those in local churches reject false authorities.

Titus 1:14

Titus 1:14 occurs in one of the pastoral epistles and, as such, has bearing on local churches. It states: "Not giving heed to Jewish fables, and commandments of men, that turn from the truth." This verse commands the rejection of pseudo-authorities and is Paul's inspired instruction to Titus and, by extension, to all of God's ministers in local churches. Paul gave similar instruction in I Timothy 1:4.[271] *Giving heed* (προσέχοντες a present active nominative masculine plural participle from προσέχω) "means 'turn one's mind to',"[272] therefore *not giving heed* means continually do not turn one's mind toward Jewish

---

[270] Gill, *The Scriptures the Only Guide in Matters of Religion Jeremiah 6:16*, 4,5.

[271] I Timothy 1:4 says, "Neither give heed to fables and endless genealogies, which minister questions, rather than godly edifying which is in faith: *so do.*"

[272] George W. Knight III, *The Pastoral Epistles: A Commentary on the Greek Text* in *The New International Greek Testament Commentary*, eds. I. Howard Marshall and W. Ward Gasque (Grand Rapids: William B. Eerdmans Publishing Company, 1992), 72.

fables and commandments of men. There must be a constant resistance against these things, for they turn from the truth.

Jewish fables are fables from a Jewish source. *Fables* is (μύθοις a masculine dative plural noun from μῦθος) "commonly rendered as a tale or a fable or that which is fabricated by the mind in contrast to reality. It is the word from which 'mythology' is derived. . . . It is mostly used in the NT denoting a fable full of falsehoods and pretenses."[273] II Timothy 4:4 also uses *fables* and teaches that it is the opposite of the truth. One of the Jewish fables promulgated by Natronai II ben-Hilai and later by Elias Levita is that of the novelty of the points (see Chapter One). These two men were Jews and the novelty of the points that they promoted is certainly a fable for Jesus taught otherwise (Matthew 5:18; Luke 16:17). The novelty of the points is one of many Jewish fables that ministers of local churches should reject. Sadly, many are doing the very opposite.

Commandments of men are commandments (ἐντολαῖς a feminine dative plural noun from ἐντολή) that come from men instead of from the Lord (cf. I Corinthians 14:37). A similar expression occurs in Matthew 15:9 and Mark 7:7 where Jesus criticizes the Pharisees for teaching the commandments of men for doctrines. The principles of textual criticism are an example of modern-day commandments of men that turn from the truth, for these commandments of men concerning textual criticism reject the teaching of the Bible regarding perfect preservation (Psalm 12:6,7).

But the Scriptures are the authority for local churches, not Jewish fables and not the commandments of men. Indeed, Peter asserted to the council and the high priest, "We ought to obey God rather than men" (Acts 5:29). Peter would not allow the commandments of men to be his authority in the matter of his practice. Likewise, a true

---

[273] Zodhiates, "3454. μῦθος."

minister of the Lord must demonstrate his faith in God's Words by continually rejecting pseudo-authorities.

Conclusion

It is not enough for local churches simply to receive the Words of God, they must also reject that which is false. False religious authorities include philosophy and vain deceit (Colossians 2:18), as well as Jewish fables and commandments of men (Titus 1:14).

Summary

Scripture is the sole authority for faith and practice in local churches. All of the New Testament concerns local churches, for, in one way or another, the Lord directs it to local churches. Furthermore, specific verses make it plain that New Testament Scripture is for local churches (Matthew 28:20; I Corinthians 14:37; I Timothy 3;14,15; II Peter 3:2; Jude 3). Old Testament Scripture is also for local churches (Matthew 28:20; Acts 7:38; Romans 15:4; I Corinthians 10:11; II Peter 3:2). Indeed, all of the Words of God are for local churches (II Timothy 3;16,17; 4:2). Local churches and local church saints have the obligation to submit to the authority of God's Words, recognizing that the Bible is the sole authority for faith and practice and rejecting false religious authorities (Colossians 2:8; Titus 1:14).

Scripture Is the Authority for Jesus' Life

The true disciple of the Lord Jesus Christ is to deny himself, take up his cross, and follow Jesus (Matthew 16:24); therefore, the true disciple of Jesus should adopt Jesus' attitude toward Scripture. Since the Words of God were the authority for Jesus' life, then these Words should also be the authority in the disciple's life. Also, since Jesus refuted and rejected false authorities, so likewise should the disciple. Concerning faith and practice, the Words of God were the authority for Jesus' life both positively and negatively – positively in that He submitted to the Bible's authority, and negatively in that He refused to submit to other authorities.

Positively

Several passages demonstrate that God's Words were the authority for Jesus' life. The author could have presented many more passages, but these should suffice to demonstrate the point at hand, among these verses are Psalm 138:2; Matthew 2:23; 4:4, 7, 10, 12-15; 5:17; 8:16, 17; 12:15-21; 13:34, 35; 21:1-5; 26:53, 54; Luke 22:37; 24:44; John 13:18; 15:25; 19:28; and Hebrews 10:7.

Psalm 138:2

In Psalm 138:2, David writes under inspiration that God has magnified His Word above all His name. Chapter Four presents a more detailed look at Psalm 138:2, but for now suffice it to say that it teaches that God, and Jesus since He also is God (Hebrews 1:8), has put Himself under the authority of His Own Word. Jesus repeatedly demonstrates submission to the Word of God in His response and actions towards the Word of God.

Matthew 2:23

Matthew 2:23 says, "And he came and dwelt in a city called Nazareth: that it might be fulfilled which was spoken by the prophets, He shall be called a Nazarene." Nazareth was a despised place, for Nathanael asked, "Can there any good thing come out of Nazareth?" (John 1:46). It had a bad reputation. The prophets in general did teach that people would despise and reject Jesus as evident from Psalm 22; Isaiah 53; and Zechariah 11:12,13. No one prophet in particular uses the exact words *He shall be called a Nazarene*, but Jesus' being called a Nazarene is in fulfillment of that which was spoken *by the prophets*. That is, Jesus' being called a Nazarene is something that more than one Old Testament prophet said about Jesus and, therefore, indicates what the prophets in general taught about Jesus. Therefore, *He shall be called a Nazarene* is a general summation of the message of several prophets, as opposed to being the specific words of one single prophet. Broadus states:

> Had he been called Jesus the Bethlehemite, it would have seemed honourable; but to be called Jesus the Nazarene, would at once awaken the contempt of the Jews, and would be a *prima facie* argument against his claims' to be regarded a Messiah, the son of David; and we know that such an argument was once actually used (John 7:41).[274]

For someone to call a person a Nazarene was something that was despicable, but to fulfill the prophecies concerning His being despised and rejected, Jesus willingly dwelt in Nazareth. Despite the ridicule that would come His way from dwelling in Nazareth, Jesus submitted to the authority of the Word of God. One must submit to the authority of God's Words, although it may result in some discomfort, ridicule, and lack of recognition.

Matthew 4:4,7,10

In Matthew 4 is the account of Satan tempting Jesus for forty days and forty nights. Matthew relates three of the temptations. In each of these three cases, Jesus confronted Satan's temptation by quoting a verse and then subsequently submitting to the teaching of that verse. In Matthew 4:4, Jesus quoted from Deuteronomy 8:3. In Matthew 4:7, He quoted from Deuteronomy 6:16.[275] And in Matthew 4:10, Jesus quoted from Deuteronomy 6:13. In confronting these temptations, Jesus did not rely upon His Own authority as being God

---

[274] John A. Broadus, *Commentary on Matthew* (Philadelphia: American Baptist Publication Society, 1886, Reprinted, Grand Rapids: Kregel Publications, 1990), 28.

[275] It is interesting that before Jesus' response in Matthew 4:7, Satan first quoted a passage (Psalm 91:11,12). In addition to misquoting it, Satan also took the passage out of the overall context of the Old Testament. Jesus by quoting Deuteronomy 6:16 demonstrates that one must rightly divide and rightly apply Scripture for it to be a true authority.

in the flesh (I Timothy 3:16), but He relied upon and submitted to the authority of Scripture. Scripture was the authority for Jesus' actions.

Matthew 4:12-15

Matthew 4:12-15 relates that after Jesus heard of John being imprisoned, that He went to dwell in Capernaum, so as to fulfill a prophecy from Isaiah 9:1,2. Jesus allowed the Words of God to direct His movements. He was conscious of the fact that He had to act in accordance to those Words and submit to their authority.

Matthew 5:17

In Matthew 5:17, Jesus states, "Think not that I am come to destroy the law, or the prophets: I am not come to destroy, but to fulfil." Jesus submitted fully to what the Word of God said, for He came to fulfill it, not to destroy it. Therefore, He did not establish an alternate authority, but submitted to the present authority of the written Words of God. Concerning Matthew 5:17, M'Intosh asks: "For what could so decisively and significantly declare and require the trueness [*sic*], reliability, and Divine authority and inviolability of God's Written Word as to say that the Incarnate Word of God came to fulfill it?"[276] Jesus' actions loudly proclaim that the Bible is the sole authority for faith and practice.

Matthew 8:16,17

Matthew 8:16,17 speaks of Jesus healing various people in fulfillment of Isaiah 53:4. Jesus allowed the Words of God to direct Him in the manner in which He conducted His ministry. He was not a law unto Himself.

---

[276] Hugh M'Intosh, *Is Christ Infallible and the Bible True?* (Edinburgh: T & T Clark, 1902, reprinted, Minneapolis: Klock & Klock, 1981), 175.

Matthew 12:15-21

Matthew 12:15-21 speaks of Jesus healing great multitudes and of Jesus charging them not to make Him known so that the prophecy of Isaiah 42:1-4 could be fulfilled. Matthew 12:15-21 is an interesting passage for the verse before it (Matthew 12:14) speaks of the Pharisees holding a council against Jesus to determine how they might destroy Him. If Jesus had neglected the prophecy of Isaiah and encouraged the multitudes to make Him known, might such an action have counteracted the Pharisees' plans? Consider, for instance, that the Pharisees would not speak against John the Baptist because the people took John for a prophet (Matthew 21:25,26). Might the same have happened if Jesus had neglected Isaiah 42:1-4 and encouraged the people to make Him known? Yet, Jesus did not do what might have seemed expedient, but He submitted to the Word of God, even though it would put Him at risk. The Bible is the authority, not expediency. The disciple of the Lord must submit to the authority of the Words of God regardless of the cost.

Matthew 13:34,35

Matthew 13:34,35 relates the fact that Jesus spoke to the multitude in parables in fulfillment of Psalm 78:2. Even in the teaching technique of Jesus, He submitted to the authority of Scripture. He did not do what was popular, but He followed what the Bible said. The disciples of the Lord today must do likewise. It is not the duty of disciples to tickle the ears of the listeners, though ear-tickling may increase the crowds and the popularity of the speaker. Rather, it is the duty of disciples to do God's work according to God's Words.

Matthew 21:1-5

Matthew 21:1-5 relates the account of the Triumphal Entry and Jesus instructing His disciples to get a colt so as to fulfill Zechariah 9:9. Riding upon a donkey while coming into the city of Jerusalem may seem like a little insignificant detail, but the fact is that God gave this prophecy to Zechariah and it must needs be fulfilled. Jesus fully surrendered and submitted to the authority of the Word of God, even in the littlest of details. It behooves the true servants of the Lord to do likewise.

Matthew 26:53,54

In Matthew 26:53,54, as the soldiers are about to arrest Jesus, Jesus states: "Thinkest thou that I cannot now pray to my Father, and he shall presently give me more than twelve legions of angels? But how then shall the scriptures be fulfilled, that thus it must be?" Only by Jesus submitting to the authority of Old Testament verses could He fulfill them. Some of the prophecies concern the fact that one would betray Jesus for thirty pieces of silver (Zechariah 11:12,13); the one betraying Him would be a friend (Psalm 41:9); some would smite His back, pluck off His facial hair, and spit in His face (Isa 50:6); people would reproach and despise Him (Psalm 22:6-8; Isaiah 53:3); He would be put to death (Psalm 22:15; Isaiah 53:12); His disciples would forsake Him (Zechariah 13:7); God would forsake Him (Psalm 22:1); He would be numbered with the transgressors (Isaiah 53:12); the soldiers would cast lots on His vesture (Psalm 22:18); the people at the cross would give Him gall and vinegar (Psalm 69:21); those crucifying Him would not break any of His bones (Psalm 34:20); and He would be buried (Isaiah 53:9). All of these verses had to be fulfilled and all of these verses required Jesus' submission to them in order for them to be fulfilled. He could have called more than twelve legions of angels (Matthew 26:53), but He refused to do so, for He was committed to the authority of the Words of God, even though it meant unimaginable suffering for Him.

Luke 22:37

In Luke 22:37, Jesus states: "For I say unto you, that this that is written must yet be accomplished in me, And he was reckoned among the transgressors: for the things concerning me have an end."

Jesus refers here to Isaiah 53:12. When Jesus went to the cross then He, the spotless Lamb of God, would be counted a transgressor of the worst sort. He truly did make Himself of no reputation (Philippians 2:7), and why? He did it because Scripture must yet be accomplished. Jesus submitted to the authority of the Word of God, despite the personal cost to Him. How servants of the Lord must be willing to sacrifice everything (pride, station, money, recognition, fame, etc.) and bend the knee to Scripture and let it be the authority in their lives. Yes, men, even the scholars of the day, may mock and ridicule the one who stands on the Word of God, but let the servant of the Lord take his stand with His Lord (cf. Hebrews 13:13).

Luke 24:44

In Luke 24:44 the resurrected Jesus speaks to the eleven (Luke 24:33) and reminds them that He had told them prior to His death that all things concerning Him must be fulfilled. *All things* refers to all of His sufferings leading up to the cross, the agony of the cross, and the glory that would follow (Luke 24:46,47). Jesus' statement again demonstrates the importance of fully submitting to the Word of God. Indeed, Jesus teaches the eleven that the Bible is the sole authority for faith and practice, and that one must obey the Bible regardless of personal cost or sacrifice.

John 13:18

In John 13:18, Jesus refers to the fact that one of the apostles whom He had chosen would lift up his heel against Him, that is, betray Him, which was in fulfillment of Psalm 41:9. Jesus selected His betrayer, all in accordance with the Word of God. The Word of God was the authority even in a matter such as this! Oh, how Jesus humbled Himself that He might honor and exalt the Words of God. May modern-day servants of the Lord follow His example and allow the Words of God to be the complete authority for all of faith and practice.

John 15:25

In John 15:24, Jesus refers to the fact that the people hated both Jesus and the Father and then in John 15:25, Jesus refers to Psalm 69:4 when He says: "But *this cometh to pass*, that the word might be fulfilled that is written in their law, They hated me without a cause." Jesus was willing to do things that would cause the religious leaders to hate Him. Jesus allowed Scripture to be His authority, and not popularity. So often today, men are governed by what friends, scholars, or critics think; instead of being governed by Scripture. But the example of Jesus makes it so obviously clear that Scripture is the sole authority.

John 19:28

John 19:28 says, "After this, Jesus knowing that all things were now accomplished, that the scripture might be fulfilled, saith, I thirst." John 19:28 is an amazing verse, for even while Jesus was dying, He was conscious about what the Scriptures said and how those Scriptures should govern His behaviour. The Scriptures that had to be fulfilled were Psalm 22:15 and 69:21. Even to the servant of the Lord's dying words, he must allow Scripture to be his authority.

Hebrews 10:7

Hebrews 10:7 quotes Jesus as saying, "Lo, I come (in the volume of the book it is written of me,) to do thy will, O God." Jesus came to do what was written in the Book. He put Himself under the authority of God's Words. Hebrews 10:7 refers back to Psalm 40:7, where the volume of the book, at the time, was the Pentateuch. John Owen writes about Hebrews 10:7:

> Hence are we herein directed unto the whole volume of the Law; for indeed it is nothing but a prediction of the coming of Christ, and a pre-signification of what he had to do. "That book which God has given to the church as the only guide of its faith, — the Bible; (that is, *the book*, all other books being of no consideration in comparison of it;) that book wherein all divine precepts and promises are enrolled or recorded: in this book, in the volume of it, this is the principal subject,

especially in the head of the roll, or the beginning of it, namely, in the first promise, it is so written of me."[277]

Notice how Owen refers to the Bible as the only guide for faith and it is to this only guide for faith that Jesus submitted. Jesus refused, in matters of faith, to submit to anything else. The Bible is the sole authority for faith and practice.

Conclusion

Psalm 138:2; Matthew 2:23; 4:4, 7, 10, 12-15; 5:17; 8:16, 17; 12:15-21; 13:34, 35; 21:1-5; 26:53, 54; Luke 22:37; 24:44; John 13:18; 15:25; 19:28; and Hebrews 10:7 demonstrate that throughout His earthly life, Jesus followed the Words of God. Jesus submitted to the Words of God regardless of the difficulty in so doing. Truly, the Words of God were the authority for Jesus' faith and practice.

Negatively

So much so did Jesus recognize the sole authority of Scripture in matters of faith and practice that He deliberately opposed any additions to the Words of God, such as when the Pharisees elevated the tradition of the elders to the level of being authoritative. By His actions, He was clearly indicating that Scripture is the only authority. The authority is not Scripture plus a tradition, no matter how ancient or scholarly. Several passages demonstrate that Jesus refused any additions to the Words of God among which are Matthew 12:1-8, 9-13; 15:1-6; Luke 11:37, 38; 13:10-17; 14:1-6; John 5:5-12, 16, 18; 7:22, 23; and 9:14-16.

---

[277] Owen, *An Exposition of the Epistle to the Hebrews* in vol. 22 of *The Works of John Owen*, 474.

Matthew 12:1-8 (Mark 2:23-28; Luke 6:1-5)

In Matthew 12:1-8, the Bible presents the case of Jesus' disciples being hungry and plucking ears of corn and eating them on the Sabbath (Matthew 12:1). When the Pharisees saw it, they said to Jesus, "Behold, thy disciples do that which is not lawful to do on upon the sabbath day" (Matthew 12:2). The Pharisees base their objection to the disciples' action upon their tradition, not on the Scripture. Edersheim says that the Jews divided Sabbath labor into smaller parts, and concerning Matthew 12:1-8, he writes:

> In this case there were at least two such acts involved: that of plucking the ears of corn, ranged under the sin of reaping, and that of rubbing them, which might be ranged under sifting in a sieve, threshing, sifting out fruit, grinding, or fanning. The following Talmudic passage bears on this: 'In case a woman rolls wheat to remove the husks, it is considered as sifting; if she rubs the heads of wheat, it is regarded as threshing; if she cleans off the side-adherences, it is sifting out fruit; if she bruises the ears, it is grinding; if she throws them up in her hand, it is winnowing.' {Jer. Shabb. p. 10 *a*, lines 28 to 26 from bottom.} One instance will suffice to show the externalism of all these ordinances. If a man wished to move a sheaf on his field, which of course implied labor, he had only to lay upon it a spoon that was in his common use, when, in order to remove the spoon, he might also remove the sheaf on which it lay! {Shabb. 142 *b*, line 6 from bottom.} And yet it was forbidden to stop with a little wax the hole in a cask by which the fluid was running out, {Shabb. 146 *a*.} or to wipe a wound! Holding views like these, the Pharisees, who witnessed the conduct of the disciples, would naturally harshly condemn, what they must have regarded as gross desecration of the Sabbath. Yet it was clearly not a breach of the Biblical, but of the Rabbinic Law.[278]

In other words, the Pharisees did not base their objection on the Old Testament, but on their own rule that they had added to the Bible and which rule they had made just as binding as the Bible. Jesus did not have His disciples submit to the Pharisaical addition to God's Word.

---

[278] Alfred Edersheim, *The Life and Times of Jesus the Messiah* (London: Longmans, Green, & Co., 1912), II:56.

Indeed, He defended the behaviour of His disciples (Matthew 12:3-4). In Jesus' answer to the Pharisees, He refers to the account of David's hunger from I Samuel 21 and as He does so, "Jesus lays His finger on the real trouble with these Pharisees: too much reading of the rabbinical law, not enough of divine law."[279] Many have this same problem, namely, too much reading of the scholars and the critics, not enough of the Bible. One letter of the Bible carries far more weight than all the pronouncements of the scholars, unless, of course, they are quoting the Bible. The Bible is the authority, not some tradition.

David satisfied his hunger by eating the shewbread, "which was not lawful for him to eat" (Matthew 12:4). However, since "David's hunger sets aside even a divine regulation [Leviticus 24:5-9]; shall not the hunger of the disciples set aside mere rabbinical notions that lack all binding force to begin with?"[280] Poole writes:

> The law concerning the shewbread was but a ritual law, and that part of it which restrained the use of it when taken off from the holy table was of lightest concern, as it commanded it should be eaten by the priests only, and by them in the holy place. Where the life, or necessary relief, of men was concerned, the obligation of the ritual law ceased, and that was lawful, both for David and the high priest, which in ordinary cases had not been lawful. Works necessary either for the upholding of our lives, or fitting us for sabbath services, are lawful upon the sabbath day. . . . David in a case of necessity might make a common use of that holy bread, so the disciples in a case of like necessity might make use of a little of that holy time, in such necessary servile work as might fit them for their sabbath service. Thus it was lawful by the law of God, and if the Pharisees had not been ignorant, or had understood what they had read, they would never have disputed this, the instance of holy David might have satisfied. So that this little kind of labour could only be a breach of one of their bylaws, by which

---

[279] R. C. H. Lenski, *The Interpretation of St. Luke's Gospel* (Minneapolis: Augsburg Publishing House, 1961), 324.

[280] Ibid., 325.

they pretended to expound the law of God, in which he showeth they had given a false interpretation.[281]

Matthew 12:1-8 teaches that neither Jesus nor His disciples submitted to the Jewish oral tradition. They did not allow the Jewish oral tradition to rule their faith and practice. And disciples today should reject Jewish oral traditions, especially the tradition concerning the transmission of the vowels to the Masoretes.

Matthew 12:9-13 (Mark 3:1-6; Luke 6:6-11)

Matthew 12:9-13 relates the account of Jesus healing on the Sabbath a man with a withered hand. Before the healing, those in the synagogue asked Jesus, "Is it lawful to heal on the sabbath days?" (Matthew 12:10). The purpose of their question was so "that they might accuse him" (Matthew 12:10). Concerning healing on the Sabbath, the Pharisees did not think it lawful. In this case, Edersheim writes:

> According to some, disease of the ear, {Debar. R. 10.} according to some throat-disease, {Yoma 8:6.} while, according to others, such a disease as angina, {Yoma 84 a.} involved danger, and superseded the Sabbath-Law. All applications to the outside of the body were forbidden on the Sabbath.[282]

The man with the withered hand was not in danger of dying, therefore, the Pharisees would conclude that healing him on the Sabbath was unlawful.

Jesus confronts the hypocrisy of the Pharisees when He says, "What man shall there be among you, that shall have one sheep, and if it fall into a pit on the sabbath day, will he not lay hold on it, and lift *it* out? How much then is a man better than a sheep? Wherefore it is

---

[281] Matthew Poole, *A Commentary on the Holy Bible* (McLean, VA: MacDonald Publishing Company, n. d.), III: 53.

[282] Edersheim, II:59.

lawful to do well on the sabbath days" (Matthew 12:11,12). Concerning Jesus' questions, Edersheim observes:

> Although the man with the withered hand could not be classed with those dangerously ill, it could not have been difficult to silence the Rabbis on their own admissions. Clearly, their principle implied, that it was lawful on the Sabbath to do that which would save life or prevent death. To have taught otherwise, would virtually have involved murder. But if so, did it not also, in strictly logical sequence, imply this far wider principle, that it must be lawful to do good on the Sabbath? For, evidently, the omission of such good would have involved the doing of evil. Could this be the proper observance of God's holy day? There was no answer to such an argument; St. Mark expressly records that they dared not attempt a reply. {St. Mark 3:4.}[283]

The Pharisees themselves seemed to know that they were on shaky ground, but they would not admit it. Though Jesus had silenced them, they still clung to their tradition. Once men adopt another authority besides the Bible, they are sometimes loathe to reject it, which may be also the case in the matter of the vowel points.

Here again Jesus refused to allow the Pharisees' additions to the Bible to bind Him. In fact, Jesus deliberately healed the man. He, knowing all things, could have avoided going to the synagogue, but, no, He walked right into their trap, so as deliberately to refute their false authority. Lenski writes: "But could Jesus not wait and do his healing on a weekday? To have waited would have left a totally wrong impression on the people: as if it were unlawful to heal on the Sabbath. This was the very error Jesus wished to eradicate."[284] Jesus boldly confronted their false authority and smashed it to pieces. The Bible is the sole authority for faith and practice, not the Bible plus ancient traditions.

---

[283] Edersheim, II:59,60.

[284] Lenski, *The Interpretation of St. Luke's Gospel*, 332,333.

Matthew 15:1-6 (Mark 7:1-9)

In Matthew 15:2, the scribes and Pharisees came to Jesus and asked, "Why do thy disciples transgress the tradition of the elders? for they wash not their hands when they eat bread." Lightfoot writes:

> The undervaluing of the washing of hands is said to be among those things for which the Sanhedrin excommunicates: and therefore that R. Eleazar Ben Hazar was excommunicated by it, שפקפק בנטילת ידים *because he undervalued the washing of hands*; and that when he was dead, by the command of the Sanhedrim, a great stone was laid upon his bier {Bab. Berac. fol. 46.2}. "Whence you may learn (say they) that the Sanhedrim stones the very coffin of every excommunicate person that dies in his excommunication {*Leusden's edition*, vol. ii. p. 331}."[285]

Lightfoot's comment illustrates what importance the Pharisees placed upon the washing of hands. However, the Old Testament does not command that one wash his hands before eating; therefore, the washing of hands is something that the tradition of the elders demanded. The Jews highly regarded the tradition and placed spiritual significance upon it, for the Sanhedrin could excommunicate a person for undervaluing it. Jesus was, therefore, wise not to have His disciples submit to this addition to Scripture, lest He should seem to give credibility to the tradition and should seem to regard it as the authority for faith and practice.

Not only does Jesus not submit to the tradition of the elders, but also He directly declares that the scribes and Pharisees "made the commandment of God of none effect by" their "tradition" (Matthew 15:6), for by following their tradition, they disobeyed commandments concerning the honoring of parents (Matthew 15:4,5). McClintock and Strong's Cyclopedia state about the Jewish tradition:

---

[285] John Lightfoot, *Hebrew and Talmudical Exercitations upon St. Matthew* in vol. 2 of *A Commentary on the New Testament from the Talmud and Hebraica* (Peabody, MA: Hendrickson Publishers, 2003, reprint London: Oxford University Press, 1859, formerly titled *Horae Hebraicae Et Talmudicae*), 223.

> The Jews pretend that, besides their written law contained in the Pentateuch, God delivered to Moses an oral law, which was handed down from generation to generation. The various decisions of the Jewish doctors or priests on points which the law had either left doubtful or passed over in silence were the true sources of their traditions. They did not commit their numerous traditions (which appear to have been a long time in accumulating) to writing before their wars against the Romans under Hadrian and Severus. The Mishna, the Gemara, and perhaps the Masorah were collected by the rabbins of Tiberias and later schools.[286]

Some accommodationists follow Jewish oral tradition when they claim that the Jews conveyed the vowels by oral tradition and that the Masoretes added the oral tradition of the vowels to the written record of the consonants (see Chapter One under Levita and Cappellus). In following Jewish tradition, they also make the commandment of God of none effect. The commandment of God teaches that the Word of God is the sole authority for faith and practice, not the Word of God plus a Jewish oral tradition. Furthermore, the commandment of God forbids adding to the Words of God (Deuteronomy 4:2; 12:32; Proverbs 30:6), but the tradition about the vowel points makes these commands of none effect.

In Matthew 15:6, *of none effect* (ἠκυρώσατε a second aorist active indicative second person plural from ἀκυρόω) means "to render void, deprive of force and authority."[287] Zodhiates comments that Jesus "did not mean that it ceases to be the law of God, but that it had no value, worth, or lordship over them."[288] In other words, the Pharisees' tradition became more important than the Words of God. Why did the Pharisees give precedence to the tradition of the elders above the Bible? The answer is that no man can serve two masters (Matthew 6:24), one of the two must have the preeminence. The Pharisees elevated the

---

[286] "Tradition" in *Cyclopedia*, X:517.

[287] Thayer, 24.

[288] Zodhiates, "208. ἀκυρόω."

tradition of the elders above the Words of God, and many modern-day Fundamentalists are also elevating the tradition of the scholars above the Words of God. All such activity makes the Word of God of none effect. Jesus refused to give any credence to such a system that honored the tradition of men above the Words of God, and so must His disciples, for the Bible is the sole authority for faith and practice.

Luke 11:37,38

In Luke 11:37,38 a Pharisee invited Jesus to dine with him and as Jesus did so, He did not wash before dinner. See above under Matthew 15:1-6 for the importance that the Pharisees placed on the washing of hands. Lenski writes:

> This ritualistic washing of the hands was part of the tradition of the elders, a requirement that was considered more binding than those of the divine law itself. . . . For this reason Jesus could not observe the practice. This Pharisee and the others present would have thought that Jesus, too, considered the practice to be binding. So Jesus did not wash his hands before he reclined to dine. Already his action spoke with no uncertain voice."[289]

Jesus very emphatically and publicly would not comply with the tradition. Even as a guest of a Pharisee, He would in no wise give any idea that the oral tradition was valid. In so doing, He was not afraid of offending His host. How the disciples of the Lord need to have similar courage and take a stand on the absolute authority of the Word of God.

Luke 13:10-17

Luke 13:10-17 presents another case of Jesus healing on the Sabbath. In this case, the sick woman was not dying from her ailment, therefore for Jesus to heal her would violate the tradition of the elders (see above under Matthew 12:9-13). Jesus could have avoided this

---

[289] Lenski, *The Interpretation of St. Luke's Gospel*, 657.

situation altogether, but, instead, He called the woman to Himself, laid hands on her, and thereby healed her – all in plain sight of His opponents. Jesus very clearly demonstrates that tradition has absolutely no authority in matters of faith and practice and that He will in no wise submit to such additions to the Words of God.

Luke 14:1-6

Luke 14:1-6 presents another case of Jesus healing on the Sabbath. The man in this case had the dropsy and was not dying from his illness, yet Jesus went contrary to Jewish tradition in healing him (see above under Matthew 12:9-13). In fact, Jesus deliberately and openly healed the man. Jesus was not afraid to refuse to submit to extra-Biblical authority. He was not afraid of the religious leaders, for He was most concerned with pleasing the God the Father and honoring the Father's Word. May today's disciples of the Lord be unafraid of the religious leaders and adhere closely to the Words of God, instead of submitting to the commandments and doctrines of men.

John 5:5-12,16,18; 7:22,23

John 5 presents yet another case where Jesus healed on the Sabbath. In this case, the impotent man was not dying from his ailment, yet Jesus directly ignored the tradition of the elders and healed him. Jesus did not have to heal the man, but He did. It seems as if Jesus deliberately challenged the tradition of the elders. He knew that the Pharisees did not care for His Sabbath healings, but He persisted. What is the lesson? One unmistakable lesson is that tradition is not the authority.

After healing the man, Jesus told him to take up his bed and walk (John 5:8), which the Jews claimed was not lawful (John 5:10). The fact that Jesus told the man to take up his bed and walk means that it was not at all unlawful. About this incident, Lenski writes:

> It is plainly Jesus' intention to oppose, openly and positively, both the human traditions and the false spirit of the Jewish leaders. . . . They

found thirty kinds of labor forbidden on the Sabbath and they insisted on these prohibitions, deduced by their own wisdom, in such a way as to lose sight of the law's chief requirements and true spiritual intention. Jesus could have lived in peace with these men only by submitting to their spirit and their methods, and this was an utter impossibility. So he even invites the conflict.[290]

Lenski further states that this miracle and the man's walking with his bed

> was a *sign* to the Jews. As such it was intended, while in no way transgressing God's law, to run counter to the false Jewish traditions and thus to turn men's hearts - if they would be turned at all - to the true authority of Jesus, who, while upholding God's law, brought to view the mercy which both heals the sufferer's body and sets free his soul from spiritual bondage.[291]

Jesus opposed their false authority and sought to lead them to submit to true authority, but they refused. Again, once men set up a false authority, it can be very difficult for them to reject it.

John 9:14-16

John 9:14-16 records a fifth account of Jesus healing on the Sabbath. In this case, a man born blind was not in any danger of dying from his blindness, yet Jesus still healed him in direct disobedience to the tradition of the elders (see above under Matthew 12:9-13). Concerning this incident, Edersheim writes:

> Presently they bring him to the Pharisees, not to take notice of his healing, but to found on it a charge against Christ. Such must have been their motive, since it was universally known that the leaders of the people had, of course informally, agreed to take the strictest measures, not only against the Christ, but against any one who professed to be His disciple {ver. 22}. The ground on which the present charge against Jesus would rest was plain: the healing involved a manifold breach of the Sabbath-Law. The first of these was that He had made

---

[290] R. .C. H. Lenski, *The Interpretation of St. John's Gospel* (Minneapolis: Augsburg Publishing House, 1961), 366.

[291] Ibid., 367.

clay {Shabb. 24:3}. Next, it would be a question whether any remedy might be applied on the holy day. Such could only be done in diseases of the internal organs (from the throat downwards), except when danger to life or the loss of an organ was involved {Jerus. Shabb. 14 *d*}. It was, indeed, declared lawful to apply, for example, wine to the outside of the eyelid, on the ground that this might be treated as washing; but it was sinful to apply it to the inside of the eye. And as regards saliva, its application to the eye is expressly forbidden, on the ground that it was evidently intended as a remedy {Jer. Shabb. u. s.}.[292]

Rabbinism was on its great trial. The wondrous fact could neither be denied nor explained, and the only ground for resisting the legitimate inference as to the character of Him Who had done it, was its inconsistency with their traditional law. The alternative was: whether their traditional law of Sabbath-observance, or else He Who had done such miracles, was Divine? Was Christ not of God, because He did not keep the Sabbath in their way? But, then; could an open transgressor of God's Law do such miracles?[293]

Jesus directly attacked the tradition of the elders and demonstrated that He would not submit to its authority in the least.

Conclusion

Jesus repeatedly and openly refused to submit to the tradition of the elders. Six times He attacked the false ideas of Sabbath work (Matthew 12:1-8, 9-13; Luke 13:10-17; 14:1-6; John 5:5-12, 16, 18; 7:22, 23; 9:14-16). Twice He attacked the importance that the Jews put on the washing of hands (Matthew 15:1-6; Luke 11:37,38). Five times He attacked the restrictions about healing on the Sabbath (Matthew 12:9-13; Luke 13:10-17; 14:1-6; John 5:5-12, 16, 18; 7:22, 23; 9:14-16). Jesus repeatedly attacked and refuted the false notion that the tradition of the elders had any authority in matters of faith and practice. It behooves Bible believers to reject any additions to the

---

[292] Edersheim, II:181,182.

[293] Ibid., 182.

Words of God, no matter how well-meaning. It is the Bible and the Bible alone that is the sole authority for faith and practice.

Scripture Is the Authority for All of Faith and Practice

II Timothy 3:16,17 is the *locus classicus* for the teaching that the Bible is the sole authority for all of faith and practice. This passage states: "All scripture *is* given by inspiration of God, and *is* profitable for doctrine, for reproof, for correction, for instruction in righteousness: that the man of God may be perfect, throughly furnished unto all good works." Both *Scripture* and *inspiration* point to authority. The authority is the rule for faith and practice, with *doctrine* referring to faith and *reproof, correction, instruction in righteousness, perfect,* and *throughly furnished unto all good works* referring to practice.

Scripture

II Timothy 3:16 speaks of God giving all Scripture by inspiration. Thayer defines *scripture* (γραφή) as "a writing, thing written."[294] Warfield writes about γραφή and γραφαί:

> This term, in singular or plural, occurs in the New Testament some fifty times (Gospels twenty-three, Acts seven, Catholic Epistles six, Paul fourteen) and in every case bears the technical sense in which it refers to the Scriptures by way of eminence, the Scriptures of the Old Testament. This statement requires only such modification as is involved in noting that from II Pet. iii. 16 (cf. I Tim. v. 18) it becomes apparent that the New Testament writers were perfectly aware that the term "Scripture" in its high sense was equally applicable to their own writings as to the books included in the Old Testament; or, to be more precise, that it included within itself along with the writings which constituted the Old Testament those also which they were producing,

---

[294] Thayer, 121.

as sharing with the Old Testament books the high functions of the authoritative written word of God.²⁹⁵

Scripture, then, refers to a written authority.

Inspiration

God inspired Scripture. *Inspiration* (θεόπνευστος) is a feminine nominative singular adjective from θεόπνευστος, which is a compound of Θεός (God) and πνέω (breathe), therefore, literally meaning God-breathed. About *inspiration*, M'Intosh observes:

> Besides infallible truth, Divine authority is implied in θεόπνευστος. It does surely seem obvious that what is given by Divine inspiration and is a Divine production, for all of which God is responsible, should possess and carry Divine authority. The Divine fulness of this pregnant expression is not adequately set forth or exhausted with this idea also, so that Divine authority appears a necessary constituent element of it as well as truthfulness; for surely what God breathes and produces by His breathing and embodied by His Spirit's inspiration must not only be truth, but also carry and possess Divine authority. Besides, God's purpose in giving Scripture by inspiration was that it might convey a true, trustworthy, and authoritative revelation of His will in the form in which He wished it to be expressed. And since this was the supreme end of the Divine inspiration of the Bible, the θεόπνευστος must imply and include Divine authority. Therefore the expression "All Scripture is given by inspiration of God," is equivalent to "All Scripture is the Word of God, - true, trustworthy, and of Divine authority."²⁹⁶

Inspiration, then, speaks of authority.

Profitable

God gave the written and inspired authority of the Scripture so that it would be profitable in several areas. *Profitable* (ὠφέλιμος a

---

[295] Benjamin Breckinridge Warfield, *Revelation and Inspiration*, in vol. 1 of *The Works of B. B. Warfield* (NY: Oxford University Press, 1932. Reprint, Grand Rapids: Baker Book House Company, 2003), 121.

[296] M'Intosh, 385, 386.

nominative masculine singular adjective from ὠφέλιμος) means " 'useful,' in the sense of yielding a practical benefit."[297] Scripture yields a practical benefit in doctrine, reproof, correction, and instruction in righteousness; all of which indicate that Scripture is the authority for faith and practice. Zodhiates, commenting on these four things, states:

> First of all, the word of God is presented as doctrine (*didaskalía*), instruction, authoritative teaching, i.e., truth. Secondly, as truth it is ethically persuasive (*élegchos*, proof, conviction) convincing us of our error. Thirdly, it then places us in a correct moral posture. Fourthly, the word of God continues to provide discipline (*paideía*, training, discipline, chastisement) in righteousness.[298]

Matthew Henry writes:

> It is *profitable* to us for all the purposes of the Christian life, *for doctrine, for reproof, for correction, for instruction in righteousness*. It answers all the ends of divine revelation. It instructs us in that which is true, reproves us for that which is amiss, directs us in that which is good. It is of use to all, for we all need to be instructed, corrected, and reproved: it is of special use to ministers, who are to give instruction, correction, and reproof; and whence can they fetch it better than from the scripture?[299]

Profitable, then, speaks of the fact that God wants the Scripture to be the authority for doctrine (that is, faith), for reproof, for correction, and for instruction in righteousness (that is, practice).

---

[297] Knight, 449.

[298] Zodhiates, "1882. ἐπανόρθωσις."

[299] Matthew Henry, *Gal. – Rev.*, vol. 10 in *Commentary on the Whole Bible* in *The Master Christian Library*, version 8 [CD-ROM] (Rio, WI: Ages Software, 2000), 455.

Purpose

II Timothy 3:17 starts with Ἵνα, which "declares the purpose which Scripture is to serve."³⁰⁰ The purpose, as the rest of the verse indicates, is to make the man of God perfect, throughly furnished unto all good works. The purpose demonstrates that Scripture is the only authority for faith and practice as well as being the authority for all of faith and practice.

Perfect (ἄρτιος a nominative masculine singular adjective) means "completely qualified."³⁰¹ *Throughly furnished* (ἐξηρτισμένος a perfect passive participle from ἐξαρτίζω) means "to furnish or fit completely."³⁰² Concerning the use of these two words (*perfect* and *throughly furnished*), *The New International Dictionary of New Testament Theology* states: "The adj. *artios* [*perfect*] occurs only at 2 Tim. 3:17, together with the perfect pass. participle *exērtismenos* [*throughly furnished*]. In the OT scriptures the church of the New Testament has an indispensable, God-given guide to living, through which the man of God may achieve an appropriate state, viz. be equipped for every work of love."³⁰³ In other words, the Scripture is the authority for the man of God's practice.

The man of God does not need the Scripture plus psychology in order to be throughly furnished unto all good works, no, all he needs is the Scripture. He does not need the Scripture plus a creed, commentary, or papal edict in order to be throughly furnished unto all good works. He does not need the written Scripture and some sort of oral

---

³⁰⁰ J. E. Huther, *The Pastoral Epistles* in *Critical and Exegetical Commentary on the New Testament*, by Heinrich August Wilhelm Meyer (Edinburgh: T & T Clark, 1881), 308.

³⁰¹ Zodhiates, "739. ἄρτιος."

³⁰² Ibid., "1822. Ἐξαρτίζω."

³⁰³ R. Schippers, "ἄρτιος" in *New International Dictionary of New Testament Theology*, ed. Colin Brown (Grand Rapids: Zondervan, 1978), III:350.

tradition passed down from antiquity in order to be perfect, thoroughly furnished unto all good works. No, all he needs is the Scripture. Matthew Poole writes:

> The Scripture . . . is so full a direction, that Christians need not go down to the Philistines to whet their tools, nor be beholden to unwritten traditions, or to the writings of pagan philosophers, for directions what to do, how to worship God, or manage any part of their conversation, either as to their general calling, or as to their particular relations.[304]

The purpose of Scripture indicates that it is the authority for practice. In fact, it is the authority for all of practice.

Conclusion

II Timothy 3:16,17 teaches that the Bible is the sole authority for all of faith and practice, as evident from several considerations. First, *Scripture* refers to a written authority. Second, *inspiration* speaks of authority. Third, *profitable* speaks of the fact that God designed Scripture to be the authority for doctrine (that is, faith), for reproof, for correction, and for instruction in righteousness (that is, practice). And, fourth, the purpose of Scripture in making the man of God perfect and throughly furnished unto all good works indicates that it is the authority for practice.

Summary

Scripture is the sole authority for faith and practice. First, Scripture is the authority in the matter of salvation, for Scripture is able to produce faith (Romans 10:17), make a person wise unto salvation (II Timothy 3:15), and is the means by which a person is born again (I Peter 1:23).

---

[304] Poole, *Matthew – Revelation*, vol. 3 of *A Commentary on the Holy Bible*, 797.

Second, Scripture is the authority for judging, for it is the standard by which one should judge all actions, as many verses testify. Isaiah 8:20 is representative of these verses when it clearly states: "To the law and to the testimony: if they speak not according to this word, *it is* because *there is* no light in them."

Third, Scripture is the sole authority for faith and practice in local churches. New Testament Scripture is for local churches (Matthew 28:20; I Corinthians 14:37; I Timothy 3;14,15; II Peter 3:2; Jude 3). All of the New Testament concerns local churches, for, in one way or another, the Lord directs it to local churches. Furthermore, the Old Testament Scripture is for local churches (Matthew 28:20; Acts 7:38; Romans 15:4; I Corinthians 10:11; II Peter 3:2); therefore, all of the Word of God is for local churches (II Timothy 3;16,17; 4:2). But churches must be diligent to follow the Bible and at the same time dogmatically reject false religious authorities (Colossians 2:8; Titus 1:14).

Fourth, Scripture is the authority for Jesus' life, which is most significant since the disciple of Jesus is to deny himself, take up his cross, and follow Him (Matthew 16:24). Jesus repeatedly submitted Himself to the authority of God's Word in matters of faith and practice (Psalm 138:2; Matthew 2:23; 4:4, 7, 10, 12-15; 5:17; 8:16, 17; 12:15-21; 13:34, 35; 21:1-5; 26:53, 54; Luke 22:37, 44; John 13:18; 15:25; 19:28; Hebrews 10:7). Not only did Jesus submit Himself to the authority of God's Word, but also He very clearly rejected any other authority for faith and practice (Matthew 12:1-13; 15:1-6; Luke 11:37, 38; 13:10-17; 14:1-6; John 5:5-12, 16, 18; 7:22, 23; 9:14-16).

And fifth, as II Timothy 3:16,17 asserts, Scripture is the authority for all of faith and practice.

The above verses, which are representative of many in the Word of God, demonstrate clearly, conclusively, and concisely that Scripture is the sole authority for faith and practice. There is no need for any other authority or authorities in the matter of faith and practice. Spurgeon wrote:

> It is in the word that we must find wisdom and power: "because the foolishness of God is wiser than men; and the weakness of God is stronger than men" [I Corinthians 1:25]. The faintest whisper of Jehovah's voice should fill us with solemn awe, and command the deepest obedience of our souls. Brethren, how careful should we be that we do not set up in God's temple anything in opposition to his Word, that we do not permit the teachings of a creature to usurp the honor due to the Lord alone. "Thus saith antiquity;" "thus saith authority;" "thus saith learning;" "thus saith experience"; these be but idol-gods which defile the temple of God, be it yours and mine as bold iconoclasts to dash them in pieces without mercy, seeing that they usurp the place of the Word of God.[305]

Yes, let the man of God follow Scripture and at the same time boldly and thoroughly reject false authorities.

Scripture is the authority for faith and practice. Therefore, when Scripture speaks of its perfect preservation (Psalm 12:6,7), then despite all other evidence to the contrary, historical or otherwise; Scripture should settle the issue. When Scripture speaks of simply receiving the text as it does in John 17:8, instead of restoring the text; then despite the rantings and ravings of the textual critics, one should simply receive the text. Scripture speaks of the writers of Scripture recording what the Lord spake (Exodus 34:27), which, therefore, teaches that they recorded the vowels along with the consonants. Despite what the scholars declare about the vowels, one should simply believe what the Bible teaches. If the Bible is truly the sole authority for faith and practice, and if one will really honor the authority of the Bible, then he will let it guide him in the matter of preservation, the text, and the vowel points. To do otherwise is for him to rebel against the Bible's authority. Sadly, many have rebelled against the authority

---

[305] Spurgeon, " 'Thus Saith the Lord,' or the Book of Common Prayer Weighed in the Balances of the Sanctuary," 534.

of the Words of God. The author can say the same of them as what Jeremiah said of some in his day: "They have rejected the word of the LORD; and what wisdom is in them?" (Jeremiah 8:9). Many have demonstrated a lack of wisdom in deviating from the doctrine that Scripture is the sole authority for faith and practice.

DEVIATION FROM THE DOCTRINE

Various non-Baptist groups have other things besides the Bible as authorities, and more and more Fundamentalists and even Fundamentalist Baptists are looking to other things besides the Bible as the authority, such as history, textual critics, and oral tradition.

In Non-Baptist Groups

Various non-Baptist groups such as the Eastern Orthodox, Catholics, Lutherans, and others look to other things besides the Bible for authority.

Eastern Orthodox

The Eastern Orthodox have as their authority for faith and practice the "Bible and their tradition to [the year] 787."[306] According to *Handbook of Denominations of the United States*:

> The Nicene Creed in its original form is central to the Orthodox faith in all its branches. ... It is the long tradition of the church ... that defines what is orthodox. This tradition includes the decisions of the seven Ecumenical Councils as well as the tradition of the Divine Liturgy itself.[307]

---

[306] Roger Peterson, "Baptist Distinctives among other denominations" (Minneapolis: Central Baptist Theological Seminary, n.d.), centerfold of booklet.

[307] Frank S. Mead and Samuel S. Hill, *Handbook of Denominations in the United States*, 11th ed., rev. Craig D. Atwood (Nashville: Abingdon Press, 2001), 246.

The seventh of these Ecumenical Councils ended in 787 AD. The Orthodox have as their authority, the Bible plus these seven ecumenical councils, therefore, the Orthodox do not see the Bible as the only authority for faith and practice, for they add other authorities to the Bible.

Catholics

The Catholics have the "Pope (*ex cathedra*), greatest authority, then tradition, and finally the Bible."[308] According to *Handbook of Denominations of the United States*:

> The faith and doctrine of the Roman Catholic Church are founded upon what the First Vatican Council referred to as "that deposit of faith given to it by Christ and through his apostles, sustained by the Bible and by tradition." Thus, like other Catholic and Orthodox bodies, the church accepts the decisions of the first seven ecumenical councils; however, for Roman Catholics, the later councils of the Western church, such as the Fourth Lateran Council (1215), are also authoritative.[309]

The Catholics think that they need more than just the Bible to be their authority. In his 1998 encyclical *Fides et Ratio*, the Pope said,

> There are also signs of a resurgence of fideism, which fails to recognize the importance of rational knowledge and philosophical discourse for the understanding of faith. . . . One currently widespread symptom of this fideistic tendency is a "biblicism" which tends to make the reading and exegesis of Sacred Scripture the sole criterion of truth.[310]

The Pope argues against simply following the Bible (fideism) and advocates the use of reasoning in order to understand doctrine. But should not the Bible be the sole authority for faith and practice (II Timothy 3:16,17)?

---

[308] Peterson.

[309] Mead and Hill, 95.

[310] Ibid., 34.

Lutherans

The Lutherans have the "Bible and creeds of the church"[311] as their authority. According to *Handbook of Denominations of the United States*:

> Lutherans maintain that the Bible is the inspired Word of God and the rule and standard of faith and practice. They confess their faith through the three general creeds of Christendom (Apostles', Nicene, and Athanasian), which they believe to be in accordance with the scriptures. They also believe that the Augsburg Confession is a correct exposition of the faith and doctrine of evangelical Lutheranism, although there is disagreement over which version is preferred. The two catechisms of Luther, the Schmalkald Articles, and the Formula of Concord are held to be faithful interpretations of Lutheranism and of the Bible.[312]

In other words, Lutherans add other authorities to the Words of God including a number of creeds and catechisms. They do not see the Bible as the only authority for faith and practice.

Others

The Episcopalians have the "Bible, creeds, tradition" as their authority. The Methodists have the "Bible and creeds." The Congregationalists have the "Bible and tradition of the denomination." The Pentecostalists have the "Bible and personal experience."[313]

Conclusion

The Eastern Orthodox, Catholics, Lutherans, Episcopalians, Methodists, Congregationalists, and Pentecostalists all think that they need more than just the Bible as their authority for faith and practice.

---

[311] Peterson.

[312] Mead and Hill, 206.

[313] Peterson.

Amongst Fundamentalist Baptists

Some Fundamentalist Baptists seem to think, as do Protestants and Catholics, that they need more than just the Bible to serve as the authority for faith and practice. The position of some Fundamentalist Baptists concerning preservation, the text, and the vowel points demonstrate their reliance on extra-Biblical authorities.

In the Matter of Preservation

The Bible teaches that God has perfectly preserved His inspired Words (Psalm 12:6,7). However, rather than allow the Bible to be the sole authority in the matter of preservation, some look to history as the authority. Dell Johnson observes that those who will not let the Bible speak for itself on the matter of its own preservation try to resolve this theological issue by appealing to historical sources. Appealing to historical sources, Johnson declares, is the essentially Liberal technique of traditionalism.[314] Some Fundamentalist Baptists have succumbed to traditionalism in that they appeal primarily to history to support their position on preservation as opposed to letting the Bible speak for itself. For instance, in the book *One Bible Only?*, written by professors of the Central Baptist Theological Seminary (a Fundamentalist Baptist institution), are some statements which reveal a reliance on history to settle the preservation issue. Kevin Bauder says, "As this book has shown, the Bible contains no promise whatsoever that includes the preservation of all the words of the *autographa* (without addition or deletion) in a single, publicly accessible source."[315] Such a statement fails to take into account a proper understanding of Psalm 12:6,7; Matthew 5:18; John 10:35; II Timothy 3:15-17; and other

---

[314] Dell Johnson, *Preservation of the Bible: A Bible Foundational Doctrine* (Pensacola: Pensacola Christian College, 3/7/02), cassette.

[315] Kevin T. Bauder, "An Appeal to Scripture" in *One Bible Only? Examining Exclusive Claims for the King James Bible*, eds. Roy E. Beacham and Kevin T. Bauder (Grand Rapids: Kregel Publications), 158.

verses, but in believing that Scripture does not settle the issue, *One Bible Only?* appeals to history to decide the matter of preservation, for W. Edward Glenny in the same book writes,

> The Scriptures do not teach that God has perfectly preserved every word of the original autographs in one manuscript or text type. A proper understanding of the doctrine of preservation is a belief that God has providentially preserved His Word in and through all of the extant manuscripts, versions, and other copies of Scripture. *This conviction is based on the evidence of history* [emphasis mine]. . . . No passage of Scripture states that God has used multiple manuscripts to preserve His Word, but *the evidence of history leaves no doubt that such is the case* [emphasis mine].[316]

Glenny holds to preservation not because it is Scriptural, but because it is based on the evidence of history.

Glenny further writes:

> Obvious from *the evidence of history* [emphasis mine] is the fact that God has providentially preserved His Word for the present generation. However, also obvious from *the evidence of history* [emphasis mine] is the fact that God has not miraculously and perfectly preserved every word of the Biblical text in any one manuscript or group of manuscripts, or in all of the manuscripts.[317]

Why do not these Fundamentalist Baptists get their Bibliology from the Bible? They appeal to history. Of course, from history one can prove just about anything, no wonder appealing to history is a Liberal tactic. Why would Fundamentalist Baptists adopt such a tactic? Could it be that since a proper exegesis of the verses on preservation teach the preservation of all the words of the *autographa* and since, for whatever reason, these Fundamentalist Baptists do not want to hold to this Scriptural position, they are relegated, then, to rely on history? It seems that this is the case.

---

[316] W. Edward Glenny, "The Preservation of Scripture and the Version debate" in *One Bible Only?*, 121,122.

[317] Ibid., 126.

In the Matter of the Text

Another area in which Fundamentalist Baptists depart from Scripture being the sole authority for faith and practice is in the matter of the text. In the message by Johnson (see previous section) he refers to a paper entitled, "Trusted Voices on Translation" published in 2001, which appeals to historical leaders of the Fundamentalist movement showing their belief that Bible students can use other translations. Johnson observes that apparently without any help from the Bible one can settle the text issue! Is not this typical Liberalism where what the Bible says does not matter at all? Johnson concludes his remarks with a rebuke based on Mark 7:9: "Full well ye reject the commandment of God, that ye may keep your own tradition."[318] It seems that some Fundamentalist Baptists are more concerned with being true to their Fundamentalist tradition, than with being true to Scripture. In the matter of the text, these Fundamentalist Baptists have other things beside the Bible as their authority.

To illustrate further that Fundamentalists allow other things to be authorities in the matter of the text, consider David Sorenson's observation:

> Modern textual criticism accordingly has become the supreme court determining what is the Word of God and what is not. . . . The committees of modern textual critics issue their verdicts whether a given word, verse, or portions of a chapter should be a part of the Bible. Truly the collective judgments of the critics have determined the composition of the critical text of the New Testament. Modern text critics are the supreme court justices and none are Fundamental Baptists. Moreover, those of this position clearly teach that we must rely upon the findings of these text critics.[319]

---

[318] Johnson, *Preservation of the Bible*, cassette.

[319] David H. Sorenson, *Touch Not The Unclean Thing: The Text Issue and Separation* (Duluth, MN: Northstar Baptist Ministries, 2001), 60.

In other words, modern textual criticism is a greater authority in the minds of some than the Bible itself! For some it is not enough that the Bible declares that the Scripture is inspired and perfectly preserved (Psalm 12:6,7) and that all one has to do is to receive it (John 17:8). Some seem to think it necessary to walk by the sight of scholarship. So much do some follow scholarship that instead of having the sole authority of Scripture, they have at least two authorities: the written words and the words of the textual critics.

Mark Minnick, a Fundamentalist Baptist pastor of Mount Calvary Baptist Church in Greenville, South Carolina, and a professor at Bob Jones University[320] makes a revealing statement when he admits: "As a preacher of God's Word" he "must rely upon the findings of textual critics."[321] Writing in the same book, John Ashbrook, speaking of his car, states: "When it comes to diagnosis, tune-ups, and the onboard computer, I have to turn to men with special training. The same is true in the realm of the text."[322] Ashbrook places the Word of God seemingly on the same level as a car. But the Bible is no car, it does not need diagnosis, it simply needs receiving (John 17:8). But with both of these men looking to the textual critics, does not the ultimate authority become the textual critic, just as Sorenson stated earlier?

Spurgeon makes an insightful comment when he writes:

> Are these correctors of Scripture infallible? Is it certain that our Bibles are not right, but that the critics must be so? The old silver is to be de-

---

[320] *Bob Jones University Undergraduate Catalog 06 07* (Greenville: n. p., 2006), 358. On this same page is the information that Minnick became a University faculty member in 1980.

[321] Mark Minnick, "Let's Meet the Manuscripts" in *From the Mind of God to the Mind of Man: A Layman's Guide to How We Got Out Bible*, 3d ed., ed. James B. Williams (Greenville, SC: Ambassador-Emerald International, 1999), 85.

[322] John E. Ashbrook, "The History of the Textus Receptus" in *From the Mind of God to the Mind of Man*, 108. Ashbrook is the pastor emeritus of Bible Community Church in Mentor, Ohio. While this is not a Baptist church in name, he is a Fundamentalist.

preciated; but the German silver, which is put in its place, is to be taken at the value of gold. . . . Are we now to believe that infallibility is with learned men? Now, Farmer Smith, when you have read your Bible, and have enjoyed its precious promises, you will have, tomorrow morning, to go down the street to ask the scholarly man at the parsonage whether this portion of the Scripture belongs to the inspired part of the Word, or whether it is of dubious authority. It will be well for you to know whether it was written by the Isaiah, or whether it was by the second of the 'two Obadiahs.' All possibility of certainty is transferred from the spiritual man to a class of persons whose scholarship is pretentious, but who do not even pretend to spirituality. We shall gradually be so bedoubted and becriticized, that only a few of the most profound will know what is Bible, and what is not, and they will dictate to all the rest of us. I have no more faith in their mercy than in their accuracy: they will rob us of all that we hold most dear, and glory in the cruel deed. This same reign of terror we shall not endure, for we still believe that God revealeth himself rather to babes than to the wise and prudent, and we are fully assured that our own old English version of the Scriptures is sufficient for plain men for all purposes of life, salvation, and godliness. We do not despise learning, but we will never say of culture or criticism, "These be thy gods, O Israel!" [323]

One does not need the word of a man, no matter how good, for him to know that he has the written Words of God. He can simply take God at His Word that He inspired His Words (II Timothy 3:16) and preserved those inspired Words (Psalm 12:6,7) so that all he has to do is to receive them (John 17:8). He does not need to wait upon some official pronouncement that he has God's Words, or else his trust is ultimately in man's pronouncement rather than in God's promises. And if he is trusting in the pronouncement of man to assure him that he has the Words of God, then he is exalting the opinion of man and diminishing the authority of the Words of God. Such an action is very dangerous, for the Bible says, "Thus saith the LORD; Cursed be the man that trusteth in man, and maketh flesh his arm, and whose heart departeth from the LORD" (Jeremiah 17:5). Indeed, one may as well

---

[323] Charles H. Spurgeon, *The Greatest Fight in the World* in *The Charles H. Spurgeon Library*, version 2 [CD-ROM] (Albany, OR: Ages Software, 1998), 17-19.

put himself back under the pronouncements, pontifications, and predicaments of priestcraft and popery as to rely on the textual critics to tell him that he has the Words of God.

The previous quotation from Sorenson speaks of the New Testament text, but the same is true of the Old Testament text. When David Doran of Detroit Baptist Theological Seminary, a Fundamentalist Baptist seminary, asked Randy Jaeggli of Bob Jones University, "Is it accurate to say or act like textual criticism is unnecessary in the Old Testament text?" Jaeggli responded, "Absolutely not."[324] Jaeggli then gave examples where he thinks the Bible student must use textual criticism in the Old Testament text. In both the New Testament and in the Old Testament, some Fundamentalist Baptists have abandoned the teaching that the Bible is the sole authority, as they look to textual critics, instead of simply to the Bible.

In looking to the textual critics, Fundamentalist Baptists are all too willing to abandon certain passages and teachings of Scripture. Practically speaking, the Pharisees did the same thing with the Word of God, for by their tradition they made the Word of God of none effect (Matthew 15:6; Mark 7:13). *Of none effect* (ἠκυρώσατε a second aorist active indicative second person plural from ἀκυρόω) means "to render void, deprive of force and authority."[325] Zodhiates comments that Jesus "did not mean that it ceases to be the law of God, but that it had no value, worth, or lordship over them."[326] The Pharisees considered their tradition more important than the command of the Word of God to honor their parents. God's Word is clear about honoring father and mother, but the Pharisees had a tradition by which they could avoid

---

[324] *Fundamentalism and the Word of God* (Allen Park, MI: Coalition for the Defense of the Scriptures), videocassette.

[325] Thayer, 24.

[326] Zodhiates, "208. ἀκυρόω."

obeying God's command, and therefore ignore God's command so that it had no authority. And so it is with Fundamentalists who ignore God's promises of preservation and put more value on the theories of textual criticism. By their scholarly tradition, they have made Psalm 12:6,7; 119:89; Matthew 5:18; 24:35; and other verses of none effect.

In the Matter of the Vowel Points

As Chapter One presented and as subsequent chapters further present, many verses teach the inspiration, preservation, and necessity of vowels in the Old Testament. Some Fundamentalist Baptists, however, will not allow the Bible to be the sole authority about the vowel points but, instead, rely on other authorities and, therefore, reject the inspiration of the vowel points. Two Fundamentalist Baptists proponents for rejecting the inspiration of the vowel points are Larry Oats and David Sorenson. But such a position has several problems including a reliance on extra-Biblical authority, oral tradition, additions to the Bible, and fables.

Proponents

Two Fundamentalist Baptist proponents for saying that the vowel points are not inspired are Larry Oats and David Sorenson. Larry Oats, a professor at Maranatha Baptist Bible College, a Fundamentalist Baptist college, in a review of *Thou Shalt Keep Them*, writes:

> This book argues for the inspiration of the vowel points in the Hebrew text. Most scholars acknowledge that Hebrew had no vowels until the spoken language began to be lost after the destruction of Jerusalem. The Masoretes (Jewish scribes who were the preservers[327] of the writ-

---

[327] Oats statement here that the Masoretes were the preservers of the Old Testament is incorrect. While God had committed the oracles of God to the Jews (Romans 3:2), in the Great Commission and in other verses, the Lord relegated the keeping or preserving of His Words to local churches (Matthew 28:20; John 14:15; I Timothy 6:14; Jude 3). The Masoretes, while transmitting the true text of the Hebrew Old Testament, were not the preservers of that text.

ten Old Testament) developed vowels to preserve the pronunciation of the words.[328]

Herein Oats announces that he does not regard the vowel points to be inspired.

Sorenson, a Fundamentalist Baptist pastor of Northstar Baptist Church in Duluth, Minnesota, makes similar statements in a letter to the author when he writes: "I frankly believe the Masoretic vowel points (1) are not inspired and (2) were not part of the originals."[329] And in another letter to the author, Sorenson writes:

> My *theory* regarding the vowel points since the second millennium AD is that God used Jewish scribes of his choosing, perhaps the Masoretes or some other unknown scribes, to invent the pointing to (1) help Jews in danger of losing their language and (2) to help gentile Christians such as you and I understand Hebrew better. (Perhaps the scribes and rabbis did not have that in mind, but I think that God did.) In distinction to what I wrote earlier, I am willing to entertain the possibility that God even superintended the insertion of the vowel points along the way. Call that whatever you may wish.[330]

Herein Sorenson makes it clear that he does not regard the points to be inspired.

Problems

Oats and Sorenson's position on uninspired vowel points faces several problems, among which are a reliance on extra-Biblical authority, oral tradition, additions to the Bible, and fables.

Reliance on Extra-Biblical Authority

Oats reveals that he relies, at least partially, upon the opinion of "most scholars" as an authority in the matter of the vowel points,

---

[328] Larry Oats, *Thou Shalt Keep Them: A Review by Larry R. Oats* (Watertown, WI: Maranatha Baptist Bible College, 2003), 6.

[329] David Sorenson, letter to the author, January 31, 2004.

[330] David Sorenson, letter to the author, March 1, 2004.

which is very similar to those who look to textual critics as their authority in the matter of the text. It has become with some Fundamentalist Baptists, "Thus saith the scholars," instead of, "Thus saith the Scriptures." Scripture must be the sole authority for faith and practice, not scholars.

Sorenson is also not willing to allow Scripture to be the sole authority in the matter of the vowel points, but, instead, is relying on his own thinking, as he says, "My *theory* regarding the vowel points." However, one should not rely on what he thinks, but on what God says, especially in light of the fact that God says, "For my thoughts *are* not your thoughts, neither *are* your ways my ways, saith the LORD" (Isaiah 55:8). Man's thoughts are not a reliable authority when it comes to matters of faith and practice.

Reliance on Oral Tradition

Both Oats and Sorenson mention the Masoretes as the inventors of the vowel pointing, which, Oats says that the Masoretes did in order "to preserve the pronunciation of the words" and which Sorenson says that the Masoretes or some other unknown scribes invented "to help Jews in danger of losing their language." The implication of these statements is that there was some sort of oral tradition, as Levita and Cappellus argued (see Chapter One), which maintained the proper pronunciation of the words through the years. Supposedly as the oral tradition with its proper pronunciation of the words was about to fade off the stage of history, the Masoretes came to the rescue and recorded the oral tradition about the proper pronunciation of the words of the Old Testament and added it to the Old Testament. Oats believes that the work of the Masoretes preserves the pronunciation of the words. Sorenson thinks that God guided in the process of adding the vowels to the consonants. Therefore, both men are placing at least some authority in the work of the Masoretes, which means that both Oats and Sorenson are relying on oral tradition.

Whitfield observes about Cappellus: "By making those vowel and accent-sounds . . . to depend upon oral tradition, he makes the sense and interpretation, and so the whole authority thereof, to depend on the same: that is, he does, by necessary consequence, make the whole Scripture, as to the use and application, to be merely of human authority."[331] Christ, however, firmly rejected any reliance on an oral tradition in matters of faith and practice (Matthew 12:1-13; 15:1-9; Luke 11:38; 13:10-16; 14:1-6; John 5:5-18; 7:22,23; 9:14-16), and so should Fundamentalist Baptists, especially if they want to have the same Bibliology as Christ.

Reliance on Additions to the Bible

If Oats and Sorenson are right that God did not inspire the vowels, then to add vowels to the text, presents another problem, namely, it violates God's commands not to add to His Words (Deuteronomy 4:2; 12:32; Proverbs 30:5,6; Revelation 22:18). If the written Hebrew Old Testament only had consonants, then it should remain that way. Men who are not acting under the influence of the inspiration of God have no business adding to the Words of God. If the Masoretes were the inventors of the vowel points, they lacked any authority to add written vowels to a consonantal text. As such, if it be true that the *autographa* of the Old Testament only had consonants, then the consistent position would be to advocate a removal of the written vowels and stick with what God originally inspired. Jesus in His rejection of the Pharisaical oral tradition continually sought to strip from the Bible their additions to the Bible. Likewise, if the vowel points really are an addition to the Old Testament text, then let these Fundamentalist Baptists have the courage of their convictions and argue for the complete removal of the vowel points from the Hebrew Old Testament text.

---

[331] Whitfield, 21.

However, they have not done so. Instead, they choose to walk in the middle of the road. Let them be either hot or cold, but the lukewarm accommodation position cannot be pleasing to the Lord (Revelation 3:15,16).

Something else also becomes very clear and that is this: since the accommodationists claim that the points are not inspired, and since they say that the points were added, and since they are willing, either fully or partially, to place authority in such points; then they are placing authority in an addition to the Bible, which serves to demonstrate, again, that the Bible is not their sole authority for faith and practice. May Fundamentalist Baptists repent and get back to the Bible.

Reliance on Fables

A further problem with the idea that an oral tradition preserved the proper pronunciation of the words of the Old Testament is that such an idea smacks of a Jewish fable. Concerning belief amongst the Jewish Orthodox about the vowel points, an internet web-site observes:

> One basic belief of the Orthodox community in general is that it is the latest link in a chain of Jewish continuity extending back to the giving of the Torah to Moses at Mount Sinai. It believes that two guides to laws were given to the Israelites at that time: the first, known as *Torah she-bi-khtav*, or the "Written Law" is the Tanakh (Jewish Bible) as we know it today; the second, known as *Torah she-ba'al peh*, is the exposition as relayed by the scholarly and other religious leaders of each generation. The interpretation of the Oral Law is considered as the authoritative reading of the Written Law.[332]

In other words, the Orthodox Jews see two guides: a written law and an oral law. Are not the accommodationists in the same position? They look to the written Old Testament to convey the consonants and to oral tradition to convey the vowels. However, Jesus only recognized the written law as the only authority for faith and practice (Matthew 2:23;

---

[332] "Ultra-Orthodox-Judaism," http://www.nationmaster.com/encyclopedia (Internet).

4:4, 7, 10, 12-15; 5:17; 8:16, 17; 12:15-21; 13:34, 35; 21:1-5; 26:53, 54; Luke 22:37; 24:44; John 13:18; 15:25; 19:28; Hebrew 10:7) and rejected any oral authority (Matthew 12:1-13; 15:1-6; Luke 11:37, 38; 13:10-17; 14:1-6; John 5:5-12, 16, 18; 7:22, 23; 9:14-16), therefore, the contention of the Jews of there being two authoritative guides or traditions is not the truth, but a fable, and a Jewish one at that. By receiving such Jewish fables, these Fundamentalist Baptists have been turned "from the truth" (Titus 1:14).

Conclusion

Fundamentalist Baptists who hold to the accommodation position concerning the vowel points have several problems with the teaching that the Bible is the sole authority for faith and practice. Instead of having the Bible as their sole authority, they have several other authorities such as scholars, their own thinking, oral tradition, additions to the text, and fables. This is clearly unbiblical.

Summary

The Bible teaches that Scripture is the sole authority for faith and practice. Many groups, however, deviate from the teaching that the Bible is the sole authority, among them being Eastern Orthodox, Lutherans, Catholics, Episcopalians, Methodists, Congregationalists, Pentecostalists, and even some Fundamentalist Baptists. Some Fundamentalist Baptists rely on another authority in the matter of preservation, namely, history. Some Fundamentalist Baptists rely on another authority in the matter of the text, namely, Fundamentalist tradition and textual critics. And some Fundamentalist Baptists rely on other authorities in the matter of the vowel points; namely, scholars, their own thinking, oral tradition, additions to the Bible, and fables. By rejecting the sole authority of Scripture for faith and practice and by relying upon other authorities in the matters of preservation, the text, and the vowel points; these Fundamentalist Baptists manifest a Bibliology that is more in agreement with that of Pharisees, Catholics, and Protestants. If they will truly be Baptists, then let them reject these other authorities and let them cling to the Bible as the sole authority for faith and practice. There is no need for other things to be authorities for faith and practice for "all scripture *is* given by inspiration of God, and *is* profitable for doctrine, for reproof, for correction, for instruction in righteousness: that the man of God may be perfect, throughly furnished unto all good works" (II Timothy 3:16,17).

CONCLUSION

Scripture is the sole authority when it comes to salvation (Romans 10:17; II Timothy 3:15; I Peter 1:23). Scripture is the sole authority for judging (Genesis 2:17; Exodus 5:1; Leviticus 10:1,2; Deuteronomy 4:1; 7:11; 27:26; I Samuel 15:3,22; Isaiah 8:20; John 5:39; 12:48; Acts 17:11; Hebrews 8:5). Scripture is the sole authority in local churches (Matthew 28:20; Acts 7:38; Romans 15:4; I Corinthians 10:11; 14:37; Colossians 2:8; I Timothy 3:14,15; II Timothy 3:16,17; 4:2; Titus 1:4; II Peter 3:2; Jude 3). Scripture was the sole authority for Jesus' life, both negatively as He rejected the false authority of the oral tradition (Matthew 12:1-13; 15:1-6; Luke 11:37, 38; 13:10-17; 14:1-6; John 5:5-12, 16, 18; 7:22, 23; 9:14-16), and positively as He followed the written Words of God (Psalm 138:2; Matthew 2:23; 4:4, 7, 10, 12-15; 5:17; 8:16, 17; 12:15-21; 13:34, 35; 21:1-5; 26:53, 54; Luke 22:37; 24:44; John 13:18; 15:25; 19:28; Hebrews 10:7). Clearly, the Bible teaches both by precept and example, both negatively and positively, and both in the Old and in the New Testaments that Scripture is the sole authority for faith and practice. Scripture is the sole authority for faith and practice, but many Protestants, Catholics, and Fundamentalist Baptists deviate from this teaching. Particularly do Fundamentalist Baptists deviate from the teaching of the Bible being the sole authority when they approach the matters of preservation, the text, and the vowel points.

To emphasize: both the accommodation and non-authoritative positions ultimately rely on uninspired writings, rather than relying on the Bible being the sole authority for faith and practice; therefore, both positions are unbiblical. First, consider the accommodation position about authority. The accommodationists do not believe that the vowels are inspired, yet place some authority in the vowels, which means that they are trusting, at least in part, uninspired writings. Furthermore, the accommodationists rely on Jewish oral tradition to convey these vowels to Masoretes, who, without authority, inserted them into the Old Testament text. Placing authority in what they claim to be uninspired vowels and relying on Jewish oral tradition is contrary to the teaching that the Bible is the sole authority for faith and practice and reveals that the accommodation position about the vowel points cannot possibly be correct. Fundamentalists who supposedly are champions for the Bible need to rethink their position about the points.

Now, consider the non-authoritative position about authority. The non-authoritative position believes that the points are of no authority. But if the points are non-authoritative, then where is the authority? Specifically, if the points that are written in the text are not authoritative, then where does one look for authority? Is authority in one's favorite commentator or Bible teacher? What if another commentator or Bible teacher seems more persuasive, does he now become the authority? Indeed, if the points are not authoritative, then authority shifts away from the Bible to some other source and the Bible is no longer the sole authority for faith and practice. Whitfield observes:

> In case of different apprehensions; which would be quite unavoidable; whose judgment shall prevail? Must every one make an interpretation of Divine Authority to himself? We should, this way, soon have a multitude or inconsistent copies of the Holy Scriptures, to the utter subversion of all Divine Authority of Holy Writ.[333]

---

[333] Whitfield, 101.

> What havoc must be made of the Old Testament, if we reject the authority of the punctuations, without which a great part of the most obvious passages will be, as Morinus observes, capable of various senses; and the more difficult poetical and prophetic writings will be, for the most part, quite unintelligible, and consequently of no Authority at all.[334]

For proof that without the vowel points many verses would be of no authority at all, see the next chapter. Clearly, the non-authoritative position about the points cannot possibly be correct, for it would destroy the teaching that the Bible is the sole authority for faith and practice.

Since the Bible is the sole authority for faith and practice and since both the accommodation and non-authoritative positions must rely on authorities other than the Bible, then from a Biblical perspective these positions in regard to the vowel points cannot be correct. Therefore, the *autographa* position concerning the points is the only Biblical option. Adherents of the accommodation and non-authoritative views should abandon these views for the more Biblical *autographa* view.

---

[334] Whitfield, 106. In this quote, Whitfield mentions Morinus, which is probably *Morin* Latinized and most likely refers to Jean Morin who "attacked the integrity of the Hebrew text" ("Morin, Jean" in *Cyclopedia*, VI: 612). Apparently, Morin admitted that without the points, many verses in the Hebrew Bible would be of various senses and of no authority, by which argument he could overthrew the Hebrew and in its place put the LXX.

CHAPTER THREE – UNCERTAINTY

If the non-authoritative view about the vowel points is correct, then it would result in tremendous uncertainty about many words in the Old Testament and would have the result of overthrowing the authority of the Old Testament. John Owen observes that those who hold to the non-authoritative position are in essence saying:

> The points or vowels, and accents, are but lately invented, of no authority; without their guidance and direction nothing is certain in the knowledge of that tongue; all that we know of it comes from the translation of the LXX.; the Jews have corrupted the Old Testament; there are innumerable various lections both of the Old and New; there are other copies differing from those we now enjoy that are utterly lost.[335]

In other words, the result of saying that the points are of no authority is that the Hebrew Old Testament is totally uncertain and of no authority. But an uncertain and unauthoritative Old Testament is an impossibility, for the Bible teaches that Scripture is the sole authority for faith and practice.

It is the purpose of this chapter to demonstrate the uncertainty that would arise if there are no vowel points in the Hebrew text and, by so doing, further demonstrate that the non-authoritative position is completely unbiblical. Some claim that an unpointed Hebrew text would have no uncertainty or ambiguity such as Walton, who writes:

> It is to be observed, that although the reading of divers words unpointed, considered by themselves, might be dubious and subject to diverse readings, yet this ambiguity is taken away by the antecedents &

---

[335] John Owen, "Of the Divine Original, Authority, Self-Evidencing Light, and Power of the Scriptures; with an Answer to that Inquiry, How We Know the Scriptures to be the Word of God" in vol. 16 of *the Works of John Owen*, ed. William H. Goold (Carlisle, PA: The Banner of Truth Trust, 1968), 286.

> consequents, so that in the context, as they are parts of a sentence, the reading which is in it self ambiguous, is determined to one sense and meaning.[336]

That is, Walton seems to think that the context could resolve any possible ambiguity that might result from an unpointed text. Others may also hold to the fanciful notion that the context can remove the ambiguity that exists in an unpointed Hebrew text; however, such is not the case in many places. It is now that this chapter presents over one hundred instances of ambiguity in the Hebrew text, if there are no vowel points. In each of these cases, the context cannot decide the correct pointing and; therefore, the correct word is debatable, with the result that the verse loses much or all authority. This is exactly where the devil wants the Words of God as he said in the Garden, "Yea, hath God said?" (Genesis 3:1). However, such cannot be the state of the Words of God, for the Bible repeatedly asserts that Scripture is the sole authority for faith and practice.

Before presenting these verses, the reader should be aware that just because a commentator mentions an alternate reading for a word in a verse this does not mean that the commentator agrees with the change, although many times he does. In some cases, the commentator may just be mentioning a variation for sake of completeness. However, the fact that such variations exist demonstrates the ambiguity and subsequent loss of authority that would result if the text is not pointed.

The author presents this chapter with two major divisions: the comments of the commentators and the comments of the author. In the section concerning the comments of the commentators, the author presents many of these comments with little or no comment of his own. The majority of the author's comments come in the section entitled "Comments of the Author."

---

[336] Walton, *The Considerator Considered*, 215.

THE COMMENTS OF THE COMMENTATORS

This section presents in Biblical order the comments of commentators and other writers on various verses of the Old Testament. This section limits itself to what writers have actually published, as opposed to listing ambiguities that one could invent in the absence of vowels, of which there would literally be thousands.

Genesis 10:6

Concerning *Mizraim*, McClintock and Strong write:

> The sons of Ham are stated to have been "Cush," and Mizraim, and Phut, and Canaan" (Gen. x, 6; comp. 1 Chron. i, 8). It is remarkable that a dual form (Mizraim) should occur in the first generation, indicating a country, and not a person or a tribe, and we are therefore inclined to suppose that the gentile noun in the plural מִצְרִים, differing alone in the pointing from מִצְרַיִם originally stood here, which would be quite consistent with the plural forms of the names of the Mizraite tribes which follow, and analogous to the singular forms of the names of the Canaanite tribes, except the Sidonians, who are mentioned, not as a nation, but under the name of their forefather Sidon.[337]

By way of explanation, what McClintock and Strong advocate here is to repoint, that is, change the vowels, in the word *Mizraim* to make it a plural form, rather than a dual form. The dual form indicates a pair of or two of something, whereas the plural of a countable noun indicates more than one. Gill observes: "The word is of the dual number, and serves to express Egypt by, which was divided into two parts, lower and upper Egypt."[338]

---

[337] "Ham" in *Cyclopedia*, IV: 36.

[338] Gill, *An Exposition of the Old Testament* (London: Mathews & Leigh, 1810. Reprinted Paris, Arkansas: The Baptist Standard Bearer, Inc., 1989), I: 73.

Genesis 47:31

Genesis 47:31 has "upon the bed's head." Murphy states: "The Septuagint has the rendering ἐπὶ τὸ ἄκρον τῆς ῥάβδου αὐτοῦ, 'on the top of his staff,' which is given in the Epistle to the Hebrews (xi. 21). This is obtained by a mere change in the vowel pointing of the last word."[339]

Calvin writes:

> This is one of those places from which we may conclude that the points were not formerly used by the Hebrews; for the Greek translators could not have made such a mistake as to put staff here for a bed, if the mode of writing was then the same as now. No doubt Moses spoke of the head of his couch, when he said על ראש המטה but the Greek translators rendered the words, "On the top of his staff" as though the last word was written, *mathaeh*.[340]

Homer Kent writes:

> The statement that Jacob worshipped upon the top of his staff is drawn from Genesis 47:31, but employs the wording of the Septuagint, rather than the Massoretic Hebrew text which reads "bed" instead of "staff." The problem arose from the fact that the ancient Hebrew Scriptures were written in a consonantal text, and the addition of vowels to indicate pronunciation (i.e., vowel pointing), such as are found in the present text, was not done until by the Massoretic scholars between the sixth and ninth centuries A.D. It so happens that the consonants for "bed" and "staff" are exactly the same in Hebrew.[341]

Genesis 49:10

For "until Shiloh come," the *English Standard Version* has, "Until tribute comes to him," which it bases on "a slight revocaliza-

---

[339] James G. Murphy, *A Commentary on the Book of Genesis*, vol. 1 of *Barnes' Notes*, Heritage Edition (London: Blackie & Son, 1847, reprinted Grand Rapids: Baker Books, 2005), 499, 500.

[340] Calvin, *The Commentaries on the Epistle of Paul to the Hebrews*, 290.

[341] Kent, *The Epistle to the Hebrews: A Commentary*, 233.

tion,"³⁴² that is, on changing the vowels. The *New Revised Standard Version* also has "until tribute comes to him."

Exodus 2:25

In a comment on this verse, McClintock and Strong state: "In many cases (e.g. Exod. ii, 25; Nahum iii, 8) the Sept. has possibly preserved the true pronunciation and sense where the Masoretic pointing has gone wrong."³⁴³

Leviticus 24:11

In this verse is the account of the man who blasphemed the name of the Lord. On this verse, *The Pulpit Commentary* comments:

> Wherever the Name occurred in Scripture, that of *Adonai*, meaning *Lord*, was substituted for it in public reading, the consonants only of the original name, Y H V H, being preserved in the written text, and the vowels of *Adonai*, namely a o a, being written underneath them in lieu of the original vowels. From the consonants Y H V H and the vowels a o a would be formed Yahovah or Jahovah, but the laws of the Hebrew language required the first *a* to be changed into *e*, and hence the name Jehovah. It is almost certain that the original vowels were *a* and *e*, which would form the name Yahveh.³⁴⁴

If the above comment is correct, then there would be no certainty about the proper pronunciation of the Lord's name.

Deuteronomy 33:27

For "the eternal God is *thy* refuge, and underneath *are* the everlasting arms," the *English Standard Version* has a footnote that

---

³⁴² *The Holy Bible, English Standard Version* (Wheaton, IL: Good News Publishers, 2001), 42.

³⁴³ "Septuagint" in *Cyclopedia*, IX: 542.

³⁴⁴ F. Meyrick, *Leviticus* in vol. 2 of *The Pulpit Commentary*, ed. H. D. M. Spence and Joseph S. Exell (Peabody, MA: Hendrickson Publishers, n.d.), 383.

states: "Revocalization of verse 27 yields *He subdues the ancient gods, and shatters the forces of old.*"[345] The *New Revised Standard Version* follows the reading of the *English Standard Version* footnote.

Joshua 4:24

About the words, "that ye might fear," *The Pulpit Commentary* observes:

> The construction here is unusual. Instead of the imperfect or infinitive with לְמַעַן we have the perfect. Therefore Ewald, Maurer, and Knobel (who says that the second member of the sentence ought to correspond with the first) have altered the pointing in order to bring this passage into conformity with the supposed necessities of grammar.[346]

Altering the pointing would have the result of changing "that ye might fear" to "that ye feared."

I Samuel 1:7

Concerning "and *as* he did so year by year," *The Pulpit Commentary* writes:

> In ver. 7 there is a strange confusion of subject, owing to the first verb having been read as an active instead of a passive. It should be, "And so it happened year by year: when she (Hannah) went up to the house of Jehovah she (Peninnah) thus provoked her, and she wept and did not eat." It must be remembered that the Hebrews had no written vowels, but only consonants; the vowels were added in Christian times, many centuries after the coming of our Lord, and represent the traditional manner of reading of one great Jewish school. They are to be treated with the greatest respect, because as a rule they give us a sense confirmed by the best authorities; but they are human, and form no part of Holy Scripture. The ancient versions, the Septuagint, the Syriac, and the Vulgate, which are all three older than the Masoretic vowels,

---

[345] *English Standard Version*, 177.

[346] J. J. Lias, *Joshua* in vol. 3 of *The Pulpit Commentary*, 65.

translate, "And so she (Peninnah) did year by year;" but this requires a slight change of the consonants.[347]

I Samuel 18:11

Concerning the statement, "Saul cast the javelin," *The Pulpit Commentary* writes: "The Septuagint in the Alexandrian codex and the Chaldee render *lifted, i.e.* retaining the same consonants, they put vowels which refer the verb to another root."[348] This suggestion would change the words, "Saul cast the javelin" to read: "Saul lifted the javelin."

I Samuel 20:14,15

About these two verses, *The Pulpit Commentary* writes:

> The construction of this passage is very difficult if we retain the three negatives of the Masoretic text; but most commentators, following the reading of the Syriac as regards at least one of them, consider that the Masoretes have been mistaken in the vowels which they have attached to the consonants (see on 1 Samuel 1:7). Read with other vowels, two of these negatives become interjections of desire.[349]

I Samuel 20:17

In regard to "and Jonathan caused David to swear again," *The Pulpit Commentary* observes: "The Septuagint and Vulgate, by altering the vowels, read, 'And Jonathan sware again to David'."[350]

---

[347] R. Payne Smith, *I Samuel* in vol. 4 of *The Pulpit Commentary*, 3.

[348] R. Payne Smith, *I Samuel* in vol. 4 of *The Pulpit Commentary*, 341.

[349] Ibid., 378.

[350] Ibid., 378.

II Samuel 24:9

Concerning the numbers in this verse, *eight hundred thousand* and *five hundred thousand*, Youngblood writes: "Most commentators, however, sense that the numbers are inordinately large when interpreted literally. Payne therefore proposes to revocalize *'elep* ('thousand') as *'allup* ('specially trained warrior') in light of their description as 'able-bodied men who could handle a sword'."[351] While Youngblood claims that the change would only involve a revocalization, which is bad enough, it actually also involves the addition of a consonant. *Thousand* is אֶלֶף, whereas *specially trained warrior* is אַלּוּף, which adds a *waw* (ו). For more information about this change involving the addition of a consonant, see the author's footnote on I Kings 20:29.

I Kings 13:12

Concerning "had seen," *The Pulpit Commentary* notes: "Or *showed*. LXX. δεικνύουσιν. Similarly most of the versions. A very slight change in the vowel points וַיַּרְאוּ for וַיִּרְאוּ would give this sense."[352] The *English Standard Version*, the *New International Version*, and the *New Revised Standard Version* all have "showed" in this verse, instead of "had seen." Apparently, these versions are following a change in the vowel points, instead of adhering to the Traditional Text.

---

[351] Ronald F. Youngblood, *1, 2 Samuel* in vol. 3 of *The Expositor's Bible Commentary*, ed. Frank E. Gaebelein (Grand Rapids: Zondervan, 1992), 1099. However, according to Youngblood's suggestion, Joab only numbered 1300 officers, instead of 1,300,000 men. The question then arises, why did it take Joab "nine months and twenty days" (II Samuel 24:8) to number 1300 men? Youngblood suggests, "It is perhaps best to understand *'elep* here in the sense of 'military unit'," but this still does not explain why it would take Joab nearly 300 days to number only 1300 military units. The best course of action is to receive these numbers as correct.

[352] J. Hammond, *I Kings* in vol. 5 of *The Pulpit Commentary*, 295.

I Kings 17:1

I Kings 17:1 reads: "Tishbite . . . inhabitants," about which words Cook comments:

> The two words rendered "Tishbite" and "inhabitant" are in the original (setting aside the vowel points) "exactly alike." The meaning consequently must either be "Elijah the stranger, of the strangers of Gilead," or (more probably) "Elijah the Tishbite, of Tishbi of Gilead."[353]

It is interesting that both the *English Standard Version* and the *New Revised Standard Version* have "Elijah the Tishbite, of Tishbe in Gilead." The *New International Version* is similar with "Elijah the Tishbite, from Tishbe in Gilead."

I Kings 17:4

Concerning "the ravens," Cook writes: "This is the translation of most of the ancient versions; others, omitting the points, which are generally allowed to have no authority, read 'Arabians'."[354]

In regard to the same words, *The Pulpit Commentary* states: "A very slight change in the vowel points — עֲרָבִים instead of עֹרְבִים — yields the meaning 'Arabians'."[355]

Also, Farrar, apparently trying to remove the teaching of the miracle that the ravens fed Elijah, writes:

> But besides all this, the word rendered ravens (*Orebim*, ערבים) only has that meaning if it be written with the vowel points. But the vowel points are confessedly not "inspired" in any sense, but are a late Masoretic invention. Without the change of a letter the word may equally well mean people of the city Orbo, or of the rock Oreb (as was suggested even in the Bereshith Rabba by Rabbi Judah); or "merchants," as in Ezekiel 27:27; or Arabians. No doubt difficulties might be sug-

---

[353] F. C. Cook, ed., *I Samuel to Esther*, abridged and edited by J. M. Fuller in vol. 2 of *Barnes' Notes*, 200.

[354] Ibid., 201.

[355] J. Hammond, *I Kings* in vol. 5 of *The Pulpit Commentary*, 383.

gested about any of these inter*pretations*, *but which would* be most reasonable, the acceptance of such small difficulties, or the literal acceptance of a stupendous miracle, unlike any other in the Bible, by which we are to believe on the isolated authority of a nameless and long subsequent writer, that, for months or weeks together, voracious and unclean birds brought bread and flesh to the Prophet twice a day? The old naturalistic attempts to explain the miracle are on the face of them absurd; but it is as perfectly open to any one who chooses to say that "Arabians," or "Orbites," or "merchants," or "people of the rock Oreb" fed Elijah, as to say that the "ravens" did so.[356]

I Kings 20:29

In regard to "an hundred thousand footmen in one day," Wiseman, in *Tyndale Old Testament Commentaries*, states: "The casualties at *a hundred thousand* may be symbolic of a massive number, for the total Aramean army group at Qarqar was 62,900. However, the 'thousand' (*'elep*) might be revocalized without change of consonants to 'officer' (*'allup*). One hundred casualties a day in ancient warfare was heavy."[357] Wiseman's suggestion would involve a change of vowels and a change in the consonants. While Wiseman claims that the alteration would not involve a change of consonants, yet this is not the case, for אֶלֶף (*thousand*) would be repointed and have a *waw* (ו) added to make אַלּוּף (*leader*).[358]

---

[356] Frederick W. Farrar, *The First Book of Kings*, in vol. 2 of *The Expositor's Bible*, ed. W. Robertson Nicoll (Grand Rapids: Eerdmans, 1947), 303.

[357] Donald J. Wiseman, *1 & 2 Kings*, vol. 9 of *Tyndale Old Testament Commentaries*, ed. D. J. Wiseman (Downers Grove, IL: Inter-Varsity Press, 1993), 178. The number of 62,900 apparently comes from historical records, for the Bible does not mention it. The Bible does state that Benhadad who commanded the opposing army had thirty-two kings in league with him (I Kings 20:1) and that God delivered "all this great multitude into" the hand of the Israelites (I Kings 20:28). It is best to believe the Bible.

[358] In Hebrew ו represents the vowel for u and is composed of a dot in the bosom of the *waw*. The addition of the *waw* is something that would have to be added to the Hebrew consonantal text, therefore, the writer asserts that Wiseman's suggestion would involve the addition of a consonant to the text.

I Kings 20:30

About the number, "twenty and seven thousand," Wiseman, continuing the comment from the above verse, writes: "Similarly the 27,000 killed in Aphek would include everyone in the city when the walls fell. This would remind the Israelites of the victory at Jericho (Jos. 6), otherwise the number might represent twenty-seven officers killed."[359]

I Chronicles 4:10

"By alteration of the vowels of the Masoretic text,"[360] Bennett proposes changing the prayer of Jabez from reading, "And that thou wouldest keep *me* from evil" to read: "To provide pasture."

I Chronicles 7:4

On the number, "six and thirty thousand men," Payne comments:

> For Izrahiah and his four sons, even with "many wives," to have "36,000" warriors seems unlikely, as does the total (vv. 2-5) of 145,600 for just one tribe of the Twelve. This appears to be the first of nine passages in Chronicles (see Appendix B) where *'elep* ("thousand") might better be interpreted as *'allûp* ("chief").[361]

What Payne suggests would result in the repointing as well as the adding of a consonant (*waw*, ו) to the word for *thousand* (אֶלֶף) to make it into the word for *chief* (אַלּוּף), which would change the reading from *six and thirty thousand men* to *six and thirty chiefs*. The other passages wherein Payne, in his Appendix B, suggests this same repointing

---

[359] Wiseman, 178.

[360] W. H. Bennett, *The Books of Chronicles*, in vol. 2 of *The Expositor's Bible*, ed. W. Robertson Nicoll (Grand Rapids: Eerdmans, 1947), 488.

[361] J. Barton Payne, *1, 2 Chronicles* in vol. 4 of *The Expositor's Bible Commentary*, 357. The Appendix B to which this quote makes reference is an appendix in *The Expositor's Bible Commentary*.

are I Chronicles 12:24-37; 27:1-15; II Chronicles 13:3,17; 14:8,9; 17:14-18; 25:5-6; 26:12,13; 28:6,8.[362]

II Chronicles 17:14-18

Concerning the use of *thousand* six times in these verses, Payne writes:

> The king's "experienced fighting men" that he "kept in Jerusalem" (v. 13) involved five groups, that consisted respectively of 300, 280, 200, 200, and 180 specially trained leaders (rendering in each verse, *'allûp*, "leader," rather than *'elep*, "thousand" . . . . The total was thus 1,160 (not 1,160,000).[363]

Again, the suggested change would result in repointing as well as the adding of a consonant (*waw*, ו) to the word for *thousand* (אֶלֶף) to make it into the word for *chief* (אַלּוּף).

Ezra 8:26

Concerning "and silver vessels an hundred talents," the *English Standard Version* has "and silver vessels worth 200 talents," which it bases on a "revocalization."[364]

Job 3:5

About *blackness*, Delitzsch comments:

---

[362] Payne, 562. Concerning II Chronicles 14:9, the *New International Version*, while not using a repointing yet does not give the number of the army. The *King James Version* has "with an host of a thousand thousand," whereas the *New International Version* has "with a vast army."

[363] Ibid., 497.

[364] *English Standard Version*, 395. It is worth noting that on these same words the *New Revised Standard Version* has, "and one hundred silver vessels worth . . . talents." The ellipsis is in this quote is original. It seems that the *New Revised Standard Version* believes that a word or words are missing in Ezra 8:26, thereby revealing its lack of faith in God's promise of Psalm 12:6,7.

Instead of כְּמִרְרֵי (the *Caph* of which seems pointed as *praepos*), we must read with Ewald (§157, a), Olshausen, (§187, b), and others, יְרֵי־כַּמְר, after the form חַכְלִיל, darkness, dark flashing (vid., on Ps 10:8), שַׂפְרִיר, tapestry, unless we are willing to accept a form of noun without example elsewhere.[365]

Job 5:15

Concerning "from the sword, from their mouth," Barnes writes:

> The phrase "from the sword, from their mouth," has been variously interpreted. Dr. Good renders it,
>
>> So he saveth the persecutors from their mouth,
>> And the helpless from the hand of the violent.
>
> Noyes,
>
>> So he saveth the persecuted from their mouth,
>> The oppressed from the hand of the mighty.
>
> This rendering is obtained by changing the points in the word מֵחֶרֶב, *from the sword*, to מָחֳרָב, making it the Hophal participle from חרב, to make desolate. This was proposed by Capellus, and has been adopted by Durell, Michaelis, Dathe, Doederlein, and others.[366]

The changing of the points here would change the reading, "From the sword" to read: "To make desolate."

---

[365] F. Delitzsch, *The Book of Job*, trans. Francis Bolton, in vol. 5 of *Commentary on the Old Testament* (Peabody, MA: Hendrickson Publishers, 1996), 285.

[366] Barnes, *Job*, vol. 1, in vol. 3 of *Barnes' Notes*, 165. The *Capellus* that Barnes mentions is Louis Cappellus one of the early proponents for the novelty of the points (see Chapter One).

Job 6:18

About *paths*, Delitzsch states: "As the text is pointed, אָרְחוֹת, v. 18, are the paths of the torrents. Hitz., Ew., and Schlottm., however, correct אֹרְחוֹת, caravans."[367]

Job 15:23

The Pulpit Commentary, concerning "he wandereth about for bread," observes: " 'He wanders abroad *to be the food of vultures*' is a translation of the passage suggested by some moderns (as Merx), and has the support of the Septuagint, κατατέτακται δὲ εἰς σῖτα γυψίν. But it requires a slight change in the pointing."[368] The *New International Version* seems to follow this change in pointing since it reads: "He wanders about – food for vultures."

Job 21:23

Concerning *at ease*, Delitzsch writes: "In v. 23b the pointing שַׁלְאֲנַן (*adj.*) and שָׁלְאֲנַן (3 *praet.*) are interchanged in the Codd.; the following verbal adjective favours the form of writing with Kametz."[369] However, the form with the Kametz (שָׁלְאֲנַן) is not the form in the Traditional Hebrew text.

Job 21:24

About the words *are full of milk*, Barnes comments: "Many of the versions, however, here render this 'fat.' The change is only in the pointing of the Hebrew word."[370]

---

[367] Delitzsch, *The Book of Job*, in vol. 5 of *Commentary on the Old Testament*, 307.

[368] G. Rawlinson, *Job* in vol. 7 of *The Pulpit Commentary*, 263, 264.

[369] Delitzsch, *The Book of Job*, 468.

[370] Barnes, *Job*, vol. 1, in vol. 3 of *Barnes' Notes*, 356.

Job 24:12

About the word *men* at the beginning of the verse, Fausset writes: "Rather, 'mortals' (not the common Hebrew for 'men'); so the Masoretic vowel points read as the English version (מְתִים). But the vowel points are modern. The true reading is, *The dying* (מֵתִים): answering to 'the wounded' in the next clause."[371] Both the *New International Version* and the *New Revised Standard Version* vote for re-pointing the word as they have *the dying*, instead of *men*.

On the words, "Yet God layeth not folly to *them*," Barnes writes:

> The word rendered *folly* (תִּפְלָה) means folly; and thence also wickedness. If this reading is to be retained, the passage means that God does not lay to heart, that is, does not regard their folly or wickedness. He suffers it to pass without punishing it; compare Acts xvii. 30. But the same word, by a change of the points, (תְּפִלָּה), means *prayer*; and many have supposed that it means, that God does not regard the prayer or cry of those who are thus oppressed. This, in itself, would make good sense, but the former rendering agrees better with the connection.[372]

The *New Revised Standard Version* also sides with the re-pointing as it has *prayer*, instead of *folly*.

Job 27:19

Regarding "but he shall not be gathered," Delitzsch comments:

> Since, therefore, only an unsuitable, and what is more, a badly-expressed thought, is gained by this reading, it may be that the expression should be regarded with Hahn as interrogative: is he not swept away? This, however, is only a makeshift, and therefore we must see whether it may not perhaps be susceptible of another pointing.[373]

---

[371] A. R. Fausset, *Job-Isaiah*, in *A Commentary Critical, Experimental, and Practical on the Old and New Testaments* (Grand Rapids: William B. Eerdmans Publishing Company, 1984), 60.

[372] Barnes, *Job*, vol. 2, in vol. 3 of *Barnes' Notes*, 29.

[373] Delitzsch, *The Book of Job*, 533.

Job 31:18

Concerning "he was brought up with me," Delitzsch states: "The brevity of the form גְּדֵלַנִי, brief to incorrectness, might be removed by the pointing גִּדְּלַנִי (Olsh.): from my youth up he (the fatherless one) honoured me as a father."[374]

Job 36:33

About the word *vapour*, Barnes states:

But with a slight variation in the pointing עַוְלָה — instead of עוֹלֶה, the word means *evil, wickedness, iniquity* — from our word *evil*; Job xxiv. 20; vi. 29; xi. 14; xiii. 7; and it may, without impropriety, be regarded as having this signification here, as the points have no authority.[375]

The *New Revised Standard Version* seems to agree with Barnes that the points are of no authority as it has *iniquity*, instead of *vapour*.

Job 37:23

Regarding "he will not afflict," Barnes comments, "Some manuscripts vary the reading here so as to mean 'he will not answer;' that is, he will not give any account of what he does. The change has relation only to the points, but the above is the usual interpretation, and accords well with the connection."[376]

Job 39:16

About "she is hardened," Delitzsch writes:

The difficulty of הִקְשִׁיחַ (from קָשַׁח, Arab. *qsḥ*, hardened from קָשָׁה, Arab. *qsâ*) being used of the hen-ostrich in the *masc.*, may be removed

---

[374] Ibid., 590.

[375] Barnes, *Job*, vol. 2, in vol. 3 of *Barnes' Notes*, 177.

[376] Ibid., 190.

by the pointing הַקְשִׁיחַ (Ew.); but this alteration is unnecessary, since the Hebr. also uses the *masc.* for the *fem.* where it might be regarded as impossible (vid., v. 3b, and comp. e.g., Isa 32:11f.).[377]

Psalm 2:9

On "thou shalt break," Barnes states:

The Vulgate renders this "thou shalt rule;" the Septuagint, "thou shalt feed" — ποιμανεῖς; that is, thou shalt feed them as a shepherd does his flock; thou shalt exercise over them the care and protection of a shepherd. This rendering occurs by a slight change in the *pointing* of the Hebrew word, though the most approved mode of pointing the word is that which is followed in our common translation.[378]

Concerning these same words, the *English Standard Version* has a footnote that states: "Revocalization yields (compare Septuagint) *You shall rule.*"[379] This is a change that the *New International Version* adopts as it reads: "You will rule."

Psalm 7:11

Concerning the second use of *God* in this verse occurring in the phrase *God is angry with the wicked every day*, Clarke observes: "אֵל el, with the vowel point tsere, signifies GOD: אַל al, the same letters, with the point pathach, signifies not. Several of the versions have read it in this way: 'God judgeth the righteous, and is NOT angry every day'."[380]

---

[377] Delitzsch, *The Book of Job*, 675.

[378] Barnes, *Psalms*, vol. 1 in vol. 5 of *Barnes' Notes*, 22.

[379] *English Standard Version*, 448.

[380] Clarke, *Job Through Song of Solomon*, 463.

Psalm 29:9

Concerning "maketh the hinds to calve," the *English Standard Version* has a footnote that states: "Revocalization yields *makes the oaks to shake.*"[381] The *New Revised Standard Version* follows the revocalization as it reads: "Causes the oaks to whirl" as does the *New International Version*, which reads: "Twists the oaks."

Psalm 33:7

About "as an heap," Maclaren observes: "The old versions and interpreters, followed by Cheyne, read 'as in a bottle' for 'as an heap,' vocalising the text differently from the present pointing."[382] The *New Revised Standard Version* follows the different vocalising as it reads: "As in a bottle." The *New International Version* also deviates from the Traditional Text here as it reads: "Into jars."

Psalm 42:2

Concerning "and appear before God," the *English Standard Version* has a footnote that states: "Revocalization yields *and see the face of God.*"[383] The *New Revised Standard Version* apparently follows the revocalization since it reads: "And behold the face of God."

Psalm 52:5

About "he shall take thee away," which in Hebrew is יַחְתְּךָ, Tomasino reasons:

> In this case its meaning seems to be totally unrelated to the idea of removing coals from the fire, but more generally with the notion of "taking." Since the use of this vb. for something other than coals is

---

[381] *English Standard Version*, 461.

[382] Alexander Maclaren, *The Psalms*, in vol. 3 of *The Expositor's Bible*, ed. W. Robertson Nicoll (Grand Rapids: Eerdmans, 1947), 88.

[383] *English Standard Version*, 469.

unique and unexpected in light of the NE cognates, perhaps the pointing of the vb. should be emended to יְחִיתְכָה, he will destroy you, reading a form of the vb. חָתַת, "to be shattered" (Kraus, 508-9). [384]

Notice that in the above case not only would the points be different, but also there would be an insertion of two extra consonants – a י between the ח and the ת and a ה at the end of the word.

Psalm 58:1

About "sons of men," an *English Standard Version* footnote declares: "Or *mighty lords* (by revocalization)."[385]

Psalm 59:10

Concerning "the God of my mercy shall prevent me," Maclaren comments:

> For himself, he is sure that his God will come to meet him with His lovingkindness, and that, thus met and helped, he will look on, secure, at their ruin. The Hebrew margin proposes to read "The God of my lovingkindness will meet me" — an incomplete sentence, which does not tell with what God will meet him. But the text needs only the change of one vowel point in order to yield the perfectly appropriate reading. "My God shall meet me with His lovingkindness," which is distinctly to be preferred.[386]

Psalm 60:8

Instead of the reading: "Philistia, triumph thou because of me," the *English Standard Version* reads: "Over Philistia I shout in tri-

---

[384] Anthony Tomasino, "חָתָה H3149" in *New International Dictionary of Old Testament Theology and Exegesis*, ed. Willem A. VanGemeren [CD-ROM] (Grand Rapids: Zondervan, 2001).

[385] *English Standard Version*, 477.

[386] Maclaren, 157.

umph," which it bases on a "revocalization."[387] Both the *New Revised Standard Version* and the *New International Version* seemingly follow the revocalization since they both read: "Over Philistia I shout in triumph."

Psalm 69:22

Concerning "a snare before them: and *that which should have been* for *their* welfare, *let it become* a trap"; an *English Standard Version* footnote states: "A slight revocalization yields (compare Septuagint, Syriac, Jerome) *a snare, and retribution and a trap.*"[388] The *New International Version* seems to follow the revocalization as it reads: "A snare; may it become retribution and a trap."

Psalm 109:17

Instead of reading, "So let it come unto him," the *English Standard Version* through a "revocalization"[389] reads: "Let curses come upon him." The *New International Version* agrees with the revocalization since it reads: "Let curses come on him."

Psalm 110:3

Referring to "in the beauties of holiness," Clarke states: "This is a very difficult place, and the rendering of it is so various, so perplexed by the several modes of pointing it, that the difficulty is increased."[390]

---

[387] *English Standard Version*, 478.

[388] Ibid., 483.

[389] Ibid., 508.

[390] Clarke, *Job Through Song of Solomon*, 1306.

Psalm 119:118

Concerning *their deceit*, Hartley observes: "The reading of the MT, 'their deceitfulness is false,' is usually considered a tautology. Thus, many emend MT תַּרְעִיתָם, their deceitful treatment, to תַרְעִיתָם, their thought, based on LXX, Syr, and Jerome."[391]

Psalm 147:17

The last part of Psalm 147:17 says: "Who can stand before his cold," about which Barnes says: "Or, hail. The word is the same, except in pointing, as the preceding word rendered ice."[392]

Proverbs 1:7

Proverbs 1:7 starts with the words, "The fear of the LORD." *LORD* in the Traditional Hebrew Text is יְהֹוָה, that is, *Jehovah*. Steveson gives the word for *LORD* as Yahweh[393] and in so doing is accepting a repointing of the word as if it were pointed יַהְוֶה. Steveson, while upholding many times the Masoretic Text, does not do so in this case. However, his basis for usually upholding the Masoretic Text seems to be rationalistic, for he says, "Where the MT makes sense, there is no need to adopt other readings."[394] Seemingly, it is only if the MT makes sense that Steveson receives it, which is a faulty basis upon which to receive the Traditional Hebrew Text. Should not one receive the text by faith in Jesus' promise (Matthew 5:18)?

---

[391] John E. Hartley, "תַּרְעִית H9569" in *New International Dictionary of Old Testament Theology and Exegesis*.

[392] Barnes, *Psalms*, vol. 3 in vol. 5 of *Barnes' Notes*, 331.

[393] Peter A. Steveson, *A Commentary on Proverbs* (Greenville, SC: BJU Press, 2001), 7.

[394] Ibid., xx.

Proverbs 6:24

About "from the evil woman," an *English Standard Version* footnote states: "Revocalization (compare Septuagint) yields *from the wife of a neighbour*."[395] The *New Revised Standard Version* approves of this revocalization since it reads: "From the wife of another."

Proverbs 10:4

"The Septuagint, with a different pointing, reads, 'Poverty humbleth a man',"[396] instead of *he becometh poor*.

Proverbs 11:23

"The LXX., pointing differently, for 'wrath' reads 'shall perish'."[397]

Proverbs 12:19

The Pulpit Commentary, concerning "the lip of truth shall be established for ever," observes: "Septuagint, 'True lips establish testimony,' pointing the last word *ad* as *ed*."[398]

Proverbs 14:1

The Pulpit Commentary writes: "A different pointing of the word translated 'wise' *(chakhmoth)* will give 'wisdom' *(chokhmoth)*, which it seems best to read here."[399]

---

[395] *English Standard Version*, 531.

[396] W. J. Deane and S. T. Taylor – Taswell, *Proverbs* in vol. 9 of *The Pulpit Commentary*, 195.

[397] Ibid., 217.

[398] Ibid., 237.

[399] Ibid., 268.

Proverbs 21:4

Concerning "the plowing," Cook comments: "The Heb. word, with a change in its vowel-points, may signify either: **(1)** the 'fallow field,' the 'tillage' of xiii. 23, or **(2)** the lamp."[400] The *New American Standard Version*, the *New International Version*, and the *New Revised Standard Version* apparently approve of this change in vowel points, as they all have "the lamp."

Proverbs 23:7

Concerning "for as he thinketh in his heart, so *is* he," "the Septuagint, pointing differently, translates, 'For as if one should swallow a hair, so he eats and drinks'."[401] The *New Revised Standard Version* seems to accept this different pointing since it has "for like a hair in the throat."

Proverbs 25:27

By pointing the word for "their own glory," which in the Traditional Text is כְּבֹדָם as כָּבֵד, Delitzsch renders the last part of this verse, "But as an inquirer to enter on what is difficult is honor,"[402] instead of "so *for men* to search their own glory is *not* glory."

Proverbs 26:23

Instead of "silver dross," the *English Standard Version* "by revocalization"[403] has "glaze," as do the *New Revised Standard Version* and the *New International Version*.

---

[400] F. C. Cook, ed., *Proverbs* in vol.5 of *Barnes' Notes*, 59.

[401] W. J. Deane and S. T. Taylor – Taswell, *Proverbs* in vol. 9 of *The Pulpit Commentary*, 441.

[402] Delitzsch, *Proverbs* in vol. 6 of *Commentary on the Old Testament*, 379.

[403] *English Standard Version*, 548.

Proverbs 29:14

Concerning "his throne shall be established for ever," "the LXX., pointing differently, have [sic], 'His throne shall be established for a testimony' *(lahed*, instead of *lahad)*."[404]

Proverbs 30:1

About *and Ucal* (וְאֻכָל), McClintock and Strong observe that Hitzig "points the last word וָאֵכֶל, and renders, 'and I became dull'."[405] Instead of *and Ucal* at the end of Proverbs 30:1, the *English Standard Version* through a "revocalization"[406] has *and worn out*.

Proverbs 30:1 & 31:1

About the word *prophecy*, Cook writes in a footnote:

> Some have maintained that allusion is here made to a "land" of Massa (Gen. xxv. 14; 1 Chr. i. 30); that its inhabitants were among the "children of the East," whose wisdom had become proverbial (1 K. iv. 30); and that their words were therefore thought worthy of being appended to those of the sage by whom they were surpassed. With the help of some changes in the vowel-points of the original, xxx. 1 is transformed into "Agur, the son of her to whom Massa is obedient," i.e., the queen of Massa; and Proverbs 31:1 appears as "The words of (or "for") Lemuel, king of Massa, which his mother taught him." Agur and Lemuel are thus made out to be brothers, and the queen is made the possessor of a wisdom which places her on a level with the queen of the South, or with the son of David himself. The hypothesis is ingenious rather than satisfying.[407]

---

[404] W. J. Deane and S. T. Taylor – Taswell, *Proverbs* in vol. 9 of *The Pulpit Commentary*, 555.

[405] "Ucal" in *Cyclopedia*, X: 624.

[406] *English Standard Version*, 551.

[407] Cook ed., *Proverbs* in vol. 5 of *Barnes' Notes*, 7.

Ecclesiastes 3:21

Ecclesiastes 3:21 reads: "Who knoweth the spirit of man that goeth upward, and the spirit of the beast that goeth downward to the earth?" On this verse, Cook writes:

> The A. V. of this verse is the only rendering which the Hebrew text, as now pointed, allows. It is in accordance with the best Jewish and many modern interpreters. A slightly different pointing would be requisite to authorize the translation, "Who knows the spirit of the sons of man whether it goes above, and, the spirit of the beast whether it goes down below?" etc., which, though it seems neither necessary nor suitable, is sanctioned by the LXX and other versions and by some modern interpreters.[408]

The *New International Version*, the *New Revised Standard Version*, and the *English Standard Version* evidently follow the different pointing. The *New International Version* has: "Who knows if the spirit of man rises upward and if the spirit of the animal goes down into the earth?" The *New Revised Standard Version* reads: "Who knows whether the human spirit goes upward and the spirit of animals goes downward to the earth?" The *English Standard Version* has: "Who knows whether the spirit of man goes upward and the spirit of the beast goes down into the earth?"

Song of Solomon 1:2

The Pulpit Commentary, concerning "let him kiss me," observes: "Some, as Hitzig and Bottcher, would read יַשְׁקֵנִי, changing the pointing, and translating, 'Let him give me to drink'; but there is no necessity for a reading so forced and vulgar."[409]

---

[408] Cook, ed., *Ecclesiastes* in vol. 5 of *Barnes' Notes*, 97.

[409] R. A. Redford, *Song of Solomon* in vol. 9 of *The Pulpit Commentary*, 2.

Song of Solomon 7:9

On this verse, *The Pulpit Commentary* notes: "Luther strangely renders, 'which to my friend goes smoothly down and speaks of the previous year' (pointing יְשֵׁנִים as יְשָׁנִים)."[410]

Isaiah 1:2

Speaking of *hath spoken* in Isaiah 1:2, which is a Piel perfect third masculine singular, Clarke states: "I render it in the present time, pointing it דבר dober,"[411] that is, to a Qal active participle, *speaking*. The *New American Standard Version* seems to follow the suggestion of Clarke since it has *speaks*.

Isaiah 1:8

About "as a besieged city," Barnes' states:

> *As a besieged city.* כְּעִיר נְצוּרָה. Lowth. 'As a city taken by siege.' Noyes. " 'So is the delivered city.' This translation was first proposed by Arnoldi of Marburg. It avoids the incongruity of comparing a city with a city, and requires no alteration of the text except a change of the vowel points. According to this translation, the meaning will be, that all things round about the city lay desolate."[412]

Isaiah 16:4

Concerning "let mine outcasts dwell with thee, Moab," Barnes writes: "It may be observed, however, that Lowth, by setting the points aside, supposes that this should be read, 'Let the outcasts of Moab sojourn with thee, O Zion.' So Noyes."[413]

---

[410] Ibid., 164.

[411] Clarke, *Isaiah – Malachi*, vol. 4 in *Clarke's Commentary*, 37.

[412] Barnes, *Isaiah*, vol. 1, in vol. 6 of *Barnes' Notes*, 65.

[413] Ibid., 300.

Isaiah 19:10

Isaiah 19:10 reads, "And they shall be broken in the purposes thereof, all that make sluices *and* ponds for fish." On this verse, Barnes writes:

> There has been a great variety of opinion in regard to the interpretation of this verse, and much difficulty in the construction of the Hebrew words. The Vulgate renders it, "And its wet places shall fail; all who make ponds to take fish." The LXX, "And all who make beer (ζῦθον) shall lament, and shall afflict their souls." This ζῦθον was a sort of malt liquor made of fruits by fermentation, and was used in Egypt in the place of wine, since the grape did not flourish there. Jerome on this place says, that this was much used also in Dalmatia and Pannonia, and was commonly called *Sabaium*. The Chaldee renders this, "And the place where they weave cloth shall be trodden down, and the place where they make fish ponds, and where they collect waters, each one for his own life." This variety of reading arises chiefly from the different modes of *pointing* the Hebrew words.[414]

Also in this verse concerning *all that make sluices*, Barnes writes:

> There has been quite as great a variety in the interpretation of this passage as in the former. The word rendered 'sluices' (שֶׂכֶר), our translators understand in the sense of places where the water would be retained for fish ponds — made by artificial banks confining the waters that overflow from the Nile. This sense they have given to the word, as if it were derived from שָׂכַר (sâkhăr), *to shut up, to enclose*. The LXX reads it as if it meant the Hebrew שֵׁכָר (shēkhâr), or strong drink; and so also the Syriac renders it — as if from שָׁכַר (shâkhăr), *to drink*. There is no doubt that by a difference of pointing it may have this signification.[415]

Isaiah 21:13

Barnes comments on *in Arabia*:

---

[414] Ibid., 334.

[415] Ibid.

213

The LXX, the Vulgate, and the Chaldee, understand this of the *evening* — 'In the evening.' The word עֶרֶב, with different points from those which the Masoretes have used here, means *evening*, but there is no necessity of departing from the translation in our English version.[416]

Isaiah 27:7

Concerning "them that are slain by him," *The Pulpit Commentary* writes: "Rather, *them that slew him* (so Lowth, Ewald, Knobel, and Mr. Cheyne). But, to obtain this meaning, the pointing of the present text must be altered. The law of parallelism seems, however, to require the alteration."[417]

Isaiah 30:8

Of the words "for ever and ever," *The Pulpit Commentary* states: "Modern critics observe that the phrase, *lâ'ad 'ad 'olâm*, never occurs elsewhere, and suggest a change of the pointing, which would give the sense of 'for a testimony forever'."[418] Several versions seem to follow this change of the pointing. The *New American Standard Version*, the *New Revised Standard Version*, and the *English Standard Version* all have "as a witness forever." The *New International Version* has "an everlasting witness."

Isaiah 40:6

Instead of "and he said," the *English Standard Version* through "revocalization based on Dead Sea Scroll, Septuagint, [and] Vulgate"[419] has "and I said." Both the *New Revised Standard Version* and the *New International Version* both follow suit.

---

[416] Ibid., 358.

[417] G. Rawlinson, *Isaiah*, vol. 1, in vol. 10 of *The Pulpit Commentary*, 434.

[418] Ibid., 490.

[419] *English Standard Version*, 599.

Isaiah 62:5

Concerning "thy sons," Fausset writes: "*Lowth* prefers changing the points, which are of no authority in Hebrew: 'thy builder' or 'restorer' (*Bonaik* for *Banaik*. The plural form, 'thy *builders*,' is used of God, to express *His infinite fulness*, as Hebrew in Isa. liv. 5, 'thy Maker is thy *Husbands*'), i.e., God."[420] Concerning the same words, Barnes writes:

> Lowth renders this, "So shall thy restorer wed thee." He supposes that the word rendered in our common version, "thy sons" (בָּנָיִךְ), should be pointed בֹּנַיִךְ, as a participle from בָּנָה, "to build," rather than from בֵּן, "a son." The parallelism requires some such construction as this; and the unusual form of expression, "*thy sons* shall be wedded to thee," seems also to demand it. The LXX renders it, "As a young man cohabits (συνοικῶν) with a virgin (bride) (παρθένῳ), so shall thy sons dwell with thee (κατοικήσουσιν οἱ υἱοί σου)." So the Chaldee. . . . To me it seems that there is much force in the conjecture of Lowth, and that the reference is to God as the "builder," or the restorer of Jerusalem, and that the sense is that he would be "married," or tenderly and indissolubly united to her. If it be objected that the word is in the plural בֹּנַיִךְ it may be observed that the word commonly applied to God (אֱלֹהִים) is also plural, and that an expression remarkably similar to the one before us occurs in Isaiah 54:5, "For thy Maker is thy husband" (Hebrew, בֹעֲלַיִךְ, "Thy husbands.") It is not uncommon to use a plural noun when speaking of God. It should be remembered that the points in the Hebrew are of no authority, and that all the change demanded here is in them.[421]

The *New Revised Standard Version* seemingly also thinks that the points are of no authority as it has "your builder."

---

[420] Fausset, *Job-Isaiah* in *A Commentary Critical, Experimental, and Practical*, 754.

[421] Barnes, *Isaiah*, vol. 2, in vol. 6 of *Barnes' Notes*, 382.

Jeremiah 2:16

About "have broken," *The Pulpit Commentary* states: "Rather, *shall brea*k, or (for the pointing in the Hebrew Bible requires this change) *shall feed off* (or *depasture*)."[422]

Jeremiah 8:13

Concerning "and *the things that* I have given them shall pass away from them," *The Pulpit Commentary* comments: "The construction, however, which this rendering implies is not perfectly natural, though supported by most of the ancient versions (except the Septuagint, which omits the words), and it is better to alter a single vowel-point, and render 'And I will give them to those who shall pass over them'."[423]

Jeremiah 10:18

On "that they may find *it so*," *The Pulpit Commentary* observes: "The Vulgate apparently reads the text with different vowels, for it renders *ut inveniantur* [i. e., that they may be found]; the Septuagint has 'that thy stroke may be found'."[424] The *New American Standard Version* seems to have used different vowels for it has "that they may be found."

Jeremiah 15:19

The Pulpit Commentary on "then will I bring thee again" comments: "Viz. into the right relation to me, so as to be my minister (Keil). But by altering one of the vowel-points (which form no part of

---

[422] T. K. Cheyne, *Jeremiah*, vol. 1, in vol. 11 of *The Pulpit Commentary*, 24.

[423] Ibid., 215.

[424] Ibid., 270.

the text), on the authority of the Septuagint, we get a more satisfactory sense, *I will give thee a settled place.*"[425]

Jeremiah 23:17

The Pulpit Commentary, in regard to "unto them that despise me, The LORD hath said," declares:

> The Septuagint and the Syriac render the same text (the consonants are alone the text) with different vowels, thus: "Unto those who despise the word of the Lord." In favor of this it may be urged that the phrase, "The Lord hath said," is nowhere else used in this abrupt way to introduce a real or supposed revelation, and Hitzig and Graf accordingly accept it.[426]

Both the *English Standard Version* and the *New Revised Standard Version* evidently use different vowels for both have "to those who despise the word of the LORD."

Jeremiah 25:24

About "mingled people," Fausset writes: "By a different pointing it may be *translated* the *Arabs.*"[427]

Jeremiah 48:4

The Pulpit Commentary, on "her little ones," comments: "The received text, as it stands, is untranslatable, and our choice lies between the correction suggested by the vowel points, and the reading of the Septuagint and a few of the extant Hebrew manuscripts, 'unto Zoar'."[428]

---

[425] Ibid., 376.

[426] Ibid., 515.

[427] Fausset, *Jeremiah-Malachi* in *A Commentary Critical, Experimental, and Practical*, 87.

[428] T. K. Cheyne, *Jeremiah*, vol. 2, in vol. 11 of *The Pulpit Commentary*, 227.

Jeremiah 48:15

The Pulpit Commentary, concerning "Moab is spoiled, and gone up *out of* her cities," writes:

> The latter part of this clause in the Hebrew is extremely difficult; the Authorized Version is indefensible. It is even doubtful whether it can be translated at all consistently with grammar, though Hitzig, a good grammarian, has adopted the suggestion of Grotius, rendering, "and her cities have gone up," viz. *in smoke, i.e.* they have been burnt; comp. Judges 20:40, the end of which verse ought to run thus: "The whole city went up to heaven." But even if the verb in third masc. sing. be allowable after the plural noun, it is very harsh to give it such an interpretation, when the context says nothing about fire or smoke. J. D. Michaelis and Ewald, therefore, propose to change the vowel points of the first word, rendering, "The spoiler of Moab and of her cities is gone up;" and Dr. Payne Smith inclines to follow them. We thus obtain a striking antithesis; the enemy has "gone up," and Moab's young men **are gone down,** *i.e. are* felled by murderous hands (comp. Isa. xxxiv. 7).[429]

Both the *New Revised Standard Version* and the *English Standard Version* apparently adopt a change of vowel points here. The *New Revised Standard Version* reads: "The destroyer of Moab and his towns has come up." The *English Standard Version* has "the destroyer of Moab and his cities has come up."

Jeremiah 48:18

About "sit in thirst," *The Pulpit Commentary* states: "The expression is unexampled, and it is possible that we should alter one of the vowel points (which constitute no part of the Masoretic text), rendering, 'sit in thirsty (ground),' *i.e.* the dust (comp. the parallel passage, Isa. xlvii. 1)."[430] The *New American Standard Version*, the *New Revised Standard Version*, the *New International Version*, and the

---

[429] Ibid., 229.

[430] Ibid.

English Standard Version all have "sit on the parched ground," thereby siding with the view that the vowel points are inconsequential.

Jeremiah 49:1

Concerning "their king," Cheyne in *The Pulpit Commentary* writes: "The Septuagint, the Syriac, and the Vulgate, however, read *Milcom,* which was the name of the Ammonite deity; this is only a different vocalizing of the consonants of the text."[431] The *New King James Version*, the *New Revised Standard Version*, and the *English Standard Version* all have "Milcom," thereby favoring the different vocalizing.

Jeremiah 50:38

Concerning "a drought," Fausset comments: "Altering the pointing, this verse will begin as the three previous verses (חֶרֶב). 'A sword'."[432]

Jeremiah 51:3

About "against *him that* bendeth let the archer bend his bow," Fausset declares: "The Chaldean version and *Jerome*, by changing the vowel points, read (אַל, instead of אֶל), 'Let *not* him (the *Babylonian*) who bendeth his bow bend it.'"[433] Several modern versions also seem to follow a change of vowel points in this verse. The *New American Standard Version* has: "Let not him who bends his bow bend *it*." The *New Revised Standard Version* and the *English Standard Version* read:

---

[431] Ibid., 247.

[432] Fausset, *Jeremiah-Malachi* in *A Commentary Critical, Experimental, and Practical*, 172.

[433] Ibid., 174,175.

"Let not the archer bend his bow." The *New International Version* has "let not the archer string his bow."

Ezekiel 8:2

Instead of "the appearance of fire," the *English Standard Version* "by revocalization"[434] has "the appearance of a man." The *New American Standard Version*, the *New Revised Standard Version*, and the *New International Version* all favor the revocalization for they have respectively "the appearance of a man," "that looked like a human being," and "a figure like that of a man."

Ezekiel 16:30

Concerning "how weak is thine heart," the *English Standard Version* has a footnote that states: "Revocalization yields *How I am filled with anger against you.*"[435]

Ezekiel 23:4

Concerning *Aholah* and *Aholibah*, John Skinner writes: "It is not certain what is the exact meaning wrapped up in these designations. A very slight change in the pointing of the Hebrew would give the sense '*her* tent' for Ohola and '*my* tent in her' for Oholibah. This is the interpretation adopted by most commentators."[436]

Ezekiel 31:14

Fairbairn rejects the King James translation, "Neither their trees stand up in their height, all that drink water," and replaces it with

---

[434] *English Standard Version*, 696.

[435] Ibid., 703.

[436] John Skinner, *The Book of Ezekiel*, in vol. 4 of *The Expositor's Bible*, ed. W. Robertson Nicoll (Grand Rapids: Wm. B. Eerdmans Publishing Co., 1947), 269.

"and that no drinkers of water may stand upon their own greatness," which he bases on a repointing of אֵלֵיהֶם (their trees) to אֲלֵיהֶם (upon them).[437]

Ezekiel 34:3

Concerning *the fat*, Fausset says: "Ye eat the fat (הַחֵלֶב) – or, by differently pointing the Hebrew, 'milk' (הֶחָלָב): so the LXX."[438] The *New International Version* seems to favor the different pointing as it has "the curds."

Ezekiel 36:5

On the last words of this verse, "to cast it out for a prey," Fairbairn comments:

> The common rendering of this latter clause is, "that it may be cast forth as a prey." But this is a very unnatural expression to be used of a land. Therefore taking מִגְרָשָׁהּ, not as an Aramaic inf., but as the substantive, and changing thus the pointing of לָבַז [this is what he suggests for the new pointing, the pointing in the Traditional Text is לְבַז], so as to make it the inf. instead of the noun, we have the sense: in order to plunder its pasturage; a quite suitable meaning.[439]

The *New King James Version*, the *New Revised Standard Version*, and the *New International Version* all seem to favor Fairbairn's suggestion as they have respectively "in order to plunder its open country," "because of its pasture, to plunder it," and "so that they might plunder its pastureland."

---

[437] Patrick Fairbairn, *Commentary on Ezekiel* (Grand Rapids: Kregel Publications, 1989), 350.

[438] Fausset, *Jeremiah-Malachi* in *A Commentary Critical, Experimental, and Practical*, 332.

[439] Fairbairn, *Commentary on Ezekiel*, 395, 396.

Ezekiel 39:26

About "they have borne," Wakely writes: "It is preferable to retain the pointing of MT וְנָשׂוּ, and they will take upon themselves, rather than accept the emendation וְנָשׁוּ, and they will forget. The bestowal of mercy is not a call to blind forgetfulness but to careful, remorseful remembrance."[440] Though Wakely argues for the retention of the reading in the Traditional Text, several modern versions accept an emendation of the text. The *New American Standard Version* has "and they shall forget." The *New Revised Standard Version* and the *English Standard Version* both have "they shall forget." The *New International Version* has "they will forget."

Daniel 7:4

Concerning "eagle's wings," Thomson in *The Pulpit Commentary* states: "It may be objected that the 'eagle's wings,' גַפִּין *(gappeen)*, are in the dual. Yet the number two is not mentioned. That the word was in the dual in the pre-Masoretic text does not appear from the versions, so the correctness of the dual pointing may be doubted."[441] The reader should note that גַפִּין is the dual form in the Aramaic. Since eagles have two wings, the translation *eagle's wings* is perfectly acceptable. What is not acceptable is Thomson's attitude toward the pointing.

Daniel 9:27

In regard to "and for the overspreading of abominations he shall make *it* desolate," Barnes states:

> The Masoretic pointing, also, may be disregarded, and then the real idea would be better expressed by some such translation as the fol-

---

[440] Robin Wakely, "מַעַל H5085" in *New International Dictionary of Old Testament Theology and Exegesis*.

[441] J E. H. Thomson, *Daniel* in vol. 13 of *The Pulpit Commentary*, 208.

lowing: "He shall cause the sacrifice and the offering to cease. And — upon the wing — the porch of the temple — abominations! And a desolator!"[442]

The *New International Version* seems to disregard the Masoretic pointing for it reads: "He will put an end to sacrifice and offering. And on a wing *of the temple* he will set up an abomination that causes desolation."

Daniel 11:6

Concerning "and he that begat her," Barnes writes:

> Margin, "or, *whom she brought forth.*" The margin expresses the sense more correctly. . . . According to the present pointing, indeed, the literal meaning would be, "and he who begat her;" but this pointing is not authoritative. Dathe, Bertholdt, Dereser, DeWette, and Rosenmuller suppose that the reading should be וְהַיַלְדָּה. Then the sense would be, "her child," or "her offspring."[443]

The *New Revised Standard Version* apparently agrees with Barnes that the pointing is not authoritative as it has "and her child."

Hosea 13:7

On "will I observe," Fausset observes: "Several manuscripts, the LXX, *Vulgate, Syriac,* and *Arabic* read, by a slight change of the *Hebrew* vowel pointing, 'by the way *of Assyria*' (אַשּׁוּר [Assyria], for אָשׁוּר [I will observe]) a region abounding in leopards and lions. The English Version is better."[444]

---

[442] Barnes, *Daniel,* vol. 1, in vol. 7 of *Barnes' Notes,* 188.

[443] Ibid., 214. The pointing in the Traditional Text is הְיִלְדָהּ.

[444] Fausset, *Jeremiah-Malachi* in *A Commentary Critical, Experimental, and Practical,* 504.

Joel 1:18,19

Concerning these two verses, Smith notes: "The two verses generally held to be historic, 18 and 19, Merx takes to be the continuation of the prayer of the priests, pointing the verbs so as to turn them from perfects into futures."[445]

Obadiah 3

About "hath deceived," Deane notes: "Septuagint, ἐπῆρε, 'elated'; Vulgate, *extulit* [i.e., it is carrying out]. The pointing varies."[446]

Micah 2:7

About "is the spirit of the LORD straitened," *The Pulpit Commentary* observes: "Professor Driver (*Expositor,* April, 1887) obtains the very suitable meaning, *Num dicendum,* 'Shall it be said, O house of Jacob, Is the ear of the Lord shortened?' etc., by the change of a vowel point. Somewhat similarly Orelli, 'Is this the speech of the house of Jacob?'"[447]

Micah 6:9

Concerning "shall see thy name," Deane in *The Pulpit Commentary* observes:

> The versions read "fear" for "see." Thus the LXX., Σώσει φοβουμένους τὸ ὄνομα αὐτοῦ, "Shall save those that fear his Name;" Vulgate, *Salus erit timentibus Nomen tuum* [i.e., salvation shall be to the one fearing thy Name]; Syriac, "He imparts instruction to those that fear his Name;" Chaldee, "The teachers fear his Name." This

---

[445] George Adam Smith, *The Book of the Twelve Prophets* in vol. 4 of *The Expositor's Bible*, 656.

[446] W. J. Deane, *Obadiah* in vol. 14 of *The Pulpit Commentary*, 1.

[447] W. J. Deane, *Micah* in vol. 14 of *The Pulpit Commentary*, 18.

reading depends upon a change of vowel pointing. Orelli renders, "Happy is he who fears thy Name."[448]

The *New American Standard Version*, the *New Revised Standard Version*, the *New International Version*, and the *English Standard Version* all have "fear," thereby indicating that they are relying on a change of vowel pointing.

Micah 6:11

Concerning "shall I count *them* pure," which is a translation of הַאֶזְכֶּה, a Qal imperfect first common singular with interrogative particle from זָכָה, Averbeck observes: "The NIV follows the pi., 'Shall I acquit (זָכָה) a man with dishonest scales, with a bag of false weights?'"[449] The *English Standard Version* also has "shall I acquit."

Nahum 3:8

In a comment on this verse, McClintock and Strong state: "In many cases (e.g. Exod. ii, 25; Nahum iii, 8) the Sept. has possibly preserved the true pronunciation and sense where the Masoretic pointing has gone wrong."[450]

Habakkuk 1:8

About "evening wolves," Deane observes: "Septuagint (with a different pointing), 'wolves of Arabia'."[451]

---

[448] Ibid., 88.

[449] Richard E. Averbeck, "זָכָה H2342" in *New International Dictionary of Old Testament Theology and Exegesis*. In the quote, Averbeck gives the root for *shall I acquit*, instead of the Piel form of the verb. The Piel form of the verb with interrogative particle is הַאֲזַכֶּה.

[450] "Septuagint" in *Cyclopedia*, IX: 542.

[451] W. J. Deane, *Habakkuk* in vol. 14 of *The Pulpit Commentary*, 2.

Zephaniah 3:8

Concerning "until the day that I rise up to the prey," *The Pulpit Commentary* notes: "The LXX., pointing the last word differently (עֵד), renders, εἰς ἡμέραν ἀναστάσεώς μου εἰς μαρτύριον: 'until the day of my rising up for testimony'."[452] Both the *New Revised Standard Version* and the *New International Version* favor pointing the last word differently as they respectively have "for the day when I arise as a witness" and "for the day I will stand up to testify."

Haggai 1:11

Concerning "I called for a drought," *The Pulpit Commentary* writes: "The Lord punished them with 'drought' (*choreb*). The Septuagint and Syriac, pointing differently, translate this last word "sword," but this is not suitable for the context, which speaks of the sterility of the land only."[453]

Zechariah 9:8

About "because of the army," Deane observes in *The Pulpit Commentary*: "It may also be translated 'against,' or 'from'; *i.e.* to defend it from the hostile army. Others, pointing differently, render, 'as a garrison,' or 'rampart'."[454] It seems that the *New Revised Standard Version* and the *English Standard Version* point it differently for they both have "as a guard."

Malachi 2:3

About "I will corrupt your seed," Deane writes:

---

[452] W. J. Deane, *Zephaniah*, in vol. 14 of *The Pulpit Commentary*, 50.

[453] W. J. Deane, *Haggai*, in vol. 14 of *The Pulpit Commentary*, 3.

[454] W. J. Deane, *Zechariah* in vol. 14 of *The Pulpit Commentary*, 91.

God would mar the promise of their crops; but, as the priests did not concern themselves with agriculture, such a threat would have had no particular application to them. It is best, therefore, to take the pointing of some of the versions, and to translate, *I will rebuke your arm;* i.e. I will take from you the power of performing, or, I will neutralize your official duties, the arm being the instrument of labour, offering, and blessing.[455]

Conclusion

The comments of the commentators concern Genesis 10:6; 47:31; 49:10; Exodus 2:25; Leviticus 24:11; Deuteronomy 33:27; Joshua 4:24; I Samuel 1:7; 18:11; 20:14,15,17; II Samuel 24:9; I Kings 13:12; 17:1,4; 20:29,30; I Chronicles 4:10; 7:4; 12:24-37; 27:1-15; II Chronicles 13:3,17; 14:8,9; 17:14-18; 25:5-6; 26:12,13; 28:6,8; Ezra 8:26; Job 3:5,6; 5:15; 6:18; 15:23; 21:23,24; 24:12; 27:19; 31:18; 36:33; 37:23; 39:16; Psalm 2:9; 7:11; 29:9; 33:7; 42:2; 52:5; 58:1; 59:10; 60:8; 69:22; 109:17; 110:3; 119:118; 147:17; Proverbs 1:7; 6:24; 10:4; 11:23; 12:19; 14:1; 21:4; 23:7; 25:27; 26:23; 29:14; 30:1; 31:1; Ecclesiastes 3:21; Song of Solomon 1:2; 7:9; Isaiah 1:2,8; 16:4; 19:10; 21:13; 27:7; 30:8; 40:6; 62:5; Jeremiah 2:16; 8:13; 10:18; 15:19; 23:17; 25:24; 48:4,15,18; 49:1; 50:38; 51:3; Ezekiel 8:2; 16:30; 23:4; 31:14; 34:3; 36:5; 39:26; Daniel 7:4; 9:27; 11:6; Hosea 13:7; Joel 1:18,19; Obadiah 3; Micah 2:7; 6:9,11; Nahum 3:8; Habakkuk 1:8; Zephaniah 3:8; Haggai 1:11; Zechariah 9:8; and Malachi 2:3. The total is one hundred fifty two (152) verses. Six (6) of the verses are from the law (Genesis to Deuteronomy); fifty-three (53) from the prophets (Joshua to II Kings, Isaiah, Jeremiah, Ezekiel, and the Minor Prophets), and ninety-three (93) from the writings (I Chronicles to Song of Solomon, Lamentations, and Daniel), covering thirty of the thirty-nine books of the Old Testament. Though the number of verses involved in

---

[455] W. J. Deane, *Malachi* in vol. 14 of *The Pulpit Commentary*, 19. Deane understands *seed* to refer to agricultural seed, but it could as well refer to human seed, that is, to their offspring.

changes to the vowel points may seem like a lot, one should not think that these are the only verses that have words that commentators and others question. Further research of other commentaries would reveal many more.

THE COMMENTS OF THE AUTHOR

In addition to comments the author has already made in the previous section, he now presents other comments. If one were to follow the comments of the commentators, then the Bible would be full of uncertainty, ambiguity, and malignancy. It would also result in the one adopting the views of the commentators to be thinking rationalistically and unbelievingly.

Uncertainty

The above examples demonstrate that without inspired vowel points, the Word of God becomes extremely uncertain. As one clear example of the uncertainty that would reign in the Word of God without inspired points, consider Clarke's comment on Psalm 7:11. With the vowels in the present Traditional Text, Psalm 7:11 reads, "God is angry *with the wicked* every day." Clarke reveals that a changing of the vowel pointing for *God* produces the word *not* and results in the verse teaching the very opposite, that is, that God is not angry every day.[456] These are two completely opposite teachings. How contrary this is to the teaching that in Christ, Who is the Word of God (Revelation 19:13), is not yea and nay, but yea (II Corinthians 1:19).

All of the examples demonstrate that if the points are not inspired, then uncertainty abounds concerning the Words of God,. The fact is that without the pointing no one knows exactly what the word-

---

[456] Clarke, *Job Through Song of Solomon*, 463.

ing should be. And with uncertainty concerning the Words of God, of what authority are those Words? Indeed, they would have very little, if any, authority. Chapter Two of this work demonstrates that with the Word of God being the sole authority for faith and practice, there must be certainty about its Words. Furthermore, Chapters Four and Five present promises and statements about the Old Testament that make it clear that the Old Testament text is absolutely certain, which demands the presence of the vowel points. Whom will one believe, the conjectures of the commentators, the theories of the translators, or the sure promises of God Almighty?

Ambiguity

The examples in this chapter also serve to demonstrate that without vowel points the Old Testament would be full of ambiguity. While ambiguity is synonymous with uncertainty, the author gives a separate heading to discuss ambiguity because *ambiguity* is the word that Walton uses when he claims that without the points there is no ambiguity.[457] But without the points, as the examples in this chapter demonstrate, ambiguity would reign, for there would be no conclusive way of determining the correct reading in these verses: not even the context can decide the correct reading. Such ambiguity would be the Devil's delight for he is the one who first asked, "Yea, hath God said?" (Genesis 3:1).

Malignancy

This chapter's examples further demonstrate that without the points a malignancy, that is, a disease that threatens health, would permeate Scripture, casting down a word here and a word there, robbing Scripture of its ability to give (I Peter 1:23) and to maintain life

---

[457] Walton, *The Considerator Considered*, 215. The introduction to this chapter gives the full quote from Walton.

(Matthew 4:4). Also, this malignancy would perpetuate itself throughout Scripture, infecting and destroying many other words.

Permeates

If there are no points, then a malignancy permeates the Old Testament. As the author demonstrates in his conclusion to the comments of the commentators, the repointing of words comes from a great variety of places. These repointed words are not just from one book, but from all over the Old Testament. Indeed, it seems that no portion of Scripture is exempt from those who might want to find different words by changing the points. It is clear that no portion of the Old Testament is safe from such tampering.

Perpetuates

Once one allows for uninspired vowel points, then seemingly nothing would be safe. The examples of repointing could easily perpetuate themselves to thousands of other verses, verbs, and even consonants.

To Other Verses

To demonstrate that the examples presented in this chapter could perpetuate themselves to thousands of other verses, consider the Hebrew words for *LORD*, *thousand*, and *milk*.

LORD

The Hebrew word for *LORD* according to the Masoretic Text is יְהֹוָה (*Jehovah*), but there are those who repoint this to יַהְוֶה (*Yahweh*). See, for instance, the comments of the commentators under Leviticus 24:11 and Proverbs 1:7. Some may not think that repointing יְהֹוָה (*Jehovah*) is a very serious matter, but in light of the fact that the Lord commands that people are not to take His name in vain (Exodus 20:7), to call upon His name (I Chronicles 16:8), to give the glory due unto His name (I Chronicles 16:29), to exalt His name (Psalm 34:3), to sing forth the honour of His name (Psalm 66:2), to sing praises to His name (Psalm 68:4), to bless His name (Psalm 96:2), and to praise His name (Psalm 149:3); then the name of the Lord is very important. If one were to repoint יְהֹוָה (*Jehovah*) as יַהְוֶה (*Yahweh*), then it would affect five thousand five hundred twenty one (5,521) verses in which *Jehovah* occurs six thousand five hundred nineteen (6,519) times! This should demonstrate that once one starts to repoint words, it, like leaven in bread, will permeate every nook and cranny of Scripture.

Thousand

A couple of commentators suggest changing the pointing of the word אֶלֶף (*thousand*) to אַלּוּף (*leader*),[458] which would involve revocalization and a change in consonants since the Hebrew word for *leader* adds a *waw* (ו) to the word for *thousand*. The verses where the commentators suggest such a change are I Kings 20:29, 30; I Chronicles 7:4; 12:24, 25, 26, 27, 29, 30, 31, 33, 34, 35, 36, 37; 27:1, 2, 4, 5, 7, 8, 9, 10, 11, 12, 13, 14, 15; II Chronicles 13:3, 17; 14:8, 9; 17:14, 15, 16, 17, 18; 25:5, 6; 26:12, 13; 28:6, 8. The total is forty-three (43) verses.

The adding of a consonant illustrates that the malignancy would spread to consonants as well, but more on that later. For right now, consider this: if one were to apply the suggestion of these commentators to other passages where the word for *thousand* refers to people, then this could involve a number of other verses such as Joshua 4:13; 8:3; Judges 5:8; 8:10; 15:15, 16; 20:2, 15, 17, 21, 25, 44, 46; 21:10; I Samuel 4:10; 6:19; 11:8; 13:5; 15:4; II Samuel 8:4, 5; 10:6, 18; 17:1; 24:15; I Kings 5:13; 10:26; 12:21; II Kings 24:16; I Chronicles 5:21; 18:4, 5; 19:18; 21:5, 14; II Chronicles 11:1; 13:3, 17; 14:8, 9; 25:5, 6; 26:13; 28:6, 8. Following the suggestion of the commenta-

---

[458] See Youngblood's comment on II Samuel 24:9, Wiseman's comment on I Kings 20:29, as well as on I Kings 20:30; and Payne's comment on I Chronicles 7:4 and II Chronicles 17:14-18 earlier in this chapter.

tors would involve at least forty-five (45) verses, in which it would be difficult to decide from the context if the reading should be *thousand* or *leader*. Add the forty-five (45) verses to the forty-three (43) verses from the previous paragraph where commentators do suggest a change from *thousand* to *leader*, then the total amount of verses infected would be eighty-eight (88). Though eighty-eight verses is not nearly as many as would be affected if one were to repoint the word for *LORD*; it is still a significant number of verses and demonstrates how the malignancy of changing the vowels can perpetuate itself. The malignancy would spread from the forty-three (43) that the commentators mention to another forty-five (45) verses.

Milk or Fat

Some suggest a repointing of *milk* (חָלָב) to get the word *fat* (חֵלֶב), such as Barnes on Job 21:24; or of repointing *fat* to *milk* as does Fausset on Ezekiel 34:3. Both of these words have the same consonants, but different vowels. The word for *milk* occurs in forty-four (44) verses. If the points are not inspired, then in five verses (Exodus 23:19; 34:26; Deuteronomy 14:21; Job 10:10; 21:24) one would not be able to decide if the word should be *milk* or *fat*. This is assuming that one could discern in an unpointed text what words should be in the context. If one could, then there would be five (5) instances where even the context could not decide between *milk* and *fat*. The word for *fat* occurs ninety-three times in seventy verses. If the points are not inspired, then in three (3) verses (Genesis 45:18; Psalm 63:6; Ezekiel 34:3) one would not be able to decide if the word should be *fat* or *milk* or *curds* as the *New International Version* has in Ezekiel 34:3. In all, eight (8) verses are involved in this discussion about whether the word should be *milk* or *fat*. The commentators mention two of these verses, yet, if their contention is true that the points are not inspired, then the lack of certainty about the reading being *milk* or *fat* would spread to six other verses. The malignancy would perpetuate itself to other verses.

Now one may ask, "What difference does this make, whether it is *milk* or *fat?*" Three of the passages involve commands of God (Exodus 23:19; 34:26; Deuteronomy 14:21) about not seething a kid in his mother's milk. However, if there are no points, then how would one have known how to please God in the matter of handling a kid? Furthermore, all of God's Words are important, even the ones that men might consider insignificant, for God stated that His Words are pure Words and that He will preserve them (Psalm 12:6,7). If there is uncertainty as to whether a reading should be *milk* or *fat*, then God has not kept His promise. And if God did not keep His promise, then serious theological implications arise.

Summary

Repointing just the three words *Lord, thousand,* and *milk* could affect over five thousand six hundred (5,600) verses of the Old Testament! But this may be just scratching the surface, for this section only examined three words. The commentators suggest that many more words could or should be repointed, which, if extrapolated would involve many more verses. Also, the author has not examined the comments of all commentators, translators, and writers of the Old Testament. No doubt, such a search would turn up many more words that the critics want to repoint, with the result that these words would affect other verses. It is clear that one cannot tamper with even one single word in the Bible without it affecting some other part or teaching of the Bible.

To Other Verbs

The malignancy present in the comments of the commentators involves verbs and the malignancy could easily perpetuate itself to many other verbs throughout the Old Testament. Many of the examples listed under the comments of the commentators suggest a change of pointing in verbs. For instance, *The Pulpit Commentary* on Joshua 4:24 notes that some suggest a repointing of a verb to change it from the perfect to some other form. Clarke repoints a verb in Isaiah 1:2 to change it from a Piel perfect to a Qal active participle, a change that the *New American Standard Version* also follows. The *English Standard Version*, the *New International Version*, and the *New Revised Version* suggest a change in a verb in Isaiah 40:6. Fairbairn in Ezekiel 36:5 repoints an infinitive to make it a substantive, a change that the *New King James Version*, the *New Revised Standard Version*, and the *New International Version* also follow. Wakely notes that some suggest a change in the pointing of a verb in Ezekiel 39:26, a change that the *New American Standard Version*, the *English Standard Version*, the *New International Version*, and the *New Revised Standard Version* perpetuate. Smith on Joel 1:18,19 writes of one who changes the pointing to change the verbs from perfects into futures. Averbeck on Micah 6:11 observes that the *New International Version* repoints a verb from a Qal to a Piel. The English Standard Version also agrees with this change. Deane suggests changing the pointing of a verb in Malachi 2:3. *The Pulpit Commentary* notes changes in verbs by repointing in I Samuel 20:17; I Kings 13:12[459]; Song of Solomon 1:2; Isaiah 27:7; Jeremiah 2:16; 8:13; 10:18[460]; 15:19; and Micah 6:9.[461] Barnes suggests or notes repointing verbs in order to get different verbs in Job 37:23; Psalm 2:9[462]; Isaiah 19:10; Daniel 11:6[463]; as does Delitzsch on Job 31:18; 39:16; and as does the LXX in I Samuel 18:11; Proverbs 23:7; Obadiah 3. These changes involve twenty-seven (27)

---

[459] The *English Standard Version*, the *New International Version*, and the *New Revised Standard Version* agree with the change in I Kings 13:12.

[460] The *New American Standard Version* follows the change in Jeremiah 10:18.

[461] The *New American Standard Version*, the *English Standard Version*, the *New International Version*, and the *New Revised Standard Version* adopt the modification in Micah 6:9.

[462] The *English Standard Version* and the *New International Version* embrace the alteration in Psalm 2:9.

[463] The *New Revised Standard Version* adheres to the change in Daniel 11:6.

verses. Changes such as these could easily perpetuate themselves to thousands of other verses, especially when one considers the nature of Hebrew verbs.

Strouse, referring to the nature of Hebrew verbs, writes:

> The speculation that the vowels were not inspired is ludicrous in light of the complexity of the Hebrew language. Biblical Hebrew demands the linguistic necessity for distinguishing Hebrew verbs and nouns. Hebrew verbs are made up of seven stems, of which are the *Qal* stem and six derived stems, including the *Niphal, Piel, Pual, Hithpael, Hiphil,* and *Hophal*. These stems apply equally to both the strong and weak verbs. The differentiation of some of these stems is based on complex vowel pointing, without which tremendous confusion abounds. The *Piel* and *Pual* differ from each and the *Qal* stem only by vowels and diacritical marks. The *Niphal* perfect 3ms (3rd person, masculine, singular), *Niphal* imperfect 1cp (1st person, common, plural), and *Niphal* participle ms differ by vowel points alone, and may be confused with the *Qal* imperfect 1cp except for the points. The imperfect forms for all of the stems except the *Hiphil* and *Hithpael* are identical without points and consequent confusion would abound with the divinely preserved vowel points. If the stems are significant, which they must be, then their respective vowel differences are significant, and must be carefully maintained to make sense of any given passage.
>
> For example, in Gen. 1:26, Scripture uses the first of several Qal imperfect 1cp verbs (na`eseh) for God to express "let us make" man. However, without authoritatively inspired vowels this verb could be "he was made" (Niphal [passive] perfect 3ms) or "we will be made" (Niphal imperfect 1cp). Furthermore, the Niphal participle masculine singular without the pointing would be the same consonants and mean "being made." Although some might say that the context would always show which conjugation and tense was divinely inspired, in this case the context would probably eliminate only the participle. Did Jehovah say "let us make" man, or man "he was made," or "we [i.e., the Godhead] will be made" man?[464]

Gill observes:

---

[464] Thomas M. Strouse, "Lk. 16:17 – One Tittle" in *Emmanuel Baptist Theological Journal* 2 (Spring 2006), 16,17.

The nature and genius of the *Hebrew* language require points; without these the difference can't be discerned between nouns and verbs, in some instances, as דבר, with many others; between verbs active, and verbs passive, between some conjugations, moods, senses, and persons, *Kal, Piel, Pual;* imperatives and infinitives, are proofs hereof; nor can the *Vau* conversive of senses be observed, which yet is used frequently throughout the Bible, and without which, the formation of some of the tenses by letters would be useless. *Morinus* himself says "that without the points a grammar cannot be written, as *Elias* rightly observes; for example, describe the conjugation *Kal* without points, and immediately you'll be at a stand, and much more in *Piel.*"[465]

Whitfield in writing about the different conjugations of the Hebrew verb states:

A great part of the variety, force and elegance of the language, consists in the variations of the verbs, in these different conjugations, etc. But sure it is; that a great part of the differences of these conjugations, moods, and tenses, consists merely in the diversity of the punctations: so that, if we reject the points, a great part of the inflexion of the verbs will be quite lost.[466]

Whitfield continues:

Upon the rejection of the points, we should have a still greater confusion in the future tenses of the Hebrew verbs. For in that case, the future tenses of the Kal, (when that is wrote with Hholem without the ו as is very frequently the case) of Niphal, of Pihel, of Pyhal, and Hophal, will be exactly the same, there being no difference, in that all, besides the variety of the punctation; and the future of the conjugation Hiphil, will coincide with the rest, when ever Hirech magnum is changed into Pathach, Tseri, or Hirech parvum; as it very frequently is.[467]

---

[465] Gill, *Dissertation*, 259,260. The Morinus citation is from *Epist Buxtorsio* in *Antiqu. Ecclesiastes Oriental*, 392. Morinus is probably *Morin* Latinized and most likely refers to Jean Morin who "attacked the integrity of the Hebrew text" ("Morin, Jean" in *Cyclopedia*, VI: 612). Although he attacked the integrity of the text, he was willing to admit the importance of the points.

[466] Whitfield, 47,48.

[467] Ibid., 48.

Strouse, Gill, and Whitfield verify that without the points, mass confusion would reign amongst the Hebrew verbs. In light of this, the malignancy present in the comments of the commentators about verbs could easily perpetuate itself many times over.

To Consonants

The malignancy evidenced in the comments of the commentators involves consonants and the malignancy could easily perpetuate itself to many other consonants. Some of the comments of the commentators suggest a change of the consonants. As the author has already shown earlier those who suggest a change of the word אֶלֶף (*thousand*) to אַלּוּף (*leader*) not only would change the pointing, but also add a consonant. In I Kings 20:29, 30 Wiseman advocates such a change; as does Youngblood in II Samuel 24:9; and as does Payne in I Chronicles 7:4 and II Chronicles 17:14-18. Additionally, Payne suggests changing *thousand* to *leader* in I Chronicles 12:24-37; 27:1-15; II Chronicles 13:3, 17; 14:8, 9; 25:5-6; 26:12-13; and 28:6, 8. In addition to these examples, *The Pulpit Commentary* on I Samuel 1:7 notes that the LXX, the Syriac, and the Vulgate suggest a change that not only involves the vowels, but also "a slight change of the consonants." Also, on Psalm 52:5 Tomasino suggests not only a change in the pointing of the verb, but also the insertion of two additional consonants.

Not included in the comments of the commentators is a comment by Wakely, who observes: "In Jer 23:29, *NEB*, *JB*, and *BHS* (followed by several commentators, e.g., Nicholson, 199) emend כֹּה to כֹּנֶה, the masc. sing. q. act. part. of כָּנָה."[468] Notice that the change would not only involve a change in the vowels, but also the addition of a consonant, that is, a *waw* (ו).

---

[468] Robin Wakely, "כָּנָה H3917" in *New International Dictionary of Old Testament Theology and Exegesis*. *NEB* refers to the *New English Bible*, *JB* refers to the *Jerusalem Bible*, and *BHS* refers to *Biblia Hebraica Stuttgartensia*.

In light of the above examples, it seems that if a change of vowels does not produce the desired result, then one can also add a consonant or two whenever needed. If such is the case, then where would the malignancy stop? Indeed, the malignancy could perpetuate its cancer to almost every word of the Old Testament.

To Translations

Forty-one (41) of the one hundred fifty-two cases of repointing words find their way into one or more of the modern versions. The forty-one cases occur in Genesis 49:10; Deuteronomy 33:27; I Kings 13:12; 17:1; Ezra 8:26; Job 15:23; 24:12; 36:33; Psalm 2:9; 29:9; 33:7; 42:2; 60:8; 69:22; 109:17; Proverbs 6:24; 21:4; 23:7; 26:23; 30:1; Ecclesiastes 3:21; Isaiah 1:2; 30:8; 40:6; 62:5; Jeremiah 10:18; 23:17; 48:15; 48:18; 49:1; 51:3; Ezekiel 8:2; 34:3; 36:5; 39:26; Daniel 9:27; 11:6; Micah 6:9,11; Zephaniah 3:8; and Zechariah 9:8. The fact that the repointing of words finds its way into modern versions demonstrates that the problem of repointing words is not confined to scholars, books, dissertations, schools, or academia. The fact that repointed words occur in modern versions means that these repointed words find their way into the hands of unsuspecting readers, which has the further effect of denying to the reader all of God's inspired and preserved Words. It should be of the utmost concern for the reader of Scripture to make sure that he has all of God's Words since Jesus stated: "Man shall not live by bread alone, but by every word that proceedeth out of the mouth of God" (Matthew 4:4). The best recourse for an English reader of the Bible is to stick with the *King James Version*, which is a faithful translation of the Traditional Texts.

Summary

If the points are not inspired, then a malignancy permeates the Old Testament as the examples from the commentators demonstrate. The malignancy would perpetuate itself many times over to other words, verbs, consonants, and translations. With malignancy permeating the Bible, then of what value is the Word of God? If one can change Scripture at will, why even bother consulting Scripture? If a person can alter the Bible in any place, he has made the Words of God of none effect (Mark 7:13). Furthermore, if one can change Scripture at will, then how is this any different from the time of the Judges when every man did that which was right in his own eyes (Judges 17:6; 21:25)? It seems that those who change Scripture according to their own whims and fancies are setting themselves up in the place of God, claiming that their rendering of the Bible is the correct one. Instead of allowing the Word of Truth (II Timothy 2:15) to correct them (II Timothy 3:16,17), they are acting as if Scripture is the word of error, which they, with their so-called masterful brilliance, must correct. Such an attitude is devilish (Genesis 3:1), destructive (II Peter 3:16), disobedient (Revelation 22:18,19), discouraging (I Timothy 1:4), disrespectful (Psalm 138:2), and is something that every believer should discard (Colossians 2:8).

Rationalism

The examples from the commentators demonstrate that some, based on rationalism, reject the points. The rationalism evinces itself in the matters of miracles, numbers, and grammar.

Concerning Miracles

Farrar on I Kings 17:4 suggests changing *ravens* either to *merchants*, *Arabians*, *Orbites*, or *the people of the rock Oreb*, which he claims would be far more reasonable than to accept a stupendous miracle of the ravens feeding Elijah. Seemingly, because something in Scripture does not make sense to the mind of man, it is okay to alter it, that is, to explain it away. What if one were to apply this technique to other miracles in the Bible? Maybe he could remove those miracles from the pages of Scripture as well. This is nothing more than rank rationalism. The Lord, however, commands that the just live by faith (Hebrews 10:38), which involves faith in His Word.

Concerning Numbers

In a previous section concerning malignancy, the author mentioned those who would repoint as well as add a consonant to *thousand* to get *leader*. What would be the motivation behind such a change? From Youngblood's comment on II Samuel 24:9 it is clear that many commentators think that the numbers of *eight hundred thousand* (800,000) and *five hundred thousand* (500,000) are too large. From Wiseman's comment on I Kings 20:29 it seems that some would find it hard to believe that in ancient warfare there could be one hundred thousand (100,000) casualties in one day. From Payne's comment on I Chronicles 7:4 the number of *six and thirty thousand* (36,000) seems unlikely. These men are just not willing to hear the number of them (Revelation 7:4; 9:16) because it does not fit what they know of ancient warfare, seems too large, or seems unlikely. Rather than walk by faith, they allow their rationalism to control them so that they not only change the vowels, but are also willing to insert an extra consonant! Do they have any shame? They are disregarding the Words of God so that they may promote their rationalism.

Concerning Grammar

McClintock and Strong suggest a repointing of *Mizraim* in Genesis 10:6 to change it from a dual to a plural form so that it will agree with the other plurals in the context. On Joshua 4:24 *The Pulpit Commentary* states: "The construction here is unusual." Therefore, it suggests a change in pointing to make the verse grammatically conform to man-made grammatical rules. On I Samuel 1:7 *The Pulpit Commentary* says, "There is a strange confusion of subject, owing to the first verb having been read as an active instead of a passive." *The Pulpit Commentary* on I Samuel 20:14,15 writes: "The construction of this passage is very difficult if we retain the three negatives of the Masoretic text." On Job 3:5 Delitzsch suggests a change of pointing so as not "to accept a form of noun without example elsewhere." On Jeremiah 8:13 *The Pulpit Commentary* suggests a change in the pointing because the present pointing leads to a rendering that "is not perfectly natural." On Jeremiah 48:15 *The Pulpit Commentary* urges a repointing because it is doubtful that the present pointing "can be translated at all consistently with grammar." Herein are seven (7) examples where commentators note or advocate that one should repoint a word due to the grammar of the passage. While grammar is a valuable tool in spotting patterns in the construction of languages, if God's Word chooses to do something contrary to the usual pattern, one should allow for such "irregularities," since it is God Who gave language. One should receive by faith these grammatical constructions as coming from God, instead of following his own reasoning and rejecting them.

Summary

Some, while walking by sight (rationalism) rather than by faith (fideism), reject the points, for, according to them, the present pointing does not make sense. Approaching the Words of God with a rationalistic frame of mind some seek to remove miracles, others try to reduce the largeness of numbers, and still others seek to bring the Bible into conformity to man-made grammatical rules. If one were to apply these techniques to the rest of the Words of God, then how much would stand? Such rationalistic thinking would continually feed the malignancy already present in questioning the points.

The criteria in many of these cases seems to be that if the present pointing does not make sense to the commentator, then this is reason enough to change it. However, in such a case does not the reason of man become the authority? Whatever happened to walking by faith, instead of by sight? If so many of these cases existed in the Old Testament, then why did not Jesus suggest such corrections? Is one to believe that Jesus' Hebrew Old Testament was perfectly preserved, but that from Jesus' time to this present age, the text became corrupt? If it was kept pure from Moses' day to Jesus' day, then why not from Jesus' day to this day? Or, is one to believe that Jesus knew of these places, but kept quiet about them, and at the same time led people to believe that there were absolutely no problems (Matthew 5:18; John 17:17)? Both options are absurd and unbiblical. The best conclusion is to believe that the Old Testament is pointed as it should be and to receive it by faith, not to do so, results in logically questioning the veracity and then even the deity of the Lord Jesus Christ!

Unbelief

The examples from the commentators demonstrate that some have unbelief – unbelief in the promises and statements of the Bible about the Old Testament. The next two chapters present many of these promises and statements. These promises and statements, over thirty-six, prove that the points are inspired, therefore, authentic and authoritative, and that these points are preserved, therefore, present in the Traditional Text. However, in spite of these promises and statements, some express the opinion that the points are of no authority. For instance, Cook says on I Kings 17:4 that the points "are generally allowed to have no authority." Barnes on Job 36:33 writes: "The points have no authority." Fausset states on Job 24:12: "But the vowel points are modern." Fausset makes a similar statement on Isaiah 62:5. *The Pulpit Commentary* on Jeremiah 15:19 writes that the points "form no part of the text" and on Jeremiah 48:18 that the vowel points "constitute no part of the Masoretic text." These commentators should promote faith and confidence in the Words of God, rather than questions (I Timothy 1:4). Instead of attacking the foundation of the faith, the commentators should be showing how solid that foundation is, for "if the foundations be destroyed, what can the righteous do?" (Psalm 11:3).

Summary

It is very dangerous to claim that the points are not inspired, to do so results in uncertainty, ambiguity, malignancy, rationalism, and unbelief. With no points then no one can be certain as to what the text should read, at which point a person must look to another authority, which then results in him no longer having the Bible as his sole authority for faith and practice. With no inspired vowel points ambiguity would reign, in spite of the claims of some who fancy that the context can settle all disputes as to what a particular reading should be. However, as many of the verses from the commentators demonstrate, the context is powerless to decide conclusively what a word should be. With no points, a malignancy permeates the Old Testament for all parts of the Old Testament are infected. Furthermore, the malignancy perpetuates itself a thousand times over so that almost none of the nearly twenty-three thousand verses of the Old Testament would escape unscathed. With no points, rationalism rules the day, for if the points are not inspired, then one can change the points to eliminate miracles, large numbers, and unique grammatical constructions. Instead of walking by faith and receiving the preserved Words of God, one, by changing the points, could cater to his flesh as he walks by sight. Also with no points, unbelief would rule the day, for one would have to reject the statements and promises that the Bible makes about itself – promises that declare that the Bible is preserved, sure, certain, faithful, true, and much more (see the next two chapters for these promises).

The fruit that would come up from the soil in the garden of no points is not good fruit at all. In light of the fact that Jesus said, "By their fruits ye shall know them" (Matthew 7:20), let one and all know that the claim that the points are uninspired is not good or godly. It would seem to the writer that no one who would claim to be a lover of the Bible, would want to be in any way, shape, or form associated with such things.

CONCLUSION

This chapter has presented over one hundred actual examples where various writers note or suggest a repointing of the Old Testament Hebrew/Aramaic text. The examples cover every portion of the Old Testament. Such repointing results in uncertainty, ambiguity, malignancy, rationalism, and unbelief. The examples demonstrates that in an unpointed text uncertainty would predominate, resulting in overthrowing the authority of the Old Testament. Such a result is Biblically untenable, for the Bible, which includes the Old Testament, is the sole authority for faith and practice. Since the Bible being the sole authority for faith and practice demands that there be certainty in the text, and since an unpointed text produces uncertainty and a lack of authority, then the Old Testament text, to be authoritative, must have inspired vowel points. The previous chapter already devastated the non-authoritative position, this present chapter further buries it.

CHAPTER FOUR – BIBLICAL CONSIDERATIONS

Chapter Two shows that the Bible is the sole authority for faith and practice. Since the accommodation and non-authoritative positions about the points must rely on other authorities, then Chapter Two eliminates them as Biblical positions concerning the points. Chapter Three further proves the implausibleness of the non-authoritative position, for without authoritative points, uncertainty would rule in almost every verse of the Old Testament. Chapters Two and Three, on Biblical grounds, eliminate from consideration the non-authoritative and accommodation positions on the vowel points. This leaves only the third position standing, that is, the *autographa* position, which regards the points as inspired of God. Not only has the author established negatively that the *autographa* position correct by Biblically refuting the accommodation and non-authoritative positions, but also the author is able to establish positively that the *autographa* position is the correct position by presenting a number of verses that demand inspired vowel points, which is the subject of the next two chapters. This chapter presents a number of verses from both the Old and New Testaments, which demand inspired vowel points. The next chapter concentrates on Matthew 5:18, wherein Jesus directly teaches the presence and preservation of the vowel points.

For now, this chapter presents Biblical considerations for why the vowel points are part of the *autographa*. These considerations include Old Testament verses, New Testament verses, and New Testament examples. Those who deny that the points are inspired must answer these considerations; however, rather than answer these considerations, many ignore them.

OLD TESTAMENT VERSES

Many Old Testament verses demand the inspiration of the vowel points. These verses not only demand the inspiration of the vowel points, but also present the teaching that these vowels were inscripturated and will be preserved.

Exodus 4:22

Exodus 4:22 states: "And thou shalt say unto Pharaoh, Thus saith the LORD, Israel *is* my son, *even* my firstborn." This is the first of four hundred thirty (430) times wherein the Bible says, "Thus saith the Lord," or the equivalent. *Saith* is from אָמַר ('amar) and is a Qal perfect third masculine singular verb. Its "primary idea is to bear forth, to bring out to light, hence to utter, to say."[469] If there are no vowels, then how are the Words of God able to bear forth and bring to light? Indeed, as the last chapter demonstrates, without vowels a lot is hidden and dark. אָמַר (*saith*) "always indicates reasonable statements by a subject which may be heard and understood by others;"[470] therefore, *saith the LORD* means that the Lord spoke in an understandable way. Speaking in an understandable way indicates that the Lord vocalized His words and, therefore, used vowels, or else how would the hearers have understood Him? Furthermore, the writers of Scripture wrote the words that were uttered in the *thus saith the LORD* statements, that is, what they wrote is the equivalent of what God had said, therefore, what

---

[469] William Wilson, *Wilson's Old Testament Word Studies* (Peabody, MA: Hendrickson Publishers, n. d.), 368.

[470] Siegfried Wagner, "אָמַר" in *Theological Dictionary of the Old Testament*, eds. G. J. Botterweck and Helmer Ringgren, trans. John T. Willis (Grand Rapids: Eerdmans Publishing Co., 1990), I: 329.

they wrote contained vowels as well.[471] This all points to God giving the vowels by inspiration.

Those who do not believe in the inspiration of the vowels face a daunting task. They must show one of two things. Either they must demonstrate that what the writers of Scripture wrote was not equivalent to what God said and, therefore, Scripture does not mean what it says when it says, "Thus saith the LORD"; or they must demonstrate that when God spoke He did not use vowels and yet made reasonable statements that were understood by others. Far better it is just to believe the teaching of Scripture.

Exodus 24:4

Exodus 24:4 states, "And Moses wrote all the words of the LORD, and rose up early in the morning, and built an altar under the hill, and twelve pillars, according to the twelve tribes of Israel." *Words* (דִּבְרֵי) is a masculine singular construct noun from דָּבָר (*dābar*). The Bible often connects *words* with the content of what the Lord saith, that is, דָּבָר and אָמַר both occur in the same verse with both referring to what the Lord saith. For instance, Jeremiah 1:4 states: "Then the word (דְּבַר, masculine singular construct noun from דָּבָר) of the LORD came unto me, saying (לֵאמֹר, Qal infinitive construct with preposition לְ from אָמַר)." Since אָמַר "always indicates reasonable statements by a subject which may be heard and understood by others,"[472] and since דָּבָר and אָמַר often occur in the same verse with both referring to what God said; then דָּבָר also refers to that which may be

---

[471] In other words, each time the Bible uses *thus saith the LORD*, it records what the Lord saith. But if there are no vowels, then in what way does the Bible record what the Lord saith? If there are no vowels, but only consonants, then it seems that such a system would truncate what the Lord saith, and not accurately record what the Lord saith. And, since without vowels the true sense is lost, then how would anyone know for sure what the Lord saith?

[472] Wagner, "אָמַר" in *Theological Dictionary of the Old Testament*, I: 329.

heard and understood by others and, therefore, had to have vowels. Other verses that demonstrate the same relationship between דָּבָר and אָמַר are Genesis 15:4; Exodus 20:1; Numbers 12:6; I Samuel 15:10; II Samuel 7:4; I Kings 6:11; 12:22; 13:2,9; 16:1; 17:2,8; 18:31; 19:9; 21:17,28; II Kings 7:1; 15:12; 20:4; I Chronicles 22:8; II Chronicles 11:2; 12:7; Isaiah 38:4; Jeremiah 1:4,11,13; 2:1; 7:1; 11:1; 13:3,8; 16:1; 18:1,5; 21:1; 23:16; 24:4; 26:1,2; 27:1; 28:12; 29:30; 30:1,2; 32:6,26; 33:1,19,23; 34:1,12; 35:1,12; 36:1,27; 37:6; 43:8; 44:26; 49:34; Ezekiel 3:16; 6:1; 7:1; 11:14; 12:1,8,17,26; 13:1; 14:2,12; 15:1; 16:1; 17:1,11; 18:1; 20:2,45,47; 21:1,8,18; 22:1,17,23; 23:1; 24:1,15,20; 25:1,3; 26:1; 27:1; 28:1,11,20; 29:1,17; 30:1,20; 31:1; 32:1,17; 33:1,23; 34:1; 35:1; 36:4,16; 37:15; 38:1; Amos 3:1; Jonah 1:1; 3:1; Haggai 1:1,3; 2:1,10,20; Zechariah 1:1,7; 4:6,8; 6:9; 7:4,8; 8:1,18.

Here in Exodus 24:4, a connection exists between what the Lord wanted Moses to write and what the Lord spoke. From Exodus 3:4-7, 12, 14, 15; 4:2-4, 6, 7, 11, 14, 19, 21; 6:1, 2, 26; 7:1, 14; 8:16, 20; 9:1, 8, 13, 22; 10:1, 12, 21; 11:1, 9; 12:43; 14:15, 26; 16:4, 28; 17:5, 14; 19:9, 10, 21, 24; 20:22; 23:13; 24:1, it is obvious that up to the time of Exodus 24:4 where the Bible states that Moses wrote all the Words of the Lord that the Lord regularly spoke with Moses and communicated His Words to Moses by speaking to him. In fact, each of these verses before Exodus 24:4 use the Hebrew verb אָמַר to refer to the Lord's speaking to Moses. Therefore, the context of Exodus connects דָּבָר (*word*) and אָמַר (*said*) indicating that the words Moses was to write in Exodus 24:4 were the spoken Words of the Lord. Since speaking requires vocalization, which requires vowels, and since Moses wrote these words, then he used vowels as well as consonants. God, therefore, inspired the vowels as well as the consonants, for Moses wrote words, not abbreviations of words. But if there were no vowels, then in what sense did Moses write all the Words of the Lord?

Exodus 34:1

Exodus 34:1 states: "And the LORD said unto Moses, Hew thee two tables of stone like unto the first: and I will write upon *these* tables the words that were in the first tables, which thou brakest." The words that Moses was to write were words which God spoke (אָמַר) according to Exodus 20:1 and, therefore, He vocalized them with vowels, which demands that the writing of these inspired words also had vowels.

Exodus 34:27

In Exodus 34:27, the Lord said to Moses: "Write thou these words: for after the tenor of these words I have made a covenant with thee and with Israel." Exodus 34:27 teaches that God mouthed, therefore, vocalized the words, and that Moses wrote these mouthed words, teaching that he wrote consonants as well as vowels. The God-inspired Words that Moses wrote had vowels. The reader should consult the beginning of Chapter One for more information on this verse.

Deuteronomy 6:6-9; 11:18,19; & 30:13,14

Deuteronomy 6:6-9 commands the common people to write God's Words upon the posts of their houses and on their gates. Deuteronomy 11:18,19 commands these same people to lay up God's Words in their hearts and to teach the Words of God to their children. And Deuteronomy 30:13,14 states that the Word of God was near to them, implying that the common person in Israel had access to the Words of God, could read them, and could understand them. But if there are no vowels in the Old Testament, then how could the common Israelites obey these commands? Reasoning from these verses Whitfield makes a good statement:

> The reading of the Hebrew text, without the vowel marks, [is] to be attended with so much difficulty, as to make it always, as to the greatest part of the people, absolutely impracticable; yet, to read the Scrip-

tures, was a duty universally enjoined; and, consequently, there must have always existed vowel and accent marks.[473]

In other words, since the common people were to read the Word of God, and since vowels facilitate the reading of the Word of the God, then from the very beginning God gave His Words with the vowels, that is, He inspired the vowels.

Deuteronomy 27:8

Deuteronomy 27:8 states: "And thou shalt write upon the stones all the words of this law very plainly." *Very plainly* (בַּאֵר הֵיטֵב) is the combination of a Piel infinitive absolute (*plainly*, בַּאֵר, meaning "make distinct, plain"[474]) and a Hiphil infinitive absolute (*very*, הֵיטֵב, meaning to "do well or thoroughly"[475]). The combination of these two words then means to make thoroughly distinct. How could the people make the words thoroughly distinct with no vowels? Those who do not hold to the inspiration of the vowels must answer this question, for as the previous chapter demonstrates, without the vowels many things are not thoroughly distinct, but, instead, are very confused. Bishop writes: "This must include the vowel-marks, as well as consonants, for on them, most of all, the plainness must depend. There are innumerable passages where, without the vowel-points, no man alive can tell the meaning of the Holy Ghost, nor know the mind of God."[476]

---

[473] Whitfield, 69, 70.

[474] Francis Brown, S. R. Driver, and Charles A. Briggs, *A Hebrew and English Lexicon of the Old Testament: with an Appendix Containing the Biblical Aramaic* (Oxford: Clarendon Press, 1980), 91.

[475] Ibid., 405, 406.

[476] Bishop, 48.

Deuteronomy 31:24

Deuteronomy 31:24 states: "And it came to pass, when Moses had made an end of writing the words of this law in a book, until they were finished." As Exodus 24:4 indicates (see above), the words that Moses wrote were words that God had spoken to Moses and as such were vocalized with vowels. *Finished* (תֻּמָּם, a Qal infinitive construct with a third person masculine plural suffix from תָּמַם) has the "fundamental idea of completeness."[477] Therefore, *finished* indicates that not only did Moses write all the words, but also that he did not use some sort of cipher system or shorthand notation or just consonants. That is, Moses wrote out the full words for all the words of the law. The inspired words that Moses wrote had vowels.

Those who claim that the vowels are not inspired must answer a couple of questions. First, if there are no vowels, then how did Moses write words? And second, if there are no vowels, then how did he finish writing the words? If he did not use vowels, it would seem that he used a shortcut. However, how would using a shortcut be writing the words "until they were finished"?

Joshua 1:8

Joshua 1:8 states: "This book of the law shall not depart out of thy mouth; but thou shalt meditate therein day and night, that thou mayest observe to do according to all that is written therein: for then thou shalt make thy way prosperous, and then thou shalt have good success." *Book of the law* refers to something that is written, for the verse later speaks of *all that is written therein*. *Mouth* is the instrument of pronouncing words. The fact that book of the law was not to depart out of Joshua's mouth, which is the instrument of vocalization,

---

[477] J. Barton Payne, "2522 תָּמַם" in *Theological Wordbook of the Old Testament*, eds. R. Laird Harris, Gleason L. Archer, Jr., and Bruce K. Waltke (Chicago: The Moody Bible Institute, 1980), II: 973.

argues for God originally having given vowels in the book of the law. That is, God inspired the book of the law with vowels as well as consonants. Another factor that leads to this interpretation is that the Bible says that Joshua was to meditate on what was written in the law. *Meditate* (הָגִיתָ, a Qal perfect second person masculine singular with waw consecutive from הָגָה) "implies that kind of mental rumination which is apt to vent itself in an *audible sound* of the voice."[478] The meaning of *meditate*, again, presents the idea of pronunciation and vocalization. The thing in which Joshua was to meditate was that which is written, indicating that the written words had vowels and that the vowels were inspired of God.

Another verse that mentions meditating in the law of the Lord is Psalm 1:2, which states: "But his delight *is* in the law of the LORD; and in his law doth he meditate day and night." Concerning Psalm 1:2, Strouse writes: "The word 'meditate' comes from *hagah* that means, 'to mutter' and suggests the deliberate pronunciation of the words of Scripture. It is impossible to recite meaningfully consonants without vowels and it is equally impossible to delight (*chaphatz*) in consonants with non-authoritative vowels."[479]

Judges 12:6

In Judges 12:6, the Gileadites demanded that the Ephraimites say *Shibboleth* (שִׁבֹּלֶת), but the Ephraimites could not pronounce it correctly and, instead, said *Sibboleth* (סִבֹּלֶת). Hebrew uses a dot over the upper right corner of שׁ to indicate the *sh* (שׁ) in *Shibboleth*, but if there were no points, then how did the writer of Judges convey the distinction between *Shibboleth* and *Sibboleth*? A dot on the upper left corner of שׂ would indicate *s* (שׂ), which is very similar to ס, the first letter of

---

[478] George Bush, *Notes, Critical and Practical on the Book of Joshua*, 2nd ed. (NY: Newman & Ivison, 1852, reprinted Minneapolis: Klock & Klock, 1981), 22.

[479] Strouse, "Luke 16:17 – One Tittle," 15,16.

סִבֹּלֶת (*Sibboleth*). Kelley notes that ס and שׁ both represent *S* as in *Set*,[480] therefore, it seems that a point was necessary to convey the proper meaning. However, *Gesenius' Hebrew Grammar* claims, "שׁ and שׂ were originally represented (as is still the case in the unpointed texts) by only *one* form שׁ."[481] However, if such were the case, then how would the distinction in Judges 12:6 be clear? Gill, in referring to Judges 12:6, cites column 1792 of Schindler's *Lexicon Pentaglott*: "Schindler is of the opinion that from hence it appears, that the point on the right and left hand of שׁ, was then in use and so by consequence the other points also."[482] In other words, the writer of Judges under the influence of inspiration placed the dot above the upper right corner of שׁ to indicate the *sh* (שׁ) in *Shibboleth*. On this verse, Moncrieff observes:

> The Jews were well acquainted with some points or marks correspondent with those in our pointed Bibles, by which they were guided in this particular word, to pronounce the שׁ as sh, to double the ב, to add an o after it, and to use an e after the ל, making the word "Shibboleth," as it appears in our English translation, and not "Sebelet," as it must be pronounced, according to the mode of reading without Points.[483]

Other verses indicate the necessity of the distinction between שׁ (the Hebrew letter *shin*) and שׂ (the Hebrew letter *sin*). Strouse observes:

> In Psalm 119, the *sin/shin* stanza (vv. 161-168), displays an illustration of the necessity for diacritical markings (i.e., tittles [Lk. 16:17]). The sibilant or "s" consonant designated *sin* looks like a three-pronged comb with a dot over the left tooth (שׂ). The *shin* has the same consonantal form but has the diacritical dot over the right tooth (שׁ) and produces the "sh" sound and spelling. The psalmist declared in v. 164

---

[480] Kelley, *Biblical Hebrew: An Introductory Grammar*, 1.

[481] A. E. Cowley, *Gesenius' Hebrew Grammar As Edited and Enlarged by the late E. Kautzsch*, 2nd ed. (Oxford: Clarendon Press, 1982), 33.

[482] Gill, *Dissertation*, 253.

[483] Moncrieff, 37.

"Seven times a day do I praise thee because of thy righteous judgments." Without the diacritical dot over the right tooth of the first consonant in the noun *sheva`* ("seven"), the word could be the perfect verb *sava`* ("he is satisfied"). Therefore the Hebrew text could read "He is satisfied in the day I do praise thee because of thy righteous judgments." The context cannot render an authoritative solution and hence the text becomes as wax ready to be twisted by every interpreter.[484]

Another illustration of the necessity of the distinction between שׁ and שׂ occurs in Isaiah 19:10. In that verse are the words *all that make sluices*, about which Barnes writes:

> There has been quite as great a variety in the interpretation of this passage as in the former. The word rendered 'sluices' (שֶׁכֶר), our translators understand in the sense of places where the water would be retained for fish ponds — made by artificial banks confining the waters that overflow from the Nile. This sense they have given to the word, as if it were derived from שָׂכַר (sâkhăr), *to shut up, to enclose*. The LXX reads it as if it meant the Hebrew שֵׁכָר (shēkhâr), or strong drink; and so also the Syriac renders it — as if from שָׁכַר (shâkhăr), *to drink*. There is no doubt that by a difference of pointing it may have this signification.[485]

Barnes' comment refers to not only a change in the vowels שֶׁכֶר in the Traditional Text to שֵׁכָר, but also to a change in the first letter from שׂ to שׁ, which involves moving the dot from the upper left corner to the upper right corner. In other words, with no certainty about the dot in שׁ and שׂ and with no certainty about the vowels, one would not be able to determine the proper meaning of Isaiah 19:10.

Judges 12:6; Psalm 119:164; and Isaiah 19:10 illustrate the necessity to have a dot above the שׂ and the שׁ. If these dots are necessary, then it must be true of the other points as well, all of which demands the inspiration of the points in the first place.

---

[484] Strouse, "Luke 16:17 – One Tittle," 19.

[485] Barnes, *Isaiah*, vol. 1, in vol. 6 of *Barnes' Notes*, 358.

Nehemiah 8:8

Nehemiah 8:8 states: "So they read in the book in the law of God distinctly, and gave the sense, and caused *them* to understand the reading." *Distinctly* is מְפֹרָשׁ, a Pual masculine singular absolute participle from פָּרַשׁ. In addition to the usage here in Nehemiah, the Bible uses this word four other times. Only one of those times does the Bible use it in the Pual, namely Numbers 15:34 where the Bible uses the Pual perfect in referring to the case of keeping a Sabbath stick-gatherer "in ward, because it was not declared (פֹרַשׁ) what should be done to him." The Israelites would not act against this man, until they clearly knew what to do. The idea, then, behind the Pual form of פָּרַשׁ is to make things clear and distinct.

In Nehemiah 8:8 various men read in the book in the law of God distinctly. In order for them to do this, then what was written in the book had to be clear or distinct, otherwise, as the previous chapter demonstrates they could have had various and contradictory readings. Gill observes: "The scribes, which were assistant to Ezra in reading the law, cannot well be thought to read, at least so well, to read it distinctly, and cause the people to understand the reading of it, even men, women, and children, without the points."[486] The preserved copy of the inspired law of God was distinct in Nehemiah's day, demonstrating the presence of the vowels in Nehemiah's copy of the law of God and reflecting the presence of those vowels in the inspired *autographa*.

Psalm 12:6,7

Psalm 12:6,7 state: "The words of the LORD *are* pure words: *as* silver tried in a furnace of earth, purified seven times. Thou shalt keep them, O LORD, thou shalt preserve them from this generation for ever." *Words* occurs twice in this passage and in both cases is from the

---

[486] Gill, *Dissertation*, 252.

Hebrew אִמְרָה and means "utterance, speech, word."[487] It is related to the verb אָמַר, indicating speech that one can hear and understand (see above under Exodus 4:22). Clearly, אִמְרָה indicates the presence of vowels, since it refers to speech. A number of conclusions are obvious: (1) since *the words of the LORD* refers to words that have come from the Lord, then these words are inspired words; (2) since the word for *words* indicates the presence of the vowels, then these inspired words must have had vowels; and (3) since God promises to keep and to preserve these words, then God has preserved the vowels as well.

Speaking of the preservation of the pure Words of the Lord, *thou shalt preserve them* is a Qal imperfect second masculine singular with a third masculine singular suffix from נָצַר. In this context, it has "the concept of 'guarding with fidelity'."[488] *Preserve* has a third masculine singular suffix, referring to the fact that God preserves each individual word. Those who do not believe in the inspiration of the vowels have some questions to answer. If the vowels are not authoritative, then how has God preserved each individual word "from this generation for ever" (Psalm 12:7)? Without inspired vowels, many words are in dispute and seemingly unpreserved. If there are no vowels, then can one really trust God's promise in Psalm 12:6,7? And if one cannot trust the promise in Psalm 12:6,7; then what about other promises of God?

Psalm 19:7

Psalm 19:7 states: "The law of the LORD *is* perfect, converting the soul: the testimony of the LORD *is* sure, making wise the simple." *Perfect* (תְּמִימָה, a feminine singular adjective from תָּמִים) derives from

---

[487] Brown, *Hebrew and English Lexicon*, 57.

[488] Walter C. Kaiser, "1407 נָצַר" in *Theological Wordbook of the Old Testament*, 2:595.

the verb תָּמַם, which has the "fundamental idea of completeness"[489] (see above under Deuteronomy 31:24). The adjective "refers to animals which are without blemish; also translated as such related adjectives as full, whole, upright, perfect."[490] The Law of the Lord being perfect indicates that it is without blemish. That is, there is nothing to detract from it. The Law of the Lord is complete and whole. Such teaching demands that the God-inspired Law of the Lord has vowels, for without vowels it would not be complete, whole, and without blemish. Indeed, without vowels it would have many blemishes that the commentators, translators, and textual critics think they must bandage with the insertion of their own vowels.

Sure (נֶאֱמָנָה) is a Niphal feminine singular participle from אָמַן and means "verified, confirmed."[491] "The basic root idea is firmness or certainty."[492] "In the Niphal conjugation the meaning is 'to be established'(2Sam 7:16; 1Chr 17:23; 2Chr 6:17; Isa 7:9). The Niphal participle means 'to be faithful, sure, dependable' . . . . This form is also used to describe that upon which all certainty rests: God himself (Deut 7:9), and his covenant (Psa 89:28 [H 29])."[493] God's testimonies are certain. Again, the certainty of God's testimonies demands that the God-inspired testimonies have vowels, for as the previous chapter demonstrates without the vowels there is a great deal of uncertainty about God's testimonies. The fact that God's testimonies are certain and that they were certain at the time of David, which was several hundred years after God gave those testimonies, argues for the preservation of those inspired vowel points as well.

---

[489] J. Barton Payne, "2522 תָּמַם" in *Theological Wordbook of the Old Testament*, II: 973.

[490] Ibid., II: 974.

[491] Brown, *Hebrew and English Lexicon*, 53.

[492] Jack B. Scott, "116 אָמַן" in *Theological Wordbook of the Old Testament*, I:51.

[493] Ibid.

Speaking of the certainty of God's testimonies, Spurgeon wrote: "Oh, what a mercy that is! What could our souls do with *ifs*, *buts*, and *perhapses*? But the teachings of God's Word are certain, positive, infallible."[494] And Spurgeon wrote again:

> God's witness in his Word is so sure that we may draw solid comfort from it both for time and eternity, and so sure that no attacks made upon it however fierce or subtle can ever weaken its force. What a blessing that in a world of uncertainties we have something sure to rest upon! We hasten from the quicksands of human speculations to the *terra firma* of Divine Revelation.[495]

May the reader note that in addition to earlier statements showing that the points were written prior to Ezra, Psalm 19 provides another proof of that. Psalm 19 is a Psalm of David meaning that before the time of David the Law of the Lord was perfect and His testimonies sure. Therefore, the vowels were present before the time of David and Ezra or the exilic prophets did add them later. One could apply this same argumentation to many of the verses that this chapter presents, for many of the verses speak of a time before Ezra.

The result of God making His Law perfect and His testimonies sure is that His Law and testimonies make wise the simple. But in the absence of vowels how would the simple even be able to understand what God said? And how could they derive wisdom from it, if the meaning is uncertain (cf. I Corinthians 14:9-11)?

---

[494] Charles H. Spurgeon, "Exposition by C. H. Spurgeon on Psalm 19" in vol. 50 of *The Metropolitan Tabernacle Pulpit* (Pasadena, TX: Pilgrim Publications, 1978), 84.

[495] Charles H. Spurgeon, *The Treasury of David: Containing an Original Exposition of the Book of Psalms; a Collection of Illustrative Extracts from the Whole Range of Literature; a Series of Homiletical Hints upon Almost Every Verse; and Lists of Writers upon Each Psalm* (Peabody, MA: Hendrikson Publishers, n. d.), I:272.

Psalm 93:5

Psalm 93:5 states: "Thy testimonies are very sure: holiness becometh thine house, O LORD, for ever." *Sure* (נֶאֶמְנוּ) is a Niphal third common plural perfect verb from אָמַן. The discussion under Psalm 19:7 indicates that *sure* refers to something that is firm, certain, and established. *Very* (מְאֹד) "is found in many combinations, all expressing the idea of exceeding."[496] With the use of *very*, the Bible presents an heightened idea of firmness and certainty. Concerning Psalm 93:5, Spurgeon writes:

> As in providence the throne of God is fixed beyond all risk, so in revelation his truth is beyond all question. Other teachings are uncertain, but the revelations of heaven are infallible. As the rocks remain unmoved amid the tumult of the sea, so does divine truth resist all the currents of man's opinion and the storms of human controversy; they are not only sure, but *very sure*. Glory be to God, we have not been deluded by a cunningly devised fable: our faith is grounded upon the eternal truth of the Most High.[497]

Psalm 93:5 argues very strongly for the inspiration of the vowel points, since without them, as the previous chapter demonstrates, the Words of God are not only unsure, but also very unsure.

Psalm 111:7

Psalm 111:7 states: "The works of his hands *are* verity and judgment; all his commandments *are* sure." *Sure* (נֶאֱמָנִים) is a Niphal masculine plural participle and again denotes that which is certain, firm, and established (see above under Psalm 19:7). Spurgeon writes about Psalm 111:7, "He is no fickle despot, commanding one thing one day and another another, but his commands remain absolutely unal-

---

[496] Walter C. Kaiser, "1134 מאד" in *Theological Wordbook of the Old Testament*, I:487.

[497] Spurgeon, *The Treasury of David*, II:135.

tered."[498] For God's commands to remain unaltered requires the presence and preservation of the original inspired vowel points.

Psalm 119:86

Psalm 119:86 states: "All thy commandments *are* faithful: they persecute me wrongfully; help thou me." *Faithful* (אֱמוּנָה, a feminine singular absolute noun from אֱמוּנָה) means steadfastness.[499] This word "applies to God himself (Deut 32:4) to express his total dependability. It is frequently listed among the attributes of God (I Sam 26:23; Ps 36:5 [H 6]; Ps 40:10 [H 11]; Lam 3:23). It describes his works (Ps 33:4); and his words (Ps 119:89; 143:1)."[500] Psalm 119:86 teaches the absolute steadfastness and dependability of God's Words and, therefore, requires the inspiration of the vowel points, because, as the last chapter demonstrates, the Words of God are not steadfast and dependable if there are no vowel points. Furthermore, since the commandments were still faithful at the time of the writing of Psalm 119, then the inspired vowel points must have been preserved as well.

Psalm 119:89

Psalm 119:89 states: "For ever, O LORD, thy word is settled in heaven." This is quite a verse as it relates to the vowel points. An examination of the various words in this verse will lead to a correct understanding of this verse.

---

[498] Spurgeon, *The Treasury of David*, III:4.

[499] Brown, *A Hebrew and English Lexicon*, 53.

[500] Jack B. Scott, "116 אָמַן" in *Theological Wordbook of the Old Testament*, I: 52.

Thy Word

Thy word (דְּבָרְךָ) is a masculine singular construct noun with a second person masculine singular suffix from דָּבָר referring to God's Word.

Is Settled

Is settled (נִצָּב) is a niphal participle from נָצַב. The niphal has a passive idea, so that *thy word* is the recipient of the action, not the cause of the action. Presumably, the cause of the action is God, Who has magnified His Word above all His name (Psalm 138:2). Barnes states:

> The word rendered "settled" means properly "to set, to put, to place;" and then, to stand, to cause to stand, to set up, as a column, Genesis 35:20; an altar, Genesis 33:20; a monument, 1 Samuel 15:12. The meaning here is, that the word — the law — the promise — of God was made firm, established, stable, in heaven; and would be so forever and ever. What God had ordained as law would always remain law; what he had affirmed would always remain true; what he had promised would be sure forever.[501]

Since *settled* means to set and to establish, then it would require the vowels, for without the vowels, as the previous chapter demonstrates, the Words of God would not at all be set and established.

Spurgeon writes: "There is not a new divine word, or a new gospel, or a new law; but it is a settled gospel, a settled law, a settled revelation, 'settled in heaven,' stereotyped, fixed, made permanent. If perfect, then unalterable, if alterable, then would it be imperfect."[502] In short, God has established His Word, it is not subject to change. The fact that God has established His Words requires that the vowels be

---

[501] Barnes, *Psalms*, vol. 3, in vol. 4 of *Barnes' Notes*, 204.

[502] Spurgeon, "Expositions by C. H. Spurgeon: Psalm 119:81-96" in vol. 58 of *Metropolitan Tabernacle Pulpit* (Pasadena, TX: Pilgrim Publications, 1979), 408.

present, for without the vowels the Words of God are not established and are subject to great change.

For Ever

For ever refers to the abiding quality of God's Words. I Peter 1:23-25 reiterates this idea when it states: "Being born again, not of corruptible seed, but of incorruptible, by the word of God, which liveth and abideth for ever. For all flesh *is* as grass, and all the glory of man as the flower of grass. The grass withereth, and the flower thereof falleth away: But the word of the Lord endureth for ever. And this is the word which by the gospel is preached unto you." God's Words endure. Just as Psalm 119:89 states that God's Word is for ever settled, so I Peter states that the Word of God abideth for ever.

In Heaven

When examining *in heaven* it is necessary to consider a couple of things. Does *in heaven* mean that the for-ever-settled Word of God is only in heaven? Or, is the for-ever-settled Word of God also here on earth?

Only in Heaven

Is the for-ever-settled Word of God only in heaven? Psalm 119:89 does not use the word *only*, therefore, it is not restricting the for-ever-settled Word of God only to the realm of heaven, but it is merely stating that it is in heaven. Therefore, a for-ever-settled copy of the Word of God is in heaven. In other words, a complete and perfect Bible is in heaven. Other verses that teach the heavenly existence of the Word of God are Daniel 10:21; John 17:8; and Revelation 1:1,2.

Despite the fact that Psalm 119:89 does not limit the for-ever-settled Word of God to heaven, Central Baptist Theological Seminary produced a book entitled *One Bible Only?* in which they state about this verse: "Even if this verse did teach the perfect preservation of the text of God's Word, it would mean that the text is perfectly preserved in heaven, which is no help to those who want to argue for preservation of the KJV, TR, or Majority Text."[503] If Psalm 119:89 were teaching that the for-ever-settled Word of God is only in heaven, then would it not also indicate that those on earth have a sub-standard Bible and that the saved would have to wait to get to heaven to find out for certain what God's Words really said? Of course, this would be assuming that people on earth had enough correct Words from God in order to get saved so that later they could go to heaven. To claim that the Words of God are only preserved in heaven, would have disastrous consequences.

On Earth Also

The Words of God are not only settled in heaven, but also here on earth as Psalm 12:6,7; Isaiah 30:8; 40:8; Matthew 5:18; 24:35; and other verses attest. Poole wrote on Psalm 119:89: "God's word delivered to his people upon earth, which is of the same nature, must needs be of equal certainty and stability."[504] And indeed it is, as Daniel 10:21 and 11:2 illustrate.

In Daniel 10:21, an angel informs Daniel: "But I will shew thee that which is noted in the scripture of truth: and *there is* none that holdeth with me in these things, but Michael your prince." *Noted* (הָרָשׁוּם) is a Qal passive participle with the article from רָשַׁם. It "literally means 'is inscribed'."[505] The Qal passive participle indicates that

---

[503] W. Edward Glenny, "The Preservation of Scripture and the Version Debate" in *One Bible Only?* eds. Roy E. Beacham and Kevin T. Bauder (Grand Rapids: Kregel, 2001), 117. The writer argues for the preservation of the TR, not the KJV, which is a translation of the TR, and not the Majority Text, which is a text that differs with the TR in 1,838 words.

[504] Poole, "Psalms" in vol. 2 of *A Commentary on the Holy Bible*, 187.

[505] Thomas M. Strouse, *But Daniel Purposed in His Heart: An Exegetical Commentary on Daniel* (Newington, CT: Emmanuel Baptist Theological Press, 2001), 150.

it was noted in the past and was present as the angel spoke to Daniel, meaning that the *Scripture of truth* existed before this encounter with Daniel. *Scripture of truth* is "literally 'the writing of truth'."[506] The angel showed Daniel some things from the *Scripture of truth*. What the angel showed Daniel forms the content of Daniel 11:2 and following.

In Daniel 11:2 the angel says to Daniel: "And now will I shew thee the truth. Behold, there shall stand up yet three kings in Persia; and the fourth shall be far richer than *they* all: and by his strength through his riches he shall stir up all against the realm of Grecia." Further establishing the connection between Daniel 10:21 with Daniel 11:2 is the fact that *I will shew thee* (אַגִּיד לְךָ) and *truth* (אֱמֶת) are in each verse. Therefore, what the angel showed to Daniel in Daniel 11:2 and following was already in a book, a book called *The Scripture of Truth*. Daniel then wrote what was in the *Scripture of truth* and placed it in the earthly book of Daniel, so that the earthly book of Daniel was a replica of the *Scripture of truth*.

Presumably, the *Scripture of truth* is the same as the forever-settled Word of God in heaven. Oliver B. Greene states: "God has 'the Scripture of truth' reserved and protected in heaven, and it cannot be destroyed or discredited. God has a record, eternally protected in heaven, of everything He said to Daniel, and all that He made known to him through Gabriel."[507] When Daniel recorded the content of the heavenly *Scripture of truth*, then the Bible on earth was the same as the Bible in heaven. Since the forever-settled Word of God in heaven has vowels, then what Daniel wrote also had vowels. The inspired words that Daniel wrote had vowels.

---

[506] Ibid.

[507] Oliver B. Greene, *Daniel: Verse by Verse Study* (Greenville, SC: The Gospel Hour, Inc., 1964), 408-409.

Conclusion

The for-ever-settled Word of God in heaven is the same as the Word of God here on earth. Since the for-ever-settled Word of God in heaven is for ever settled, then it is established and stable, which attests to it having vowels, for without the vowels it would not be established and stable as the previous chapter demonstrates. When God gave His Word to the prophets, as the case in Daniel illustrates, that Word was the same as the for-ever-settled Word of God in heaven; therefore, God inspired the vowels as well as the consonants. And since God has promised to preserve His Words, then those inspired vowels are still part of God's Words here on earth to this day.

Psalm 119:105

Psalm 119:105 states: "Thy word *is* a lamp unto my feet, and a light unto my path." *Unto my path* is לִנְתִיבָתִי, which is a feminine singular construct noun with the preposition ל from נְתִיבָה. Earlier, the Psalmist uses this same word in asking God to make him "to go in the path of " God's commandments (Psalm 119:35). But, if there are no inspired vowels, then how would the Psalmist know exactly God's commandments? For instance, in Exodus 23:19 is the prohibition against seething a kid in his mother's milk. One could repoint the word *milk* (חֲלֵב) to get *fat* (חֵלֶב).[508] Without the vowel points it would be impossible to know which word it should be and, therefore, it would be impossible to know wherein to walk. In this case, without the vowel points, Scripture would not provide very good light in directing the Psalmist in the path of God's commandments. For Scripture to be truly a light unto the path, the vowels are necessary.

---

[508] Some commentators suggest such a change where *milk* occurs in other verses, such as Barnes on Job 21:24 (see comments on Job 21:24 in the previous chapter).

Another verse with similar teaching as Psalm 119:105 is Proverbs 6:23, which states: "For the commandment *is* a lamp; and the law *is* light; and reproofs of instruction *are* the way of life."

Psalm 119:138

Psalm 119:138 states, "Thy testimonies *that* thou hast commanded *are* righteous and very faithful." The word for *Thy testimonies* (עֵדֹתֶיךָ, a feminine plural construct noun with a second person masculine singular suffix from עֵדָה) is always in the plural in the Traditional Text and always refers to "laws as divine testimonies or solemn charges."[509] As an example of this, Deuteronomy 6:17, 20 uses *testimonies* to refer to the very testimonies that God had commanded for the children of Israel. *Testimonies*, then, are inspired commandments from God. These inspired commandments are righteous and very faithful. *Faithful* is אֱמוּנָה, a feminine singular absolute noun and means "firmness, fidelity, steadfastness, steadiness."[510] Here the Bible modifies it with the word *very* (מְאֹד, an adverb), which, as an adverb, means "very, much, greatly, exceedingly, thoroughly" and "gives a strengthening quality."[511] The use of *very* heightens the idea of faithfulness and teaches that God's inspired commandments are exceedingly firm and steadfast. Another teaching is that at the time God commanded His testimonies back in Deuteronomy, for example, they were firm and steadfast, and they continued firm and steadfast into the Psalmist's day. Furthermore, as Psalm 119:152 (see further) teaches, the testimonies would continue firm and steadfast for ever. However, as the previous chapter demonstrates, if there are no vowels, many of

---

[509] Brown, *A Hebrew and English Lexicon*, 730.

[510] "0530 אמונה" in *Online Bible Hebrew Lexicon* in *Online Bible*, version 1.33 (Winterbourne, Ontario: Timnathserah Inc., 2003).

[511] Robin Wakely, "H4394 מְאֹד" in *New International Dictionary of Old Testament Theology*.

God's testimonies are not exceedingly firm and steadfast. From Psalm 119:138 comes the teaching that not only did God inspire the vowels, but that He also preserved them.

Psalm 119:152

Psalm 119:152 states: "Concerning thy testimonies, I have known of old that thou hast founded them for ever." On *Thy testimonies* see above under Psalm 119:138. Of the testimonies the Psalmist says, "I have known of old that Thou hast founded them for ever." God has founded for ever His inspired testimonies. *Thou hast founded them* is a Qal perfect second masculine singular verb with a third masculine plural suffix referring back to *testimonies*[512] from יָסַד (*yāsad*). "The primary meaning of *yāsad* is 'to found, to fix firmly,' from which the major nominal meaning derives, i.e., 'foundation' especially of a building."[513] "There are overtones of solidity and permanence in many passages where the qal or niphal of *ysd* appears; this is almost always true in connection with the creation of the earth (cf. Ps. 24:2 and figuratively 119:152)."[514] *Thou hast founded them* is, then, speaking of the permanence and preservation of God's testimonies. Such teaching demands the inspiration as well as the preservation of the vowel points, for without the vowels in what way has God founded His testimonies for ever? Indeed, without the vowels, it seems that many of God's testimonies are, instead, lost for ever. The Psalmist knew of old that God

---

[512] The masculine plural suffix pronoun, *them*, refers to *testimonies*, a feminine plural noun. The same construction occurs in Psalm 12:6,7 where the verb, *thou shalt keep them*, also has the masculine plural suffix pronoun and just as in Psalm 119:152 where the masculine pronoun refers to a feminine noun, so in Psalm 12:7 the masculine pronoun refers to the feminine noun *words* in verse 6.

[513] Paul R. Gilchrist, "875 יָסַד," in *Theological Wordbook of the Old Testament*, 1:384.

[514] R. Mosis, "יָסַד," in *Theological Dictionary of the Old Testament*, 6:116.

had founded His testimonies, but many at the time of the writing of this book are refusing to walk in the old paths (Jeremiah 6:16).

Psalm 119:160

Psalm 119:160 states: "Thy word *is* true *from* the beginning: and every one of thy righteous judgments *endureth* for ever." The word for *true*, אֱמֶת, "carries [the] underlying sense of certainty, dependability . . . it is frequently applied to God as a characteristic of His nature . . . [and] it is a term fittingly applied to God's Words (Ps 119:142, 151, 160; Dan 10:21)."[515] "The meaning 'to be true' has arisen from the original meaning 'to be constant, permanent, faithful.' Truth is that which is constant and unchangeable."[516]

> As creator, God "keeps *'emeth*," and man can rely on Him "for ever" (Ps. 146:6). . . . He is great in *chesedh* and *'emeth* (Ex. 34:6; Ps. 86:15). Thus, *'emeth* belongs to God. This applies to the word of God in particular. The word of man may be often deceitful, but God's speech is *'emeth*! . . . a person can rely on His words. . . . Frequently the poet of Ps. 119 emphasizes the reliability of the divine word (vv. 43, 160), divine instruction (v. 142), and divine commandments (v. 151; cf. Ps. 19:10[9]; Neh. 9:13).[517]

The meaning of the word *true* necessitates the preservation as well as the inspiration of the vowel points, for without the vowel points God's Words are not certain, constant, unchangeable, and reliable.

But more than this, Psalm 119:160 states that God's Word is true from the beginning. *Beginning* is רֹאשׁ, a masculine singular construct noun from ראשׁ, and when the Bible uses this word temporally, as it does here, it refers to the beginning of something such as "the beginning of time (Prov 8:23), the first month of the year (Exod 12:12), the

---

[515] Jack B. Scott, "116 אָמַן" in *Theological Wordbook of the Old Testament*, 1:52.

[516] Alfred Jepsen, "אָמַן" in *Theological Dictionary of the Old Testament*, 1:310.

[517] Ibid., 313.

first day of a month (Num 28:11), and the beginning of a year (Ezek 40:1)."[518] At the very first, that is, at the very start and beginning of God giving His Word, it was true, meaning that it was certain, dependable, and permanent. Psalm 119:160 is a very strong verse in support of the inspiration of the vowel points. When God first gave His Word it was certain, and, therefore, had to have the vowels. As the previous chapter demonstrates without the vowels, God's Word is not certain.

The last part of the verse states: "And every one of thy righteous judgments *endureth* for ever." The translators have supplied *endureth* and rightly so, for the word *true* in the first part of the verse and the words *for ever* at the end of the verse, teach that God's judgments endure. But if there are no vowels, then many of God's judgments are lost forever and have not at all endured. In the light of Psalm 119:160, one must decide if he is going to believe what God, the Author of the Bible, says of the Bible, or if he will think that human scholars know more about the Bible than God and decide to follow them. It boils down this: will a man savour the things that be of God, or those that be of men (Matthew 16:23)?

Psalm 138:2

Psalm 138:2 states: "I will worship toward thy holy temple, and praise thy name for thy lovingkindness and for thy truth: for thou hast magnified thy word above all thy name." In this verse, David says that he will worship the Lord as well as praise His name because of God's lovingkindness and truth. And then David gives a reason for his praise and worship of the Lord as he says, "For thou hast magnified they word above all thy name." This is an astounding statement. As much as God is jealous over His name and as important as is God's name, yet this verse states that there is something that God has magni-

---

[518] Harry F. van Rooy, "רֹאשׁ (H8031)" in *New International Dictionary of Old Testament Theology and Exegesis.*

fied above all His name and that something is His Word. An examination of the various words in this verse will lead to a correct understanding of this verse.

Thou Hast Magnified

Thou hast magnified (הִגְדַּלְתָּ) is an Hiphil perfect second masculine singular from גָּדַל. "The root is used for physical growth of people and other living things as well as for the increase of things tangible and intangible whether objects, sounds, feelings, or authority."[519] "In both Piel and Hiphil stems, however, it bears the meaning 'to magnify' or 'consider great'."[520] "Generally speaking *gdl* in the hiphil means to bring about the process suggested by the finite verb in the qal: to prove oneself to be great actually and effectively."[521] Therefore, the magnifying of God's Word above all His name is something that has actually occurred. Other verses in the book of Psalms uses the Hiphil in a negative sense of people magnifying themselves against another (Psalms 38:16; 41:9; 55:12), but Psalm 138:2 uses it in a positive sense of God elevating or esteeming His Word above all His name.

Thou in *thou hast magnified* points back to the Lord as the subject of the action. Therefore, the teaching is that God has voluntarily exalted His Word above all His name. The Hiphil verb also indicates that God Himself is the cause of the action, it is not just David's opinion, but it is the truth. Waltke and O'Connor translate thusly: "You *caused* your word . . . *to be great*."[522]

---

[519] Elmer B. Smick, "315 גָּדַל" in *Theological Wordbook of the Old Testament*, I:151.

[520] Ibid.

[521] R. Mosis, "גָּדַל" in *Theological Dictionary of the Old Testament*, II:404.

[522] Bruce K. Waltke and M. O'Connor, *An Introduction to Biblical Hebrew Syntax* (Winona Lake, Indiana: Eisenbrauns, 1990), 437.

Thy Word

Thy Word (אִמְרָתֶךָ) is a feminine singular construct noun with a second masculine singular suffix. Psalms repeatedly uses this noun of the Word of God (Psalm 12:6; 119:11, 41, 58, 67, 76, 116, 123, 133, 148).

Above

God has magnified His Own Word above all His name. *Above all thy name* in Hebrew is עַל־כָּל־שְׁמֶךָ. *Above* (עַל) is a preposition that can have several possible meanings including "upon, and hence on the ground of, according to, on account of, on behalf of, concerning, beside, in addition to, together with, beyond, above, over, by, on to, towards, to, against."[523] What meaning does *above* have in this context? "It denotes *elevation* or *pre-eminence* ... with words ... such as ... גדל."[524] גדל compose the base consonants of the root for *thou hast magnified* (הִגְדַּלְתָּ), which is an Hiphil perfect second masculine singular from גָּדַל. In light of this, the King James translators have correctly translated עַל (ʿal-) with *above*.

All

All (כָּל) is a masculine singular construct noun.[525] The genitive of this construct relationship is *thy name* (שְׁמֶךָ). When the Bible uses *all* in the construct state, it signifies " 'the whole of something'."[526] *All* "with foll[owing] gen[itive] (as usually) [means] *the whole of*, to be rendered, however, often in our idiom, to avoid stiff-

---

[523] Brown, *A Hebrew and English Lexicon*, 752.

[524] Ibid., 755.

[525] John Joseph Owen, *Analytical Key to the Old Testament* (Grand Rapids: Baker, 1991), 3:503.

[526] John N. Oswalt, "985 כָּלַל" in *Theological Wordbook of the Old Testament*, 1:441.

ness, *all* or *every*."⁵²⁷ When a determinate genitive follows *all*, then *all* "has the meaning of *the entirety*, i.e., *all, the whole*."⁵²⁸ The Hebrew word following *all* is *thy name*. Since *thy name* has the second masculine singular pronoun suffix, then it is a determined noun, or definite noun, or "genitive determinate."⁵²⁹ In light of this, *all* means entirety, therefore, God has magnified His Word above the entirety of His name. Whatever God's name conveys, God has magnified His Word above that.

Thy Name

Thy name (שִׁמְךָ a masculine singular construct noun with a second person masculine singular suffix from שֵׁם) refers to God's name and "signifies the whole self-disclosure of God in his holiness and truth (Ps 22:22)."⁵³⁰ In Psalm 22:22 the Hebrew uses the same expression as in Psalm 138:2, that is, *thy name* (שִׁמְךָ), therefore, in Psalm 138:2 *thy name* also signifies the whole self-disclosure of God. According to Wilson, "The name is supposed to correspond to the nature of a person or thing; or to express some qualities or circumstances relating to them . . . . Hence the name of God sometimes signifies the nature, and properties, and attributes of God, as his power, wisdom, goodness, majesty, holiness, justice, and truth."⁵³¹ Ross observes: "שֵׁם can also signify the nature or attributes of the person named. This is especially true with regard to God."⁵³² In light of these statements,

---

⁵²⁷ Brown, *A Hebrew and English Lexicon*, 481.

⁵²⁸ A. E. Cowley, *Gesenius' Hebrew Grammar*, 411.

⁵²⁹ Ibid., 410.

⁵³⁰ Walter C. Kaiser, "2405 שֵׁם" in *Theological Wordbook of the Old Testament*, II:934.

⁵³¹ Wilson, 284.

⁵³² Allen P. Ross, "(H9005) שֵׁם" in *New International Dictionary of Old Testament Theology and Exegesis*.

God's very name or title indicates something about God's nature. For example, *Almighty* (Genesis 49:25) indicates that God is omnipotent. *Jehovahjireh* indicates that God will provide (Genesis 22:14). *I AM* indicates that God is ever-present and eternal (Exodus 3:14). In each of these cases, the actual title is truly indicative of God's nature. Indeed, there are no titles for God that do not truly agree with His nature or character.

God the Father has magnified His Word above all His name. In what way is that God has magnified His Word above all His name? The answer is that whenever God makes a promise, He binds Himself to that promise. Indeed, He places Himself under the obligation to perform that promise. If He were to fail to keep His Word, then He would cease to be God. Therefore, all of God's name and all that God's name signifies are subordinate to His Word.

Conclusion

Psalm 138:2 means exactly what it says, that is, that God has magnified His Word above all His Name. With God magnifying His Word above all His name, then a number of conclusions follow. First, since God "cannot lie" (Titus 1:2), and since God has magnified His Word above all His name, then His Word must also be true. Indeed, Jesus stated, "Thy word is truth" (John 17:17).

Second, since God's "way is perfect" (II Samuel 22:31), and since He has magnified His Word above all His name, then His Word must also be perfect. Indeed, the Bible states, "The words of the LORD *are* pure words: *as* silver tried in a furnace of earth, purified seven times" (Psalm 12:6). In light of the perfection of God, the Bible must be free of so-called scribal errors.

Third, since "God is not *the author* of confusion" (I Corinthians 14:33), and since He has magnified His Word above all His name, then His Word must also be free of confusion. God not being the author of confusion demands that God inspired the Old Testament with vowels, for without the vowels confusion would reign. Therefore, the Lord instructed Moses to "write upon the stones all the words of this law very plainly" (Deuteronomy 27:8) and Habakkuk to "write the vision, and make it plain upon tables" (Habakkuk 2:2). These commands from God for a clear representation of His Word extend to all the writers of the Old Testament (Matthew 5:18; Luke 16:17).

Fourth, since God is eternal (Deuteronomy 33:27), and since He has magnified His Word above all His name, then His Word is eternal as well. The Bible states in I Peter 1:23 that the Word of God "liveth and abideth for ever." Also, I Peter 1:25 states, "The word of the Lord endureth for ever." The Word of God will last, not a part of it will be lost, which indicates that the vowels along with the consonants that compose the words will endure, that is, that God preserves the vowels and consonants of the words. If there are no vowels and if the lack of vowels, therefore, results in uncertainty about the wording of the Bible, then in what sense can it be that God's Word liveth and abideth for ever? Without the vowels, the Word does not live and abide.

Proverbs 22:20,21

Proverbs 22:20,21 states: "Have not I written to thee excellent things in counsels and knowledge, That I might make thee know the certainty of the words of truth; that thou mightest answer the words of truth to them that send unto thee?" Solomon wrote so that his reader might know the certainty of the words of truth. *Truth* (אֱמֶת) also occurs in Psalm 119:160 and refers to that which is constant and unchangeable. But if there are no vowels, then in what way are these words constant and unchangeable?

Words (אִמְרֵי) a masculine plural construct noun from אָמַר) in Proverbs 22:20,21 refers to written words, as the first part of verse 20 indicates, but in other verses refers to spoken words, which, because they were spoken, were vocalized. For instance, Deuteronomy 32:1 states: "Give ear, O ye heavens, and I will speak; and hear, O earth, the words (אִמְרֵי) of my mouth." Other verses that teach that *words* refer to spoken words are Numbers 24:4,16; Joshua 24:27; Job 8:2; 22:22; 23:12; Psalm 5:1; 19:14; 54:2; 78:1; 138:4; 141:6; Isaiah 32:7; 41:26; and Hosea 6:5. Of particular interest are the times that the book of Proverbs uses אָמֵר to clearly refer to the spoken word (Proverbs 1:21; 2:16; 4:5,10; 5:7; 6:2; 7:5,24; 8:8; 15:26; 16:24; 17:27; 19:7; and 23:12). In several of these verses Proverbs refers to the spoken words of knowledge and counsel (Proverbs 1:21; 4:5,10; 5:7; 7:24; 19:27; 23:12), which, according to Proverbs 22:20 are the words that Solomon wrote. Since the spoken word requires vowels, and since these spoken words of counsel and knowledge were written, then these written, inspired words must also have vowels. The inspired Words of God that Solomon wrote had vowels. Not only is this a valid conclusion from the meaning of אָמֵר itself, but also from the word for *truth*, which emphasizes that these words are certain and unchanging. Certain and unchanging words require vowels.

Furthermore, the word *certainty* establishes that these written words have vowels. *Certainty* (קֹשְׁטְ, a masculine singular construct noun from קֹשֶׁט) means "exact, precise truth; weighed, as it were, in the evenest balance."[533] But as the previous chapter demonstrates, without the vowels, the words are not at all exact.

For those who argue that the vowels are uninspired, a couple of questions arise. First, if there are no vowels, then in what way did Solomon convey words? Also, if there are no vowels, then in what way did Solomon make known the certainty of the words of truth?

Isaiah 30:8

Isaiah 30:8 states: "Now go, write it before them in a table, and note it in a book, that it may be for the time to come for ever and ever:" In the following verses are the words that God commanded Isaiah to

---

[533] Wilson, 456.

write. Not only did Isaiah write the words, but he also recorded the command to write those words and the purpose for the writing them. The purpose for writing these words is that they might be for the time to come for ever and ever. Therefore, God's method of preserving His Words is through writing, not through an oral tradition. Such a method demands that Isaiah also wrote the vowels, for, as the previous chapter demonstrates, without the vowels some words are not for ever and ever, but, instead, are for ever lost. The inspired Words of God that Isaiah wrote had vowels.

Some ignore the clear teaching of Isaiah 30:8 and proceed to tamper with it. For example, *The Pulpit Commentary* states: "Modern critics observe that the phrase, *lâ'ad 'ad 'olâm* [*for ever and ever*], never occurs elsewhere, and suggest a change of the pointing, which would give the sense of 'for a testimony forever'."[534] Such critics show a brazen disregard for Scripture. While one might initially think that *for ever and ever* and *for a testimony forever* have the same meaning, they do not. Isaiah 30:8 in the Traditional Text teaches that what Isaiah wrote would be for ever and ever, that is, that the very words themselves would be for ever and ever, which speaks of verbal preservation. What the critics suggest, however, with their repointing is that Isaiah's writing would be for a testimony forever, in other words, that Isaiah's message would continue, but not necessarily Isaiah's very words. The change suggested by the critics promotes conceptual preservation, that is, preservation of the concepts, but not of the actual words. Conceptual preservation does not necessarily require the vowels, whereas verbal preservation does, and it is verbal preservation that the Bible teaches (Psalm 12:6,7).

---

[534] G. Rawlinson, *Isaiah*, vol. 1, in vol. 10 of *The Pulpit Commentary*, 490.

Isaiah 40:8

Isaiah 40:8 states: "The grass withereth, the flower fadeth: but the word of our God shall stand for ever." In what way can Isaiah claim that the Word of God shall stand for ever, if there are no vowels? Indeed, if there are no vowels, then many of the words are not standing at all, for no one could know certainly what the words are.

E. J. Young, commenting on this verse, says,

> To God's word there is a permanent character. Unlike the flesh of man, which withers and fades, it stands forever. It rises up, stands, and endures. In contrast to all flesh with its perishable nature, the word of God is imperishable and endures forever. The thought is similar to that of our Lord's, "The Scripture cannot be broken." When God speaks, His word expresses the truth; and that truth cannot be annulled or changed.[535]

Such a permanent character of the Words of God of which Isaiah speaks requires the vowels, for without the vowels the words are not permanent, but are in a state of flux, as the previous chapter demonstrates.

Isaiah 59:21

Isaiah 59:21 states: "As for me, this *is* my covenant with them, saith the LORD; My spirit that *is* upon thee, and my words which I have put in thy mouth, shall not depart out of thy mouth, nor out of the mouth of thy seed, nor out of the mouth of thy seed's seed, saith the LORD, from henceforth and for ever." God put His Words in Isaiah's mouth and stated that these Words would not depart out of Isaiah's mouth, or out of the mouth of Isaiah's seed, nor out of the mouth of the seed of Isaiah's seed. Four times the Lord uses *mouth*. *Mouth* refers to vocalized words, that is, words having both consonants and vowels.

---

[535] E. J. Young, *The Book of Isaiah* (Grand Rapids: Eerdmans, 1978), 3:35.

These mouthed words will continue for ever. God promises to preserve these mouthed words, indicating a promise to preserve both the consonants and the vowels.

Jeremiah 30:2

Jeremiah 30:2 states: "Thus speaketh the LORD God of Israel, saying, Write thee all the words that I have spoken unto thee in a book." God commands Jeremiah to write the words that He had spoken, therefore, these words were vocalized, and God wanted these vocalized words written. Since speaking necessitates the presence of vowels and consonants, and since Jeremiah was to write these spoken words, then Jeremiah wrote both vowels and consonants. The inspired words that Jeremiah wrote had vowels.

Jeremiah 36:1-4,6

Jeremiah 36:1-4 states: "And it came to pass in the fourth year of Jehoiakim the son of Josiah king of Judah, *that* this word came unto Jeremiah from the LORD, saying, Take thee a roll of a book, and write therein all the words that I have spoken unto thee against Israel, and against Judah, and against all the nations, from the day I spake unto thee, from the days of Josiah, even unto this day. It may be that the house of Judah will hear all the evil which I purpose to do unto them; that they may return every man from his evil way; that I may forgive their iniquity and their sin. Then Jeremiah called Baruch the son of Neriah: and Baruch wrote from the mouth of Jeremiah all the words of the LORD, which he had spoken unto him, upon a roll of a book." In what way could it be true that Baruch wrote from the mouth of Jeremiah all the words that the Lord spoke unto Jeremiah, if he used no vowels? The Lord spoke and Jeremiah spoke, both of which necessitate the use of vowels, then Baruch wrote what the Lord spoke to Jeremiah. If Baruch did his job faithfully, he had to use vowels. Indeed, as the previous chapter indicates, if there are no vowels, then it is very difficult in certain places to know the exact words that the Lord spoke. The inspired Words of God that Baruch wrote had vowels.

Jeremiah 36:6 has a similar application. It states: "Therefore go thou, and read in the roll, which thou hast written from my mouth, the words of the LORD in the ears of the people in the LORD'S house upon the fasting day: and also thou shalt read them in the ears of all Judah that come out of their cities." M'Intosh observes: "The written word of God is the same in character with the spoken word."[536] In other words, since the spoken Word of God requires vowels, then the written Word of God also must have vowels, all of which demands inspired vowel points.

Habakkuk 2:2

Habakkuk 2:2 states: "And the LORD answered me, and said, Write the vision, and make *it* plain upon tables, that he may run that readeth it." *Plain* (בָּאֵר a piel masculine singular imperative) is from the same Hebrew word for *plainly* in Dt 27:8 (see above) meaning to make plain, distinct, clear. In what way could Habakkuk write the vision and make it plain, distinct, and clear, if he did not use vowels? Furthermore, the last part of the verse states that Habakkuk is to write it so clearly "that he may run that readeth it." God's desire was that the writing would be so plain and so clear that even a person running would be able to discern what Habakkuk had written. Again, in what way could Habakkuk accomplish this, if he did not use vowels? Habakkuk 2:2 leads to the conclusion that the inspired Words of God that Habakkuk wrote had vowels.

Summary

This section presents from the Old Testament twenty-seven (27) passages in detail and additionally alludes to several other pas-

---

[536] M'Intosh, 393.

sages. From these verses a couple of conclusions become obvious. First, the inspired Words of God had vowels (Exodus 4:22; 24:4; 34:1, 27; Joshua 1:8; Judges 12:6; Psalm 12:6; 19:7; 93:5; 111:7; 119:86, 89, 105, 138, 152, 160; 138:2).

Second, the God-inspired Words that various writers wrote had vowels. The God-inspired Words that Moses wrote had vowels (Exodus 24:4; 34:1, 27; Deuteronomy 31:24). The God-inspired Words that Solomon wrote had vowels (Proverbs 22:20,21). The God-inspired Words that Isaiah wrote had vowels (Isaiah 30:8). The God-inspired Words that Jeremiah wrote had vowels (Jeremiah 30:2). The God-inspired Words that Baruch wrote had vowels (Jeremiah 36:1-4, 6). The God-inspired Words that Daniel wrote had vowels (Psalm 119:89; Daniel 10:21; 11:2). The God-inspired Words that Habakkuk wrote had vowels (Habakkuk 2:2).

Third, the vowels that God inspired were preserved and will be preserved (Nehemiah 8:8; Psalm 12:6, 7; 19:7; 111:7; 119:86, 89, 138, 152, 160; 138:2; Isaiah 30:8; 40:8; 59:21).

These verses present a compelling case for the inspiration, inscripturation, and preservation of the vowels of the Hebrew Old Testament.

NEW TESTAMENT VERSES

Just as many Old Testament verses require the inspiration of the vowel points, so do many New Testament verses. This section presents several of these verses.

Matthew 4:4

Matthew 4:4 states: "But he answered and said, It is written, Man shall not live by bread alone, but by every word that proceedeth out of the mouth of God." From this verse a number of teachings are clear. First, Matthew 4:4 speaks of words that proceedeth out of the mouth of God. Words proceeding out of the mouth require the use of vowels, therefore, God used vowels. Second, *every word that proceedeth out of the mouth of God* is an adequate description of inspiration, therefore, God inspired the vowels. Third, since man needs the Words of God, then the Words are available. The availability of the Words of God speaks of the preservation of the Words and, therefore, the preservation of the vowels. The way by which God has chosen to make these words available is through the writing of His Words (Isaiah 30:8), therefore, the written words must have the vowels.

Those who do not believe in the inspiration of the vowel points must answer this question: if there are no inspired vowels, then many of God's Words are in doubt, how, then, would man have every word that proceedeth out of the mouth of God? It is clear from the previous chapter that without inspired, preserved, and authoritative vowels many of God's Words would not be available to man.

Matthew 22:31

In Matthew 22:31 the Lord Jesus Christ said to the Sadducees, "But as touching the resurrection of the dead, have ye not read that which was spoken unto you by God, saying." In the following verse (Matthew 22:32), Jesus refers to the inspired Words of God in Exodus 3:6, where the Lord said, "I am the God of Abraham, and the God of Isaac, and the God of Jacob." These Words are Words that God spoke and said. *Spoken* and *saying* involve the vocalizing of words, which necessitate the use of vowels. A conclusion that arises now is that since God spoke words, which involves the use of vowels; and since these words are inspired words; then God inspired the vowels.

The vocalized words of Exodus 3:6, though spoken by God to Moses approximately fifteen hundred years earlier, not only had a message for Moses, but were also intended for the Sadducees of Christ's day! Woudstra, based on Matthew 22:31, observes: "Through the medium of Scripture the Words of God originally spoken to Moses under the solemn circumstances of the burning bush are also spoken to the Sadducees."[537] The vocalized words continued through the medium of writing so that the Sadducees were able to read them. In other words, Jesus equates what the Sadducees could read, that is, what is written, with what God spoke and said many years earlier. The above facts lead to a couple more conclusions: (1) the inspired vowels that God spoke in Moses' day were inscripturated so that the Sadducees could read them at a later date; and (2) the inspired vowels that God spoke were preserved so that they were available for the Sadducees to read some fifteen hundred years later.[538]

Jesus dogmatically appeals to the it-is-written record of what God said to teach the Sadducees the truth of the resurrection. If, however, there are no vowels, as the previous chapter demonstrates, then many of the Words of God become uncertain and one can no longer dogmatically appeal to them. Jesus' authoritative use of the words of the Old Testament demands the presence of the vowels in His copy of

---

[537] Marten H. Woudstra, "The Inspiration of the Old Testament" in *The Bible – The Living Word of Revelation*, ed. Merrill C. Tenney (Grand Rapids: Zondervan, 1968), 137.

[538] It is true that in some cases the New Testament writers do not always give a verbatim quotation of a passage from the Old Testament, but rather allude to it, or paraphrase it. At other times, the Holy Spirit gave them additional revelation concerning the meaning of Old Testament words and moved them to use different words so as to bring forth the meaning of the verse (e.g., Hebrews 10:5,6 referring to Psalm 40:6). But such cases do not invalidate the point that the writers of the Old Testament wrote what God said, and since speaking requires vowels, then the writing of such speaking also requires vowels. The requirement for vowels becomes even more evident when one considers the use of present tense and perfect tense verbs to refer to the speaking or saying (Acts 7:48,49; 8:32-34; Romans 9:29; 12:19; 14:11; II Peter 3:2), indicating that the prophet or the Lord is still saying these words. But where are they still saying these words? They are still saying them in the written Word of God, so that the written Word of God echoes their vocalized words. For more information on the subject of how New Testament writers quoted the Old Testament see the author's *Those So-Called Errors* (Newington, CT: Emmanuel Baptist Theological Press, 2003), p. 43 footnote 57, p. 93 footnote 157, and pp. 170-174.

the Old Testament, that is, the Traditional Text of the Old Testament had vowels.

Matthew 22:31-32 presents the teaching of inspired vowels, inscripturated vowels, preserved vowels, and authoritative vowels. Other verses present the same teaching.

> Luke 24:25 – "Then he said unto them, O fools, and slow of heart to believe all that the prophets have spoken." This refers to what the prophets spoke about Jesus. Their God-inspired spoken and, therefore, vocalized words were written.
>
> John 1:23 – "He said, I *am* the voice of one crying in the wilderness, Make straight the way of the Lord, as said the prophet Esaias." Here John the Baptist refers to Isaiah's prophecy written in Isaiah 40:3. In referring to this written record, he states that it is something that Isaiah said. The God-inspired vocalized Words of Isaiah continue in the preserved written record.
>
> John 12:38 – "That the saying of Esaias the prophet might be fulfilled, which he spake, Lord, who hath believed our report? and to whom hath the arm of the Lord been revealed?" The God-inspired vocalized Words of Isaiah are written in Isaiah 53:1, involve the use of vowels, and are authoritative.
>
> Acts 3:22 – "For Moses truly said unto the fathers, A prophet shall the Lord your God raise up unto you of your brethren, like unto me; him shall ye hear in all things whatsoever he shall say unto you." See also Acts 7:37. The God-inspired vocalized Words of Moses are written in Deuteronomy 18:15.
>
> Acts 7:48,49 – "Howbeit the most High dwelleth not in temples made with hands; as saith the prophet, Heaven *is* my throne, and earth *is* my footstool: what house will ye build me? saith the Lord: or what *is* the place of my rest?" What the prophet Isaiah said (*saith*) is written in Isaiah 66:1. *Saith* (λέγει) is a present active indicative verb. Since the Word of God liveth and abideth for ever (I Peter 1:23-25), it is as if Isaiah is still saying it. Isaiah's spoken and, therefore, vocalized Words from God are still reverberating in the pages of Holy Scripture.
>
> Acts 8:32-34 - "The place of the scripture which he read was this, He was led as a sheep to the slaughter; and like a lamb dumb before his shearer, so opened he not his mouth: In his humiliation his judgment was taken away: and who shall declare his generation? for his life is

taken from the earth. And the eunuch answered Philip, and said, I pray thee, of whom speaketh the prophet this? of himself, or of some other man?" Here the eunuch is reading Isaiah 53:7,8. *Speaketh* (λέγει) is a present active indicative verb once again indicating that Isaiah's spoken Words from God are still resounding in the written Words.

Acts 28:25 - "And when they agreed not among themselves, they departed, after that Paul had spoken one word, Well spake the Holy Ghost by Esaias the prophet unto our fathers," The following words in Acts 28:26,27 are written in Isaiah 6:9,10. Again, the vocalized Words of God through Isaiah are in the written record. See also Matthew 13:14,15.

Romans 9:29 - "And as Esaias said before, Except the Lord of Sabaoth had left us a seed, we had been as Sodoma, and been made like unto Gomorrha." Romans 9:29 refers to Isaiah 1:9. *Said before* (προείρηκεν from προλέγω) is a perfect active indicative, indicating that what Isaiah had said in the past still continued in the present. Therefore, what Isaiah spoke continued, that is, even the vocalization continued. But if there are no vowels in the written record, then in what way does the speech of Isaiah continue?

Romans 12:19 – "Dearly beloved, avenge not yourselves, but *rather* give place unto wrath: for it is written, Vengeance *is* mine; I will repay, saith[539] the Lord." Romans 12:19 refers to what is written in Deuteronomy 32:35. The vocalized Words of the Lord are written, which would be impossible if what is written has no vowels.

Romans 14:11 – "For it is written, *As* I live, saith[540] the Lord, every knee shall bow to me, and every tongue shall confess to God." This is from Isaiah 45:23 and again presents the teaching that what the Lord saith was written, therefore, the written record must include the vowels.

I Corinthians 9:10 - "Or saith he *it* altogether for our sakes? For our sakes, no doubt, *this* is written: that he that ploweth should plow in hope; and that he that thresheth in hope should be partaker of his hope." This verse indicates that what God said (*saith*) is written,

---

[539] Concerning the importance of *saith*, see above in this list on Acts 7:48,49.

[540] Concerning the importance of *saith*, see above in this list on Acts 7:48,49.

which would be impossible, if the vowels are not present in the written account.

Hebrews 3:7 – "Wherefore as the Holy Ghost saith,[541] To day if ye will hear his voice." Hebrews 3:7 and the following verses are from Psalm 95:7-11. The vocalized Words of the Spirit of God continue in the written record, where He is still saying them.

II Peter 3:2 - "That ye be mindful of the words which were spoken before by the holy prophets, and of the commandment of us the apostles of the Lord and Saviour." *Spoken before* is a perfect passive participle, which indicates "permanence, the speaking still continues in Holy Writ."[542] "The perfect tense . . . underlines the permanence of these prophetic utterances; the speaking still continues in the inspired Scriptures."[543] These Words of God spoken in the past remain speaking into Peter's day. Since the prophets vocalized the words that they spoke, and since these spoken Words continue, then the vowels must also continue.

These thirteen (13) passages, along with Matthew 22:31, all support the teaching that God inspired the vowels, these vowels were inscripturated, these vowels are preserved, and these vowels are authoritative.

Matthew 24:35

Matthew 24:35 states: "Heaven and earth shall pass away, but my words shall not pass away." In this verse, the word for *words* is λόγοι, which is a nominative masculine plural from λόγος. The Bible uses λόγος in reference to Jesus' sayings (Matthew 7:24, 26, 28; 15:12; 19:1, 11, 22; 26:1; Mark 8:32; 10:22; Luke 6:47; 9:28, 44; John 6:60; 7:36, 40; 8:51, 52, 55; 10:19; 14:24); casting out spirits with His Word (Matthew 8:16); asking a thing (Matthew 21:24; Luke 20:3); talk (Matthew 22:15); words He prayed (Matthew 26:44; Mark 14:39);

---

[541] Concerning the importance of *saith*, see above in this list on Acts 7:48,49.

[542] Lenski, *The Interpretation of I and II Epistles of Peter, the Three Epistles of John, and the Epistle of Jude*, 337.

[543] Hiebert, *Second Peter and Jude*, 139.

preaching (Mark 2:2; 4:33; Luke 5:1; 10:39; 22:61; John 2:22; 4:41, 50; 5:24, 38; 8:31, 37, 43; 12:48; 15:3); words (Matthew 24:35; Mark 8:38; 10:24; 12:13; Luke 4:22, 32; 9:26; 20:20; 24:44; John 14:23); and asking a question (Mark 11:29). Obviously, all of these instances involved vocalized words, therefore, necessitating the use of vowels.

While *words* applies to Jesus' New Testament canonical Words,[544] it also applies to Old Testament words for Jesus spoke in the Old Testament. Jesus, as the Angel of the Lord, spoke on several occasions in the Old Testament.[545] Furthermore, the Bible teaches that the Spirit of Christ worked in the Old Testament prophets. I Peter 1:10,11 says, "Of which salvation the prophets have enquired and searched diligently, who prophesied of the grace that should come unto you: searching what, or what manner of time the Spirit of Christ which was in them did signify, when it testified beforehand the sufferings of Christ, and the glory that should follow." The Spirit of Christ was in the Old Testament prophets testifying to them about the sufferings and glory of Christ. The testifyings of the Spirit of Christ to the Old Testament prophets are the Words of Christ and, therefore, are included in the promise of Christ that His Words shall not pass away. Waite states:

> The Lord is talking of His *Words*, the New Testament. Not the Masoretic Hebrew Old Testament only, but His Words will not pass away. That means the promise extends to the New Testament. I believe, personally that the Lord Jesus was the Source and Author of every He-

---

[544] Thomas M. Strouse, "The Translation Model Predicted By Scripture" (Newington, CT: Emmanuel Baptist Theological Seminary, 2000), 9,10.

[545] Various verses make it evident that the Old Testament Angel of the Lord is the Lord Himself (Genesis 16:7-13; 22:1, 2, 11, 12, 15, 16; Exodus 3:2-7, 13-16 (cf. Acts 7:30-32); Judges 2:1 (cf. Exodus 20:2); 6:11-20; 13:3, 8-22; Zechariah 12:8). Several verses make it clear that the Old Testament Angel of the Lord is the Lord Jesus Christ (Exodus 3:14 (cf. John 8:58); Judges 13:18 (cf. Isaiah 9:6); John 1:18).

brew Old Testament text. He was the Revelator. He is the Word of God. Truly, therefore, His *Words* include the entire Old Testament.[546]

The Spirit of Christ testifying to the prophets refers to the process of inspiration where the Spirit of Christ gave words to the prophets. Since the Words of Christ include vowels then the words of these testifyings also had vowels, indicating the inspiration of the vowels.

Pass away, παρέλθωσι, is an aorist active subjunctive third person plural from παρέρχομαι, which Matthew 24:35 uses "metaphorically" meaning "to pass away" or to "perish."[547] *Not* in *shall not pass away* uses the double negative, οὐ μή. Zodhiates says that οὐ μή is "a double neg[ative] strengthening the denial, meaning not at all, no never. . . . When these two neg[atives] are coupled together they refer to emphatic negations as to the fut[ure], meaning not at all, by no means, construed particularly with the fut[ure] indic[ative] or more commonly with the aor[ist] subjunctive,"[548] which is exactly the tense Matthew uses here. The teaching is that Jesus' very Words will not at all perish. The imperishability of Jesus' Words demands the presence of the vowels, or else, if there are no vowels as the previous chapter demonstrates, many of these Old Testament words have perished. What Jesus guarantees here is the preservation of the vowels along with the consonants.

At this point, one has a decision to make: will he believe Jesus about the vowels, or the scholars? Jesus, Who is the Living Word, is certainly the Authority on the written Word. Despite what critics say, one cannot go wrong believing in Jesus. To believe Jesus may involve some reproach (Hebrews 13:13), but it is far better to be with Jesus, than against Him.

---

[546] Donald A. Waite, *Defending the King James Bible* (Collingswood, NJ: The Bible for Today Press, 1992), 11.

[547] Zodhiates, "3928. παρέρχομαι."

[548] Zodhiates, "3364. οὐ μή."

John 10:35

In John 10:35, Jesus said: "The scripture cannot be broken." *Scripture* here refers to the Old Testament.[549] In the Greek, *cannot be broken* is οὐ δύναται λυθῆναι. *Can be* is the translation of δύναται, which is a present middle indicative from δύναμαι, and means "to be able, have power."[550] An aorist passive infinitive (λυθῆναι *broken*) follows δύναται, and in such cases δύναται is "implying transient or momentary action, either past or pres[ent]."[551] Also, since the negative particle (οὐ) accompanies δύναται, then it is denying that Scripture is able to be momentarily broken, let alone permanently broken. The fact that God's Words cannot be broken speaks of the continuing and abiding quality of the Words of God, which is something of which Peter also speaks in I Peter 1:23: "Being born again, not of corruptible seed, but of incorruptible, by the word of God, which liveth and abideth for ever." It is impossible to stamp out any part of the Word of God even momentarily. *Broken*, λυθῆναι, means "to loose, loosen what is fast, bound, meaning to unbind, untie," and "by implication, to destroy . . . figuratively of a law or institution, to loosen its obligation, i.e., either to make void, to do away."[552] The teaching of John 10:35 is clear: it is impossible to do away with or make void the Old Testament, therefore, it is fully preserved and completely authoritative.[553] Robert Lightner commenting on John 10:35 states,

---

[549] See previous discussion on II Timothy 3:16,17 in Chapter Two, as well as the author's treatment of the word *Scripture* in John 10:35 in *Those So-Called Errors* (Newington, CT: Emmanuel Baptist Theological Press, 2003), 83, 84.

[550] Zodhiates, "1410. δύναμαι."

[551] Ibid.

[552] Zodhiates, "3089. λύω."

[553] Being fully preserved and completely authoritative would equally apply to the New Testament text since it too is Scripture (I Timothy 5:18; II Timothy 3:16; II Peter 3:16).

> The word "cannot" expresses a Divine and moral impossibility. The point is, Scripture cannot be annulled, dissolved, abrogated, or rendered void because it declares the will and purpose of God. Of equal importance in Christ's statement is the word "broken." By this expression He emphasizes not only the Divine authority but also the unity and solidarity of Scripture. What cannot happen to one minute part cannot happen to the whole.[554]

If, however, the Hebrew Old Testament text has no inspired vowels, then in what way is the Old Testament Scripture preserved and authoritative? As the previous chapter demonstrates, with no inspired vowel points, the text is riddled with uncertainty. If the Old Testament has no inspired vowels, then it is broken in many places and needs the attention of many scholars to mend it. Even then, they are not able to mend it fully; therefore, the Old Testament always has a shadow of doubt and suspicion surrounding it. Such is the place where the devil would want God's Words: broken and powerless. Thank God that such is not the case, for Jesus has promised that the Scripture cannot be broken. Such a promise asserts that the Words of God are settled and if they are settled, then the words must have the vowels.

Acts 7:38

In Acts 7:38, Stephen spoke of the fathers "who received the lively oracles to give unto us." The fathers, that is, the Old Testament Jews received the lively oracles (Romans 3:2). *Lively* (ζῶντα a present active participle accusative neuter plural from ζάω) refers metaphorically in the participle to things that are "living, lively, active, also enduring, opposed to what is dead, inactive, and also transient."[555] *Lively*, being a present participle, indicates that at the time Stephen spoke in Acts 7 that these oracles were still lively. They had not lived in the past and then died, but were still alive. *Oracles* (λόγια an accu-

---

[554] Robert Lightner, *The Saviour and the Scriptures* (Philadelphia: Presbyterian and Reformed Publishing Co., 1978), 102.

[555] Zodhiates, "2198. ζάω."

sative neuter plural noun from λόγιον) refers to "the declarations of God."[556] These declarations of God from the Old Testament are living, they are not dead declarations, but they have a vitality about them. Furthermore, Stephen declares that these oracles are "unto us." *Us* includes Stephen, a local church member (Acts 6:1-5, cf. I Timothy 3:8-15). Therefore, by implication the oracles are for all local church members. The oracles are given *unto us* via the written Words of God.[557] If, however, the words have no vowels, then in what way are these oracles still lively and in what way are they *unto us*? Why, if the Old Testament words do not have inspired and preserved vowels, then it would seem that many of the oracles have died and are hidden from the view of New Testament saints. But the teaching of Acts 7:38 is that believers of this day do not have dead words that various doctors of the law and specialists must resuscitate, reconstruct, and revive. Oh, no, believers of this day have words that are robust, words that are full of life and able to impart life (I Peter 1:23-25). Such teaching demands that the words have inspired, preserved, and authoritative vowels.

II Timothy 3:16,17

II Timothy 3:16, 17 states: "All scripture *is* given by inspiration of God, and *is* profitable for doctrine, for reproof, for correction, for instruction in righteousness: That the man of God may be perfect, throughly furnished unto all good works." II Timothy 3:16-17 teaches that the Bible is the authority (see Chapter Two). However, if the Old Testament has no inspired and preserved vowels, then many of its words are uncertain, and if many of its words are uncertain, then what authority does it have? Whitfield in commenting on II Timothy 3:16 states:

---

[556] Zodhiates, "3051. λόγιον."

[557] It is obvious that the written Words of God transmit *unto us* the oracles since Stephen in Acts 7 is quoting from the written Old Testament.

> The Apostle here speaks principally of the Scriptures of the Old Testament; for those only were what Timothy had been instructed in from a child [II Timothy 3:15]. But this authority can be of no service, with respect to Scriptures, which are not understood. A man can neither be taught, nor reproved, nor reformed, nor instructed, by writings unintelligible or of uncertain signification. . . . But if any part of this Divine revelation, be supposed to be of a dubious and equivocal interpretation, no one assumed sense can, under Divine authority, claim our faith and obedience; so long as the ambiguity of its meaning remains. And as this is the case with respect to the Hebrew Scriptures; if the points be not allowed to be essential to them, we must, upon that supposition, bid farewell to all pretence of the Divine authority, of any one interpretation of them.[558]

In other words, if there are no vowel points, then the Old Testament lacks authority. However, II Timothy 3:16,17 teaches that the Bible is the sole authority. For the Old Testament to be part of that sole authority, it must have inspired vowels.

Hebrews 4:12

Hebrews 4:12 states: "For the word of God *is* quick, and powerful, and sharper than any twoedged sword, piercing even to the dividing asunder of soul and spirit, and of the joints and marrow, and *is* a discerner of the thoughts and intents of the heart." *Quick* (ζῶν) is a present active nominative masculine singular participle from ζάω, which is the same root that Acts 7:38 uses and comments from that verse equally apply here as well. The Word of God is still alive. But if there are no inspired and preserved vowels, then in what way is the Bible quick?

I Peter 1:23

I Peter 1:23 states: "Being born again, not of corruptible seed, but of incorruptible, by the word of God, which liveth and abideth for

---

[558] Whitfield, 89,90.

ever." *Liveth* (ζῶντος) is a present active masculine genitive singular participle from ζάω, which is the same root that Acts 7:38 uses and comments from that verse equally apply here as well. Again, if there are no inspired and preserved vowels, then in what way does the Bible live?

I Peter 1:23 also teaches that the Word of God abideth for ever, which speaks of the preservation and continuance of God's Words. But if there are no vowels in the Hebrew Old Testament, then in what way do God's Words abide for ever? If there are no vowels, then it seems that many of God's Words are gone for ever.

II Peter 1:19

II Peter 1:19 states: "We have also a more sure word of prophecy; whereunto ye do well that ye take heed, as unto a light that shineth in a dark place, until the day dawn, and the day star arise in your hearts." In the previous verses, Peter refers to the time when he, along with James and John, was on the Mount of Transfiguration and heard the voice of God the Father say, "This is my beloved Son, in whom I am well pleased" (cf. Matthew 17:1-8). They heard the voice of God the Father. However, in verse 19, Peter indicates that believers[559] have something more sure than what Peter, James, and John heard with their ears, namely, believers have a more sure word of prophecy. In the next verse, Peter defines this more sure word of prophecy as being the prophecy of Scripture, that is, written prophecy. Also, as Peter further elaborates in verse 21, the prophecy came in old time, therefore, referring to Old Testament prophecy.

---

[559] D. Edmond Hiebert on page 76 of *Second Peter and Jude* (Greenville: Unusual Publications, 1989) referring to p. 97 of Lenski's commentary on II Peter states, "Some like Lenski, would limit this 'we' to all the apostles; but since in the remainder of the verse Peter speaks to believers generally, it is more natural to understand 'we' to include all true believers."

The written Old Testament prophecy[560] is more sure than what the apostles heard on the mount. Some, as Hiebert alludes in the quote following, ignore the comparative that Peter presents in II Peter 1:19. Hiebert writes:

> "Made more sure" (*bebaioteron*) renders a comparative adjective that is in the predicate position and placed emphatically forward, "we have more sure the prophetic word." It ascribes to the prophetic word the quality of being "more sure," "firm" or "reliable." One should not construe this comparative as the equivalent of the positive degree, "a sure word," nor treat it as a subjunctive with the elative force, "a very sure word." To do so simply evades the difficulty presented by the comparative. But how should one understand it? . . . In view of the coordinating "and" (*kai*), it seems more natural to render, "And we have [as] more sure the prophetic word." Then the meaning is that we have another source of assurance that is even more reliable than the testimony of the apostles, namely, "the prophetic Word."[561]

Several other commentators also observe that what is written in the Old Testament is more sure than what the apostles saw with their eyes and what they heard with their ears. For instance, Vincent writes: "We have the word of prophecy as a surer confirmation of God's truth than what we ourselves saw, i.e., Old-Testament testimony is more convincing than even the voice heard at the transfiguration."[562]

---

[560] Hiebert contends that *the word of prophecy* "was 'a current expression embracing the OT as a whole and not simply the prophets proper.' [Hiebert is referring to J. N. D. Kelly, *A Commentary on the Epistles of Peter and of Jude*, in *Harper's New Testament Commentaries* (NY: Harper & Row, 1969), 321]. The adjective 'prophetic' (*prophētikon*), used only here and in Romans 16:26, describes this written 'word' as having the character of prophecy, that is, including a predictive element. All parts of the Old Testament contain prophecies about the coming Messiah (cf. Luke 24:27, 44). The definitive article marks this as a body of prophecy with which the readers were familiar, while the singular number groups all the Old Testament prophecies together and views them in their unity, all bearing witness to the coming Messiah" (Hiebert, 76).

[561] Hiebert, 76,77. Brackets around *as* are from Hiebert.

[562] Marvin R. Vincent, "The Second General Epistle of Peter" in vol. 1 of *Word Studies in the New Testament* in *The Master Christian Library*, version 8 [CD-ROM] (Rio, WI: Ages Software, 2000), 672.

Wuest writes, " 'More sure' is the comparative of *bebaios*, 'stable, fast, firm,' metaphorically, 'sure, trusty.' The idea here is of something that is firm, stable, something that can be relied upon or trusted in. The idea in the Greek text is, 'We have the prophetic word as a surer foundation' than even the signs and wonders which we have seen."[563]

Lillie writes, "The prophetic word is represented as a surer evidence of 'the power and coming of our Lord Jesus Christ' than is afforded by the apostolic testimony in regard to the Transfiguration. And this is no doubt the only sense that can fairly be got out of the clause at is lies before us."[564]

Spurgeon writes: "Can anything be more sure than that which an eye-witness sees? Well Peter says that this prophetic Book, in which Holy Scripture is stored up is better to us than if we had even seen Christ himself. If any one thing be more sure than another, it is this blessed book-revelation of the Christ of God."[565] Spurgeon also writes:

> Surely, nothing could be more sure than the evidence presented to the apostles in the holy mount. Yet Peter thus writes to express his utmost confidence in the Word of God. Surer than the light he saw, which dazzled him; surer than the voice he heard, which he never failed to remember, and to which he ever bore unfaltering witness; surer even than these things is that divine Book which is still preserved to us: "We have also a more sure word of prophecy."[566]

---

[563] Kenneth S. Wuest, "The Exegesis of Second Peter" in *In These Last Days* in volume 2 of *Wuest's Word Studies from the Greek New Testament for the English Reader* (Grand Rapids: Wm. B. Eerdmans Publishing Company, 1973), 34.

[564] John Lillie, *Lectures on the First and Second Epistles of Peter* (Minneapolis: Klock & Klock Christian Publishers, 1978), 414.

[565] Spurgeon, "Exposition by C. H. Spurgeon on 2 Peter 1:9-21" in vol. 57 of *Metropolitan Tabernacle Pulpit* (Pasadena, TX: Pilgrim Publications, 1979), 216.

[566] Spurgeon, "Exposition by C. H. Spurgeon on 2 Peter 1:16-21; 2:1-10" in vol. 41 of *Metropolitan Tabernacle Pulpit* (Pasadena, TX: Pilgrim Publications, 1975), 575.

II Peter 1:19 teaches that what is written in the Old Testament is more sure than the spoken word the apostles heard on the mount. However, if what is written in the Old Testament has no vowels, then in what way is it more sure than what was spoken? When people speak, they use vowels, so that it is clear what word they are saying. But if what is written has no vowels, then one cannot be sure what words are intended, and in such a case, what is written would not at all be more sure than the spoken words. The conclusion is clear: for the Old Testament prophecy to be more sure than the spoken word, it has to have vowels; vowels that are inspired, preserved, and authoritative.

II Peter 1:21

II Peter 1:21 states, "Holy men of God spake *as they were moved by the Holy Ghost.*" Also, I Corinthians 2:13 states, "Which things also we speak, not in the words which man's wisdom teacheth, but which the Holy Ghost teacheth; comparing spiritual things with spiritual." That is, the Holy Ghost, as He moved in holy men of old, used words. But if the Hebrew Old Testament only has consonants, then in what sense did the Holy Ghost move these men to speak and to write words? Bishop writes: "The Bible asserts the inspiration of the very vowel-points, because it says, 'Words which the Holy Ghost teacheth'—the *words*. 'Words,' notice, not '*half*-words'—not wind-swept skeletons, which wait to be filled in by human conjecture."[567]

Summary

This section presents ten (10) passages and alludes to many more from the New Testament that point to the inspiration, preservation, and authority of the vowels of the Old Testament. The New Testament is in agreement with the consistent teaching of the Old Testament. Several of these New Testament verses come right from the lips

---

[567] Bishop, 4.

of the Lord Jesus Christ (Matthew 4:4; 22:31; 24:35; John 10:35). Those who would dispute that God inspired the vowels of the Old Testament find themselves in the unenviable position of fighting against the Lord Jesus Christ. Far better would it be for these disputers to submit to the teaching of the Lord Jesus Christ and to believe Him above all others.

NEW TESTAMENT WORDS

New Testament writers were aware of the pointing of Hebrew words as evidenced by how they vocalized various words from the Old Testament. Both Gill and Strouse give illustrations to substantiate this claim.

Gill's Illustrations

Gill observes:

> The words of Christ expressed on the cross, *Eli, Eli,* etc. and the names of persons in the genealogies of the Evangelists, and in Heb. xi. and in other places of the New Testament, seem to confirm the modern punctuation [that is, the vowel pointing]. The *Dagesh forte* appears, and is preserved in many words in those times, as in *Immanuel,* Mat. i. 23, *Matthew, Lebbaeus, Thaddaeus,* Matt. x. 3, *Hosanna,* Matt. xxi. 9, *Ephphatha,* Mark vii. 34, *Anna,* Luke ii. 36, *Matthat, Matthathias,* Luke iii. 24, 25, *Matthias,* Acts i. 23, *Abaddon,* Rev. ix. 11, *Armageddon,* Rev. xvi. 16, *Sabbaton,* Matt. xii. 5, *Lamma,* Mark xv. 34, with others, and the *Dagesh lene* in *Capernaum, Sarepta,* and others; and even the use of the *Pathach Genubah* appears in the pronunciation of *Messias* and *Siloam* as well as the other points, John i. 41, and ix. 7, 11.[568]

In this quote, Gill gives several proofs for the presence of vowel points among them being the words *Eli, Eli*; names of persons; the *dagesh*

---

[568] Gill, *Dissertation,* 225.

forte; the *dagesh lene*; and the *pathach genubah*. The next sections examine some of these proofs in more detail.

Eli, Eli

The words *Eli, Eli* are words that Jesus spoke on the cross according to Matthew 27:46, and are the English transliteration of the Greek transliteration of Jesus' Hebrew words. Psalm 22:1 prophesied that Jesus would speak these words. In Psalm 22:1 the words for *my God, my God* are אֵלִי אֵלִי (*'ēlî 'ēlî*), which the Greek transliterates as Ἠλί, Ἠλί, reflecting exactly the vocalization of the Hebrew words. The next word that Christ spoke at this time, *lama*, also has the same vocalization as the word in Psalm 22:1. *Lama* in Greek is λαμά and in Hebrew is לָמָה (*lāmāʰ*). In this case, the Greek drops the final *hey* (ה), allowing the vowel to predominate, which is a common practice.[569] The last word that Jesus spoke in this sequence is *sabachthani*. This word is not Hebrew, but Aramaic[570] and, therefore, does not follow the exact vocalization of the Hebrew עֲזַבְתָּנִי (*ʿăzabʾtānî*) in Psalm 22:1. Jesus' Hebrew Words on the cross, *Eli, Eli, lama*, match the vowels of their Old Testament counterparts. Here are three (3) words in the Greek New Testament that match the Hebrew vowels present in the Old Testament.

---

[569] Strouse, "Luke 16:17 – One Tittle," 21. Some further examples of the Greek dropping a consonant and allowing the vowel to predominant are with the words *Abel* (הֶבֶל – heḇel; Ἄβελ), *Hosea* (הוֹשֵׁעַ - hôšēaʿ, Ὡσηέ), and *Hagar* (הָגָר – hāḡār, Ἁγάρ). In these examples the end vowel predominates, rather than the beginning vowel, but the same principle applies.

[570] Gill, *Matthew* in vol. 1 of *An Exposition of the New Testament* (London: Mathews & Leigh, 1810. Reprinted Paris, Arkansas: The Baptist Standard Bearer, Inc., 1989), 363.

Names of Persons

Many names from the Old Testament retain their exact vocalization when brought over into the New Testament. There are some cases, however, where the New Testament writers do not follow exactly the vowels present in the Hebrew spelling of a name. For more information on such cases, see Chapter One in the section detailing problems with the *Autographa* position. This section presents a list of names with the English, the Hebrew spelling along with its transliteration, the Old Testament verse in which the name appears, the Greek counterpart, and the New Testament verse in which the name appears.

English	Hebrew	Verse	Greek	Verse
David	דָּוִד (*dāwīd*)	I Ki 2:24	Δαβὶδ	Mt 1:1
Abraham	אַבְרָהָם (*ʾaḇrāhām*)	Gen 17:5	Ἀβραάμ	Mt 1:1
Isaac	יִצְחָק (*yiṣḥāq*)	Gen 17:19	Ἰσαάκ	Mt 1:2
Jacob	יַעֲקֹב (*yaʿăqōḇ*)[571]	Gen 25:26	Ἰακώβ	Mt 1:2
Pharez	פֶּרֶץ (*pāreṣ*)	Gen 38:29	Φάρες	Mt 1:3
Zarah	זֶרַח (*zāraḥ*)	Gen 38:30	Ζαρὰ[572]	Mt 1:3
Tamar	תָּמָר (*tāmār*)	Gen 38:6	Θάμαρ	Mt 1:3
Salmon	שַׂלְמוֹן (*śalmôn*)	Ruth 4:21	Σαλμών	Mt 1:4
Jesse	יִשַׁי (*yīshay*)	Ruth 4:17	Ἰεσσαί[573]	Mt 1:5
Ruth	רוּת (*rût*)	Ruth 1:4	Ῥούθ	Mt 1:5

---

[571] In this case, the Greek does not transliterate the *ayin* (ע) because there is no equivalent for it in Greek, but the Greek does follow the vowels.

[572] In this case, the Greek drops the final *cheth* (ח), allowing the vowel to predominate, which is a common practice (Strouse, "Luke 16:17 – One Tittle," 21, 22).

[573] Here the Greek uses two *sigmas* (σ) to represent the Hebrew *shin* (שׁ), which is the *sh* sound. Greek does not have a single letter for *sh*, therefore, in this case uses two *sigmas*. Another example of the Greek using two *sigmas* to represent the Hebrew *shin* (שׁ) is with the name *Naasson* (Ναασσών).

Asa	אָסָא (ʾāsāʾ)	I Ki 15:8	Ἀσά	Mt 1:7
Jehoshaphat	יְהוֹשָׁפָט (yəhôšāpāṭ)	I Ki 22:2	Ἰωσαφάτ	Mt 1:8
Joram	יוֹרָם (yôrām)	I Chr 3:11	Ἰωράμ	Mt 1:8
Ahaz	אָחָז (ʾāḥāz)	II Ki 15:38	Ἄχάζ	Mt 1:9
Amon	אָמוֹן (ʾāmôn)	II Ki 21:18	Ἀμών	Mt 1:10
Eliakim[574]	אֶלְיָקִים (ʾelyāqîm)	II Ki 18:18	Ἐλιακείμ	Mt 1:13
Abihud[575]	אֲבִיהוּד (ʾăbîhûḏ)	I Chr 8:3	Ἀβιούδ	Mt 1:13
Abel	הֶבֶל (hāḇel)	Gen 4:2	Ἄβελ[576]	Heb 11:4
Enoch	חֲנוֹךְ (ḥănôḵ)	Gen 4:17	Ἐνώχ[577]	Heb 11:5
Joseph	יוֹסֵף (yôsēp̄)	Gen 30:24	Ἰωσήφ	Heb 11:22
Jericho	יְרִיחוֹ (yərîḥô)	Josh 3:16	Ἰεριχώ	Heb 11:30
Barak	בָּרָק (bārāq)	Jud 4:6	Βαράκ	Heb 11:32
Israel	יִשְׂרָאֵל (yiśrāʾēl)	Gen 32:28	Ἰσραήλ	Rev 2:14
Sabaoth	צְבָאוֹת (ṣəbāʾôṯ)	Isa 6:3	Σαβαώθ[578]	Jas 5:4
Corban	קָרְבָּן (qorbān)	Lev 1:2	Κορβάν	Mk 7:11
Gabriel	גַּבְרִיאֵל (gaḇrîʾēl)	Dan 9:21	Γαβριήλ	Lk 1:19
Abiathar	אֶבְיָתָר (ʾeḇyāṯār)	I Sam 22:20	Ἀβιάθαρ	Mk 2:26
Aaron	אַהֲרֹן (ʾahărōn)	Ex 4:14	Ἀαρών	Heb 5:4
Adam	אָדָם (ʾāḏām)	Gen 2:19	Ἀδάμ	I Tim 2:13
Baal	בַּעַל (baʿal)	Num 22:41	Βάαλ	Rom 11:4

---

[574] The references for *Eliakim* are not to the same person.

[575] The references for *Abihud* are not to the same person.

[576] In this case the Greek drops the *hey* (ה), allowing the vowel to predominate, which is a common practice (Strouse, "Luke 16:17 – One Tittle," 21).

[577] In this case the Greek drops the *cheth* (ח), allowing the vowel to predominate, which is a common practice (Strouse, "Luke 16:17 – One Tittle," 21, 22).

[578] In this case, the Greek renders the half-vowel *shewa* (ְ) with an α (*a*), which is perfectly acceptable since Greek does not have half vowels.

Balak	בָּלָק (bālāq)	Num 22:2	Βαλάκ	Rev 2:14
Gad	גָּד (gāḏ)	Gen 30:11	Γάδ	Rev 7:5
Gog[579]	גּוֹג (gôḡ)	Ezek 38:2	Γὼγ	Rev 20:8
Eber	עֵבֶר (ʿēḇer)	Gen 10:24	Ἐβέρ	Lk 3:35
Eliezer[580]	אֱלִיעֶזֶר (ʾĕlîʿezer)	Gen 15:2	Ἐλιέζερ	Lk 3:29
Enos	אֱנוֹשׁ (ʾĕnôš)	Gen 5:11	Ἐνώς	Lk 3:38
Ephraim[581]	אֶפְרַיִם (ʾep̄rāyim)	Gen 41:52	Ἐφραὶμ	Jn 11:54
Jephthah	יִפְתָּח (yip̄tāḥ)	Jud 11:1	Ἰεφθάε	Heb 11:32
Joel	יוֹאֵל (yôʾēl)	Joel 1:1	Ἰωήλ	Acts 2:16
Cain	קַיִן (qayin)	Gen 4:3	Κάϊν	I Jn 3:12
Kish	קִישׁ (qîš)	I Sam 9:1	Κίς	Acts 13:21
Levi	לֵוִי (lēwî)	Gen 29:34	Λευΐ	Heb 7:5
Lot	לוֹט (lôṭ)	Gen 11:27	Λώτ	II Pet 2:7
Magog[582]	מָגוֹג (māḡôḡ)	Ezek 39:6	Μαγώγ	Rev 20:8
Michael	מִיכָאֵל (mîḵāʾēl)	Dan 10:21	Μιχαὴλ	Jude 9
Nathan	נָתָן (nāṯān)	II Sam 5:14	Ναθάν	Lk 3:31
Nachor	נָחוֹר (nāḥôr)	Josh 24:2	Ναχώρ	Lk 3:34
Rachel	רָחֵל (rāḥēl)	Gen 29:6	Ῥαχὴλ	Mt 2:18
Zadok[583]	צָדוֹק (ṣāḏôq)	II Sam 8:17	Σαδώκ	Mt 1:14
Salem	שָׁלֵם (šālēm)	Gen 14:18	Σαλήμ	Heb 7:1
Saul[584]	שָׁאוּל (šāʾûl)	Gen 36:37	Σαούλ	Acts 9:4

[579] These references to *Gog* are not to the same place.

[580] These references to *Eliezer* are not to the same person.

[581] These references to *Ephraim* are not to the same person or place.

[582] These references to *Magog* are not to the same place.

[583] These references to *Zadok* are not the same person.

[584] These references to *Saul* are not the same person.

Seth	שֵׁת (shēṯ)	Gen 4:25	Σήθ	Lk 3:38
Shem	שֵׁם (shēm)	Gen 5:32	Σήμ	Lk 3:36
Hosea	הוֹשֵׁעַ (hôshēaᵃ)	Hos 1:2	Ὡσηὲ	Rom 9:25
Heli[585]	עֵלִי (ʿēlî)	I Sam 1:3	Ἡλὶ[586]	Lk 3:23
Er[587]	עֵר (ʿēr)	Gen 38:3	Ἤρ	Lk 3:28
Esau	עֵשָׂו (ʿēśāw)	Gen 25:25	Ἠσαῦ	Heb 11:20
Obed	עוֹבֵד (ʿôḇēḏ)	Ruth 4:17	Ὠβὴδ	Mt 1:5

The above list contains fifty-eight (58) names all demonstrating that the writers of the New Testament were aware of the vowel pointing for these names.

Dagesh Forte

Gill presents fourteen (14) examples of *dagesh forte*, which is the doubling of a consonant due to the presence of a dot in that consonant. Seven (7) of Gill's examples occur in the Old Testament, therefore, it is possible to verify that these cases actually do reflect the *dagesh forte*. These seven cases are *Immanuel, Abaddon, Armageddon, Anna, Matthan, Mattathias*, and *Sabbaton*. While the other seven words (*Matthew, Lebbaeus, Thaddaeus, Hosanna, Ephphatha, Matthat, Matthias, Lamma*), do not occur in the Old Testament, yet they reflect Hebrew words or in the case of *Ephphatha* and *Lamma* Aramaic words and, therefore, may give evidence of the *dagesh forte*. The seven examples that do not occur in the Old Testament may give evi-

---

[585] These references to *Eli/Heli* are not to the same person.

[586] In this case, the initial consonant in the Hebrew word *ayin* (ע) does not come through in the Greek, rather the Greek simply gives the vowel under the *ayin*. This is a common practice. In fact, as Moncrieff relates there are two ways to handle the *ayin* when transliterating from Hebrew into Greek: (1) simply convey the vowel under the *ayin*; or (2) render it with a g (γ), since "g is a component of its sound as a guttural" (Moncrieff, 29).

[587] These references to *Er* are not to the same person.

dence of the *dagesh forte* because there are cases when the Greek doubles the consonant in translating a Hebrew word even though the Hebrew word does not have the *dagesh forte* such as *Joppa*, which in Hebrew is יָפוֹ (*yāpô* see Jonah 1:3), whereas the Greek has Ἰόππη (Acts 9:36). Other examples are *Jesse* (Matthew 1:5), *Naasson* (Matthew 1:4), and *Rebecca* (Romans 9:10).[588] Two more Greek translations of Aramaic words that are not in the Old Testament but that may demonstrate the *dagesh forte* are *Abba* in Mark 14:36 and *Barabbas* in Matthew 27:16. Other Greek translations of Hebrew names that are not in the Old Testament but that may reflect the presence of the *dagesh forte* are *Gennesaret* in Matthew 14:34, *Janna* in Luke 3:24, *Nagge* in Luke 3:25, *Addi* in Luke 3:28, *Annas* in Luke 3:2, *Emmaus* in Luke 24:13, and *Gabbatha* in John 19:13. The rest of this section discusses the seven examples from Gill that occur in the Old Testament as well as one more that Gill did not mention, which together with the other words in this section give a total of twenty-four (24) words that lend evidence for the presence of the *dagesh forte*.

Emmanuel (Ἐμμανουήλ) occurs in Matthew 1:23, which is a quote of Isaiah 7:14 where the Hebrew has עִמָּנוּ אֵל (*ʿimmānû ʾēl*). Of particular note in this example are the two *m*'s, which the Hebrew conveys with a dot in the bosom of the מ, which grammarians call the *dagesh forte*. Without the dot, the New Testament would have spelled *Emmanuel* with only one *m*, that is, *Emanuel*.

Abaddon is a Hebrew word that occurs in Revelation 9:11. *Abaddon* is in the Hebrew text of Job 26:6; 31:12; and Proverbs 15:11 where the English translates the Hebrew word *destruction*. In the Hebrew the word is אֲבַדּוֹן (*ʾăḇaddôn*) where the *dagesh forte* in the *d* (ד) indicates a doubling, something that the Greek replicates.

Armageddon occurs in Revelation 16:16 where the Greek has Ἀρμαγεδδών, which is the combination of two Hebrew words. The

---

[588] In these cases, the Greek is giving an alternate spelling for these words.

first of the words is הַר (*har*), which the Bible often translates as *mount* (for example, Genesis 10:30). The second word is מְגִדּוֹן (*məḡiddôn*), which the Bible translates as *Megiddon* in Zechariah 12:11. *Armageddon* follows the vowels of these two Hebrew words and has the doubling of the *d* due to the *dagesh forte*.

Anna is from the Hebrew word חַנָּה (*ḥannāʰ*, cf. I Samuel 1:2). The Greek for *Anna* is "Αννα (cf. Luke 2:36). In this case the beginning *cheth* (ח) and the ending *hey* (ה) of the Hebrew are not carried over into the Greek allowing the vowels to predominate, which is a normal occurrence.[589] The Greek doubles the *n* (ν) since in the Hebrew it has the *dagesh forte*.

Matthan (Ματθάν in Matthew 1:15) has an Old Testament counterpart in *Mattan* (מַתָּן - *mattān* in II Chronicles 23:17). These references are not referring to the same person, but the Greek here is recognizing the *dagesh forte* of the Hebrew name with its spelling.

Concerning the name *Mattathias* (Ματταθίου in the genitive case in Luke 3:25), it is following the *dagesh forte* present in the Old Testament spelling of *Mattithiah* (מַתִּתְיָה - *mattityāʰ* in I Chronicles 9:31). These references are not to the same person, which could account for the variations in other parts of the spelling. However, the fact remains that there is a recognition here of the *dagesh forte*.

Sabbaton (σάββατον), which occurs in Matthew 12:5, is the Greek translation of the Hebrew word *Sabbath*. In Hebrew *Sabbath* (שַׁבָּת) has a *dagesh forte* in the *b* (ב). The Greek recognizes the *dagesh forte* by doubling the *b* in its translation of the Hebrew. As to why the Greek has *Sabbaton* rather than *Sabbath*, it is possible that the Greek bases its translation on the Hebrew word שַׁבָּתוֹן in Exodus 16:23, which the English translates as "rest," which is exactly what *Sabbath* means. If the Greek refers to שַׁבָּתוֹן, then the Greek duplicates exactly the vowels as well as the *dagesh forte* of the Hebrew.

---

[589] Strouse, "Luke 16:17 – One Tittle," 21, 22.

Manasseh is an additional example of the New Testament writers recognizing the *dagesh forte* of the Old Testament spelling. In Genesis 41:51, the Hebrew has מְנַשֶּׁה (*mənašše^h*), which has the *dagesh forte* in the *shin* (שׁ). The Greek recognizes the *dagesh forte* by doubling the *s* (Μανασσῆ in Matthew 1:10).

Twenty-four (24) words demonstrate that the Greek New Testament writers knew of the *dagesh forte*. In researching material about the *dagesh forte*, the author has come across two instances where the Greek New Testament writers do not follow the *dagesh forte* present in the Hebrew Old Testament. The two examples are (1) *Amminadab*, which in Hebrew is עַמִּינָדָב ('*ammînāḏāḇ*, see Ruth 4:20), but the Greek has Ἀμιναδάβ (*Aminadab*, see Matthew 1:4); and (2) *Gaza*, which in Hebrew is עַזָּה ('*azzā^h*, see Genesis 10:19), whereas the Greek has Γάζαν (Acts 8:26). Apparently, these spellings are alternate spellings for these words. Be this as it may, twenty-four (24) words provide examples of where the Greek writers were aware of the *dagesh forte*.

Before leaving this discussion of the *dagesh forte*, Whitfield makes an interesting observation when he writes concerning the *dagesh forte* in Psalm 73:28:

> Was it ever writ in Ps. 73.28 שתתי באדני יהיה מחסי *Shathathi baadonai Jehova mahhsi*, where we now have שַׁתִּי and which is read *Shathti* or *Shatti*, by means of the *dagesh*; without which it would only be read *Shathi*? None will ever be able to produce such an instance of writing, and consequently the *dagesh* must always have had this use; or the Masters of Tiberias must have purposely corrupted the reading.
>
> But I shall be answered, that the learned Jews of old, knew, by oral tradition, and force of memory, where the letters were to be founded double; as well as with what vowel and accent sounds they were to be read . . . . And I may here add, that it is almost as easy to suppose, that the whole text might have been retained, by tradition and memory, as that the vowels and accents with which every word was to be pronounced, and all the *dageshes*, and other points, to regulate the reading, should be so retained: and yet this is the only foundation, upon

which, Elias Levita and his followers depend for the truth of their doctrine.[590]

Whitfield makes a good observation here. It is also a significant observation especially when one considers that all the books of the Old Testament use the *dagesh forte* (for example, Genesis 41:51; Exodus 16:23; Leviticus 1:2; Numbers 1:10; Deuteronomy 3:13; Joshua 10:41; Judges 1:18; Ruth 4:20; I Samuel 1:2; II Samuel 1:2; I Kings 1:1; II Kings 20:21; I Chronicles 9:31; II Chronicles 23:17; Esther 1:2; Nehemiah 1:3; Ezra 10:30; Job 26:6; Psalms 73:28; Proverbs 15:11; Ecclesiastes 1:10; Song of Solomon 1:2; Isaiah 7:14; Jeremiah 47:1; Lamentations 1:1; Ezekiel 48:4; Daniel 1:8; Hosea 1:1; Joel 1:5; Amos 1:6; Obadiah 2; Jonah 1:1; Micah 1:2; Nahum 1:1; Habakkuk 1:1; Zephaniah 2:4; Haggai 1:3; Zechariah 12:11; Malachi 1:1). If manuscripts did not originally have points, then it would it seem that somewhere there would be manuscripts where, instead of the *dagesh forte*, the writer doubled the consonants. But are there such manuscripts? Whitfield observes that no such manuscripts exist.

Dagesh Lene

The *dagesh lene* of which Gill speaks is a dot in the bosom of certain letters and results in a hard pronunciation.[591] An example of the *dagesh lene* is *Capernaum*. *Capernaum* is the combination of two Hebrew words כָּפַר (*kapar*) and נָחוּם (*naḥûm*). The first of these words (כָּפַר) has a dot in the first letter (כ) which gives a pronunciation of *k*, instead of *kh* if it were without the dot. Greek reflects this *dagesh lene* when it has Καπερναούμ (*Capernaum*) in Matthew 4:13. Not only does the first letter reflect the use of the *dagesh lene*, but also the vowels of the Hebrew find their way into the Greek word. *Capernaum* pre-

---

[590] Whitfield, 20.

[591] Kelley, *Biblical Hebrew*, 3.

sents one (1) example of where the Greek writers of the New Testament take note of the *dagesh lene*.

Pathach Genubah

The *Pathach Genubah* of which Gill speaks is the same as the *Pathaḥ furtive*. *Gesenius' Hebrew Grammar* explains: "The vowel sign stands regularly *under* the consonant, *after* which it is to be pronounced . . .. The *Pathaḥ* called *furtivum* alone forms an exception to this rule, being pronounced *before* the consonant."[592] An example of *Pathaḥ furtive* occurs in the word *Messiah*. In Hebrew it is מָשִׁיחַ (see Daniel 9:25). Underneath the last letter (ח) is a *pathaḥ* (ַ), which one pronounces before the ח, instead of after it. The Greek, cognizant of the *Pathaḥ furtive*, places an α before the last consonant (Μεσσίαν) as in John 1:41, instead of after the last consonant. Another example of *Pathaḥ furtivum* is in the word *Siloam* (Luke 13:4). The Hebrew behind the Greek for *Siloam* is שִׁלֹחַ (*shīlōᵃḥ* – see Isaiah 8:6). The Greek recognizing the *Pathaḥ furtivum* places an α before the last consonant, instead of after it. *Messiah* and *Siloam* present two (2) examples of where the Greek writers take note of the *Pathaḥ furtivum*.

Strouse's Illustration

Strouse writes, "Paul knew the pointing of the inspired Hebrew word behind the inspired Greek *arrabon* ('earnest') in Eph. 1:14 because he doubled the 'r' (*rho*) in his inspired transliterated spelling of the Hebrew word (*'errabon*) from Gen. 38:17."[593] In this particular case, the *r* in the Hebrew word *'errabon* does not have the *dagesh forte* because it is a guttural letter and as such rejects the *dagesh forte*. "When this takes place, the preceding short vowel is left in an open,

---

[592] E. Kautzsch, ed., *Gesenius' Hebrew Grammar*, 42.

[593] Strouse, "Scholarly Myths Perpetuated on Rejecting the Masoretic Text of the Old Testament," *Emmanuel Baptist Theological Journal* 1 (Spring, 2005):55.

unaccented syllable, and therefore must be lengthened."[594] In the pointed Hebrew text for Genesis 38:17, the vowel before the *r* is a long vowel, indicating that one should double the *r* when one pronouncing the word. With no vowel pointing, how would Paul know that he was to double the *r*? The word *Sara* provides another illustration. In Hebrew her name is שָׂרָה (Genesis 17:15), which has the long *a* (ָ) before the *r*. Paul, in writing Hebrews 11:11 was cognizant of the long *a* and, therefore, spells her name with two *r*'s (Σάρρα). The word *Charran* is another illustration of the doubling of the *r*. In Hebrew *Haran* (חָרָן – *ḥārrān* in Genesis 11:32) has a long *a* (ָ) before the *r* and Luke recognizing the long *a* spells the word with two *r*'s (Χαρράν in Acts 7:2). Yet another example of the doubling of the *r* is in the word *Gomorrah* (Genesis 10:19 and Romans 9:29), which has the long *o* before the *r* and Paul recognizing this, doubles the *r*. *Earnest*, *Sara*, *Haran*, and *Gomorrah* present four (4) examples of where the Greek writers were aware of the long vowel before the *r* in the Hebrew and, therefore, double the *r* in the Greek.

Summary

This section presents ninety-two (92) examples that demonstrate that the writers of the Greek New Testament were aware of the proper pointing of Hebrew and Aramaic Old Testament words. Yes, it is true that in the case of *Aminadab* and *Gaza*, the New Testament writers did not follow the *dagesh forte* in the Hebrew. However, the preponderance of the evidence shows that the New Testament writers were well aware of the points and many times used them exactly as they are in the Old Testament.

---

[594] Kelley, 23.

CONCLUSION

The verses that this chapter presents pose further problems for the accommodation and non-authoritative positions on the vowel points. The Bible teaches that God inspired words (Genesis 22:16; Exodus 24:4; Jeremiah 36:1,2), which words proceeded out of His mouth (Exodus 4:22; 34:27; Jeremiah 30:2; 36:1-4; Matthew 4:4), and, therefore, included vowels (Matthew 22:31; I Corinthians 9:10; cf. Romans 9:29; II Peter 3:2). Therefore, God inspired the vowels. These inspired words are fully preserved (Psalm 12:6,7; Isaiah 30:8; 40:8; 59:21; Matthew 5:18; 24:35; Luke 16:17), so that the words are pure (Psalm 12:6,7), perfect (Psalm 19:7), sure (Psalm 93:5; 111:7), faithful (Psalm 119:89,138), settled (Psalm 119:89), a lamp and a light (Psalm 119:105), founded for ever (Psalm 119:152), enduring for ever (Psalm 119:160), magnified above all of God's name (Psalm 138:2), certain (Proverbs 22:20,21), standing for ever (Isaiah 40:8), not passing away (Matthew 24:35), not broken (John 10:35), lively oracles (Acts 7:38), the sole authority (II Timothy 3:16,17), quick (Hebrews 4:12), liveth and abideth for ever (I Peter 1:23), and a more sure word of prophecy (II Peter 1:19). These verses demand the presence of the vowels, which then refutes the non-authoritative and the accommodation positions and asserts the *autographa* position.

In addition to the above factors that demand the presence of the vowel points, the New Testament often asserts that the written words of the Old Testament are equivalent to spoken words (Matthew 22:31; Luke 24:25; John 1:23; 12:38; Acts 3:22; 7:48,49; 8:32-34; 28:25; Romans 9:29; 12:19; 14:11; I Corinthians 9:10; Hebrews 3:7; II Peter 3:2). Since speaking requires the use of vowels, then these written words must also have vowels. Such teaching again refutes the non-authoritative and the accommodation positions and asserts the *autographa* position.

But this is not all, examples of Old Testament words in the New Testament show that the New Testament writers were aware of the points. The Words of Christ on the cross, *Eli, Eli, lama* follow the pointing of Psalm 22:1. Fifty-eight (58) Hebrew and Aramaic names in the New Testament follow the pointing that is in the Old Testament. Twenty-four (24) words indicate that the New Testament writers were aware of the *dagesh forte*. *Capernaum* shows the presence of the *dagesh lene*. The words *Messiah* and *Siloam* demonstrate the presence of the *Pathah furtive*. *Earnest, Sara, Haran,* and *Gomorrah* present four (4) examples of where the Greek writers were aware of the long vowel before the *r* in the Hebrew and, therefore, double the *r* in the Greek. In all, at least ninety-two (92) examples demonstrate that the Greek writers of the New Testament were aware of and used the points of the Hebrew Old Testament.

Old Testament verses, New Testament verses, and New Testament words all teach that God inspired the vowels of the Hebrew Old Testament. This is positive Biblical proof that the *autographa* position is the correct position in the matter of the vowel points. The next chapter presents further Biblical proof to substantiate that the *autographa* position is the correct position.

CHAPTER FIVE – ONE TITTLE

Twice in the New Testament, the Lord Jesus Christ refers to the *tittle*. In fact, these two times are the only uses of *tittle* in all of the Bible. In Matthew 5:18, He states: "For verily I say unto you, Till heaven and earth pass, one jot or one tittle shall in no wise pass from the law, till all be fulfilled." And in Luke 16:17, Jesus states: "And it is easier for heaven and earth to pass, than one tittle of the law to fail." In Matthew 5:18 and Luke 16:17, Jesus is referring to the Old Testament Scriptures and the inviolability of even one tittle. It becomes clear that just one tittle is very important. But the question arises, what is a *tittle*? It is the contention of the author that *tittle* refers to a vowel point of the Old Testament Scriptures. If this contention is true, then it would provide further Biblical support for the *autographa* position as the correct position on the vowel points. The author bases his contention that *tittle* refers to a vowel point upon lexical, contextual, etymological, Scriptural, and translational considerations.

LEXICAL CONSIDERATIONS

The word *tittle* is the translation of κεραία, a feminine nominative singular noun. Lexicons give a couple of possible meanings for κεραία.

Pasor – 1621

Pasor's lexicon lists for κεραία this entry:

κεραία, ας, ἡ. idem quod κέρας item apex, punctulũ. Mat. 5:18. Μία κεραία οὐ μὴ Παρέλθη ἀπὸ τῆ νόμη,⁵⁹⁵ unicus apex non praeterierit ex lege. Perapicem intelligitur hic punctum. Puncta vocalia ergo tempore Christi fuerunt, & non, ut quidam fingunt, recens inuenta.⁵⁹⁶

A translation of what follows after listing the entry, κεραία, ας, ἡ, is as follows: "the same as κέρας, likewise an apex, a point. Matthew 5:18. One tittle shall in no wise pass from the law, a single apex shall not pass out of the law. By which is meant here a point. Therefore vowel points existed in the time of Christ, and not, as certain ones are pretending, a recent invention." Pasor gives the meaning of *point* for κεραία, and applies it specifically to vowel points.

A statement that Pasor makes in his definition deserves further attention. In his definition, Pasor states that κεραία has the same meaning as κέρας, which is a neuter nominative singular noun. While κέρας has other meanings, it can mean *apex* or a *point*. Thayer supports Pasor's contention when he presents for his third definition on κέρας this entry: "Tropically, *a projecting extremity in shape like a horn, a point, apex.*"⁵⁹⁷ At the end of the section entitled "Etymological Considerations" is more information on κέρας.

Schrevelius – 1812

Schrevelius gives as a definition of κεραία: "a little horn, a horn, an antler; a sail-yard; a feeler *or* antenna; a bent rod; a little mark *or* point over a letter, an accent."⁵⁹⁸ This definition presents the

---

[595] These last two words, for some reason, differ from the *Textus Receptus*, which has τοῦ νόμου.

[596] George Pasor, *Lexicon Graeco-Latinum In novum domini nostri Iesu Christi testamentum, ubi omnium vocabulorum Graecorum themata indicantur, & utraque tam themata quam deriuata grammatice resolvuntur* (London: Apud Iohannem Billium, 1621), 97.

[597] Thayer, 344.

[598] Schrevelius, *The Greek Lexicon of Schrevelius Translated into English with Many Additions* (Boston: Cummings, Hilliard, and Company, 1826 in Dartmouth Col-

meanings of *horn*, a *little mark* or *point over a letter*, and *accent*. In Hebrew a little point over a letter could be as little as a dot such as the point for the Hebrew vowel for *o* (   ). Schrevelius also gives the meaning of *an accent*. Some of the Hebrew accents are very small. In fact, one Hebrew accent, the *R ᵉbhîᵃ ʽ gādôl*,[599] is as small as a dot atop the *i*.

Donnegan - 1837

Donnegan states that κεραία is a term that "*is extended to various objects from the resemblance* [to] *the feelers, or* antenna *of insects, of crabs, and shell fish of a similar kind* – a sail-yard – a mark, *or* accent over letters."[600] Donnegan's definition emphasizes the meaning of *antenna*, but it could also be a *mark* or *accent over letters*, which could include a point (see above under Schrevelius).

Fradersdorff – 1860

Fradersdorff under the word for *tittle* has "στίγμα, τό. ἀκαρές, οὖς, τό. κεραία, ἡ (*in writing, e.g. accentual mark*, apex)."[601] Fraders-

---

lege Rauner Rare Book Collection), 485. This footnote gives the date of publication as 1826, but pages vi and vii of the work state: "Schrevelius's work was originally extracted from that of Scapula (an edition of which he superintended), and seems to have been first published in 1654." However, page viii states that the current editors of the work added and/or improved "upwards of two thousand articles." There is no way of knowing if these editors had a hand in the definition of κεραία, or if this definition dates earlier.

[599] E. Kautzsch, ed., *Gesenius' Hebrew Grammar*, 61.

[600] James Donnegan, *A New Greek and English Lexicon; Principally on the Plan of the Greek and German Lexicon of Schneider: the Words Alphabetically Arranged; Distinguishing such as Are Poetical, of Dialectic Variety, or Peculiar to Certain Writers and Classes of Writers; with Examples, Literally Translated, Selected from the Classical Writers*, rev. R. B. Patton (Boston: Hilliard, Gray & Co., 1837), 751.

[601] J. W. Fradersdorff, *A Copious Phraseological English-Lexicon*, revised by Thomas Kerchever Arnold and Henry Browne, 2nd ed. (London: Rivingtons, 1860), 593.

dorff puts στίγμα, ἀκαρές, and κεραία as synonymous when one would use them of writing. According to Thayer, στίγμα is *"a mark pricked in* or *branded upon the body."*[602] If one were to use στίγμα of writing, then it could refer to a *prick*, that is, a *point*, which is very possible since Fradersdorff says, "*E.g, accentual mark.*" Some accentual marks are as small as a point (see above under Schrevelius). The next word in the definition, ἀκαρές, refers "properly of hair, *too short to be cut*, hence generally, *small, tiny*" and metaphorically of something that is "*within a hair's breadth of,*"[603] which, if one were to use this of writing, it would refer to something very small. Fradersdorff presents the meanings of *apex, accentual mark*, and possibly a *prick* or a *point*.

Thayer – 1901

Thayer states that κεραία means "*a little horn; extremity, apex, point*; used by the Grk. Grammarians of the accents and diacritical points."[604] One of Thayer's meanings is that of *point*, which certainly is descriptive of the smallest of the Hebrew vowel points, the *chirek*, which is simply a dot, that is, a point. He also states that Greek grammarians use κεραία of diacritical marks. One of the Greek diacritical marks is a diæresis (¨), which writers place over two vowels to show that one should pronounce them as two separate sounds.[605] An example of diæresis is in Revelation 19:1 with the word Ἀλληλουϊα. Clearly, according to Thayer, κεραία can refer to a point. Despite this observation, Thayer states that in Matthew 5:18 and Luke 16:17, the Bible uses κεραία "of the little lines, or projections, by which the Hebr.

---

[602] Thayer, 588.

[603] Henry George Liddell and Robert Scott, *A Greek-English Lexicon*, rev. Henry Stuart Jones (Oxford: At the Clarendon Press, 1951), I:47.

[604] Thayer, 344.

[605] William D. Mounce, *Basis of Biblical Greek Grammar* (Grand Rapids: Zondervan, 1993), 11.

Letters in other respects similar differ from each other, as ח and ה, ר and ד, ב and כ."⁶⁰⁶ Thayer's conclusion is different from Pasor's (see above). While Thayer's entry allows for the meaning of *point*, yet when it specifically comes to Matthew 5:18 and Luke 16:17, he believes that κεραία refers to little lines and not points.

Arndt and Gingrich – 1979

Arndt and Gingrich say of κεραία:

Lit[erally] 'horn'; *projection, hook* as part of a letter, a *serif* (of letters, Sib[yllina] Or[acula]⁶⁰⁷ 5, 21; 24; 25 al.; of accents and breathings in IG II 4321, 10; Apollon[ius] Dysc[olus]; Plut[arch] Numa 13, 9, Mor. 1100A. In the last-named pass[age] in the sense of someth[ing] quite insignificant: ζυγομαχεῖν περὶ Συλλαβῶν καὶ κεπαιῶν. Likew[ise]⁶⁰⁸ Dio Chrys[ostom] 14(31), 86 κεπαίαν νόμου τινός ἢ ψηφίσματος μίαν μόή συλλαβὴν ἐξαλείφειν; Philo, In Flacc. 131 τὰ γράμματα κατὰ συλλαβήν, μᾶλλον δὲ καὶ κεραίαν ἑκάστην) Mt 5:18; Lk 16:17.⁶⁰⁹

The above quote presents several sources that connect κεραία with accents and breathing marks. These sources are Apollonius Dyscolus, Plutarch, Dio Chrysostom, and Philo. Arndt and Gingrich on page xxxiii give Apollonius Dyscolus as being the same as *Grammatici Graeci II*, 1ˢᵗ, 2ⁿᵈ, 3ʳᵈ editions by R. Schneider and G. Uhlig from 1878 to 1910, which dates back to the second century. Plutarch's work as well as that of Dio Chrystrom dates to between the first and second century. Philo's work dates to the first century.

---

[606] Thayer, 344.

[607] That is, *Oracula Sibyllina*, ed. J. Geffcken, 1902.

[608] That is, likewise according to the same usage as Plutarch.

[609] William F. Arndt and F. Wilbur Gingrich, *A Greek-English Lexicon of the New Testament and Other Early Christian Literature: A translation and adaptation of the fourth revised and augmented edition of Walter Bauer's Griechisch-Deutsches Wörterbuch zu den Schriften des Neuen Testaments und der übrigen urchristlichen Literatur*, 2d ed. (Chicago: University of Chicago, 1979), 428.

Not only are these early testimonies to the use of κεραία, but they also help to delineate the meaning of κεραία. Arndt and Gingrich state that in Plutarch's work κεραία is "in the sense of someth[ing] quite insignificant: ζυγομαχεῖν περὶ συλλαβῶν καὶ κεπαιῶν," that is, "to struggle concerning syllables and tittles." Here Plutarch connects κεραία with syllables, which could involve not only accent marks, but also diacritical marks, since diacritical marks also aid in the syllabication of words, as is the case with diæresis (see above under Thayer). Since syllables have vowels, then Plutarch's connection of κεραία with syllables ultimately points back to vowels. Dio Chrysostom also places κεραία in the same context with syllables, when he states: "κεπαίαν νόμου τινός ἢ ψηφίσματος μίαν μόή συλλαβὴν ἐξαλείφειν," that is, "a tittle of a certain law or one only syllable of a decree to blot out." The quotation from Philo's work is "τὰ γράμματα κατὰ συλλαβήν, μᾶλλον δὲ καὶ κεραίαν ἑκάστην," that is, "the letters according to a syllable, but rather even (according to) each tittle." Philo indicates that *tittle* is something even smaller than a syllable, quite possibly the vowel of the syllable. These three citations connect κεραία and syllable. Since syllables have vowels, then there is ultimately a connection between vowels and κεραία.

From Arndt and Gingrich's discussion, κεραία can mean a *horn* or *serif*, or refer to something that aids in proper pronunciation of words, such as *accents* or *diacritical marks*.

Perschbacher – 1990

Perschbacher states that κεραία means "*a horn-like projection, a point, extremity*; in N.T. *an apex, or fine point*; as of letters, used for *the minutest part, a tittle*, Matt. 5:18; Luke 16:17."[610] It is interesting to note that Perschbacher, a modern-day lexicographer, uses the Eng-

---

[610] Wesley J. Perschbacher, *The New Analytical Greek Lexicon* (Peabody, MA: Hendrickson Publishers, 1990), 236.

lish word *tittle* to define κεραία. *Webster's* gives as the primary modern-day meaning for the English word *tittle* as "1. A point or small sign used as a diacritical, punctuation, or similar mark, in writing or printing; variously: a. *Obs.* A cedilla b. a tilde c. the dot over *I* or *j* d. a vowel point or accent, as in Hebrew or Arabic."[611] Here *Webster's* connects, among other things, the English word *tittle* with a Hebrew vowel point or accent. In light of the fact that Matthew 5:18 refers to the law, that is, to something written in Hebrew, Webster's definition is most significant. Furthermore, *The Oxford English Dictionary* lists as a meaning for the English word *tittle*, "The dot over the letter *i*; a punctuation mark; a diacritic point over a letter; any one of the Hebrew and Arabic vowel-points and accents; also, a pip on dice."[612] *Oxford's* definition, also, is most significant in light of Matthew 5:18. In his definition, Perschbacher gives the meanings of *horn, point,* or *tittle*.

Conclusion

Several meanings for κεραία come to the surface. From Pasor comes the meaning of *vowel point*. Schrevelius presents the meanings of *horn*, a *little mark* or *point over a letter*, and an *accent*. Donnegan gives the meanings of *antenna*, *mark over letters*, and an *accent*. Fradersdorff presents the meanings of *apex, accentual mark*, and possibly a *prick* or a *point*. Thayer gives the meaning of a *little horn* that distinguishes one Hebrew consonant from another. Arndt and Gingrich present the meanings of *horn, serif, accents,* and *diacritical marks*. Perschbacher gives the meanings of *horn, point,* or *tittle*. One can divide these meanings into one of two categories: those meanings deal-

---

[611] William Allan Neilson, ed., *Webster's New International Dictionary of the English Language*, 2nd ed. (Springfield, MA: G & C Merriam Company, Publishers, 1961), 2656.

[612] "Tittle" in *The Oxford English Dictionary*, 2nd ed., prepared by J. A. Simpson and E. S. C. Weiner (Oxford: Clarendon Press, 1989), XVIII: 159.

ing with consonants and those meanings dealing with non-consonants. The consonantal meanings for *tittle* are *horn, antenna, apex, serif,* and *mark over a letter*. These meanings, as Thayer illustrates, see the *tittle* as a horn, antenna, apex, or serif projecting or extending out of a consonant, or as a mark decorating the consonant. The non-consonantal meanings for *tittle* are *vowel point, accent,* and *diacritical mark*. The question is this: when Jesus used κεραία in Matthew 5:18 and Luke 16:17, does it refer to consonants or to non-consonants? While the lexicons allow for either possibility, only the context can decide which is correct.

CONTEXTUAL CONSIDERATIONS

The lexicons give either a consonantal or non-consonantal meaning for κεραία. As is the case with many words, only the context can definitely decide which meaning is correct. In this section the author presents three contextual arguments from Matthew 5:18 that mandate that Christ uses κεραία in a non-consonantal way. The first of the contextual arguments concerns *one jot or one tittle*, the second *till all be fulfilled*, and the third *one of the least of these commandments*. The first of the contextual arguments demands that *tittle* have a non-consonantal meaning and the next two contextual arguments demand that *tittle* include the meaning of vowel point.

One Jot or One Tittle

The first contextual argument concerns the phrase *one jot or one tittle*, which demands that *tittle* have a non-consonantal meaning. In Matthew 5:18 Jesus uses κεραία when He states: "One jot or one tittle (κεραία) shall in no wise pass from the law." There is little dispute that *jot* in Matthew 5:18 refers to the Hebrew letter *yodh* (׳), which is the smallest Hebrew consonant. A common view about the *tittle* in Matthew 5:18 is that it refers to the smallest differences between the Hebrew consonants (e.g., see Thayer above). But such an interpretation is flawed, for it has both *jot* and *tittle* referring to consonants, when to say *one jot* would have been sufficient to teach that every consonant of the Hebrew Bible is imperishable (see the next section). With that in mind, this section first presents the significance of *jot* referring to consonants and then demonstrates that *tittle* must refer to non-consonants.

Jot Refers to Consonants

Consider that when Jesus stated that one jot shall in no wise perish from the Law, He guaranteed that the littlest consonant of the Hebrew alphabet will not pass from the Law, that is, the Old Testament.[613] By saying that one jot shall in no wise pass from the Law, Jesus then guaranteed that every consonant of the Hebrew Scriptures also shall in no wise pass from the Law. Jesus elsewhere stated, "He that is faithful in that which is least is faithful also in much: and he that is unjust in the least is unjust also in much" (Luke 16:10). If the least consonant of the Hebrew alphabet shall not perish from the Law, then neither will any of the greater consonants. Therefore, no *beths* (ב) or *caphs* (כ), though similar, shall perish from the Law. No *daleths* (ד) or *reshes* (ר), though similar, shall perish from the Law. No *waws* (ו), *zayins* (ז), *gimels* (ג), or *nuns* (נ), though all similar, shall perish from the Law. No *hehs* (ה) or *cheths* (ח), though similar, shall perish from the Law. No *mems* (מ) or *samechs* (ס), though similar, shall perish from the Law. No *seens* (שׂ) or *sheens* (שׁ), though similar, shall perish from the Law.[614]

---

[613] That *law* in Matthew 5:18 refers to the entire Old Testament, consult the author's *Those So-Called Errors*, 70-76.

[614] Gray observes: "The elder Lightfoot, the Hebraist and rabbinical scholar of the Westminster Assembly time, has called attention to an interesting story of a certain letter yod found in the text of Deuteronomy 32:18. It is in the word teshi, to forsake, translated in the King James as 'unmindful.' Originally it seems to have been written smaller even than usual, i.e., undersized, and yet notwithstanding the almost infinite

Another interesting aspect about the *yodh* (׳) is that the very shape of it resembles a horn. In light of this, it is further unnecessary to have κεραία refer to a horn. Indeed κεραία must refer to something other than a horn.

Tittle Refers to Non-Consonants

Again, by saying that one jot shall in no wise pass from the Law, Jesus is also asserting that not one single consonant of the Hebrew alphabet shall pass from the Law. In light of this, there is no need for *tittle* also to refer to consonants. Indeed, in the expression *one jot or one tittle*, the word *or* (ἤ) is the disjunctive conjunction,[615] which means that it "denotes an opposition of the ideas expressed by the words or clauses it connects."[616] Therefore, *jot* and *tittle* are different things. In particular *tittle* is not referring to consonants, and if it is not referring to consonants, then in this context it must have a non-consonantal meaning, that is, a *vowel point*, *accent*, or *diacritical mark*. Strouse observes, Christ's use of "the disjunctive particle ἤ ('or'), indicates that He differentiated between the consonant jot and

---

number of times in which copies have been made, that little yod stands there today just as it ever did. Lightfoot spoke of it in the middle of the seventeenth century and although two more centuries and a half have passed since then with all their additional copies of the book, yet it still retains its place in the sacred text" (James M. Gray, "The Inspiration of the Bible – Definition, Extent and Proof" in *The Fundamentals – A Testimony to the Truth*, ed. R. A. Torrey, A. C. Dixon, and others [CD-ROM] (Rio, WI: Ages Software, 2000), II:26).

[615] Randolph O. Yeager, *Matthew 1-7* in *The Renaissance New Testament* (Gretna, LA: Pelican Publishing Co., 1986), 370. This work gives a grammatical identification for every word of every verse in the New Testament. Another work that gives a grammatical identification for every word of the Greek New Testament is *Analytical Greek New Testament* by Timothy and Barbara Friberg. The Fribergs' work identifies ἤ in Matthew 5:18 as a coordinating conjunction. May the reader note that *disjunctive conjunction* is a sub-category under the broader category of *coordinating conjunction*. In other words, the Fribergs give a more general classification, whereas Yeager gives a more specific classification.

[616] Neilson, ed., *Webster's New International Dictionary*, 641.

the vowel tittle. Redundancy would have been meaningless."[617] The previous paragraph demonstrates that "redundancy would have been meaningless." Since one jot will not pass, then neither will any of the other consonants pass; therefore there is no need for Jesus to refer to consonants twice, which would be the case if *tittle* had a consonantal meaning. The disjunctive conjunction means that *tittle* is not synonymous with *jot*; therefore, *tittle* does not have a consonantal meaning. Consequently, *tittle* does not mean a *little horn*, the *smallest differences between the letters*, a *serif*, an *ornamental marking*, or a *tagin*.[618] When Jesus stated that *one jot or one tittle shall in no wise pass from the law*, He was stating a truth about both the consonants and the non-consonants of the Hebrew Old Testament.

Various Commentators

The above truth of *tittle* referring to non-consonants is a truth that other commentators have made clear in their comments.

---

[617] Strouse, "Luke 16:17 – One Tittle," 10. Some may think that the *or* in the phrase *one jot or one tittle* necessitates that *jot* and *tittle* be completely synonymous, but such is not the case, for *or* is a disjunctive particle. Later in Matthew 5:36, Jesus uses the same word when He said, "Thou canst not make one hair white or black." *White* and *black* are not at all synonymous, yet they are connected by the word *or*.

Bishop writes, "The words of Christ, 'jot,' 'tittle' (see Matt. v:18), are no repetition of some common and exaggerated proverb, and they are no tautology" (Bishop, 3). If anyone dare claim that Jesus was using a common exaggerated proverb, then he would, in essence, be claiming that Jesus "stretched the truth," that is, that He lied. It is best to believe Jesus, instead of claiming that He lied.

[618] From the booklet *Every Jot & Tittle—A Study of Matthew 5*[17-20] by John C. P. Smith, 2001, available at www.jotandtittle.co.uk comes the theory that "Jesus probably used the Aramaic equivalent חָגִין *tāgīn* (singular *tāg*). . . . The *Encyclopedia Judaica* describes the specific nature and function of *tāgīn*: 'Tagin are special designs resembling crowns placed by a scribe on the upper left-hand corner of seven of the 22 letters of the Hebrew alphabet in a Torah, *tefillin*, or *mezuzah* scroll. A *tag* is generally composed of three flourishes or strokes, each of which resembles a small ' '*zayin*' '." That Jesus knew Aramaic is indisputable (Mark 5:41). That He may have spoken the words in Matthew 5:18 in Aramaic is speculation. Furthermore, the fact is that while the Bible could have given His words in Aramaic it did not do so, but rather used Greek.

Piscator

Piscator writes on Luke 16:17: "Hinc apparet tempore Christi Biblia scripta fuisse cum punctis,"[619] that is, "hence it appears the Bible in the time of Christ was written with points."

Broughton

Broughton comments:

> The Jews note fifteen words in the Law with Psalms and Prophets, pricked over the heads, for special deep consideration: and so written from the first copies. . . . They call them תגים [tagim]. But that term is not used in the Hebrewish of S. Mat. not in the Syriaque, or Arabique. . . . So that we are to search whether prickes as the fifteen strange: or other pricks which are vowels and accents be meant. The תגים pricks [are] only of marking, and likewise accents are not part of the word. Therefore, I trow, vowel pricks must needs be meant.[620]

Prideaux

Prideaux states on jot and tittles: "Controversia emergit ex textu, in quo iota & apices, pari censu habentur: si apices tunc temporis non fuerunt, cur eorum meminit Servator? Si eaedem fuerunt cum consanantibus, vel illarum tantum corniculares eminentia, cur hic ut res distinctae recensentur?"[621] That is, "a controversy emerges out of the text, in regard to jot and small points, they are being considered for

---

[619] Johannes Piscator, *Analysis logica evangelii secundum Lucam Una cum scholis et observationibus locorum doctrinae* (London: Richards Field, 1596), 295.

[620] Hugh Broughton, *Daniel his Chaldee visions and his Hebrew: both translated after the original: and expounded both, by reduction of heathen most famous stories unto the exact propriety of his words (which is the surest certainty what he must mean) and by joining all the Bible, and learned tongues to the frame of his work* (London: Gabriel Simson, 1597), comment on Daniel 9:26. There are no page numbers in this edition.

[621] John Prideaux, *Viginti-duae lectiones de totidem relgionis captibus, praecipue hoc tempore controversis, prout publice habebantur oxoniae in vesperiis* (Oxoniae: Excedebat Hen. Hall, Impensis Hen. Cripps, Hen. Curteyn & Thom. Robinson, 1648), 182.

equal valuation: if the small points were not at this time, why is the Saviour making mention of them? If they were the same with the consonants, or only conical eminencies of them, why are they here being reckoned as distinct things?" Prideaux poses some good questions here, which strengthen the author's contention that *tittle* has a non-consonantal meaning.

Lightfoot

Lightfoot writes: "Our Saviour in his words of one *Iota* and one small *kerai* not perishing from the Law, seems to allude to the least of the Letters, *Jod*, and the least vowel and accent."[622]

Owen

John Owen writes in reference to Matthew 5:18: "That our Savior doth here intend the *writing of the Scriptures* then in use in the church, and assure the protection of God unto the least letter, vowel, or point of it, I have proved elsewhere." [623]

Gill

Gill writes: "As the least letter in the *Hebrew* alphabet *Yod* is referred to, the least of the points in use, *Chirek*, is also."[624] Gill's identification of κεραία with *Chirek* is something to which this chapter gives more attention later.

Whitfield

Commenting on Matthew 5:18, Whitfield states:

---

[622] Lightfoot, *The Whole Works of the Rev. John Lightfoot, D.D.*, IV: 50.

[623] John Owen, "The Causes, Ways, and Means of Understanding the Mind of God as Revealed in His Word, with Assurance Therein" in *A Discourse Concerning the Holy Spirit, Continued* in *The Works of John Owen*, in vol. 4 of *the Works of John Owen*, ed. William H. Goold (Carlisle, PA: The Banner of Truth Trust, 1967), 213.

[624] Gill, *Dissertation*, 223.

This is, by some, (I think very improperly) expounded of those small flourishes added to some of the Hebrew letters, in the more elegant and modern manuscripts of the Law, merely for the greater beauty and ornament of the writing; which, by being in the general totally neglected, plainly are not, nor ever were, or could be thought, essentially necessary to the Scripture: and Father Simon, in his Critical History of the Old Testament, expressly saith, that those additional ornaments or flourishes, are not to be found in the more ancient copies, but were the fanciful invention of some modern transcribers: but the passage must be understood of the punctations [marking with points], which always were, as we have seen, so necessary to fix the adequate interpretation and true sense of the Sacred Writings.[625]

Here Whitfield eliminates the meaning of *tagim* (see above under Broughton) and argues for the meaning of vowel points.

Bengel

Bengel comments on *tittle*: "An appendage or portion of a letter, a mark by which one letter is distinguished from another, as ב *B*, from כ *K*, or ר *R*, from ד *D*, or one sound from another, as a vowel point or accent: in short, anything which in any way relates to the revelation of the Divine will in the law, or assists to explain it."[626] Bengel allows for both a consonantal and non-consonantal meaning for *tittle*, just as the lexicons, but the context, as this section presents, decides in favor of the non-consonantal meaning.

Van Doren

Van Doren states on Luke 16:17 that *tittle* is "a little '*dot*' inserted in the smallest Hebrew letter—*iota*."[627] The dot inserted in the

---

[625] Whitfield, 139,140.

[626] John A. Bengel, *New Testament Word Studies*, trans. Charlton T. Lewis and Marvin R. Vincent (Grand Rapids: Kregel Publications, 1971), I: 108.

[627] W. H. Van Doren, *A Suggestive Commentary on St. Luke: with Critical and Homiletical Notes* (NY: I . K. Funk & Co., Publishers, 1867), II: 145.

smallest Hebrew letter is the same size as the *chirek*, the smallest Hebrew vowel point.

Yeager

Yeager on Matthew 5:18 states: "Not the smallest letter or most insignificant vowel point shall pass away from the law. . . . The smallest Hebrew letter (ἰῶτα) or the smallest vowel point (κερέα) shall be held inviolate."[628] Yeager uses an alternate reading (κερέα) instead of the reading in the Received Text of κεραία; however, it is clear that Yeager identifies *tittle* as the smallest Hebrew vowel point, which is the *chirek* (see above under Van Doren).

Franklin

Franklin on Matthew 5:18 observes:

Jesus' statement concerning "one tittle" also has great significance. The word "tittle" in Matthew 5:18 is translated from the Greek κεραια (pronounced *keraia*). The meaning of this word is explained by Arndt and Gingrich in *A Greek-English Lexicon of the New Testament* (p. 428). As they attest, the literal meaning of this term is "horn, projection or hook," referring to that part of a letter which printers call a serif. Webster defines the word "serif" as "a fine line projecting from a main stroke of a letter in common styles of type." Such lines are purely stylistic and add no meaning to a word. However, historical records show that the word κεραια, or "tittle," is not limited to this basic meaning. Κεραια is used in ancient Greek inscriptions and papyri to denote **word accents and breathings**. . . .

"Accents" and "breathings" were marks that were added to words to convey the correct pronunciation of consonants and vowels. Consonants are letters that are spoken with very little resonance. Compared to a consonant, a vowel is spoken with a great deal of resonance. Thus the sound of a vowel is said to be relatively open, and the sound of a consonant is said to be relatively closed. "Breathings" were generally used to indicate the correct vowel sounds.

---

[628] Yeager, 371.

When we understand what the words "jot" and "tittle" represent, the statement that Jesus made in Matthew 5:18 becomes far more meaningful. Jesus was clearly and emphatically declaring that the words of the Old Testament, **as recorded and marked in square script in the Hebrew text**, would be **preserved intact** throughout the ages. The fact that Jesus included the "tittle" in His prophecy shows that even the **pronunciation of the words** would be preserved.

The words of Jesus Christ, as recorded by Matthew, give us absolute assurance that from the earliest times, God has safeguarded His Word. What Jesus declared in 26 AD shows that **no consonant**--not even the smallest, the "jot"--has been lost, and **no vowel sound,** or "tittle," has been lost. Not one word has been lost, and not one pronunciation has been lost![629]

The pronunciation of the Hebrew and Aramaic words depends on the vowels. Franklin argues for a non-consonantal meaning for *tittle*.

Summary

In the phrase *one jot or one tittle shall in no wise pass from the law*, Jesus, by referring to the smallest consonant of the Hebrew language (*jot*), guarantees the preservation of all the consonants of the Old Testament. *Tittle*, then, refers to something other than consonants, namely non-consonants. *Tittle* being a non-consonant receives further support from the fact that Jesus uses the disjunctive conjunction *or* (ἤ), which demands that a *tittle* is different from a *jot*, and, therefore, a *tittle* is something other than a consonant. But which of the non-consonantal meanings does *tittle* have? Is it an *accent*, a *vowel point*, or a *diacritical mark*? The next two contextual considerations demonstrate that *tittle* must include the meaning of *vowel point*.

---

[629] Carl D. Franklin, "In Defense of Jehovah: An Analysis of the Article 'FACTS and *MYTHS* About the Sacred Name' " (August 9, 1998, pages 27 and 28), available online at : http://www.biblestudy.org. Emphasis is in the original.

Till All Be Fulfilled

A second contextual argument for arriving at the proper meaning for *tittle* concerns the words *till all be fulfilled*. A proper understanding of these words demands that *tittle* include the non-consonantal meaning of *vowel point*. *Be fulfilled* (γένηται) is a third person singular second aorist middle subjunctive from γένηται and means *"come to pass"* and refers to the fact that "not the smallest part of the law shall pass away till everything (*i.e.*, everything it contains) shall come to pass. The things predicted in the law must all occur."[630] One of the non-consonantal meanings for *tittle* is that of *vowel point*. If there are only consonants and no vowels in the Hebrew Text, then can there be any certainty as to what is to occur, and can anyone know for certain that it really did come to pass? Chapter Three lists verses wherein various commentators suggest or note differences in the reading of certain verses by changing the vowel pointing of some of the words. Some of these verses concern prophecy, that is, things that are to be fulfilled. The following list presents prophecies that are uncertain if the points are not inspired.[631]

> In Malachi 2:3, is it, "I will corrupt your seed," or is it, "I will rebuke your arm"?
>
> In Zephaniah 3:8, is it, "Until the day that I rise up to the prey," or is it, "Until the day of my rising up for testimony"?
>
> In Micah 6:9, is it, "Shall see thy name," or is it, "Shall fear thy name"?
>
> In Hosea 13:7, is it, "Will I observe," or is it, "By the way of Assyria"?
>
> In Daniel 9:27, is it, "And for the overspreading of abominations he shall make it desolate," or is it, "And – upon the wing – the porch of the temple – abominations! And a desolator!"?

---

[630] John A. Broadus, *Commentary on Matthew* (Grand Rapids: Kregel, 1990), 101.

[631] For more information on the verses in the list, consult Chapter Four.

In Jeremiah 50:38, part of a prophetic passage concerning Babylon, is it, "Drought," or is it, "Sword"?

In Jeremiah 48:4, part of a prophetic passage concerning Moab, is it, "Her little ones," or is it, "Unto Zoar"?

In Jeremiah 25:24, part of a prophecy concerning judgment upon various people, is it, "Mingled people," or is it, "Arabs"?

In Jeremiah 15:19, is it, "Then will I bring thee again," or is it, "I will give thee a settled place"?

In Jeremiah 8:13, is it, "And the things that I have given them shall pass away from them," or is it, "And I will give them to those who shall pass over them"?

In Isaiah 21:13, part of a prophecy concerning Arabia, is it, "In Arabia," or is it, "In the evening"?

In Isaiah 19:10, part of a prophecy concerning Egypt, is it, "And they shall be broken in the purposes thereof, all that make sluices and ponds for fishes," or is it, "And all who make beer shall lament, and shall afflict their souls," or is it, "And the place where they weave cloth shall be trodden down, and the place where they make fish ponds, and where they collect waters, each one for his own life"?

In Proverbs 29:14, is it, "His throne shall be established for ever," is it, "His throne shall be established for a testimony"?

In Proverbs 12:19, is it, "The lip of truth shall be established forever," or is it, "True lips establish testimony"?

In Psalm 2:9, a prophecy concerning Christ, is it, "Thou shalt break," or is it, "Thou shalt rule," or is it, "Thou shalt feed"?

In Job 37:23, is it, "He will not afflict," or is it, "He will not answer"?

In Job 24:12, is it, "God layeth not folly to them," or is it, "God layeth not prayer to them"?

In I Kings 17:4, a prophecy concerning the feeding of Elijah, is it, "Ravens," or is it, "Arabians"?

In Genesis 49:10, is it, "Until Shiloh come," or is it, "Until tribute comes to him"?

From the above examples, it is clear that the vowels are essential to a proper fulfillment of the Old Testament. If there are no vowels in the Law, then multiple possibilities exist for fulfillments of Old Testament prophecy. Why, if one way of pointing did not happen, then one could appeal to another way of pointing. Is this what Jesus meant when He said, "Till all be fulfilled"? If so, He is no better than the quacks and charlatans who give such vague prophecies that almost anything can count as a fulfillment. Is this the level to which proponents of an unpointed Hebrew Old Testament want to subject the Lord Jesus Christ and the Words of God? Perish the thought. The fact that all is to be fulfilled necessitates a clear statement as to what is to be fulfilled. Since a clear statement of what is to be fulfilled demands the vowel points; since *tittle* can mean *vowel point*; since one tittle shall not pass from the law till all be fulfilled indicates an inseparable link between *tittle* with what is to be fulfilled; then here is a contextual argument demanding that *tittle* mean *vowel point*.

One of These Least Commandments

A third contextual argument for arriving at the proper meaning of *tittle* concerns the words of Matthew 5:19. A proper understanding of Matthew 5:19 demands that *tittle* includes the non-consonantal meaning of *vowel point*. Matthew 5:19 states: "Whosoever therefore shall break one of these least commandments, and shall teach men so, he shall be called the least in the kingdom of heaven: but whosoever shall do and teach *them*, the same shall be called great in the kingdom of heaven." Matthew 5:19 uses the word *therefore* (οὖν), which indicates "that something follows from another necessarily" and "hence it is used in drawing a conclusion."[632] Hence, the word *therefore* means that Matthew 5:19 derives a specific application from the teaching of Matthew 5:18, that is, since one jot or one tittle shall in no wise pass

---

[632] Thayer, 463.

from the law till all be fulfilled, then the least of the commandments is important. McClain observes:

> In verse 19 He declares that "whosoever therefore shall break one of these least commandments, and shall teach men so, he shall be called the least in the kingdom of heaven." These "commandments" are contained in "the law" referred to in verse 17, which is the Mosaic law, and of which verse 18 asserts that "one jot or one tittle" cannot pass away. As Alford points out, "These least commandments" refer to "one jot or tittle above."[633]

A proper observance of the least of the commandments depends on the jots and tittles. Specifically, some of the least of the commandments depend on the vowel pointing. One example should suffice. In Exodus 23:19, is the prohibition against seething a kid in his mother's milk. Some might classify this command as one the least of the commandments. Since one could repoint the word *milk* (חֲלֵב) to *fat* (חֵלֶב), then without the vowel pointing he, thinking that the word was *fat* instead of *milk*, could easily break this commandment and teach others also to break it. If one is not going to break one of the least of the commandments, he must have the vowel points so that he clearly knows the demands of the commandment. The vowel points are essential to a proper understanding of the least of the commandments.

Since Matthew 5:19 teaches the importance of the least of the commandments; since the least of the commandments depends on the vowel points; since Jesus bases the teaching of Matthew 5:19 on the teaching of Matthew 5:18; and since Matthew 5:18 speaks of the *tittle*, which can mean a *vowel point*; then here is another contextual reason for why *tittle* does mean *vowel point*.

---

[633]Alva J. McClain, "What Is 'The Law'?", *Bibliotheca Sacra* 110 (October 1953): 337. McClain seems to think that *law* in vs. 18 only refers to the Mosaic Law, however, this is not the case. It refers to the entire Old Testament. See the author's *Those So-Called Errors*, pp. 70-76.

Conclusion

Three contextual considerations demand that *tittle* refers to a vowel point. The first of these considerations involves the phrase, "One jot or one tittle shall in no wise pass from the law" in Matthew 5:18. Since *one jot* guarantees the preservation of all the consonants, and since *or* is a disjunctive conjunction indicating that it is different from a *jot*; then *one tittle* must have a non-consonantal meaning. The second contextual consideration involves the phrase "till all be fulfilled" in Matthew 5:18. Vowels are essential to a proper fulfillment of Old Testament prophecy, and *tittle*, which can mean a *vowel point*, Jesus inseparably links with what is to be fulfilled; therefore, the context determines that *tittle* must indeed be a vowel point. And a third contextual consideration involves Matthew 5:19 and the words "the least of one of these commandments," which commandments depend on the vowel points. Since Matthew 5:19 bases its teaching on Matthew 5:18, which mentions the *tittle*, which again can mean a *vowel point*; then Matthew 5:19 provides further contextual evidence that *tittle* does indeed mean *vowel point*. These three contextual considerations limit *one tittle* to a non-consonantal meaning, and demand that it refer to a vowel point.

ETYMOLOGICAL CONSIDERATIONS

Oats, on contextual grounds, objects to *tittle* being a vowel point. He argues: "The 'jot' is the 'yodh,' the smallest of the Hebrew consonants. While most view 'tittle' as a part of a consonant, this book [*Thou Shalt Keep Them*] argues that the word refers to vowels. It is inconsistent, however, for Jesus to use the actual name of a consonant, but not the actual name of a vowel."[634] As for Oats' contention

---

[634] Oats, *Thou Shalt Keep Them: A Review*, 6.

that *tittle* is not the actual name of a Hebrew vowel, one only need look at the definitions for *tittle* to see that it can mean *point*, as Pasor, Schrevelius, Thayer, and Perschbacher all state (see earlier), which is an apt description for the smallest of the Hebrew vowel points, the *chirek*[635] (חִירֶק), which is simply a dot or a point (.), which should be enough to end the argument. Additionally, etymological evidence connects κεραία directly to *chirek*.

Gill states: "As the least letter in the *Hebrew* alphabet *Yod* is referred to, the least of the points in use, *Chirek*, is also; between which and the *Greek* word κεραια, used by the Evangelist, is great nearness of sound, and seems to be no other than that point made Greek."[636] In other words, Gill indicates that κεραία is a transliteration into Greek of the Hebrew חִירֶק (*chirek*). Before considering Gill's contention, a question arises. Was the word חִירֶק (*chirek*) in use in the time of Christ? *Chirek* does not occur in the Hebrew Old Testament, neither do the names for any of the other the vowel points or letters; therefore, one must appeal to non-biblical, historical sources to determine if *chirek* was in use in Christ's day. With historical records being often incomplete or in dispute, the author is unable to conclusively demonstrate that *chirek* was a word in use in Christ's day. However, he can offer some information. First, as a previous footnote indicates, modern-day writers refer to the *chirek*. Second, Gill in his *Dissertation* of 1767 mentions the *chirek*. Third, Gill refers to Hutter's using

---

[635] Alternate spellings are *hireq* as in Thomas O. Lambdin, *Introduction to Biblical Hebrew* (NY: Charles Scribner's Sons, 1971), XXV; *khirik* as on www.wikipedia.com; *ḥireq* as in Kelley, 6; *ḥiriq* as in Menahem Mansoor, *Biblical Hebrew: Step by Step* (Grand Rapids: Baker Book House, 1980), I:29; and *chireq* as in Strouse, "One Tittle," 13. These spellings are just different ways for transliterating חִירֶק into English. The first letter, ח, has a *ch* sound, which comes through into English as *ch*, *kh*, *k*, or an hard *h*. The last letter, ק, has a *k* or *q* sound and, therefore, comes through into English as either *k* or *q*. The last vowel is ִ , which is a long *e* and can be represented in English as an *e* or a long *i*.

[636] Gill, *Dissertation*, 223.

chirek in his Hebrew translation of the New Testament,[637] which Hutter completed in 1600.[638] Fourth, Gill relates that Kimḥi uses the word *chirek* in a comment on Psalm 110:1, 3.[639] Kimḥi lived from 1160 to about 1240.[640] And fifth, Gill, who dates the *Zohar* at 120 AD, states of the *Zohar* that "the very names of the points and accents are mentioned in it in various places, as *Cholem, Schurek, Chirek, Pathach, Segol, Sheva, Kametz, Tzere*."[641] Concerning the dating of the *Zohar* Gill states:

> About this time [120 AD], according to the Jewish chronology, lived Simeon Ben Jochai a disciple of R. Akiba author of the book of *Zohar*; the authority and antiquity of which book is not called in question by any of the Jews, no not by Elias Levita himself, who first asserted the points to be the invention of the men of Tiberias; yet declared, if anyone could convince him that his opinion was contrary to the book of *Zohar*, he should be content to have it rejected. What may be urged in favor of the antiquity of that book, is not only, that the persons introduced speaking in it, and whose sayings are recorded, were as early or earlier than the time to which it is placed; but the neatness of the language in which it is written, which far exceeds anything written after this time; as also there being no mention made of the Talmud in it, though there is of the Targums of Onkelos and Jonathan. Some things objected to its antiquity may be only interpolations. R. Azariah says, it

---

[637] Ibid.

[638] "Hebrew Version of the New Testament," in *Cyclopedia*, xii:534.

[639] Gill, *Dissertation*, 138,139. The full quote is: "*Kimchi* observes against those that read *Adonai* lord, and *immecha* with thee, in Ps. cx. 1, 3. instead of *Adoni* my lord, and *ammeca* thy people, 'that from the rising of the sun to the setting of it, (i. e. throughout the world) you will find, in all copies, *nun* with *chirek*, and *Ain* with *pathach*'." In this quote Gill cites Apud Pocok. Porta Mosis miscell. not. p. 58.

[640] "Kimchi, David" in *Cyclopedia*, V:80.

[641] Gill, *Dissertation*, 214. Gill cites *Zohar* in Gen. fol. 1, 2. & 26, 3. & 38. 1. 2. & 71. 2. Tikkune zohar praefat, fol. 6, 2. & 7, 1.

was written before the *Misnah* was compiled. According to Masius it was written a little after the destruction of Jerusalem.[642]

If 120 AD is the correct date the *Zohar*, then this would be conclusive proof that the word *chirek* was in use at about the time of Christ. However, some question dating the *Zohar* back to 120 AD (see Chapter One under Simon ben-Jochai) and instead date it to the thirteenth century; therefore, for some, appeal to the *Zohar* is not conclusive. Be this as it may, the above evidence does establish that *chirek* is a traditional name for one of the Hebrew vowel points and to the writer's knowledge no one has established that this point was ever known by any other name. Furthermore, and more importantly, the previous chapter establishes on a Biblical basis the existence of Hebrew vowels; therefore, Christ was aware of the Hebrew vowels. Hence, His using κεραία to refer to one of those vowels presents no problem.

Now back to Gill's contention that κεραία is a transliteration into Greek of the Hebrew חִירֶק (*chirek*). For Gill's contention to be true, then (1) ח (*ch*) in Hebrew would have to be equivalent to κ in Greek; (2) י (*i*) in Hebrew would have to be equivalent to ε in Greek; (3) ר (*r*) in Hebrew would have to be equivalent to ρ (*r*) in Greek; (4) ֶ (e) in Hebrew would have to be equivalent to αι (*ai*) in Greek; and (5) ק (*q*) in Hebrew would have to be equivalent to α (*a*) in Greek. This section presents information on each of these points in order to establish that Gill's contention may be correct and that κεραία is a Greek transliteration for the Hebrew חִירֶק (*chirek*).

Ch in Hebrew Equal to K in Greek

To establish a connection between *ch* (ח) in Hebrew with κ (*k*) in Greek requires several steps. First, ח (*ch*) in Hebrew is equivalent

---

[642] Ibid., 212, 213. Gill cites *Ganz Tzemach David*, par. 1. fol. 30, 1.; Levita, *Praefatioa 3. Ad Masoret.*; *Zohar* in Gen. fol. 61, 1.; Azariah, *Imre Binah*, c. 59. fol. 179, 2.; and Masius, *Comment. in Joshua* 1, 3.

to χ (*ch*) in Greek, for יְרֵחוֹ (*yərēḥô Jericho*, Numbers 22:1) the Greek renders with Ἰεριχώ (Hebrews 11:30). Other examples involve the words *Nachor* (Joshua 24:2 and Luke 3:34), *Rachel* (Genesis 29:6 and Matthew 2:18), and *Haran / Charran* (Genesis 11:31and Acts 7:2).

Second, כ (*k*) in Hebrew is also equivalent to χ (*ch*) in Greek, for בְּרֶכְיָה (*Berechiah*, I Chronicles 3:20) the Greek renders with Βαραχίου (*Barachias*, Matthew 23:35). Other examples include the names of *Zacharias* (Matthew 23:35 and II Chronicles 24:20), *Jechonias* (Matthew 1:11 and I Chronicles 3:16), *Issachar* (Revelation 7:7 and Genesis 30:18), *Michael* (Jude 9 and Daniel 12:1), *Canaan* (Matthew 15:22 and Genesis 12:5), and the word *cherubims* (Hebrews 9:5 and Exodus 25:19).

Third, כ (*k*) in Hebrew is equivalent to κ (*k*) in Greek, for *Capernaum* is a compound of two Hebrew words (כָּפַר - *kap̄ar* and נָחוּם - *naḥûm*),[643] which the Greek renders with Καπερναούμ (Matthew 4:13).

These three steps establish that ח (*ch*) in Hebrew is, at times, equivalent with κ (*k*) in the Greek. The use of mathematical equations helps to clarify this point: from step one, ח (*ch*) = χ (*ch*); from step two, כ (*k*) = χ (*ch*); and from step three, כ (*k*) = κ (*k*); therefore, by two substitutions, ח (*ch*) = κ (*k*).

Gill takes a more direct route in establishing that ח (*ch*) = κ (*k*) when he observes that the letters חרן, which refer to the city *Haran*, are by Ptolemy, Herodian, and other Greek writers rendered καρρα.[644] Another way to connect ח (*ch*) with κ (*k*) comes from a couple of observations. First, Kelley states that ח (*ch*) and כ (*k*) have similar sounds, that is, a *ch* sound as in *Bach*.[645] Second, step three above

---

[643] Thayer, 324.

[644] Rippon, lxi.

[645] Kelley, 1.

demonstrates that the Hebrew כ (*k*) = the Greek κ (*k*). Third, by substitution, ח (*ch*) = κ (*k*).

The conclusion from this section is that *ch* (ח) in Hebrew can be equal with κ (*k*) in Greek, which establishes that the first letters of κεραία and חִירֶק correspond.

I in Hebrew Equal to E in Greek

To show that *i* (ִ) in Hebrew is equal to ε (*e*) in Greek will also take a couple of steps. First, *Jericho* has two spellings in the Hebrew Old Testament, יְרִיחוֹ (*yərîḥô* in Joshua 2:2), and יְרֵחוֹ (*yərēḥô* in Numbers 26:3). Both of the spellings have the same accent, therefore, the spelling change is not due to accent. The Hebrew spelling for *Jericho* establishes that at times ִ (*i*) is interchangeable with ֵ (*e*). Another possible example of ִ (*i*) being interchangeable with ֵ (*e*) is with the word *poverty* where in Proverbs 28:19 the word for *poverty* is רִישׁ (*rîsh*) but Proverbs 30:8 spells it as רֵאשׁ (*rēʾsh*). The author says *possible* because the accents of these two words are different. If, in these instances, the accents do not affect the spelling, then in the second spelling, an ֵ (*e*) replaces the vowel *chirek yodh* (ִ), that is, *i* of the first spelling and further establishes that ִ (*i*) is interchangeable with ֵ (*e*).

The next step in showing that *i* in Hebrew can be equivalent to *e* in Greek is to examine the word *Levi*. *Levi* in Hebrew is לֵוִי (*lēwî* in Genesis 29:34), which in Greek is Λευί (Luke 3:24), which shows that ֵ (*e*) from Hebrew is equivalent to ε (*e*) in Greek.

The last step in this process is to use substitution. Since in Hebrew *i* at times is equivalent to *e*, and since *e* in Hebrew is equivalent to *e* in Greek, then an *e* in Greek could represent an *i* from the Hebrew. Using mathematical equations, it would look like this: *i* in Hebrew = *e* in Hebrew; *e* in Hebrew = *e* in Greek; therefore, by substitution *i* in Hebrew = *e* in Greek.

R in Hebrew Equal to R in Greek

To show that *r* (ר) in Hebrew is equivalent to *r* (ρ) in Greek is easy. An example of an *r* (ר) in Hebrew being an *r* (ρ) in Greek is with the name *Berechiah* (I Chronicles 3:20 {בְּרֶכְיָה - bere$\underline{k}$yā^h} and Matthew 23:35 {Βαραχίου}).

E in Hebrew Equal to Ai in Greek

To establish that (*e*) in Hebrew is equivalent to αι (*ai*) in Greek involves a couple of steps. First, a connection between *e* ( ) and the long *a* ( ) in Hebrew comes from the word *thousand* where II Chronicles 35:7 spells the word as אֶלֶף (*'elep̄*) but Ezra 1:9 spells it as אָלֶף (*'ālep̄*), where the long *a* ( ) has taken the place of the *e* ( ). Note that both of these words have the same accent, therefore, the differences in spelling are not due to accent.

Second, a connection between (*a*) in Hebrew and αι (*ai*) in Greek comes from the word *Elisha* (אֱלִישָׁע - *'ĕlîšā'* in I Kings 19:16), which the Greek renders as 'Ελισσαίου (Luke 4:27), where the *ai* in the Greek represents the (*a*) from the end of the Hebrew word.

By substitution, then, the Greek αι (*ai*) can convey the Hebrew (*e*). Mathematically, it looks like this: *e* ( ) in Hebrew = *a* ( ) in Hebrew; *a* ( ) in Hebrew = αι (*ai*) in Greek; therefore, *e* ( ) in Hebrew = αι (*ai*) in Greek.

Q in Hebrew Equal to A in Greek

To demonstrate that ק (*q*) in Hebrew is equal to α (*a*) in Greek will also take several steps. First, the Greek renders the Hebrew ק (*q*) with a κ (*k*), as in the case of the name for *Cain*. In Hebrew *Cain* is קַיִן (*qayin*). In Greek *Cain* is Κάϊν. Notice that the Greek renders the ק (*q*) in the Hebrew with a κ (*k*). Other examples of ק (*q*) in Hebrew being equal with κ (*k*) in Greek are *Cainan* (קֵינָן – *qênān* in Genesis 5:9 and Καϊνάν in Luke 3:37); *Cis* (קִישׁ – *qîsh* in I Samuel 9:1 and Κίς in Acts 13:21); and *Core* (קֹרַח - *qōraḥ* in Exodus 6:21 Κόρε in Jude 11). From this first step, ק (*q*) in Hebrew = κ (*k*) in Greek.

Second, an earlier discussion demonstrated that the Greek renders the Hebrew כ (*k*) with κ (*k*); therefore, by substitution, the Hebrew ק (*q*) equals the Hebrew כ (*k*).

Third, also an earlier discussion demonstrated that כ (*k*) and ח (*ch*) can be interchanged, therefore, the Hebrew כ (*k*) = the Hebrew ח (*ch*). Combining this information with the previous step, then there exists a connection between ק (*q*) and ח (*ch*). That is, since the Hebrew ק (*q*) = the Hebrew כ (*k*) and since the Hebrew כ (*k*) = the Hebrew ח (*ch*); then by substitution, the Hebrew ק (*q*) = the Hebrew ח (*ch*).

Fourth, the Greek at times renders the Hebrew ח (*ch*) with α (*a*). Several examples will suffice to demonstrate this: Matthew 1:3 has Ζαρὰ (*Zara*), referring to זֶרַח (*zāraḥ*) of Genesis 38:30; Luke 3:34 has Θάρα (*Thara*), referring to תֶּרַח (*teraḥ*) of Genesis 11:26; and Matthew 1:2 has Ἰσαάκ (*Isaac*), referring to יִצְחָק (*yiṣḥāq*) of Genesis 21:3. From this step, the Hebrew ח (*ch*) = the Greek α (*a*).

Using mathematical equations, the above arguments look like this: (1) ק (*q*) in Hebrew = κ (*k*) in Greek; (2) the Hebrew ק (*q*) = the Hebrew כ (*k*); (3) the Hebrew כ (*k*) = the Hebrew ח (*ch*), therefore, by substitution, the Hebrew ק (*q*) = the Hebrew ח (*ch*); and (4) the Hebrew ח (*ch*) = the Greek α (*a*), therefore, by substitution, the Hebrew ק (*q*) = the Greek α (*a*).

Gill takes a different approach to arrive at identifying the Hebrew ק (*q*) with α (*a*). He writes, "In the *Chaldee* or Syro-Chaldean language, used in Christ's time, and before, the same word, which ends in קא, κα, has the termination of *ky*, αα, or αια. Thus *araka* is read *araa* in the same verse, Jer. x. 11."[646] In this quote, Gill mentions the *Chal-*

---

[646] Rippon, lxi.

dee language, which is another name for the Aramaic language.[647] Jeremiah 10:11, the verse to which Gill appeals, is written in Aramaic. In Jeremiah 10:11, the Bible uses the phrase *the earth* twice, which are the words to which Gill refers. In the first use of *the earth*, the Bible spells it as אַרְקָא, which Gill transliterates as *araka*. In the second use, the Bible spells *the earth* as אַרְעָא, which Gill transliterates as *araa*. In Gill's example, the Bible replaces the *ka* of the first word by an *a* in the second word, therefore, α (*a*) replaces ק (*q*), which is exactly what κεραία does in having the α (*a*) at the end of the word replace the ק (*q*) at the end of *chirek* (חִירֶק).

Conclusion

By the above steps, one could deduce that κεραία is Greek for חִירֶק (*chirek*). When Gill proposed that κεραία is a transliteration of חִירֶק (*chirek*), some thought that he mistook חִירֶק (*chirek*) for קֶרֶן (*qeren*), the Hebrew word for *horn*.[648] Some suppose that κεραία, a feminine noun, is from κέρας, a neuter noun,[649] a Greek word that can refer to *horn*, which Kedar-Kopfstein associates with the Hebrew word קֶרֶן (*qeren*).[650] Gill wrote: "To derive this word [κεραία] from the *He-*

---

[647] Otto Zockler, *The Book of the Prophet Daniel. Theologically and Homiletically Expounded*, trans., enlarged, and ed. James Strong in vol. 13 of *A Commentary on the Holy Scriptures: Critical, Doctrinal and Homiletical*, ed. John Peter Lange, trans. Philip Schaff (NY: Scribner, Armstrong & Co., 1876), 68.

[648] Rippon, lxi.

[649] For example, Alfred Plummer, *The Gospel According to S. Luke* in *The International Critical Commentary on the Holy Scriptures of the Old and New Testaments*, eds. Samuel Rolles Driver, Alfred Plummer, and Charles Augustus Briggs, 5th ed. (Edinburgh: T & T Clark, 1989), 389. Also, Pasor, who is listed under the lexical section of this chapter connects κέρας with κεραία, but he gives it the same definition as κεραία (see earlier).

[650] B. Kedar-Kopfstein, "קֶרֶן qeren; קָרַן qāran" in *Theological Dictionary of the Old Testament*, eds. G. Johannes Botterweck, Helmer Ringgren, and Heinz-Josef Fabry, trans. David E. Green (Grand Rapids: William B. Eerdmans Publishing Company, 2004), xiii: 168.

brew word קרן which signifies an *horn;* as if our Lord referred to the corniculated apices, pricks, or spikes upon the tops of some letters, not in use in his time (as Capellus and others); is mere fiction and conceit."[651] While it is possible, according to the lexical listings presented earlier in this chapter, for κεραία to mean *horn*; however, as the lexical listings also show, κεραία can mean *point* and it is this meaning that this chapter establishes that the context of Matthew 5:18 demands. *Tittle* has a non-consonantal meaning; therefore, in Matthew 5:18 it can not mean a *little horn, the smallest differences between the letters,* a *serif,* an *ornamental marking,* or a *tagin*.[652] Furthermore, the Lord Jesus Christ used the word κεραία and not the word κέρας in Matthew 5:18 and Luke 16:17. The word κεραία bears a definite similarity with the Hebrew word *chirek*, which the word κέρας does not. The Lord could have used the word κέρας, but He did not. Instead, He used a word that resembles the Hebrew word for *chirek*. Indeed, this section establishes that *tittle* derives from חִירֶק (*chirek*) and, therefore, does not derive from קֶרֶן (*qeren*).

SCRIPTURAL CONSIDERATIONS

Another factor that decides for *tittle* being a reference to a vowel point is a Scriptural consideration. The Bible is it's own best interpreter (I Corinthians 2:12,13). Previously, the writer presented over thirty passages from both the Old and New Testaments that demand the preservation of the Old Testament vowels. Of particular note are the Words of the Lord Jesus Christ, Who is the only One Who used *tittle* in the New Testament. In Matthew 24:35 Jesus stated, "Heaven and earth shall pass away, but my words shall not pass away." And in

---

[651] Gill, *Exposition*, I: lxii.

[652] See earlier section in this chapter entitled "Contextual Considerations."

John 10:35 Jesus stated, "The scripture cannot be broken." In order for Jesus' Old Testament Words not to pass away and in order for the Old Testament Scripture not to be broken, the vowels are necessary, for without the vowels how can one definitely know the exact words? And if one cannot definitely know the words, then the Scripture is broken.

Furthermore, Jesus taught that words proceeded out of the mouth of God (Matthew 4:4). Words proceeding out of the mouth involve vocalization, that is, the use of vowels. In Matthew 4:4 Jesus asserted that the proceedeth-out-of-the-mouth-of-God Words are available to man, therefore they are preserved. How are these vocalized Words from the mouth of God preserved? They are preserved in writing, as Jesus said, "It is written." In other words, Jesus teaches that the vocalized Words of God, involving both consonants and vowels, are written; therefore, the written words have both vowels and consonants.

Jesus taught the preservation of the Words of God, the preservation of which demands the vowels. Jesus defined the Words of God as something that proceeded out of God's mouth, also demanding the use of vowels. Jesus taught that the words that proceeded from God's mouth are written, which also necessitates the use of vowels. Therefore, for Jesus to use *tittle* to refer to a vowel point seems quite natural.

But there is more, *tittle* referring to a vowel point is supported by many other verses that this book has already presented. God spoke words involving the use of both vowels and consonants (Genesis 22:16; Exodus 4:22; 24:4; Jeremiah 30:2; 36:1-4). God's prophets wrote the Words of God, which necessitates their having used vowels (Exodus 34:27; Matthew 22:31; Luke 24:25; John 1:23; 12:38; Acts 3:22; 7:48,49; 8:32-34; 28:25; Romans 9:29; 12:19; 14:11; I Corinthians 9:10; Hebrews 3:7; II Peter 3:2). New Testament writers were cognizant of the vowel points (see Chapter Four). God's Words are sure, which sureness is dependent on the vowels (see Chapters Three and Four). The Bible teaches that the Scripture is the sole authority for faith and practice, which authority depends on the points (see Chapters

Three and Four). Herein is strong Scriptural support for *tittle* referring to a vowel point.

The interpretation that *tittle* refers to a vowel point is in agreement with these passages. In other words, the interpretation that *tittle* is a vowel point is a consistent interpretation with the rest of Scripture. Indeed, the author is not relying on a unique interpretation of one single verse to make his case. The overall testimony of Scripture supports the teaching that one vowel shall in no wise pass from the Law.

TRANSLATIONAL CONSIDERATIONS

Several translations of the Bible support the author's contention that κεραία is a vowel point. Though the author in this section will be referring to translations that are not in the Received Text line, one should not construe such action as an endorsement of these translations. However, in the case of Matthew 5:18, the Critical Text and the Received Text are identical. The author uses these modern translations to illustrate that others understand κεραία in the sense of a dot or point.

Tyndale – 1525

Tyndale in his address to the reader, *Pentateuch* (Mombert's Reprint, p. 3), writes:

> For they which in tymes paste were wont to loke on no more scripture then they founde in their duns or soch like develysh doctryne, have yet not so narowlye loked on my translatyon, that there is not so moch as one I therin if it lacke a tytle over his hed, but they have noted it, and nombre it unto the ignorant people for an heresye.[653]

---

[653] James Hastings, "Tittle" in *A Dictionary of the Bible Dealing with Its Language, Literature, and Contents Including the Biblical Theology*, ed. James Hastings (Edinburgh: T & T Clark, 1904), IV:781, 782.

A modern spelling of Tyndale's comment is:

> For they which in times past were wont to look on no more Scripture then they found in their duns or such like devilish doctrine, have yet not so narrowly looked on my translation, that there is not so much as one *i* therein if it lack a tittle over his head, but they have noted it, and number it unto the ignorant people for an heresy.

Herein Tyndale refers to the dot over the *i* as a *tytle*. "In quoting Mt 5:18 three pages later, he spells the word 'tittle',"[654] which is the spelling in the present King James Bible. It is clear that Tyndale understood κεραία as a dot, which is the same as the *chirek*.

Polyglot Testament – 1600

The *Polyglot Testament* is the work of Elias Hutter in which is the first translation of the entire New Testament into Hebrew. "According to the judgment of professor Delitzsch, it is of great value, and is still worth consulting, because in many places it is very correct."[655] According to Gill in this version, Hutter rendered κεραία with *chirek*.[656]

Revised Standard Version – 1952

The *Revised Standard Version* uses *dot* when translating κεραία in Matthew 5:18. The whole verse reads: "For truly, I say to you, till heaven and earth pass away, not an iota, not a dot, will pass from the law until all is accomplished."

New International Version – 1984

The *New International Version* translates Matthew 5:18 with: "I tell you the truth, until heaven and earth disappear, not the smallest

---

[654] Ibid., 782.

[655] "Hebrew Version of the New Testament," in *Cyclopedia*, xii:534.

[656] Gill, *Dissertation*, 223.

letter, not the least stroke of a pen, will by any means disappear from the Law until everything is accomplished." This version understands κεραία to be *the least stroke of a pen*, certainly descriptive of a single dot or point.

English Standard Version – 2001

In Matthew 5:18 the *English Standard Version* translates κεραία with the word *dot*. The whole verse reads: "For truly, I say to you, until heaven and earth pass away, not an iota, not a dot, will pass from the Law until all is accomplished."

Summary

These five translations all demonstrate that the translators of these translations understood κεραία as being a dot or a point. The author could have multiplied examples of translations using *tittle* as the translation for κεραία, but after the first example from Tyndale there was no need to do so. However, for those interested, translations that use *tittle* include *The Geneva Bible*, *King James Version*, *The Darby Bible*, *The Webster Bible*, *Young's Literal Translation*, *American Standard Version*, *New American Standard Version*, and *New King James Version*.

CONCLUSION

After examining lexical, contextual, etymological, Scriptural, and translational considerations; the author concludes that *tittle* refers to a vowel point of the Old Testament Scriptures. Lexically, *tittle* can have a consonantal meaning, where it is part of a consonant, or *tittle* can have a non-consonantal meaning. An examination of the context of Matthew 5:18 decides the case for *tittle* having a non-consonantal meaning, specifically that it refers to a vowel point. *Jot*, the least of the Hebrew consonants, adequately guarantees the preservation of all the consonants (see Luke 16:10), therefore, *tittle* need not refer to consonants. Also, the phrase *one jot or one tittle* with the use of the disjunctive conjunction (ἤ *or*) makes it clear that *tittle* is different from the *jot*, which further establishes that *tittle* is referring to something other than consonants or something connected to consonants. Furthermore, the expression *till all be fulfilled* refers to the fulfillment of prophecy, the exact fulfillment of which depends on the vowels.[657] Also, *one of these least commandments* in the next verse, Matthew 5:19, depends on the vowels.[658] Scripturally, God spoke words involving the use of both vowels and consonants (Genesis 22:16; Exodus 4:22; 24:4; Jeremiah 30:2; 36:1-4; Matthew 4:4). These words God's prophets wrote necessitating their having used vowels (Exodus 34:27; Matthew 22:31; Luke 24:25; John 1:23; 12:38; Acts 3:22; 7:48,49; 8:32-34; 28:25; Romans 9:29; 12:19; 14:11; I Corinthians 9:10; Hebrews 3:7; II Peter 3:2). Jesus guaranteed the perfect preservation of God's Words (Matthew 24:35; John 10:35; 17:17). These Scriptural considerations, along with the fact that God's Words are sure and are the sole authority for faith and practice demand the presence of vowels. In other words, Scripture teaches the inspiration and preservation of the vowels of the Old Testament, which teaching is in exact agreement with understanding *tittle* to be a vowel point in Matthew 5:18. Etymologically, the Greek word behind *tittle* (κεραία) is a transliteration

---

[657] Please consider Genesis 49:10; I Kings 17:4; Job 24:12; 37:23; Psalm 2:9; Proverbs 12:19; 29:14; Isaiah 19:10; 21:13; Jeremiah 8:13; 15:19; 25:24; 48:4; 50:38; Daniel 9:27; Hosea 13:7; Micah 6:9; Zephaniah 3:8; and Malachi 2:3. These verses are all prophecies that some would like to repoint, but repointing would affect the fulfillment, making it impossible to know if they are fulfilled.

[658] In Exodus 23:19, is the prohibition against seething a kid in his mother's milk. Some might classify this command as one the least of the commandments. Since one could repoint the word *milk* (חֲלֵב) to *fat* (חֵלֶב), then without the vowel pointing one, thinking that the word was *fat* instead of *milk*, could easily break this commandment and teach others also to break it. If one is not going to break one of the least of the commandments, he must have the vowel points so that he clearly knows the demands of the commandment.

into Greek of the Hebrew חִירֶק (*chirek*), wherein *chirek* is the name of the smallest Hebrew vowel point. Lastly, other translations support the contention that *tittle* is a dot, and not merely another part of a consonant.

To rephrase and to re-emphasize the teaching of this chapter, Matthew 5:18 supports the *autographa* position on the vowel points. First, *tittle* can mean *vowel point.* Second, *jot*, the least of the Hebrew consonants, adequately guarantees the preservation of all the consonants (see Luke 16:10) so that *tittle* need not refer to consonants or any part of consonants. Third, the disjunctive conjunction (ἢ *or*) differentiates the *tittle* from the *jot*, showing that it is not a consonant. Fourth, Jesus inseparably links *tittle* with prophecies that are yet to be fulfilled, the fulfillment of which depends on the vowels. Fifth, Matthew 5:18 is the foundation on which Jesus bases His teaching in Matthew 5:19 about "one of these least commandments," which commandments depend on the vowels. Sixth, God spoke words involving the use of both vowels and consonants (Genesis 22:16; Exodus 4:22; 24:4; Jeremiah 30:2; 36:1-4; Matthew 4:4). Seventh, God's prophets wrote the Words of God, which necessitates their having used vowels (Exodus 34:27; Matthew 22:31; Luke 24:25; John 1:23; 12:38; Acts 3:22; 7:48,49; 8:32-34; 28:25; Romans 9:29; 12:19; 14:11; I Corinthians 9:10; Hebrews 3:7; II Peter 3:2). Eighth, New Testament writers were cognizant of the vowel points (e.g., *Emmanuel* in Matthew 1:23; *Abaddon* in Revelation 9:11; *Capernaum* in Matthew 4:13; *Messiah* in John 1:41; and many others). Ninth, God's Words are sure, which sureness is dependent on the vowels (see Chapter Four). Tenth, the Bible teaches that Scripture is the sole authority for faith and practice, which authority depends on the points (see Chapter Three). Eleventh, Jesus elsewhere guaranteed the perfect preservation of God's Words (Matthew 24:35; John 10:35; 17:17). And twelfth, the Greek word for *tittle* (κεραία) is a transliteration into Greek of the Hebrew חִירֶק (*chirek*), wherein *chirek* is the name of the smallest Hebrew vowel point. In light of these twelve statements, the writer concludes that *tittle* refers to the Hebrew vowel point, *chirek*.

Matthew 5:18, then, is a strong foundation upon which to base the teaching of the inspiration of the Hebrew vowel points and their preservation, thereby further establishing the *autographa* position on the points as the correct view and further eliminating the accommodation and non-authoritative positions as incorrect views. Thank God that Jesus has assured one and all that the Bible is certain down to the smallest of details[659] and that it will certainly last. Why would anyone want to argue otherwise? Perhaps some are not fully aware of what the Bible teaches about the points, and it is the hope of the author that they will change their minds. The fact is that Jesus clearly and dogmatically asserts: "Till heaven and earth pass, one jot or one tittle shall in no wise pass from the law, till all be fulfilled" (Matthew 5:18). Jesus also asserts: "It is easier for heaven and earth to pass, than one tittle of the law to fail" (Luke 16:17).

---

[659] In Luke 16:17 Jesus stated: "And it is easier for heaven and earth to pass, than one tittle of the law to fail." In Luke 16:17, Jesus speaks of the biggest observable part of God's creation, heaven and earth, and states that they are easier to pass away than one tittle. Man might think that it does not matter to lose some small pieces as long as he maintains the whole, but the Lord Jesus Christ thinks otherwise, as He asserts that the preservation of the very small tittle is more important than the preservation of heaven and earth.

CHAPTER SIX – FURTHER OBJECTIONS

Some pose objections to the *autographa* position on the vowel points. Chapter One listed all of these objections and gave substantial answers to most of them. This chapter presents only those objections that need a more extensive evaluation. The writer divides these objections into two categories: historical and Biblical.

HISTORICAL OBJECTIONS

Most writers who argue against the *autographa* position often use historical arguments. Seemingly, they believe that they have won the day if they think that they have proved their assertion by using history. However, the Bible is the sole authority for faith and practice, not history. Consequently, neither a one of these historical arguments, nor all of them combined together can decide the issue about the points. But since most people walk by sight and put their trust in history, the writer must deal with these historical objections. He does so with the hope of turning people away from a humanistic and rationalistic reliance on history and toward a walking by faith in the promises of God. This section deals more fully with the historical objections concerning unpointed documents and the Joab story.

Unpointed Documents

Those who argue for the novelty of the points often refer to various unpointed documents such as newspapers, the Dead Sea Scrolls, the Samaritan Pentateuch, synagogue copies of the Law, and from other languages. Along with this argument is the reasoning that if people can or could read these documents without points, then the proponents of this argument claim that it was possible for people to read unpointed Hebrew Bibles. Perhaps some people could read unpointed Hebrew Bibles, just as an English-speaking person might be able to make sense of cn u rd ths?; but the fact that some could do this, does not mean that God did not inspire the points. What people can or cannot do should not be the factor that decides the vowel point issue, on the contrary, it should be, what does the Bible say.

Newspapers

Larry Oats, who holds to the novelty of the points, in a review of *Thou Shalt Keep Them* argues:

> A person can take unpointed Hebrew (just the consonants) and without changing or even moving a consonant add all the vowels. Gary Webb declares that without the vowels, the Old Testament would have been "an unintelligible grouping of consonants" (44). Obviously, Webb has never been to Israel and looked at their daily newspapers. There are no vowels – and no one complains that they cannot read their papers.[660]

Such an argument suffers from several weaknesses. First, the Modern Hebrew of the *Ha Aretz* and the *Jerusalem Post* are not the given-by-inspiration Words of God (II Timothy 3:16). Second, *Ha Aretz* and the *Jerusalem Post* do not have God's promise of preservation (Psalm 12:6,7). Third, *Ha Aretz* and the *Jerusalem Post* are not necessary for the Christian life (Matthew 4:4). Fourth, *Ha Aretz* and the *Jerusalem Post* are not magnified above all of God's name (Psalm 138:2). Fifth, *Ha Aretz* and the *Jerusalem Post* are not living Words (I Peter 1:23-25). In light of these facts, to compare the newspaper to the Bible is to denigrate the Bible. The Bible is no newspaper, but is the inspired, perfectly preserved (Psalm 12:6,7), essential-for-life (Matthew 4:4), magnified-above-all-of-God's-name (Psalm 138:2), and living Word of

---

[660] Oats, *Thou Shalt Keep Them: A Review by Larry Oats*, 6. Oats' review has no date, but obviously, he wrote it after the publication of *Thou Shalt Keep Them*, which was published in August of 2003.

God (I Peter 1:23-25); as such it is totally unique. Rather than try to make the Bible like any other book, as the proponents of an unpointed Hebrew Old Testament and the proponents of textual criticism attempt to do, one should try to see the excellencies of God's Words (Proverbs 22:20,21).

Trying to compare the Bible with modern-day unpointed Hebrew newspapers also suffers from a few serious misunderstandings. The first misunderstanding results from a failure to recognize that modern-day Hebrew often uses certain consonants in the place of vowels, something that Biblical Hebrew does not do. Gill observes: "In Rabbinical books, the *matres lectionis*, as א ו י are called, are used to supply the want of vowels; whereas in the Bible they are most frequently omitted, and even in places where they might be expected, and least of all should be omitted."[661] In other words, Biblical words often lack the *matres lectionis*, and instead represent vowels by points. Some examples should suffice. *Morning* in Biblical Hebrew is בֹּקֶר whereas in modern Hebrew it is בוקר.[662] Notice that in modern Hebrew ו (*waw*) takes the place of the vowel point . *Flea* in Biblical Hebrew is פַּרְעֹשׁ, but in modern Hebrew it is פרעוש.[663] *Table* in Biblical Hebrew is שֻׁלְחָן whereas in modern Hebrew it is סולחן. In this case, ו (*waw*) takes the place of . Zilberman also notes:

> Classical Hebrew had strict rules in writing. The use of 'short spelling,' (i.e. the short khirik, short kholam and kubuts) was strictly kept. Words in unpointed Hebrew were spelled like those in pointed Hebrew. For example, חִוֵּר (khiVER) (pale) in pointed Hebrew was written חור in unpointed Hebrew as well. But חור might be mistaken for (khor) (hole). Since it was sometimes difficult for the reader to identify the meaning, the 'full spelling' was introduced, and the letters

---

[661] Gill, *Dissertation*, 273,274.

[662] Shimon Zilberman, *The Compact Up-To-Date English-Hebrew Hebrew-English Dictionary* (Jerusalem: Zilberman, 2001), 179.

[663] Ibid., 107.

ו and י were used instead of vowels. Thus חִוֵר (khiVER) is now written חיוור in unpointed Hebrew.[664]

Therefore, the spelling in Modern Hebrew is often not the same as that of Biblical Hebrew. Those who try to compare the newspaper with the Bible manifest a major misunderstanding in this regard.

Another misunderstanding is the failure to recognize that at times writers point Modern Hebrew in order to avoid confusing the meaning. Zilberman writes: "Partially pointed Hebrew is sometimes used to clarify the meaning: הוא סָמֵחַ (hu saMEakh) (he is glad). סָמַח הוא (hu saMAKH) (he was glad)."[665] De' Rossi who wrote in Hebrew states: "When the vocalization of the words might be uncertain, we insert vowel points to ensure that the words are read correctly."[666] If it is necessary at times in Modern Hebrew to point consonants so as to make sure the reader gets the proper meaning, then how much more so should this be the case with Biblical Hebrew where the eternal destiny of souls is at stake?

Those who appeal to modern-day Hebrew newspapers as a reason to say that Old Testament Hebrew does not have inspired vowels are in error. They are in error because they fail to understand the uniqueness of the Words of God. They are in error because they fail to understand that modern-day Hebrew spells words differently than Biblical Hebrew. And they are in error because they fail to understand that Modern Hebrew, at times, uses points – it is not a completely pointless language.

---

[664] Zilberman, "An Introduction to Hebrew" in *The Compact Up-To-Date English-Hebrew Hebrew-English Dictionary*, 16.

[665] Ibid., 15.

[666] De' Rossi, 704.

Dead Sea Scrolls

David Sorenson, another proponent of the novelty of the points, writes: "Modern Israeli society in its entirety operates with a language (i.e., Hebrew) with no vowel points. The fact that neither synagogue copies of the Scripture nor the DSS [Dead Sea Scrolls] have pointing is troubling to me. Is not Israel the custodian of the Old Testament? Were not the Jews scrupulously careful in the copying of their own Scriptures?"[667] Sorenson's statement has several faults. First, as stated in the previous section, modern Israeli society in its entirety does not operate with a language with no vowel points. Second, what bearing does modern society have in determining matters of faith and practice? Third, while the Jews were at one time the custodians of the Old Testament Scriptures (Romans 3:2); with the Great Commission, God committed the keeping of the Scriptures, both Old and New Testaments, to local churches (Matthew 28:19, 20; I Timothy 3:15; Jude 3; Revelation 3:8, 10). Therefore, Jewish practice in the synagogue and with the first century Dead Sea Scrolls are not reliable foundations upon which to decide the vowel point issue.

Concerning local churches being the keepers of God's Words since the Great Commission, local churches received the Masoretic Text with its points, and made it the *Textus Receptus* of the Old Testament.[668] It is true that the oldest pointed manuscript in the Masoretic

---

[667] David Sorenson, personal letter to the author dated March 1, 2004.

[668] Burnett on page 170 of *From Christian Hebraism to Jewish Studies: Johannes Buxtorf (1564-1629) and Hebrew Learning in the Seventeenth Century* indicates that Jacob ben Chayyim's Hebrew text of 1525 "became accepted (at least among Christians) as the 'received text'." Ginsburg also states of this text that it "came to be recognized as the true masoretic text" (Christian D. Ginsburg, "Prolegomenon" in *Jacob Ben Chajim Inn Adonijah's Introduction to the Rabbinic Bible, Hebrew and English; with Explanatory Notes* (NY: KATV Publishing House, Inc., 1968), XI). The work of Jacob ben Chayim "was the first to present a complete Masorah – the Masoretic notes on the text – and was the second Rabbinic Bible, the only authorised Masoretic recension, becoming in time the 'textus receptus' of the Old Testament" ("Preface to the Bomberg/Ginsburg Hebrew Old Testament" in *Hebrew Old Testament* (London:

line comes from about the tenth century[669] and that the Dead Sea Scrolls outdate it by nearly one thousand years.[670] However, the fact that the Dead Sea Scrolls are older can not be a proper basis for overthrowing the *Textus Receptus* of the Old Testament, for it is clear that God's people in the local churches did not possess the Dead Sea Scrolls. The Dead Sea Scrolls were in hiding for nearly nineteen hundred years;[671] therefore, local churches did not use them, for they were not available to them. One of the promises concerning God's Words is that God's Words would be available to God's people (Matthew 4:4). The Dead Sea Scrolls do not meet the requirement of availability. Furthermore, they are drastically different from the Received Text of the Old Testament, for the Dead Sea Scrolls lack the vowel points. God's local churches made the Masoretic Text with its vowel points the Received Text, not the unpointed Dead Sea Scrolls. Despite what local churches have decided, scholars continually appeal to the Dead Sea Scrolls. Did not the same thing happen with *Codex Sinaiticus*? *Sinaiticus* is a manuscript that had been out of the hands of God's people in the local churches for at least fifteen hundred years[672] and is so drastically different from the New Testament *Textus Receptus*. Yet,

---

Trinitarian Bible Society, 1998), i). Chayyim's Hebrew text included the vowel points.

[669] Gill in his *Dissertation* on pages 143,144 refers to a pointed Hebrew manuscript of the Old Testament, which he dates in the year 900 A.D.

[670] Harry Thomas Frank in "Discovering the Scrolls" in *Understanding the Dead Sea Scrolls*, edited by Hershel Shanks (NY: Random House, 1992) on pages 7 and 8 states: "Such was the discovery of the Dead Sea Scrolls, manuscripts a thousand years older than the then oldest known Hebrew texts of the Bible, manuscripts many of which were written a hundred years before the birth of Jesus."

[671] The Dead Sea Scrolls were discovered in 1946/1947 (Frank, "Discovering the Scrolls" in *Understanding the Dead Sea Scrolls*, 3-5).

[672] Tischendorf in 1859 brought *Codex Sinaiticus* from the Convent of St. Catherine on Mount Sinai ("Sinaitic Manuscript," in *Cyclopedia*, IX: 774).

because the textual critics believe that the oldest is the best, [673] they flocked to *Sinaiticus* as well as to *Vaticanus* and used these manuscripts to overthrow the *Textus Receptus* of the New Testament.[674] Has Sorenson fallen prey to one of the textual critics' favorite mantras that the oldest is the best and, by so doing, is he working to question the inspiration of the vowels of the *Textus Receptus* of the Old Testament? The author hopes not. *The oldest is the best* is a false maxim that leaves the Words of God in a state of flux. For instance, what if scholars find an even older manuscript that differs from the current manuscripts, would such a discovery result in further changes to the Words of God? It is best to reject the oldest-is-the-best mantra and believe God. The local church is the pillar and ground of the truth (I Timothy 3:15) and local churches through the years have passed along God's Words for the Old Testament as they are in the Masoretic Text.

For one to use the Dead Sea Scrolls as an argument against inspired vowels in the Hebrew Old Testament is faulty reasoning for a couple of reasons. First, the promoters of the Dead Sea Scrolls fail to recognize that local churches have God's charge to keep the Scriptures. These local churches have adopted the Traditional Hebrew Text, which is pointed; therefore, they have rejected the unpointed Dead Sea Scrolls as the basis for the Old Testament. And second, the Dead Sea Scroll argument relies on the worn-out and unbiblical contention of the textual critics that the oldest is the best. For these reasons, one should not base his Bibliology on the Dead Sea Scrolls.

---

[673] See Wilbur N. Pickering, *The Identity of the New Testament Text*, rev. ed. (Nashville: Thomas Nelson Publishers, 1980), 121,122.

[674] For a full discussion of the appeal that some make to *Sinaiticus* and *Vaticanus* in rejection of the Greek *Textus Receptus*, the author suggests David Sorenson's "The Double Stream of Biblical Texts" in *Touch Not the Unclean Thing* (Duluth, MN: Northstar Baptist Ministries, 2001), 43-74. This is the same Sorenson that the author is criticizing in the current discussion. While Sorenson takes an excellent position on the New Testament text, it seems to the writer that he is inconsistent in his position on the Old Testament text.

Synagogue Scrolls

There are those who look at the unpointed synagogue scrolls, and from this extrapolate backwards to claim that the *autographa* did not have vowel points. Walton states that the Jews in the Synagogue "use one special book of the Law unpointed; for this end and purpose, that it may represent the Original Copy written by Moses, and laid up in the Ark, which they acknowledge was written without points; and that this book, if it be pointed, is thereby profaned, and not fit for that use."[675] Green observes: "The synagogue rolls, to which special sacredness is attached, never have the vowel points; this can only be accounted for, if the points are not an original constituent of the sacred text, but a subsequent innovation."[676] And Sorenson, as he argues for the novelty of the points, states: "The fact that neither synagogue copies of Scripture nor the DSS [Dead Sea Scrolls] have pointing is troubling to me."[677]

Several problems arise with using synagogue practice to say that the vowel points are uninspired. First, is there evidence that every synagogue throughout history had unpointed scrolls? Whitfield writes: "No one hath ever proved, that unpointed copies in the synagogue Scriptures were always used in the public assemblies of the Jews."[678] He further states: "The later writers, who have been advocates for the novelty of the points, since Elias Levita, have, I believe all, asserted this; but no one hath given any thing like a proof of it."[679] Ginsburg relates that most Jewish commentators and grammarians "maintained that the vowel-points were either given to Adam in Paradise, or com-

---

[675] Walton, *The Considerator Considered*, 241.

[676] William Henry Green, 65.

[677] Sorenson, letter to the author, March 1, 2004.

[678] Whitfield, 268.

[679] Ibid.

municated to Moses on Sinai, or were fixed by Ezra and the Great Synagogue." Ginsburg continues by stating:

> This view was all the more orthodox, since the famous *Sohar*, the sacred code of the Kabbalists, which was believed to be a revelation from God, communicated through R. Simon b. Jochai (*circa* A.D. 70-110), declared that "the letters are the body and the vowel-points the soul, they move with the motion and stand still with the resting of the vowel-points, just as an army moves after its sovereign" (*Sohar* i., 15, b.): that "the vowel-points proceeded from the same Holy Spirit which indited the sacred Scriptures, and that far be the thought to say that the scribes made the points, since even if all the prophets had been as great as Moses, who received the law direct from Sinai, they could not have had the authority to alter the smallest point in a single letter, though it be the most insignificant in the whole Bible" (*Sohar on the Song of Solomon*, 57 b, ed. Amsterdam, 1701).[680]

Margolis also states that there were those who "maintained that the Torah Pentateuch which Moses received on Sinai and delivered to Israel was furnished with vowel-points and accent signs, both of which were indeed as old as the alphabet and the language (communicated to Adam in paradise)."[681] Others held that the points came through the prophets or through Ezra, both of whom would have operated under the influence of inspiration, thereby making the points inspired. That the points originated with Ezra or with the prophets is not the position of the author, however, such a view does indicate a belief in the inspiration of the vowels, which is something to which the author does adhere. "The general belief of the Jews in the Middle Ages was that both the vocalization and accentuation originated with Ezra."[682] Ben Asher "speaks of the accents as introduced by the

---

[680] Ginsburg, "Preface" in *The Massoreth Ha-Massoreth of Elias Levita*, 47,48.

[681] Max L. Margolis, "Accents in Hebrew" in *The Jewish Encyclopedia: a Descriptive Record of the History, Religion, Literature, and Customs of the Jewish People from the Earliest Times to the Present Day*, ed. Isidore Singer (New York: Funk and Wagnalls Company, 1907), I:156.

[682] Ibid.

prophets and princes of the diaspora (the exiled Jews in Babylon), to whom the interpretation of every word (Scriptural passage) was revealed."[683] In light of this general belief about the points, which would lead to the conclusion that they are inspired, how can the advocates of the novelty of the points assert that the synagogues always used unpointed copies of the Old Testament? The burden of proof is upon those who make this assertion.

A second problem with using synagogue practice to declare that the points are uninspired is that synagogue practice is not and cannot be the authority for deciding the issue about the vowel points. The Bible is the sole authority for faith and practice. Particularly must one reject synagogue practice since God committed the keeping of His Words to New Testament churches (Matthew 28:19, 20), not to synagogues. Instead of looking to synagogues why do not scholars look instead to the God-appointed institution for keeping His Words in this current dispensation, the local church (I Timothy 3:15)? The local church, God's appointed institution for keeping His Words, has regarded the Masoretic Text with its points as the Received Text of the Old Testament.[684] What local churches have decided should be a decisive factor in arguing for the vowel points.

A third problem with using synagogue practice to say that the vowels are not part of the inspired Old Testament is that, contrary to modern-day synagogue practice, it is obvious that Jesus' Old Testament had the points (Matthew 5:18; Luke 16:17). If the synagogue leaders of Jesus' day had removed the points, it seems likely that Jesus would have dealt with this matter. Since Jesus attacked the Pharisees for violating one command of the Old Testament (Matthew 15:1-6), as well as for committing other sins (Matthew 23), surely He would have

---

[683] Ibid.

[684] For more about local churches making the Masoretic Test the Received Text of the Old Testament, see earlier section in this chapter on the Dead Sea Scrolls.

mentioned the greater sin of removing the points, which would have violated at least two commands of the Old Testament (Deuteronomy 4:2; 12:32). Jesus' silence is deafening. In light of this, the removal of the points from the synagogue scrolls must have occurred some time after Jesus.

When, why, and who removed the points is a matter of speculation. But what is not speculation is that the Bible of Jesus' day was pointed and that some time after Jesus, some of the Jews of the synagogue advocated the use of scrolls that did not have the vowel points. For example, Natronai II ben-Hilai of the ninth century AD said, "We must not put the points to the scrolls of the law."[685] It seems, then, that the Jews were responsible for leaving out the vowel points. Such a conclusion may be unthinkable in some peoples' minds,[686] but it is Biblically justifiable. The Pharisees had a higher regard for their tradition than they did for the Word of God (Matthew 15:1-6). Could they have had some reason for getting rid of the points? In a comparable case, who would have ever thought that Fundamentalists would be championing the removal of passages, verses, and words from the New Testament text, but this is exactly what they are doing when they defend the Critical Text. Many Fundamentalists have long ago departed from the Received Text, while at the same time claiming to have a high regard for Scripture. Could not the same thing be true of the Jews?

Or, could the Pharisees or some other Jews concocted the teaching that God only commanded Moses to write the consonants and conveyed the vowels orally via an oral tradition (see Chapter Two), so as to exalt the importance of their oral tradition as well as their own importance? The Pharisees believed their oral tradition to be very im-

---

[685] "Vowel-Points" in *Cyclopedia*, X:820.

[686] For instance, Sorenson in a letter to the author dated March 1, 2004, states: "Were not the Jews scrupulously careful in the copying of their own Scriptures? . . . For whatever else may be said about the Jews and their spiritual deadness, they did have a high regard for the Scriptures."

portant (Matthew 15:3; Mark 7:8-9,13). They also promoted themselves as being very important (Matthew 23:5-7). Such a thing would parallel the Roman Catholic approach to the vowel points. The Catholics during the Reformation taught that the points were not inspired and that their tradition was necessary to interpret properly the Old Testament with the help of the priests. For example, according to McClintock and Strong, Morinus, a Roman Catholic:

> Solemnly declares, in his learned *Exercitationes Biblicae et Hebraei Graecique Textus Sinceritate*, that "the reason why God ordained the Scriptures to be written in this ambiguous manner (i.e. without points) is because it was his will that every man should be subject to the judgment of the Church, and not interpret the Bible in his own way. For, seeing that the reading of the Bible is so difficult, and so liable to various ambiguities, from the very nature of the thing, it is plain that it is not the will of God that every one should rashly and irreverently take upon himself to explain it, nor to suffer the common people to expound it at their pleasure; but that in those things, as in other matters respecting religion, it is his will that the people should depend upon the priests."[687]

The Roman Catholic priests did not want vowel points in the Hebrew Old Testament so that they would be the sole arbiters of the Old Testament. Could the Pharisees or some other Jewish group have had a similar desire?

A fourth problem with relying on synagogue practice to say that the vowels of the Old Testament are uninspired is that the Jews of the synagogues continually rejected the teaching of the Old Testament. These Jews persecuted and killed those who came to them preaching God's Word (Matthew 10:17; 23:34; John 16:2). The synagogue Jews tried to kill Jesus because they did not like His correct interpretation of Isaiah 61:1,2 (Luke 4:16-29). Synagogue Jews put out of the syna-

---

[687] "Vowel-Points" in *Cyclopedia*, X: 821, citing Jean Morinus, *Exercitationes Biblicae et Hebraei Graecique Textus Sinceritate* (Paris: n.p., 1633), IV, ii, 8, 198.

gogue those who confessed Christ (John 9:22; 12:42). They opposed Stephen (Acts 6:9-15) and his correct preaching from the Old Testament (Acts 7). The Jews of the synagogue opposed Paul and Barnabas (Acts 13:42-45). There was one synagogue that Jesus called "the synagogue of Satan" (Revelation 2:9; 3:9). Clearly, this synagogue did not care for the Words of God (Genesis 3:1). In light of these things, why would anyone appeal to the synagogues to decide a matter concerning Bibliology? The synagogues rejected Christ. The synagogues persecuted and killed those who received Christ. And the synagogues rejected the true preaching of the Old Testament. Why, then, appeal to the synagogues to help decide the issue of the vowel points? The synagogues were largely apostate. To appeal to the synagogues would be akin to appealing to the Roman Catholic Church to help decide a matter on Bibliology. One should believe what the Bible says about itself, more than what the synagogues say about the Bible. The Bible adequately and abundantly testifies to the presence of the points (see Chapter Four) and this testimony decides the issue.

Other Languages and Inscriptions

Green appeals to the lack of vowel points in other languages as well as in Hebrew inscriptions as a reason for his holding to the novelty of the points. He writes, "Syriac and Arabic were originally written without vowel signs; these are a later invention. The Samaritan uses substantially the old form of the Hebrew letters, but has no vowel signs; neither have the ancient Hebrew inscriptions, nor the Phoenician monuments."[688]

Several problems are present with Green's reasoning. First, the Bible is the sole authority for faith and practice. The authority is not what other languages do or do not do. The question is what does the Bible teach. The question should not be what did the Samaritans

---

[688] William Henry Green, 65.

do. The question should not be what did the Syrians do. The question should not be what did the Arabs do. The question should not be what did the Phoenicians do. The question should not even be what did the Jews do on their inscriptions. The question ever has to be, what does the Bible teach? Repeatedly it seems that various writers think that they can decide matters about the Bible without using the Bible. By so doing, are they not bringing the Bible down and, thereby, treating it like any other book?

Second, Gill disputes Green's contention that the Samaritan language has no vowel signs, for Gill writes: "Notwithstanding what has been said to the contrary, the *Samaritan* had its points, though differing from the *Hebrew*, as *Jerome* observes, and so a later writer observes it has."[689] In light of this, there seems to be a difference of opinion about the Samaritan language having no vowel signs. Concerning Arabic, De' Rossi states:

> There are points, lines, and markers which are put above, below, and in the middle, as in Hebrew, which was the first language to have this system. It was then adopted by Arabic and Aramaic which are later corruptions of Hebrew. In the case of this second group [of languages], educated people frequently omitted the points and markers without confronting any difficulty. But this does not imply that the languages intrinsically lacked the vowel points.[690]

Here again there seems to be a difference of opinion about the Arabic language being originally written without vowels. But even if these languages did not have written vowels, it would still not clinch the case for Green, for only Scripture can decide Biblical matters.

Third, as the writer has before shown, Scripture concerns the most excellent of subjects - subjects that treat of heaven and hell, life

---

[689] Gill, *Dissertation*, 258. The citation for Jerome is from *Praefatio ad Reg. T.* 3 fol 5 L. The "later writer" citation is from *Petrus a Valle in Antiqu. Eccl. Orient.* p. 184.

[690] De' Rossi, 703.

and death; therefore, it is absolutely necessary that the testimony of the Lord be sure (Psalm 19:7) and such a fact requires the vowel points. The fact that other languages and inscriptions may be unpointed has no bearing on whether the Old Testament is pointed.

Summary

Those who argue for the novelty of the points based on unpointed documents such as newspapers, the Dead Sea Scrolls, the Samaritan Pentateuch, synagogue copies of the Law, and other languages are out of step with Scripture. Synagogue practice, Samaritan practice, Dead Sea scroll practice, modern-day practice, the custom of other languages, or even the secular customs of Jews are not what determines faith and practice for local churches. Scripture must ever be the sole authority for faith and practice. Those who appeal to other authorities in the matter of faith and practice are trying to get the churches of God off the sure foundation of the Words of God and unto a foundation of sinking and shifting sand. May local church believers stand firmly on "thus saith the Lord."

Story about Joab

Another historical argument that some advance for the novelty of the points concerns a story about Joab. This section examines the story and the problems with it.

The Story

Elias Levita relates an extra-Biblical story about Joab, in which he places great confidence because he believes that it demonstrates that there were no points in the days of Joab. This story concerns a supposed conversation between David and Joab wherein David questioned Joab as to why he only killed the Edomite males, as opposed to everybody. Joab responded by saying that his teacher had taught him to read Deuteronomy 25:19 with the word *male*, instead of *remembrance*. Levita says of the Joab story,

> What is still greater proof [that is, greater proof than the supposed silence of the Rabbins concerning vowel-points], is the following remark in the Talmud (*Baba Bathra*, 21 *b*), "Joab slew his teacher because he had performed the work of the Lord deceitfully, in reading to him זָכָר [*male*] instead of זֵכֶר [*remembrance*] (Deut. xxv. 19)." Now is it credible that he would have attempted to read זָכָר with two *Kametz*, if they had had the points, and the word in question had been pointed זֵכֶר with six points?[691]

The Problems

Since Levita placed such great confidence in the Joab story, then it behooves this book to expose the many problems present in this story. First, the story about Joab has no Biblical basis and, therefore, lacks any authority whatsoever to decide the issue about the points.

Second, the Joab story is actually an evidence for the existence of points at least as far back as 500 A.D. (the date for the Babylonian Talmud, which relates the story about Joab). "Levita thought that the vowel points and accents were invented after the composition of the Talmud."[692] However, Gill observes:

> Nor can I see how the ridiculous story, concerning *Joab's* slaying of his master for teaching him to read wrong could be related in the *Talmud* {Babylonian Talmud Bava Bathra, fol. 21. 1. 2} without the vowel-points being put to the word in it, which is told thus; after Joab had cut off every male in Edom, I Kings xi. 15, 16, when he came before David he said to him, what is the reason that thou hast so done? (i. e. that thou hast not destroyed the females, as the gloss is) he replied, because it is written (Deut. xxv. 25:19) thou shalt blot out זכר of Amaleck; David said unto him, but behold we read זכר; Joab answered, I was taught to read it זכר: he went and asked his master, saying, how didst thou teach me to read, he told him זכר; he drew his

---

[691] Levita, *Massoreth Ha-Massoreth*, 128.
[692] Burnett, 212.

> sword to kill him. Now where is the difference? they all say the same thing, David, Joab, and his master, as the bare letters of the word without the vowel-points are given. What sense can be made of this story, thus told? No doubt but in the *Talmud*, as originally written, the several vowel-points were put to this word; as said to be read by Joab, it was *zacar*, male, with two *Kametzes*; as by David and Joab's master, it was *zecer*, remembrance, with two *Segols*; and so in other cases, of a similar kind, the points were put, though in process of time left out, through the carelessness or sloth of transcribers.[693]

Contrary to the use for which Levita has for the Joab story, it does not bolster his case of the novelty of the points, indeed, it establishes that the points existed in 500 A.D., and, no doubt, some time prior.

Third, this story contradicts the premise that the Israelites could read the text accurately without the points. Concerning this premise, Levita writes:

> Now there are some who might ask, How was it possible, before the invention of the vowel-points, to teach a child the correct reading from a book which was not pointed? But this is no question. For the sacred tongue was the language which all spoke, both young and old, children and women, since they had no other language till they were led captive from their land. When, therefore, a child was being taught to know the letters, his teacher read with him from a book each verse two or three times, till be was familiar with it, and as the child was conversant with the language, he could easily remember the words which he read, and whenever he met with them again he read them without difficulty.[694]

However, according to the Joab story, Joab's teacher did not know the correct reading and neither did Joab – so much for their being able to read correctly the text without points.

Fourth, the Joab story destroys the notion that differences in reading do not matter. Whitfield writes:

> Capellus says upon the supposition, that there may be such differences of reading, without violence to the sense, he says, Quid periculi erit, si

---

[693] Gill, *Dissertation*, 156, 157.

[694] Levita, 129,130.

utramq; amplectamur punctationem, & utrumq; qui ex eâ exurget, sensum? i.e. "what harm will it be, if we take both the punctations [vowel pointings], and both the resultant senses?"[695]

But in the story about Joab, both senses were not acceptable, for one was right and the other was wrong. Whitfield asks, "If there were no points to ascertain the reading; and suppose the story true, why was not one of those senses of the place as good as the other?"[696]

Fifth, the story about Joab also destroys another premise of Levita, Capellus, and Walton, namely "that the points were invented . . . not to introduce any new method of reading, but to denote by characters of their own designation, those vowels and accents, whose use they had retained through all generations . . . to render the same perpetual and unchangeable in all time to come."[697] It seems that Levita, Cappellus, and Walton thought that the same reading persisted throughout time, but the story of Joab introduces two different readings.

Summary

The story about Joab does nothing to further the case for the novelty of the points, for it is not at all Biblical and, therefore, completely lacks any authority. Rather than further the case for the novelty of the points, the Joab story destroys the case. First, the story of Joab hints at the presence of the points at the time of the writing of the Talmud. Second, the Joab story destroys the premise that the Israelites could read the text accurately without the points. Third, the Joab story destroys the premise that differences in reading, if they exist, do not matter. And fourth, the Joab story destroys the premise that one and the same reading persisted throughout time.

---

[695] Whitfield, 60.

[696] Ibid., 258.

[697] Ibid., 224.

Conclusion

Two major historical arguments for the novelty of the points are unpointed documents and the story about Joab. Both of these arguments try to use history as a means for determining faith and practice and, therefore, are structurally weak, since the Bible is the sole authority for faith and practice. However, even when one examines these arguments for what they purport to be, they still fail to make the case for the novelty of the points.

BIBLICAL OBJECTIONS

Chapter One has already dealt with many of the Biblical objections to the teaching of inspired vowels in the Hebrew Old Testament. This section elaborates further upon a possible Biblical objection to inspired vowels. The possible Biblical objection concerns places in the Masoretic Text where there are consonants without vowels, vowels without consonants, and a lone vowel serving as the article. The author has not found anyone who uses any of these things as an argument against inspired points, but these items do deserve a treatment, especially the matter of consonants without vowels. Chapter One has already presented some information about these matters; this section presents additional material. Before presenting the additional material, one must approach this matter with the attitude of faith. Specifically one must have faith in God's statements that He inspired His Words (II Timothy 3:16; II Peter 1:21) and that He has and will preserve His Words (Psalm 12:6,7). Furthermore, the Lord Jesus Christ fully authenticated the Old Testament text by asserting that not a single consonant or vowel will pass from the Law till all be fulfilled (Matthew 5:18). Matthew 5:18 assures everyone that the text of Jesus' day was perfect and that it would continue in this state until all is fulfilled. Therefore, as one approaches a study of the Old Testament, he ought to approach it with confidence in Jesus' promise that in the Traditional

Text he has the very same text that Jesus had – a text complete and without error. With these preliminary thoughts in mind, the author will now present additional material concerning consonants without vowels, vowels without consonants, and a lone vowel acting as the article.

Consonants without Vowels

The Traditional Hebrew text has eight places where consonants are without vowels (אם in Ruth 3:12; II Samuel 13:33; 15:21; Jeremiah 39:12; נא in II Kings 5:18; את in Jeremiah 38:16; ידרך in Jeremiah 51:3; and חמס in Ezekiel 48:16). Without vowels these consonants are impossible to pronounce, therefore, technically they are not words, but rather are some type of notation. How did God convey this notation to the prophet? And what is the purpose of this notation?

Method of Conveying This Notation

It seems that there are at least two methods of how God could have conveyed to the prophet the notation of unpointed consonants. God could have conveyed this notation at the time of the vision, or later at the time of writing.

At the Time of the Vision

Often when the Lord gave revelation, He both spoke and presented a vision to the prophet. In Numbers 12:6 the Lord states: "Hear now my words: If there be a prophet among you, *I* the LORD will make myself known unto him in a vision, *and* will speak unto him in a dream." In light of this, the one receiving revelation from God, could both hear something as well as see something. Normally the prophet could convey the vision through words. Such was the case when Nathan spoke to David about building the Temple where the Bible says, "According to all these words, and according to all this vision, so did Nathan speak unto David" (II Samuel 7:17). But could there be instances where the prophet could only convey what he saw by means of symbols and notations, such as consonants without vowels? That the prophet, in these eight instances, did convey consonants without vowels is undeniable, for they are in the Traditional Text. But the reason for why the prophet conveyed consonants without vowels is a matter of speculation. One such speculation is that as God gave him a vision, he not only heard the Words of God, but he also saw unpointed consonants, which consonants he faithfully recorded along with the words.

At the Time of Writing

Another possibility for how God conveyed the unpointed consonants to the prophet is that the prophet did not see the unpointed consonants at the same time when he saw the vision from God. Rather, God moved the prophet to record the unpointed consonants at the time that he wrote the vision. That is, the prophet first saw a vision and heard God speaking, at which time there were no consonants without vowels. Then as the prophet set about to write the vision, the Lord moved him to add the notation of consonants without vowels. The Bible has examples where God provides additional revelation after the initial revelation. For instance, in the New Testament the Spirit of God moved writers to quote the Old Testament, and at times gave additional details into the Old Testament prophecy (cf. Matthew 2:15 with Hosea 11:1; cf. Hebrews 10:5 with Psalm 40:6).

In the Old Testament the Spirit of God moved later writers to add inspired comments to earlier inspired material. For instance in the books of Samuel, the expression *unto this day* occurs several times (I Samuel 5:5; 6:18; 27:6; 30:25; II Samuel 18:18). Of particular interest is I Samuel 27:6: "Then Achish gave him Ziklag that day: wherefore Ziklag pertaineth unto the kings of Judah unto this day." Achish giving Ziklag to David occurred in the days of David, but the comment about Ziklag pertaining unto the kings of Judah unto this day was written after the days of David. *Unto the kings of Judah* indicates that the comment was written after the Schism, when there were kings of Judah as well as kings of Israel. The comment is an inspired editorial comment added after the fact. Likewise, the Spirit of God could have moved the writer to add the unpointed consonants after the giving of the vision.

Conclusion

Whenever God gave unpointed consonants, at the time of the vision or at the time of writing, the fact is that they are from God, for God inspired them. The question now arises, why might God give this notation of unpointed consonants?

Purpose of This Notation

Without direct revelation from God, one cannot be certain why God gave unpointed consonants, but the author can suggest several possible reasons. These unpointed consonants could serve as a test to see if one will walk by faith. They could also be some sort of inspired punctuation. Or, these unpointed consonants could be present for emphasis.

A Test

One obvious purpose behind the unpointed consonants would be to see if the man of God would walk by faith. These difficulties in the text are an opportunity for a person to manifest faith and thereby please God (Hebrews 11:6). Will the Bible student savour the things of God or the things of men (Matthew 16:23)? Will he claim, contrary to the statement of Jesus in Matthew 5:18, that all of the Old Testament was originally unpointed and that the unpointed consonants are some examples where the pointers of the text missed a few places? Or, will he claim, also contrary to the statement of Jesus in Matthew 5:18, that some *tittles* are forever lost? Or, will he claim in harmony with the statement of Jesus in Matthew 5:18 that all is well with the Old Testament text? The bottom line is this: one must choose either to walk by faith and trust that this is exactly how God inspired and preserved His Words, or to walk by sight and adopt some unbelieving, rationalistic explanation for these things. Just as God purposely inspired and preserved His Words with seeming contradictions (cf., for instance, II Kings 8:26 with II Chronicles 22:2), so He has inspired and preserved His Words with what appears to be textual difficulties. Will a man really walk by faith?[698] Will a man simply and humbly believe God's Words, although he may not be able to explain all of them?

Punctuation Marks

Could it be that some of these unpointed consonants serve the purpose of inspired punctuation marks? In Hebrew, there is the sign of the accusative (אֵת), which is an untranslatable grammatical marker. In a similar fashion, could some of the unpointed consonants function as punctuation marks or to mark some other aspect of the sentence? Concerning אם in Ruth 3:12; II Samuel 13:33; 15:21; and Jeremiah 39:12; in each case it follows a כִּי and precedes an important statement in the sentence. In Ruth 3:12 אם precedes the words, "I *am thy* near kinsman." In II Samuel 13:33 אם precedes the words, "Amnon only is dead." In II Samuel 15:21 אם precedes the words, "In what place my lord the king shall be, whether in death or life, even there also will thy servant be." And in Jeremiah 39:12 אם precedes the words, "Do unto him even as he shall say unto thee." In each of these cases important words follow the אם. Could it be that אם is serving as an hyphen to indicate a pause in the speaking of the words that follow it? It seems possible. Boaz could have paused as he said to Ruth that he was her near kinsmen, while all the time knowing that there was one nearer than he (Ruth 3:12). Jonadab could have paused before telling David that Amnon was dead (II Samuel 13:33). While David was fleeing from Absalom, Ittai could have paused as he promised to David that he would be true to David (II Samuel 15:21). In each of these cases a bit

---

[698] Consider also that when God created, He created things with apparent age (Genesis 1:11,12), but despite this apparent age, the earth is only thousands of years old, not billions of years. Despite what man sees with his eyes, he must believe God by faith.

of emotion was involved and could account for such a pause. In the case of Jeremiah 39:12, Nebuchadnezzar gave orders concerning Jeremiah, in which be may have paused before commanding Nebuzaradan, the captain of the guard, to do unto Jeremiah even as Jeremiah would say unto him, a most unusual order.

נא in II Kings 5:18 occurs in the midst of the words of Naaman wherein he beseeches Elijah to pardon him when he goes into the house of Rimmon with his master. נא occurs in between the verb *pardon* (יִסְלַח) and the subject of the verb *LORD* (יְהוָה). In this verse, it is the second time in which Naaman asks for pardon. Earlier in the verse he says, "The LORD pardon" (יִסְלַח יְהוָה). In the first instance of asking for pardon there is nothing between the verb and its subject. But in the second instance of asking for pardon, could the נא be indicating a pause in the midst of a second asking for pardon? It seems possible.

את in Jeremiah 38:16 occurs in the midst of Zedekiah promising to Jeremiah that he would not put Jeremiah to death. It occurs after the words *as the LORD liveth* and before the words *that made us this soul*, which may indicate a pause as Zedekiah contemplates exactly what he will say to Jeremiah.

In six of the eight cases, the unpointed consonants could be serving as some sort of punctuation indicator to show that a speaker paused before continuing his words. The question may arise, why did not the Bible use unpointed consonants more frequently as punctuation marks to indicate a pause? An answer is Deuteronomy 29:29: "The secret *things belong* unto the LORD our God: but those *things which are* revealed *belong* unto us and to our children for ever, that *we* may do all the words of this law."

Emphasis

Another possible reason for why God inspired eight cases of unpointed consonants is that He did this to provide emphasis. For the six cases above, providing emphasis could be the reason for unpointed consonants. But particularly would the providing of emphasis apply to the remaining two cases of Jeremiah 51:3 and Ezekiel 48:16 where the unpointed consonants repeat pointed consonants that occurred immediately prior. In Jeremiah 51:3 the Hebrew text is יִדְרֹךְ ידרך. The pointed consonants represent the word *bendeth*. The unpointed consonants following the pointed consonants seem to draw attention back to this word and thereby, in an unusual way, emphasize it. Jeremiah 51:3 occurs in a prophecy about the destruction of Babylon during the time of the Lord's vengeance (Jeremiah 51:6), a reference to the Tribulation (Jeremiah 46:10). Jeremiah 51:3, 4 indicates that the bow benders in that future Babylon will die. Some of these bow benders will have been those who will have tormented God's people (Jeremiah 51:35-36, 49). The fact that the tormentors of God's people will be punished will be a tremendous triumph at that time and perhaps to emphasize this, the Lord uses an unusual construction in the writing of Jeremiah 51:3.

In Ezekiel 48:16 the Hebrew text is חֲמֵשׁ חמש. The pointed consonants represent the word *five*. The unpointed consonants following the pointed consonants seem to draw attention back to this word and thereby, in an unusual way, emphasize it. Ezekiel 48:16 speaks of the measurements of a future city, a city in which the Lord Himself will dwell (Ezekiel 48:35). Hengstenberg believes that חמש emphasizes "that the south side *equally* with the north side has 4500 cubits."[699]

Conclusion

In each of the cases of unpointed consonants, one must exercise faith in God's promises of inspiration and preservation. Indeed, these unpointed consonants could be a test to see if a person will walk

---

[699] E. W. Hengstenberg, *The Prophecies of the Prophet Ezekiel Elucidated*, trans. A. C. Murphy and J. G. Murphy (Edinburgh: T & T Clark, 1869, reprinted Eugene, OR: Wipf and Stock Publishers, n. d.), 489.

by faith instead of by sight. Additionally, these unpointed consonants could serve the purposes of being punctuation marks and of providing emphasis.

Vowels without Consonants

The Traditional Text has nine places were only vowels occur, that is, where vowels are without consonants. This should not cause any alarm since Jesus guaranteed that not even one jot shall pass from the Law (Matthew 5:18). In light of this promise, it is clear that the Lord inspired and preserved these vowel points and did not give any corresponding consonants with them. Since one can vocalize vowels, then the vowels without consonants are words, which people actually spoke. Usually Hebrew words have both consonants and vowels, but the nine cases of vowels without consonants appear to be the exception. Since they are the exception, they would have a different sound than their consonants-with-vowels equivalent. While these nine cases are the exception in Hebrew, the Greek language, on the other hand, regularly contains both one and two vowel words and even a four vowel word (e.g., ὁ, *the*; οὗ, *where*; and οὐαὶ, *woe*).

The nine places where the Traditional Text has vowels without consonants are (1) in Judges 20:13 meaning *sons of*; (2) in Ruth 3:17 meaning *unto me*; (3) in II Samuel 8:3 meaning *Euphrates*; (4) in II Samuel 16:23 meaning *man*; (5) in II Samuel 18:20 with the meaning of *thus*; (6) in II Kings 19:31 with the meaning of *hosts*; (7) in II Kings 19:37 meaning *his sons*; (8) in Jeremiah 31:38 (vs. 37 in the Hebrew) meaning *come*; and (9) in Jeremiah 50:29 meaning *thereof*. These nine different combinations are alternate ways to refer to these words. And since each unique combination has its own unique meaning, there is no way to confuse them. Those who think that the Hebrew text was originally unpointed have a real problem here for without these vowels nine words are missing from the text. And if nine words are missing from the text, then what of God's promises to preserve His Words?

Lone Vowels

Furthermore, the Traditional Hebrew text has fourteen places where just a point serves to indicate the definite article, as opposed to a ה with the appropriate point (I Samuel 14:32; II Samuel 23:9; I Kings 4:7; 7:20; 15:18; II Kings 11:20; 15:25; Isaiah 32:15; Jeremiah 10:13; 17:19; 40:3; 52:32; Lamentations 1:18; Ezekiel 18:20). Again, since Jesus promised that all the consonants of the Hebrew Old Testament are intact, then one should not surmise that in these cases a consonant disappeared from the text. Since one can pronounce the vowel points, there would be no problem in reading these words. Those, however, who think that the Hebrew text was unpointed, have a real problem here, for without these vowels, then the definite article in fourteen instances is gone from the text.

Summary

In eight places, the Traditional Text[700] has consonants without vowels. In ten places, the Traditional Text has vowels without conso-

---

[700] In speaking of the Traditional Text of the Hebrew Old Testament, the author is aware of places where different editions of the Traditional Text differ. In this footnote, he will attempt to give answers to two places where two different editions of the Traditional Text disagree. In formulating these answers one must ever keep in mind several things: (1) the promises of Jesus in Matthew 5:18 and Luke 16:17 guarantee that not one jot or tittle is missing from the Old Testament; (2) difficulties in the Words of God may be present so as to test one's faith; and (3) if one cannot provide satisfactory answers, he must wait on the Lord and realize that his understanding is limited, while God's Word is perfect With that in mind, two places where two different editions of the Traditional Text disagree are I Chronicles 1:7 and Joel 1:12.

In I Chronicles 1:7 the *Hebrew Old Testament* published by the Trinitarian Bible Society has ורודנים (*and Rodanim*), whereas *The Holy Scriptures of the Old Testament: Hebrew and English* published by The British & Foreign Bible Society has ודדנים (*and Dodanim*). In this case, the King James translators have "and Dodanim." Since local churches are the pillar and ground of the truth (I Timothy 3:15), and since they have a charge to keep God's Words (Matthew 28:20), and since local churches for nearly four hundred years have adopted the *King James Version* as their translation, and since the King James translation followed the reading in The British & Foreign Bible Society edition, ודדנים (*and Dodanim*); then the author concludes that in this

nants. And in fourteen places, the Traditional Text has a single vowel standing at the beginning of a word by itself and serving the function of the definite article. While these thirty-two places are exceptional, let no one suppose that they represent errors in the Traditional Text. Jesus promised that not one single jot or one single tittle has passed from the Law (Matthew 5:18). Therefore, let the Bible student rest comfortably in Jesus' promise and by faith believe that all is well with the Hebrew Old Testament. For anyone to suggest that these thirty-

---

case וְדֹדָנִים (*and Dodanim*) is the correct reading. Such reasoning is similar to the reasoning that Edward F. Hills applied in deciding what reading to follow when various editions of the Received Text of the New Testament differ. Hills writes: "But what do we do in these few places in which the several editions of the Textus Receptus disagree with one another? Which text do we follow? The answer to this question is easy. We are guided by the common faith. Hence we favor that form of the *Textus Receptus* upon which more than any other God, working providentially, has placed the stamp of His approval, namely, the *King James Version*, or, more precisely, the Greek text underlying the *King James Version*" (Hills, *The King James Version Defended A Space-Age Defense of the Historic Christian Faith*, 3rd ed. (Des Moines, IA: The Christian Research Press, 1979), 223).

In Joel 1:12 the Trinitarian Bible Society edition has הוֹבִישָׁה, whereas The British & Foreign Bible Society edition has הוּבִישָׁה. The difference between the two editions is the dot or absence thereof above the waw (ו). These editions are both editions of the Traditional Text, yet they differ by a single point. What is one to make of this, especially when Jesus promised that one tittle shall in no wise pass from the law (Matthew 5:18; Luke 16:17)? Jesus' promise must remain true, therefore, this leaves one of two possibilities: (1) the Trinitarian Bible Society edition is correct and the British & Foreign Bible Society edition is incorrect, in which case the British edition's rendering may be the result of a printing error, not unlike some of the printing errors that occurred with the King James Bible where in, one instance, a printer left out a *not* in one of the one ten commandments resulting in "The Adulterers' Bible" – "Thou shalt commit adultery"; or (2) the British & Foreign Bible Society edition is correct and the Trinitarian Bible Society edition is incorrect, in which case הוּבִישָׁה seems to be an alternate spelling for הוֹבִישָׁה. It is hard to know which reading the King James translators used, especially if these two words are alternate ways of spelling the same word, for then both would have the same translation. However, since in the case of I Chronicles 1:7 the *King James Version* translators followed the reading in the British & Foreign Bible Society edition, it is likely they did so here as well; therefore, at this time, the author concludes that the British & Foreign Bible Society edition has the correct reading in Joel 1:12.

two instances are errors is for him also to suggest that Jesus was in error when He spoke the words of Matthew 5:18. Such a suggestion is blasphemous and may any who lean toward this suggestion repent of it immediately.

CONCLUSION

This chapter has covered more fully with some of the historical and Biblical objections that some might use for the novelty of the points and against the inspiration of the vowel points. The historical objections concern two areas. The first of these areas involve the presence of unpointed documents such as newspapers, the Dead Sea Scrolls, the Samaritan Pentateuch, synagogue copies of the Law, and other languages. But in examining each of these historical objections, none of them either individually or corporately is able to establish the case for the novelty of the points and, therefore, that the vowel points were not inspired. The other area in the matter of historical objections concerns the story about Joab, but this story rather than further the case for the novelty of the points, destroys it. All of the historical objections rest upon a faulty foundation, namely, that non-Biblical material can decide Biblical issues. But non-Biblical material is powerless to overthrow the *autographa* position about the points, for the Bible is the sole authority for faith and practice. The historical objections do reveal a major problem with the accommodation and non-authoritative positions on the points, for the objections reveal that these positions are anchored on the shifting sands of history. Such is also the problem that the Pharisees had, for when they appealed to their historical traditions, they made the Word of God of none effect (Matthew 15:6). And so, likewise, those who advance these historical objections, while clinging to their historical traditions, are neglecting many verses of Scripture. Let them return to the solid rock of Scripture, rather than continuing adrift amidst historical uncertainty.

The Biblical objections concern consonants without vowels, vowels without consonants, and a lone vowel acting as the article. About consonants without vowels, they technically are not words but, nonetheless, God conveyed them to the prophet either at the time of a vision or at the time of writing. God's purpose for giving these consonants without vowels could be to test man's faith, to serve as punctuation marks, or to provide emphasis. About vowels without consonants, one can vocalize these vowels and, therefore, they are words, albeit, unusual words. And concerning lone vowels serving as the definite article, there is no problem here for one can vocalize these vowels as well. Here again, these objections do not overthrow the *autographa* position, but rather reveal the strength of the *autographa* position, which is that the *autographa* position seeks to walk by faith in God's Words. Indeed, this is exactly how one should approach all of the objections to the Bible, that is, with unwavering faith in God's precious promises. Periodically, there will be circumstances that could cause disciples of the Lord to doubt, but rather than be slow of heart, let the disciples of the Lord "believe all that the prophets have spoken" (Luke 24:25). Such an attitude is one that will thrill the heart of the Saviour.

CHAPTER SEVEN – CONCLUSION

The conclusion has two headings: (1) a summary of the arguments; and (2) a summary of the evidence. These two categories do overlap, but summarize the material from two slightly different perspectives. One perspective may be more effective than another in helping readers to assess the material.

ARGUMENT SUMMARY

The argument summary recaps the arguments of this work largely in the order in which the book states them. Concerning the vowel points of the Old Testament, three positions present themselves. One of these positions is, what the author calls, the *autographa* position, which believes that the points were given by inspiration and are, therefore, fully authoritative. Many have held this position among them being Simon ben-Jochai, Levi ben-Joseph, Moses the Punctuator, David Kimḥi, Johannes Isaac Levita, Antoine Rudolphe Chevalier, Azariah De' Rossi, William Fulke, Guilielmus Eyrius, Johannes Buxtorf, Sr., Valentin Schindler, Amandus Polanus Von Polandsdorf, John Weemes, John Lightfoot, Johannes Buxtorf, Jr., Gisbert Voetius, James Ussher, John Owen, Matthias Wasmuth, Joseph Cooper, Francois Turretin, Samuel Clark, Johann Gottlob Carpzov, Pierre Guarin, Peter Whitfield, John Gill, James Robertson, Adam Benedict Spitzner, John Moncrieff, George Sayles Bishop, Kent Brandenburg, Gary Webb, and Thomas Strouse. For over a period of a thousand years men have held to the inspiration of the vowel points. Some raise historical problems with the *autographa* position such as difficulty in writing the points, spelling variations, unpointed documents, silence about points, a story about Joab, vowel point names not in Hebrew, the *kethib* and *keri* readings, and the *matres lectionis*. But none of these historical objections carries any weight since it is not history that is the rule for faith and practice, but it is the Bible. Some raise Biblical problems with the *autographa* position such as the spelling of David's name, New Testament spelling of Old Testament names, *tittle* supposedly not being the name of a vowel point, the word *men* in Acts 15:17, the words *top of his staff* in Hebrews 11:21, and consonants with no vowels. David's name could have different spellings just as other names do. New Testament writers at times simply spelled Old Testament names differently just as Old Testament writers at times spelled names differently. *Tittle* is the name of the Hebrew vowel *chirek*. In Acts 15:17 the Spirit of God is giving an inspired commentary upon an Old Testament word. In Hebrews 11:21 Jacob both leaned upon the top of his staff and bowed himself upon the bed's head as Genesis 47:31 says. Concerning consonants with no vowels one should believe by faith that God has perfectly preserved His Words (Psalm 12:6,7). The Biblical problems some pose against the *autographa* position have answers and are not sufficient to overthrow the position.

A second position about the vowel points is, what the author calls, the accommodation position. This position, on the one hand, says that the vowel points are fully or partially authoritative, but, on the other hand, are not inspired. Some of the proponents of this position are Elias Levita, John Calvin, Louis Cappellus, Brian Walton, Homer A. Kent, Larry Oats, and David Sorenson. The accommodation position suffers from serious Scriptural problems. First, it relies on oral tradition to convey the vowels through history to the Masoretes; but oral tradition has no authority (Matthew 15:1-6). Second, the accommodation position relies on the additions of these vowels by the Masoretes to the Words of God; but the Bible forbids adding to it (Deuteronomy 4:2; 12:32; Proverbs 30:6; and Revelation 22:18). Third, the accommodation position neglects the written words of the Bible in that it fails to recognize that (1) God's spoken and, therefore, vocalized words, are written (Exodus 34:27; Jeremiah 36:1,2; Matthew

22:31; I Corinthians 9:10); (2) the Bible is the sole authority for faith and practice (II Timothy 3:16,17); (3) the Spirit of God used words, which necessitates vocalization, which words the prophets wrote (I Corinthians 2:13; II Peter 1:21); (4) God commanded that people write His Words very plainly, which requires the use of vowels (Deuteronomy 27:8; Habakkuk 2:2); and (5) the Words of God were for the common people, which would seem to require vowels to make it easier for one and all to understand (Deuteronomy 11:18-20). To the writer's knowledge, no one holding to the accommodation position has attempted an answer to these problems.

A third position about the vowel points is, what the author calls, the non-authoritative position, which regards the vowel points as uninspired and non-authoritative. But with uninspired points, then, as Chapter Three demonstrates, uncertainty would be present in just about every verse of the Old Testament. Therefore, one would have to rely on other authorities to decide what word or words should be in a verse. Some of the proponents of the non-authoritative position are Natronai II ben-Hilai, Louis Cappellus,[701] Albert Barnes, and most modern-day scholars. In spite of its popularity, the non-authoritative position suffers from serious Scriptural problems among which are that it fails to see that God's Words are preserved (Psalm 12:6,7; Isaiah 30:8; 40:8; Matthew 24:35; Luke 16:17); perfect (Psalm 19:7); sure (Psalm 93:5; 111:7; II Peter 1:19); settled (Psalm 119:89); a lamp and a light (Psalm 119:105; Proverbs 6:23); faithful (Psalm 119:138); founded (Psalm 119:152); enduring (Psalm 119:160); exalted above all His name (Psalm 138:2); certain (Proverbs 22:20,21); cannot be broken (John 10:35); and the sole authority (II Timothy 3;16,17). Again, to the writer's knowledge no one holding to the non-authoritative position has attempted an answer to these problems.

---

[701] The author lists Cappellus earlier under the accommodation position. Capellus initially held the accommodation position and then changed to the non-authoritative position.

Both the accommodation and the non-authoritative positions suffer from a failure to see that the Bible is the sole authority for faith and practice. However, Scripture is the sole authority when it comes to salvation (Romans 10:17; II Timothy 3:15; I Peter 1:23); to judging (Genesis 2:17; Exodus 5:1; Leviticus 10:1,2; Deuteronomy 4:1; 7:11; 27:26; I Samuel 15:3,22; Isaiah 8:20; John 5:39; 12:48; Acts 17:11; Hebrews 8:5); to local churches (Matthew 28:20; Acts 7:38; Romans 15:4; I Corinthians 10:11; 14:37; Colossians 2:8; I Timothy 3:14,15; II Timothy 3:16,17; 4:2; Titus 1:4; II Peter 3:2; Jude 3); to Jesus' life, both negatively as He rejected the false authority of the oral tradition (Matthew 12:1-13; 15:1-6; Luke 11:37,38; 13:10:17; 14:1-6; John 5:5-12,16,18; 7:22,23; 9:14-16), and positively as He followed the written Words of God (Psalm 138:2; Matthew 2:23; 4:4,7,10,12-15; 5:17; 8:16,17; 12:15-21; 13:34,35; 21:1-5; 26:53,54; Luke 22:37; 24:44; John 13:18; 15:25; 19:28; Hebrews 10:7). The authority for faith and practice is not the Bible plus oral tradition, the Bible plus the Masoretes, the Bible plus the textual critics, the Bible plus history, or the Bible plus some other uninspired work. The teaching of the Bible being the sole authority for faith and practice is devastating to the accommodation and non-authoritative positions, for the advocates of these positions do not have a Bible that is the sole authority.

The Biblical problems with the accommodation and non-authoritative positions eliminate them as correct views. The only viable position left is the *autographa* position. The *autographa* position is not the correct position merely because it is the only left, but because the Bible teaches that it is the correct view. The Bible teaches that God inspired words (Genesis 22:16; Exodus 24:4; Jeremiah 36:1,2), which words proceeded out of His mouth (Exodus 4:22; 34:27; Jeremiah 30:2; 36:1-4; Matthew 4:4), and, therefore, included vowels (Matthew 22:31; I Corinthians 9:10; cf. Romans 9:29; II Peter 3:2). These words are fully preserved (Psalm 12:6,7; Isaiah 30:8; 40:8; 59:21; Matthew 5:18; 24:35; Luke 16:17), so that the words are pure (Psalm 12:6,7), perfect (Psalm 19:7), sure (Psalm 93:5; 111:7), faithful

(Psalm 119:89,138), settled (Psalm 119:89), a lamp and a light (Psalm 119:105), founded for ever (Psalm 119:152), enduring for ever (Psalm 119:160), magnified above all of God's name (Psalm 138:2), certain (Proverbs 22:20,21), standing for ever (Isaiah 40:8), not passing away (Matthew 24:35), not broken (John 10:35), lively oracles (Acts 7:38), the sole authority (II Timothy 3:16,17), quick (Hebrews 4:12), liveth and abideth for ever (I Peter 1:23), and a more sure word of prophecy (II Peter 1:19). These verses demand the presence of the vowels. Furthermore, the New Testament asserts that the written words of the Old Testament are equivalent to the spoken Words of God (Matthew 22:31; Luke 24:25; John 1:23; 12:38; Acts 3:22; 7:48,49; 8:32-34; 28:25; Romans 9:29; 12:19; 14:11; I Corinthians 9:10; Hebrews 3:7; II Peter 3:2). Since speaking requires the use of vowels, then these written words must also have vowels. Also, various New Testament words demonstrate that New Testament writers were aware of the points: *Eli, Eli, lama* (Matthew 27:46; Psalm 22:1); *Emmanuel* (Matthew 1:23; Isaiah 7:14); *Abaddon* (Revelation 9:11; Job 26:6; 31:12; Proverbs 15:11); *Armageddon* (Revelation 16:16; Genesis 10:30; Zechariah 12:11); *Anna* (Luke 2:36; I Samuel 1:2); *Matthan* (Matthew 1:15; II Chronicles 23:17); *Mattathias* (Luke 3:25; I Chronicles 9:31); *Sabbaton* (Matthew 12:5; Exodus 16:23); *Manasseh* (Matthew 1:10; Genesis 41:51); *Capernaum* (Matthew 4:13); *Messiah* (John 1:41; Daniel 9:25); *Siloam* (Luke 13:4; Isaiah 8:6); *Gomorrha* (Romans 9:29; Genesis 10:19); *Sara* (Hebrews 11:11; Genesis 38:17); *Charran* (Acts 7:2; Genesis 11:32); *earnest* (Ephesians 1:14; Genesis 38:17); as well as fifty-eight Old Testament names that retain their exact vocalization when brought over into the New Testament. This Biblical teaching refutes the non-authoritative and the accommodation positions and asserts the *autographa* position.

A further consideration that positively establishes the *autographa* position as the correct position is a proper exegesis of Matthew 5:18. Lexical, contextual, etymological, Scriptural, and translational considerations demonstrate that *tittle* has the non-consonantal meaning of *vowel point*. Lexically, *tittle* can have a consonantal meaning, where it is part of a consonant, or *tittle* can have a non-consonantal meaning. An examination of the context of Matthew 5:18 decides the case for *tittle* having a non-consonantal meaning, specifically that it refers to a vowel point. *Jot*, the least of the Hebrew consonants, adequately guarantees the preservation of all the consonants (see Luke 16:10), therefore, *tittle* need not refer to consonants. Also, the phrase *one jot or one tittle* with the use of the disjunctive conjunction (ἢ *or*) makes it clear that *tittle* is different from the *jot*, which further establishes that *tittle* is referring to something other than consonants or something connected to consonants. Furthermore, the expression *till all be fulfilled* refers to the fulfillment of prophecy, the exact fulfillment of which depends on the vowels.[702] *Tittle*, which can mean *vowel point*, Jesus inseparably links with what is to be fulfilled and this link demands that *tittle* does, indeed, mean *vowel point*. In addition to this, *one of these least commandments* in the next verse, Matthew 5:19, also depends on the vowels.[703] Since Jesus bases the teaching of Matthew 5:19 on the teaching of Matthew 5:18; and since Matthew 5:18 speaks of the *tittle*, which can mean a *vowel point*; then this provides yet another contextual reason for why *tittle* does mean *vowel point*. Scripturally, God spoke words involving the use of both vowels and consonants (Genesis 22:16; Exodus 4:22; 24:4; Jeremiah 30:2; 36:1-4; Mat-

---

[702] Please consider Genesis 49:10; I Kings 17:4; Job 24:12; 37:23; Psalm 2:9; Proverbs 12:19; 29:14; Isaiah 19:10; 21:13; Jeremiah 8:13; 15:19; 25:24; 48:4; 50:38; Daniel 9:27; Hosea 13:7; Micah 6:9; Zephaniah 3:8; and Malachi 2:3. These verses are all prophecies that some would like to repoint, but repointing would affect the fulfillment, making it impossible to know if they are fulfilled.

[703] In Exodus 23:19, is the prohibition against seething a kid in his mother's milk. Some might classify this command as one the least of the commandments. Since one could repoint the word *milk* (חָלֵב) to *fat* (חֵלֶב), then without the vowel pointing one, thinking that the word was *fat* instead of *milk*, could easily break this commandment and teach others also to break it. If one is not going to break one of the least of the commandments, he must have the vowel points so that he clearly knows the demands of the commandment.

thew 4:4). These words God's prophets wrote necessitating their having used vowels (Exodus 34:27; Matthew 22:31; Luke 24:25; John 1:23; 12:38; Acts 3:22; 7:48,49; 8:32-34; 28:25; Romans 9:29; 12:19; 14:11; I Corinthians 9:10; Hebrews 3:7; II Peter 3:2). Jesus guaranteed the perfect preservation of God's Words (Matthew 24:35; John 10:35; 17:17). These Scriptural considerations, along with the fact that God's Words are sure and are the sole authority for faith and practice demand the presence of vowels. In other words, Scripture teaches the inspiration and preservation of the vowels of the Old Testament, which teaching is in exact agreement with understanding *tittle* to be a vowel point in Matthew 5:18. Etymologically, the Greek word behind *tittle* (κεραία) is a transliteration into Greek of the Hebrew חִירֶק (*chirek*), wherein *chirek* is the name of the smallest Hebrew vowel point. Lastly, other translations support the contention that *tittle* is a dot, and not merely another part of a consonant. For anyone who will believe it, Jesus in Matthew 5:18 settles the question of the vowel points, the perfect preservation, and the complete authority of the Traditional Hebrew Old Testament text.

EVIDENCE SUMMARY

The evidence summary presents the evidence against the accommodation and non-authoritative views and the evidence for the *autographa* view in a more direct manner. Therefore, this section does not present a chapter by chapter recap, but, rather, rearranges the evidence in such a way as to present a very forceful and direct case for the inspiration of the Hebrew Old Testament vowel points.

The inspiration of the Hebrew Old Testament vowel points rests on the foundation of the Bible being the sole authority for faith and practice. This is of paramount importance when it comes to the matter of the vowel points. Scripture is the sole authority when it comes to salvation (Romans 10:17; II Timothy 3:15; I Peter 1:23); to judging (Genesis 2:17; Exodus 5:1; Leviticus 10:1,2; Deuteronomy 4:1; 7:11; 27:26; I Samuel 15:3,22; Isaiah 8:20; John 5:39; 12:48; Acts 17:11; Hebrews 8:5); to local churches (Matthew 28:20; Acts 7:38; Romans 15:4; I Corinthians 10:11; 14:37; Colossians 2:8; I Timothy 3:14,15; II Timothy 3:16,17; 4:2; Titus 1:4; II Peter 3:2; Jude 3); to Jesus' life, both negatively as He rejected the false authority of the oral tradition (Matthew 12:1-13; 15:1-6; Luke 11:37,38; 13:10:17; 14:1-6; John 5:5-12,16,18; 7:22,23; 9:14-16), and positively as He followed the written Words of God (Psalm 138:2; Matthew 2:23; 4:4,7,10,12-15; 5:17; 8:16,17; 12:15-21; 13:34,35; 21:1-5; 26:53,54; Luke 22:37; 24:44; John 13:18; 15:25; 19:28; Hebrews 10:7). The authority for faith and practice is not the Bible plus oral tradition, the Bible plus the Masoretes, the Bible plus the textual critics, the Bible plus history, or the Bible plus some other uninspired work.

The teaching of the Bible being the sole authority for faith and practice is devastating to the accommodation and non-authoritative positions, for the advocates of these positions do not have a Bible that is the sole authority. The accommodation position neglects the Bible being the sole authority for faith and practice by (1) relying on oral tradition to convey the vowels through history to the Masoretes; however, oral tradition has absolutely no authority (Matthew 15:1-6); (2) relying on the additions of vowels by the Masoretes to the Words of God; however, the Bible forbids adding to it (Deuteronomy 4:2; 12:32; Proverbs 30:6; and Revelation 22:18); and (3) appealing to various historical arguments, such as difficulty in writing the points, spelling variations, unpointed documents, silence about points, a story about Joab, vowel point names not in Hebrew, the *kethib* and *keri* readings, and the *matres lectionis*, to prove that the points are not inspired; however, the Bible itself is the authority (II Timothy 3:16,17), and not history. Because the accommodation position neglects the Bible being the sole authority for faith and practice, it is not the right view. Those who want to honor God's Words should reject the accommodation position.

The non-authoritative position also neglects the Bible being the sole authority for faith and practice by claiming that the vowel points have no authority whatsoever. The result of such a view is to make the Words of God extremely uncertain and to strip them of all authority. This is evident in looking at verses where various writers suggest a replacing of vowels in certain words. In light of such a practice a number of questions arise.[704]

> In Genesis 47:31, is it "upon the bed's head," or "on the top of his staff"?
>
> In Genesis 49:10, is it "until Shiloh come," or "until tribute comes to him"?
>
> In Deuteronomy 33:27, is it "the eternal God is *thy* refuge, and underneath *are* the everlasting arms," or "He subdues the ancient gods, and shatters the forces of old"?
>
> In Joshua 4:24, is it "that ye might fear," or "that ye feared"?
>
> In I Samuel 1:7, is it "he did so year by year," or "so she did year by year"?
>
> In I Samuel 18:11, is it "Saul cast the javelin," or "Saul lifted the javelin"?
>
> In I Samuel 20:17, is it "Jonathan caused David to swear again," or "Jonathan sware again to David"?
>
> In II Samuel 24:9, is it "eight hundred thousand," or "eight hundred specially trained warriors"?
>
> Again, in II Samuel 24:9, is it "five hundred thousand," or "five hundred specially trained warriors"?
>
> In I Kings 13:12, is it "had seen," or "showed"?
>
> In I Kings 17:1, is it "Tishbite," or "stranger"?
>
> Again, in I Kings 17:1, is it "inhabitants," or "Tishbi"?
>
> In I Kings 17:4, is it "ravens," or "Arabians"?
>
> In I Kings 20:29, is it "an hundred thousand footmen," or "an hundred officers"?

---

[704] The author bases these questions on material from Chapter Three. The first group of words are from the *King James Version*, which are an accurate translation of the Hebrew of the Masoretic Text, and the second group of words reflect the changes in translation that would occur if one were to change the vowels.

In I Kings 20:30, is it "twenty and seven thousand," or "twenty and seven officers"?

In I Chronicles 4:10, is it "and that thou wouldest keep me from evil," or "to provide pasture"?

In I Chronicles 7:4, is it "six and thirty thousand," or is it "six and thirty chiefs"?

In I Chronicles 12:24-37, where *thousand* occurs thirteen times, is it "thousand," or "leaders"?

In I Chronicles 27:1-15, where *thousand* occurs thirteen times, is it "thousand," or "leaders"?

In II Chronicles 13:3, where *thousand* occurs twice, is it "thousand," or "leaders"?

In II Chronicles 13:7, is it "thousand," or "leaders"?

In II Chronicles 14:8-9, where *thousand* occurs thrice, is it "thousand," or "leaders"?

In II Chronicles 17:14-18, where *thousand* occurs six times, is it "thousand," or "leaders"?

In II Chronicles 25:5-6, where *thousand* occurs twice, is it "thousand," or "leaders"?

In II Chronicles 26:12-13 where *thousand* occurs thrice, is it "thousand," or "leaders"?

In II Chronicles 28:6, is it "thousand," or "leaders"?

In II Chronicles 28:8, is it "thousand," or "leaders"?

In Ezra 8:26, is it "and silver vessels an hundred talents," or "and silver vessels worth 200 talents"?

In Job 5:15, is it "from the sword," or "to make desolate"?

In Job 6:18, is it "paths," or "caravans"?

In Job 15:23, is it "he wandereth about for bread," or "he wanders abroad to be the food of vultures"?

In Job 21:24, is it "full of milk," or "full of fat"?

In Job 24:12, is it "men," or "mortals"?

Again, in Job 24:12, is it "folly," or "prayer"?

In Job 27:19, is it "but he shall not be gathered," or "is he not swept away"?

In Job 31:18, is it "he was brought with me," or "from my youth he honoured me as a father"?

In Job 36:33, is it "vapour," or "evil"?

In Job 37:23, is it "he will not afflict," or "he will not answer"?

In Psalm 2:9, is it "thou shalt break," or "thou shalt rule," or "thou shalt feed"?

In Psalm 7:11, is it "God," or "not"?

In Psalm 29:9, is it "maketh the hinds to calve," or "causes the oaks to whirl"?

In Psalm 33:7, is it "as an heap," or "as in a bottle"?

In Psalm 42:2, is it "and appear before God," or "and behold the face of God"?

In Psalm 52:5, is it "he shall take thee away," or "he will destroy you"?

In Psalm 58:1, is it "sons of men," or "mighty lords"?

In Psalm 59:10, is it "the God of my mercy shall prevent me," or "my God shall meet me with his lovingkindness"?

In Psalm 60:8, is it "a snare before them: and *that which should have been* for *their* welfare, *let it become* a trap," or "a snare, and retribution and a trap"?

In Psalm 109:17, is it "so let it come unto him," or "let curses come on him"?

In Psalm 119:118, is it "their deceit," or "their thought"?

In Psalm 147:17, is it "cold," or "hail"?

In Proverbs 1:7, and over five thousand five hundred (5,500) other verses is the Hebrew name for God "Jehovah," or "Yahweh"?

In Proverbs 6:24, is it "from the evil woman," or "from the wife of another"?

In Proverbs 10:4, is it "he becometh poor," or "poverty humbleth a man"?

In Proverbs 11:23, is it "wrath," or "shall perish"?

In Proverbs 12:19, is it "the lip of truth shall be established for ever," or "true lips establish testimony"?

In Proverbs 14:1, is it "wise," or "wisdom"?

In Proverbs 21:4, is it "the plowing," or "the fallow-field," or "the lamp"?

In Proverbs 23:7, is it "for as he thinketh in his heart, so is he," or "for as if one should swallow a hair, so he eats and drinks"?

In Proverbs 25:27, is it "so for men to search their own glory is not glory," or "but as an inquirer to enter on what is difficult is honor"?

In Proverbs 26:23, is it "silver dross," or "glaze"?

In Proverbs 29:14, is it "his throne shall be established for ever," or "his throne shall be established for a testimony"?

In Proverbs 30:1, is it "and Ucal," or "and I became dull"?

In Ecclesiastes 3:21, is it "who knoweth the spirit of man that goeth upward, and the spirit of the beast that goeth downward to the earth," or "Who knows if the spirit of man rises upward and if the spirit of the animal goes down into the earth"?

In Song of Solomon 1:2, is it "let him kiss me," or "let him give me to drink"?

In Isaiah 1:2, is it "hath spoken," or "speaking"?

In Isaiah 1:8, is it "as a besieged city," or "so is the delivered city"?

In Isaiah 16:4, is it "let mine outcasts dwell with thee, Moab," or "let the outcasts of Moab sojourn with thee, O Zion"?

In Isaiah 19:10, is it "and they shall be broken in the purposes thereof, all that make sluices *and* ponds for fish," or "and all who make beer shall lament, and shall afflict their souls"?

In Isaiah 21:13, is it "Arabia," or "evening"?

In Isaiah 27:7, is it "them that are slain by him," or "them that slew him"?

In Isaiah 30:8, is it "for ever and ever," or "for a testimony forever"?

In Isaiah 40:6, is it "and he said," or "and I said"?

In Isaiah 62:5, is it "thy sons," or "they builder," or "thy restorer"?

In Jeremiah 2:16, is it "have broken," or "shall break," or "shall feed off"?

In Jeremiah 8:13, is it "and the things that I have given them shall pass away from them," or "and I will give them to those who shall pass over them"?

In Jeremiah 10:18, is it "that they may find it so," or "that they may be found," or "that thy stroke may be found"?

In Jeremiah 15:19, is it "then will I bring thee again," or "I will give thee a settled place"?

In Jeremiah 23:17, is it "unto them that despise me, The LORD hath said," or "unto those who despise the word of the Lord"?

In Jeremiah 25:24, is it "mingled people," or "Arabs"?

In Jeremiah 48:4, is it "her little ones," or "unto Zoar"?

In Jeremiah 48:15, is it "gone up," or "gone down"?

In Jeremiah 48:18, is it "sit in thirst," or "sit on the parched ground"?

In Jeremiah 49:1, is it "their king," or "Milcom"?

In Jeremiah 50:38, is it "a drought," or "a sword"?

In Jeremiah 51:3, is it "against him that bendeth let the archer bend his bow," or "let not him who bendeth his bow bend it"?

In Ezekiel 8:2, is it "the appearance of fire," or "the appearance of a man"?

In Ezekiel 16:30, is it "how weak is thine heart," or "how I am filled with anger against you"?

In Ezekiel 23:4, is it "Aholah," or "her tent"?

Again, in Ezekiel 23:4, is it "Aholibah," or "my tent in her"?

In Ezekiel 31:14, is it "neither their trees stand up in their height, all that drink water," or "and that no drinkers of water may stand upon their own greatness"?

In Ezekiel 34:3, is it "fat," or "milk"?

In Ezekiel 36:5, is it "to cast it out for a prey," or "in order to plunder its pasturage"?

In Ezekiel 39:26, is it "they have borne," or "they will forget"?

In Daniel 9:27, is it, "And for the overspreading of abominations he shall make it desolate," or is it, "And – upon the wing – the porch of the temple – abominations! And a desolator!"?

In Daniel 11:6, is it "and he that begat her," or "whom she brought forth"?

In Hosea 13:7, is it "will I observe," or "by the way of Assyria"?

In Obadiah 3, is it "hath deceived," or "carrying out"?

In Micah 2:7, is it "is the spirit of the LORD straitened," or "is the ear of the Lord shortened"?

In Micah 6:9, is it "shall see thy name," or "shall fear thy name"?

In Micah 6:11, is it "shall I count *them* pure," or "shall I acquit"?

In Habakkuk 1:8, is it "evening wolves," or "wolves of Arabia"?

In Zephaniah 3:8, is it "until the day that I rise up to the prey," or "until the day of my rising up for testimony"?

In Haggai 1:11, is it "I called for a drought," or "I called for a sword"?

In Zechariah 9:8, is it "because of the army," or "against the army," or "from the army," or "as a garrison," or "as a rampart"?

In Malachi 2:3, is it "I will corrupt your seed," or "I will rebuke your arm"?

The above one-hundred five (105) questions well illustrate the uncertainty and lack of authority that would reign throughout the Bible if the vowels of the Hebrew Old Testament are not authoritative. Such a position is diametrically opposed to the teaching that the Bible is the sole authority for faith and practice and, therefore, cannot possibly be a correct view on the vowel points. Here again, those who want to honor God's Words should reject the non-authoritative position.

The Bible being the sole authority for faith and practice is devastating to the accommodation and non-authoritative positions. The *autographa* position, in contrast, rests firmly upon the Bible being the sole authority for faith and practice. The Bible teaches that the Words of God are vocalized and that the Words of God are sure, which teaching is in direct contradiction to the teachings of the accommodation and non-authoritative positions. God inspired words (Genesis 22:16; Exodus 24:4; Jeremiah 36:1,2), which words proceeded out of His mouth (Exodus 4:22; 34:27; Jeremiah 30:2; 36:1-4; Matthew 4:4), and, therefore, included vowels (Matthew 22:31; I Corinthians 9:10; cf. Romans 9:29; II Peter 3:2). The New Testament further asserts that the written words of the Old Testament are equivalent to the spoken Words of God (Matthew 22:31; Luke 24:25; John 1:23; 12:38; Acts 3:22; 7:48,49; 8:32-34; 28:25; Romans 9:29; 12:19; 14:11; I Corinthians 9:10; Hebrews 3:7; II Peter 3:2). Since speaking requires the use of vowels, then these written words must also have vowels. In addition to the teaching of the above verses, the Bible teaches that (1) the Spirit of God used words, which necessitates vocalization, which vocalized words the prophets wrote (I Corinthians 2:13; II Peter 1:21); (2) God commanded that people write His Words very plainly, which requires the use of vowels (Deuteronomy 27:8; Habakkuk 2:2); and (3) the Words of God were for the common people, which would seem to require vowels to make it easier for one and all to understand (Deuteronomy 11:18-20). The Bible teaches that the Words of God have vowels, which establishes the *autographa* position as the correct position.

The Words of God are fully preserved (Psalm 12:6,7; Isaiah 30:8; 40:8; 59:21; Matthew 5:18; 24:35; Luke 16:17), so that the

Words of God are pure (Psalm 12:6,7), perfect (Psalm 19:7), sure (Psalm 93:5; 111:7), faithful (Psalm 119:89,138), settled (Psalm 119:89), a lamp and a light (Psalm 119:105; Proverbs 6:23), faithful (Psalm 119:138), founded for ever (Psalm 119:152), enduring for ever (Psalm 119:160), magnified above all of God's name (Psalm 138:2), certain (Proverbs 22:20,21), standing for ever (Isaiah 40:8), not passing away (Matthew 24:35), not broken (John 10:35), lively oracles (Acts 7:38), the sole authority (II Timothy 3:16,17), quick (Hebrews 4:12), living and abiding for ever (I Peter 1:23), and a more sure word of prophecy (II Peter 1:19). These verses demand the presence of the vowels. These verses not only devastate the accommodation and non-authoritative positions, but also establish the *autographa* position.

Another fact that positively establishes the *autographa* position as the correct view is that various verses recognize the points in several words such as *shibboleth* (Judges 12:6), *Eli, Eli, lama* (Matthew 27:46; Psalm 22:1); *Emmanuel* (Matthew 1:23; Isaiah 7:14); *Abaddon* (Revelation 9:11; Job 26:6; 31:12; Proverbs 15:11); *Armageddon* (Revelation 16:16; Genesis 10:30; Zechariah 12:11); *Anna* (Luke 2:36; I Samuel 1:2); *Matthan* (Matthew 1:15; II Chronicles 23:17); *Mattathias* (Luke 3:25; I Chronicles 9:31); *Sabbaton* (Matthew 12:5; Exodus 16:23); *Manasseh* (Matthew 1:10; Genesis 41:51); *Capernaum* (Matthew 4:13); *Messiah* (John 1:41; Daniel 9:25); *Siloam* (Luke 13:4; Isaiah 8:6); *Gomorrha* (Romans 9:29; Genesis 10:19); *Sara* (Hebrews 11:11; Genesis 38:17); *Charran* (Acts 7:2; Genesis 11:32); *earnest* (Ephesians 1:14; Genesis 38:17); as well as fifty-eight Old Testament names that retain their exact vocalization when brought over into the New Testament.

Some accommodationists object to the *autographa* position by drawing attention to the spelling of David's name, New Testament spelling of Old Testament names, *men* in Acts 15:17, and *top of his staff* in Hebrews 11:21 as evidence that the points were added later. But David's name could have different spellings just as other names do. New Testament writers at times simply spelled Old Testament names differently just as Old Testament writers at times spelled names differently. In Acts 15:17 the Spirit of God is giving an inspired commentary upon an Old Testament word. Concerning Hebrews 11:21 Jacob both leaned upon the top of his staff and bowed himself upon the bed's head as Genesis 47:31 says he did. Furthermore, if the points were added later, as the accommodationists allege, then such an allegation flies in the face of the Bible being the sole authority (see earlier in this section). The accommodationists' objections to the *autographa* position are unable to overthrow the *autographa* position.

The *autographa* position also finds support from Matthew 5:18 where Jesus states, "Till heaven and earth pass, one jot or tittle shall in no wise pass from the law, till all be fulfilled." First, *tittle* can mean *vowel point*. Second, *jot*, the least of the Hebrew consonants, adequately guarantees the preservation of all the consonants (see Luke 16:10) so that *tittle* need not refer to consonants or any part of consonants. Third, the disjunctive conjunction (ἢ *or*) differentiates the *tittle* from the *jot*, showing that it is not a consonant. Fourth, Jesus inseparably links *tittle* with prophecies that are yet to be fulfilled, the fulfillment of which depends on the vowels.[705] Fifth, Matthew 5:18 is the foundation on which Jesus bases His teaching in Matthew 5:19 about "one of these least commandments," which commandments depend on the vowels.[706] Sixth, God spoke words involving the use of both vowels and consonants (Genesis 22:16; Exodus 4:22; 24:4; Jeremiah 30:2; 36:1-4; Matthew 4:4). Seventh, God's prophets wrote the Words of God, which necessitates their having used vowels (Exodus 34:27; Matthew 22:31; Luke 24:25; John 1:23; 12:38; Acts 3:22; 7:48,49;

---

[705] Please consider Genesis 49:10; I Kings 17:4; Job 24:12; 37:23; Psalm 2:9; Proverbs 12:19; 29:14; Isaiah 19:10; 21:13; Jeremiah 8:13; 15:19; 25:24; 48:4; 50:38; Daniel 9:27; Hosea 13:7; Micah 6:9; Zephaniah 3:8; and Malachi 2:3. These verses are all prophecies that some would like to repoint, but repointing would affect the fulfillment, making it impossible to know if they are fulfilled.

[706] For example, in Exodus 23:19, by changing the pointing, one can change *milk* to *fat*.

8:32-34; 28:25; Romans 9:29; 12:19; 14:11; I Corinthians 9:10; Hebrews 3:7; II Peter 3:2). Eighth, New Testament writers were cognizant of the vowel points (e.g., *Emmanuel* in Matthew 1:23; *Abaddon* in Revelation 9:11; *Capernaum* in Matthew 4:13; *Messiah* in John 1:41; and many others). Ninth, God's Words are sure, which sureness is dependent on the vowels (see Chapter Four). Tenth, the Bible teaches that Scripture is the sole authority for faith and practice, which authority depends on the points (see prior discussion in this section as well as Chapter Two). Eleventh, Jesus elsewhere guaranteed the perfect preservation of God's Words (Matthew 24:35; John 10:35; 17:17). And twelfth, the Greek word for *tittle* (κεραία) is a transliteration into Greek of the Hebrew חִירֶק (*chirek*), wherein *chirek* is the name of the smallest Hebrew vowel point. In light of these twelve statements, the writer concludes that *tittle* refers to the Hebrew vowel point, *chirek*. Why would anyone think otherwise? Some, who think otherwise, perhaps have not fully considered all that the Bible teaches on the vowel points and it is the hope of the writer that when they do fully consider these things, they will adopt the *autographa* position.

The *autographa* position stands on the foundation of the Words of God being the sole authority for faith and practice, which requires inspired vowels. The Bible teaches that God spoke words, which the prophets wrote, all of which requires vowels. The Bible teaches that God's Words are sure, which requires vowels. In light of this evidence, the writer concludes that God inspired the vowels. Thank God that He has given to His people such a wonderful Book as the Bible. "Oh that *men* would praise the LORD *for* his goodness, and *for* his wonderful works to the children of men!" (Psalm 107:8).

DEFINITIONS AND DELIMITATIONS

This section presents definitions of various terms as well as delimitations. Delimitations are limits that the author has placed upon this work, which have the effect of limiting the scope of the book.

DEFINITIONS

Apographa refers to the copies of the *autographa*.

Autographa refers to the actual inspired writings of those whom God used to give His Words. Many writers often use *autographa* and *originals* interchangeably, but in this work *autographa* will be the word of choice.

Biblicist refers to one who believes that whatever the Bible says is so. A Biblicist is one who does not question the Bible, but makes the Bible, indeed all of the Bible, his rule for faith and practice. The writer refers to himself as a Biblicist. While some use the terms *Fundamentalist* and *Biblicist* interchangeably, the writer does not. In the opinion of the writer, *Fundamentalist* is a more general term describing one who subscribes to a list of fundamental doctrines, whereas *Biblicist* is a more specific term describing one who subscribes to and defends the entire Bible. While all Biblicists are Fundamentalists, not all Fundamentalists are Biblicists.

Consonantal text refers to the Hebrew Old Testament written without vowel points.

Fundamentalist[707] refers to one who holds to the fundamentals of the faith usually defined as (1) the inspiration and inerrancy of the *autographa*; (2) the Trinity; (3) the deity of Christ; (4) the virgin birth of Christ; (5) the substitutionary atonement of Christ; (6) the bodily resurrection of Christ; (7) the ascension of Christ into heaven; (8) the second coming of Christ; (9) salvation by grace through faith in the finished work of Christ; (10) heaven; and (11) hell. In addition to holding to the fundamentals, a Fundamentalist is one who adheres to the principle of separation from error. It is the observation of the writer that one can call himself a Fundamentalist or have others think of him as a Fundamentalist even though he does not hold to baptism by immersion, eternal security, the local church as opposed to a so-called universal church, autonomy of the local church, two ordinances (baptism and the Lord's supper), inspiration of the vowels of the Hebrew Old Testament, preservation of the Scriptures, pre-tribulational rapture, as well as other doctrines. However, these doctrines are part of the "all things" that Jesus commands His disciples to teach to others (Matthew 28:20), and Fundamentalists should not ignore these doctrines by calling them non-essentials.[708]

---

[707] Robert Lightner says of Fundamentalism that it is "the movement which was born in the early part of the twentieth century in opposition to and as a reaction against liberalism. It strongly reemphasizes the fundamentals of historic Christianity. In addition to other doctrines which were held to be basic and fundamental, the area of conflict centered around: (1) the inerrancy of Scripture; (2) the deity of Christ; (3) the virgin birth of Christ; (4) the substitutionary atonement of Christ; and (5) the physical resurrection and bodily return of Christ. The term was used to designate the defense of these fundamentals when it was first coined and this is the true meaning of it today" (Robert Lightner, *Neoevangelicalism Today* (Schaumburg, IL: Regular Baptist Press, 1979), 28,29). The definition that this work gives is a more complete one and lists some of those "other doctrines" which Lightner does not list.

[708] Jesus commanded baptism in Matthew 28:19. The meaning of the word *baptism* teaches that it is by immersion, as does the example of Jesus' baptism (Matthew 3:13-16). Jesus taught eternal security (John 6:37,47; 10:27-29; 11:25,26). Jesus taught the preservation of the Words of God (Matthew 4:4; 5:18; 24:35; John 10:35; 17:17). Jesus taught the inspiration and preservation of the vowels of the Hebrew Old Testament (Matthew 4:4 – God's vocalized Words are written; Matthew 5:18; Luke

Inscripturated refers to the recording in writing of God's inspired words making them part of the *autographa*.

Inspiration refers to the process whereby God, that is, God the Father (II Timothy 3:16), God the Son (I Peter 1:11), and God the Holy Spirit (II Peter 1:21), moved in holy men to record accurately His Words so as to produce the Word of God.

Kethib / Keri refers to words of the Hebrew Bible that are either written in the text (*Kethib*) or are read or inserted from the margin (*Keri*). It is the position of this work that since God has perfectly preserved His pure, inspired words (Psalm 12:6,7[709]) that one should not

---

16:17). Jesus taught the doctrine of the local church (Matthew 16:18; 18:15-20) and its autonomy (Matthew 18:15-17). Jesus gave two ordinances (Matthew 28:19; I Corinthians 11:23-26). Jesus spoke of the rapture (Jn 14:1-3) and taught that it is pre-trib (Revelation 3:10). Clearly, these doctrines were not non-essentials to Jesus and they should not be non-essentials to the followers of Jesus.

[709] The author is aware of the controversy surrounding Psalm 12:6-7 and its application to the perfect preservation of God's Words. He realizes that some believe that both occurrences of *them* in vs. 7 refer to the poor and needy in vs. 5, rather than to *words* in vs. 6. The main argument in favor of *them* referring to *poor* and *needy* is that both of these words are masculine, whereas *words* is feminine. However, it is not out of the ordinary for a masculine pronoun to refer to a feminine noun, especially in the matter of a masculine pronoun referring back to a feminine noun that speaks of the Words of God as Psalm 119:111,129,152, and 167 demonstrate.

In Psalm 119:111, the masculine plural pronoun *them* refers back to *testimonies*, a feminine plural noun. In Psalm 119:129 the masculine plural pronoun *them* attached as a suffix to the verb *keep* refers back to *testimonies*, a feminine plural noun. In Psalm 119:152, the masculine plural suffix pronoun *them* attached to the verb *founded* refers to *testimonies*, a feminine plural noun. In Psalm 119:167, the masculine plural pronoun *them* attached as a suffix to the verb *love* refers to *testimonies*, a feminine plural noun.

In light of the above, the author asserts that both occurrences of *them* in Psalm 12:7 refer to *words* in Psalm 12:6 and that, therefore, the passage teaches the perfect preservation of God's Words. For a more complete treatment of Psalm 12:6,7, see the author's *Those So-Called Errors: Debunking the Liberal, New Evangelical, and Fundamentalist Myth that You Should Not Hear, Receive, and Believe All the Numbers of Scripture* (Newington, CT: Emmanuel Baptist Theological Press, 2003), 142-145. Also, see Strouse's article "The Permanent Preservation of God's Words" in *Emmanuel Baptist Theological Journal* 2 (Fall/Winter 2006): 27-36.

use the *Keri* or marginal readings, but should always retain the *Kethib* readings, which are already in the text.

Liberal refers to one who denies the fundamentals of the faith and, in particular, denies the miraculous, thereby seeking to explain away the miraculous in terms of naturalistic causes.

LXX refers to the Septuagint, a Greek translation of the Hebrew Old Testament.

Masorah refers to a commentary on the Old Testament whose purpose "is to indicate the correct reading of the text with respect to words, vowels, accents, etc., so as to preserve it from all corruption."[710]

Masoretes refers to a group of Jewish scribes that lived from about five hundred A.D. to nine hundred A.D. Some claim that they are the ones who added the vowel points to a consonantal text of the Old Testament.

Matres Lectionis is a Latin term meaning "mothers of reading" and refers to the using of consonants in the place of vowels to assist in reading words. Particularly as this relates to Hebrew, some suggest that scribes used the Hebrew letters י ו ה א and sometimes ע in the place of vowels. They refer to these letters as *matres lectionis*. For instance, Brian Walton asserts: "The ancient Hebrew vowels were the same before the invention of points, which are in all other Eastern tongues, as the Chaldee, Syriac, Arabic, etc., viz. י ו א which are yet commonly called *matres lectionis*, because they direct the reading in books not pointed, to which some add ה and St. Jerome ע."[711]

New Evangelical refers to one who evinces a spirit of compromise with error, even to the point of fellowshipping with Liberals. George Dollar defines New Evangelicalism as

---

[710] "Masorah, Masoreth, or Massoreth" in *Cyclopedia*, V:860.

[711] Walton, *The Considerator Considered*, 202.

an attitude or position which professes to adhere to the Fundamentals of the Faith but advocates a spirit of re-examination of the basic doctrines, an attitude of tolerance toward the Liberals and an entering into "dialogue" with them, and an emphasis on the love and mercy of God rather than on His holiness and righteousness.[712]

Preservation refers to the process by which God has insured that all the words given by Him through the process of inspiration have not been lost.

Preserved text(s), depending on the context, refers to (1) the Ben Chayyim Masoretic Text of the Old Testament; (2) the Received Text of the New Testament; or (3) both.

Punctations is a term that Whitfield often uses to refer to the vowel points.

Punctuation is a term that older writers use to refer to the vowel points.

Received Text refers to Scrivener's Annotated Greek New Testament: Being the Exact Greek Textus Receptus the Underlies the King James Bible by Frederick H. A. Scrivener.

Revocalization refers to the process of replacing the vowels of Hebrew or Aramaic words of the Old Testament to arrive at a new word.

Textual Criticism refers to the naturalistic, humanistic, and rationalistic attempts allegedly to restore the words of the *autographa*.

Traditional text and *Traditional Hebrew Old Testament* refer to the Ben Chayyim Masoretic Text of the Old Testament.[713]

---

[712] George Dollar, *A History of Fundamentalism in America* (Greenville: Bob Jones University Press, 1973), 383.

[713] Donald A. Waite, *Defending the King James Bible* (Collingswood, NJ: The Bible for Today Press, 1992), 27. Another name for Ben Chayyim Masoretic Text is the Daniel Bomberg Hebrew edition of the Masoretic text.

Vowel points refers to a system of dots (ֶ ָ ֖ ְ ִ ׃ ֻ), a ֗, or a ֮, inserted above, between, or below Hebrew consonants so as to represent vowels. For example, in the Hebrew word for earth, אֶרֶץ, the dots are vowels. In this book, when the author is referring to the Hebrew Old Testament, he uses *vowel points* and *vowels* interchangeably. He does not at all mean to suggest that somehow the vowels are different from the points. On the contrary, the points are the vowels.

Vulgate refers to the Jerome's Latin translation of the Bible dating back to the fourth century AD.

DELIMITATIONS

The author sets forth several delimitations. One delimitation is that this book receives the Traditional Text of the Old Testament and the Received Text of the New Testament as the texts that have the preserved words of the *autographa*. Furthermore, this treatise accepts the Authorized Version (KJV) as an accurate translation of the preserved texts into English. Consequently, this work does not resort to claiming that scribal errors exist in the preserved texts. In light of the above statement, this book does not engage in textual criticism. However, the author may refer to readings other than those in the Received Texts that underlie the Authorized Version in order to show the fallacy of those readings.

A second delimitation is that this treatise concerns itself with the inspiration of the vowel points of the Hebrew and, therefore, does not take up the question of the accents. Some writers argue for the inspiration or antiquity of both the vowels and the accents. The author agrees with such writers, therefore, often when making a direct quote from the Hebrew Old Testament Text, this work will include the accents. However, the whole subject of demonstrating that the accents are inspired would require a separate inquiry. For example, Lambdin writes in his *Introduction to Biblical Hebrew*, "The use of various accents is very complex and will not be taken up in this book."[714] And Waltke and O'Connor write, "The complex accentual systems added to the text by the Masoretes represent an important understanding of the text, one that complements the study of Hebrew grammar but one that needs to be taken up independently."[715] Waltke and O'Connor suggest that Masoretes were the inventors of the accents, but if God inspired the accents, then the Masoretes merely passed along these accents. The point of this quote from Waltke and O'Connor is that the study of accents would require a separate work, which is not the purpose of this work.

A third delimitation is that while this work concerns itself with the Hebrew language, it does not delve into the evolution of languages. The author of this book believes that when the Bible states that Moses wrote words (Exodus 24:4) that that is exactly what he did. Moses, therefore, had the capacity to read and to write. Not only did Moses have the capacity to read and to write, but also Adam did. Genesis 5:1 speaks of the book of the generations of Adam, indicating that Adam wrote a book. The Bible teaches that language, the comprehension of language, the writing of words, and the reading of words are abilities that the first man had; they are not things that mankind gradually developed over time.

A further delimitation is that this work does not attempt to prove the inspiration or the antiquity of the vowel points by appealing to history. This does not mean that there are not historical sources demonstrating the existence of vowel points from the most ancient of times. However, to base one's conclusion about the vowel points or about any point of doctrine, for that matter, on history is for that one to

---

[714] Thomas Lambdin, *Introduction to Biblical Hebrew* (NY: Charles Scribner's Sons, 1971), 201.

[715] Waltke and O'Connor, 633.

build upon a most precarious foundation. Many of the historical sources are obscure, incomplete, and subject to debate. For instance, those of a contrary opinion about the vowel points, that is, those who advocate the novelty or newness of the points, can summon historical arguments to support their case. One will never decide the debate about the points by history. If ever one will decide this debate, he must appeal to the Bible, for only upon the Bible does one have a sure and a solid foundation upon which to stand.

The Bible is the sole authority for faith and practice and not history (Isaiah 8:20; II Timothy 3:16,17). It is essential that one establish points of doctrine and belief with *thus saith the Lord* and not *thus saith history* or else one is elevating history to a level equal to or above Scripture. Such was the methodology of the Pharisees, who repeatedly used the Tradition of the Elders to determine matters of faith and practice, while they completely ignored the Bible (Matthew 12:1-8; 15:1-9). Many Fundamentalists of this day, that is, of the latter twentieth and early twenty-first centuries, rely on various traditions of scholars or the traditions of textual critics to prove points of doctrine. This is a most alarming trend. Because this is such a crucial point, this book presents an entire chapter on the Bible being the sole authority for faith and practice. It is a topic that has a large bearing on the vowel point issue.

In downplaying the use of history to substantiate doctrine, this does not mean that history cannot be useful. While history cannot substantiate doctrine, it can illustrate doctrine. In fact, this work refers to those in the past who have written about the vowel points, not as a way to prove that one should hold to the inspiration of these points, but as a way to illustrate that throughout history there have been those who have held to the inspiration and antiquity of the points evidencing belief in Jesus' statement that "one tittle shall in no wise pass from the law" (Matthew 5:18).

BIBLIOGRAPHY

This bibliography contains two sections: (1) Books; and (2) Articles, Sermons, and Videos. The Books section includes books on CD-ROM. The Articles, Sermons, and Videos section includes articles from periodicals, essays from books, sermons in books, and sermons on cassette.

BOOKS

Adams, Thomas. *A Commentary on the Second Epistle General of St. Peter.* Revised by James Sherman. Ligonier, PA: Soli Deo Gloria Publications, 1990.

Ainsworth, Henry. *Annotation upon the Second Book of Moses Called Exodus: wherein, by Conferring the Holy Scriptures, Comparing the Chaldee and Greek Versions, and Other Records of the Hebrewes: Moses His Wordes, Lawes and Ordinances Are Explained.* London: n. p., 1617.

Aland, Kurt, Matthew Black, Carlo M. Martini, Bruce M. Metzger, and Allen Wikgren, eds. *The Greek New Testament*, 3d ed. NY: American Bible Society, 1975.

Allen, F. Sturges ed. *Webster's New International Dictionary of the English Language.* Springfield, MA: G. & C. Merriam Company, 1923.

Arndt, William F. and F. Wilbur Gingrich. *A Greek-English Lexicon of the New Testament and Other Early Christian Literature: A translation and adaptation of the fourth revised and augmented edition of Walter Bauer's Griechisch-Deutsches Wörterbuch zu den Schriften des Neuen Testaments und der übrigen urchristlichen Literatur*, 2d ed. Chicago: University of Chicago, 1979.

Armitage, Thomas. *The History of the Baptists: Traced by Their Vital Principles and Practices, from the Time of Our Lord and Saviour Jesus Christ to the Year 1886.* 2 vols. Watertown, WI: Maranatha Baptist Press, 1980.

Balz, Horst and Gerhard Schneider, eds. *Exegetical Dictionary of the New Testament*, 3 vols. Grand Rapids: Eerdmans, 1991.

Barnes, Albert. *Barnes' Notes on the Bible*, 18 vols., in *The Master Christian Library*, version 8 [CD-ROM]. Rio, Mich.: Ages Software, 2000.

Beacham, Roy E. and Kevin T. Bauder, eds. *One Bible Only? Examining Exclusive Claims for the King James Bible*. Grand Rapids: Kregel, 2001.

Beare, Francis Wright. *The Gospel according to Matthew*. San Francisco: Harper & Row, Publishers, 1981.

Bengel, John Albert. *New Testament Word Studies*, 2 vols. Trans. by Charlton T. Lewis and Marvin R. Vincent. Grand Rapids: Kregel, 1971.

Betts, Gavin. *Teach Yourself Latin: A Complete Course*. Chicago: NTC Publishing Group, 1992.

Blass, F. and A. Debrunner. *A Greek Grammar of the New Testament and Other Early Christian Literature: A Translation and Revision of the ninth-tenth German Edition incorporating supplementary notes of A. Debrunner, by Robert W. Funk*. Chicago: The University of Chicago Press, 1961.

Boice, James Montgomery. *The Gospel of John*, 5 vols. Grand Rapids: Baker Books, 1999.

Botterweck, G. Johannes, Helmer Ringgren, and Heinz-Josef Fabry, eds. *Theological Dictionary of the Old Testament: the Authorized and Unabridged Translation of Theologisches Wörterbuch Zum Alten Testament*, 14 vols. Translated by John T. Willis, David E. Green, and Douglas W. Stott. Grand Rapids: Eerdmans, 2000.

Brandenburg, Kent, ed. *Thou Shalt Keep Them: A Biblical Theology of the Perfect Preservation of Scripture*. El Sobrante, CA: Pillar & Ground Publishing, 2003.

Broadus, John A. *Commentary on Matthew*. Grand Rapids: Kregel, 1990.

Bromiley, Geoffrey W. *Theological Dictionary of the New Testament*, abridged in one volume. Edited by Gerhard Kittel and Gerhard Friedrich. Translated by Geoffrey Bromiley. Grand Rapids: Eerdmans, 2000.

Broughton, Hugh. *Daniel his Chaldee visions and his Hebrew: both translated after the original: and expounded both, by reduction of heathen most famous stories unto the exact propriety of his words (which is the surest certainty what he must mean) and by joining all the Bible, and learned tongues to the frame of his work.* London: Gabriel Simson, 1597.

Brown, Colin, ed. *The New International Dictionary of the New Testament Theology: Translated, with additions and revisions, from the German Theologisches Begriffslexikno Zum Neuen Testament, edited by Lothar Coenen, Erich Beyreuther, and Hans Bietenhard*, 3 vols. Grand Rapids: Zondervan, 1979.

Brown, Francis, S. R. Driver, and Charles A. Briggs. *A Hebrew and English Lexicon of the Old Testament with an Appendix Containing the Biblical Aramaic: Based on the Lexicon of William Gesenius as Translated by Edward Robinson.* Oxford: Clarendon Press, 1980.

Brown, Lesley, ed. *The New Shorter Oxford English Dictionary*, 2 vols. New York: Oxford University Press, 1993.

Brown, Raymond E., Joseph A. Fitzmyer, and Roland E. Murphy, ed. *The Jerome Biblical Commentary.* London: Prentice-Hall International, Inc., 1968.

Bruce, F. F. *The Epistle to the Hebrews* in *The New International Commentary on the New Testament.* Edited by Gordon D. Fee. Grand Rapids: Eerdmans, 1990.

Burnett, Stephen G. *From Christian Hebraism to Jewish Studies Johannes Buxtorf (1564-1629) and Hebrew Learning in the Seventeenth Century.* NY: E. J. Brill, 1996.

Bushell, Michael S. and Michael D. Tan. *BibleWorks* [CD-ROM]. Norfolk, VA: BibleWorks, LLC, 2003.

Buttrick, George A., ed. *The Interpreter's Bible: The Holy Scriptures in the King James Version and Revised Standard Version with General Articles and Introduction, Exegesis, Exposition for Each Book of the Bible.* Nashville: Abingdon Press, 1953-1956.

Buxtorf, John. *Thesaurus Grammaticus Linguae Sanctae Bebraeae.* Basil: Conrad Waldkirch, 1609. In the Caspari Library of the University of Pennsylvania.

Buxtorf, John, Jr. *Tractatus de Punctorum Vocalium, et Accentuum, in Libris Veteris Testamenti Hebraicis, Origine, Antiquitata, & Authoritate: oppositus Arcano Punctationis Revelato, Ludovici Cappelli.* Basil: Martini Wagneri, 1648.

Calvin, John. *Calvin's Commentaries.* 22 vols. Edinburgh: Calvin Translation Society, n.d. Reprinted Grand Rapids: Baker Book House, 2005.

Cathcart, William, ed. *The Baptist Encyclopedia: A Dictionary of the Doctrines, Ordinances, Usages, Confessions of Faith, Sufferings, Labors, and Successes, and of the General History of the Baptist Denomination in all Lands.* Philadelphia: Louis H. Everts, 1881. Reprinted Paris, Arkansas: The Baptist Standard Bearer, 1988.

Chafer, Lewis Sperry and John F. Walvoord. *Major Bible Themes.* Grand Rapids: Zondervan, 1974.

Christian, John T. *A History of the Baptists: Together with Some Account of Their Principles and Practices.* 2 vols. Texarkana, Arkansas: Bogard Press, 1922.

Clarke, Adam. *Clarke's Commentary*, 8 vols., in *The Master Christian Library*, version 8 [CD-ROM]. Albany, OR: Ages Software, 1997.

Clark, Samuel. *The Divine Authority of the Holy Scriptures Asserted in Two Discourses: The former shewing The Nature and Extent of the Inspiration vouchsafed by the Holy Ghost to the Penmen of the Scriptures, and the distinct share of each therein. The latter shewing the Divine Authority of the Vowels and Accents in the Hebrew Text; by new and intrinsic Arguments: in a Discourse concerning the Division of the Bible into Chapters and Verses.* London: St. Paul's Church-yard, 1699.

Cloud, David W. *Things Hard to be Understood: A Handbook of Biblical Difficulties.* Port Huron, MI: Way of Life Literature, 2001.

Collett, Sidney. *All About the Bible: Its Origin—Its Language—Its Translation—Its Canon—Its Symbols—Its Inspiration—Its Alleged Errors and Contradictions—Its Plan—Its Science—Its Rivals.* Westwood, NJ: Fleming H. Revell, 1964.

Comfort, Philip Wesley, ed. *The Origin of the Bible.* Wheaton, IL: Tyndale House Publishers, Inc., 1992.

Cooper, Joseph. מפתח בית משה או סיג לתורה *Hoc est Domus Mosaicae Clavis, sive Legis Sepimentum: In quo punctorum Hebraicorum adstruitur antiquitas: Eaque omnia, cum accentualia tum vocalia, ipsis literis fuisse coaeva, argumentis, undique petitis, demonstratur. Quae vero in contrarium ab Elia Levita Primipilo, Ludovia Capelli, D. Doctore Waltone* . . . . London: T. R., 1673.

Cramp, J. M. *Baptist History: from the Foundation of the Christian Church to the Close of the Eighteenth Century.* Philadelphia: American Baptist Publication Society, n.d.

Dana, H. E. and Julius R. Mantey. *A Manual Grammar of the Greek New Testament.* Toronto: MacMillan, 1957.

Davidson, Benjamin. *The Analytical Hebrew and Chaldee Lexicon.* Grand Rapids: Zondervan, 1970.

Davies, W. D. and Dale C. Allison. *A Critical and Exegetical Commentary on The Gospel According to Saint Matthew,* 3 vols., in *The International Critical Commentary on the Holy Scriptures of the Old and New Testaments.* Edited by J. A. Emerson, C. E. B. Cranfield, and G. N. Stanton. Edinburgh: T & T Clark, 1988.

Davis, John. *A Short Translation to the Hebrew Tongue, Being a translation of the Learned John Buxtorfius' epitomi of his Hebrew Grammar: that those which are ignorant of the Latin tongue, may attaine by this English introduction to the knowledge and apprehension of the originall Text of Scripture.* London: Roger Daniel, 1655.

De' Rossi, Azariah. *The Light of the Eyes.* Translated from the Hebrew with an introduction and annotations by Joanna Weinberg. New Haven, CT: Yale University Press, 2000.

Donnegan, James. *A New Greek and English Lexicon; Principally on the Plan of the Greek and German Lexicon of Schneider: the Words Alphabetically Arranged; Distinguishing such as Are Poetical, of Dialectic Variety, or Peculiar to Certain Writers and Classes of Writers; with Examples, Literally Translated, Selected from the Classical Writers.* Revised by R. B. Patton. Boston: Hilliard, Gray & Co., 1837.

Driver, S. R. *Notes on the Hebrew Text and Typography of the Books of Samuel.* Oxford: At the Clarendon Press, 1913.

Dunbar, George. *A New Greek and English and English and Greek Lexicon with An Appendix, Explanatory of Scientific Terms, &c.* Edinburgh: Maclachlan, Stewart, and Co., 1840. In Dartmouth College Rauner Rare Book Collection.

Easton, M. G. *Easton's Bible Dictionary* in *The Master Christian Library*, version 8 [CD-ROM]. Albany, OR: Ages Software, 1996.

Edersheim, Alfred. *Bible History Old Testament.* Peabody: Hendrickson Publishers, Inc., 1995.

_____. *Sketches of Jewish Social Life.* Updated edition. Peabody: Hendrickson Publishers, Inc., 1994.

_____. *The Life and Times of Jesus the Messiah*, 2 vols. New York: Longmans, Green, and Co., 1912.

Elliger, Karl and Wilhelm Rudolph, eds. *Biblia Hebraica Stuttgartensia.* Stuttgart: Deutsche Bibelstiftung, 1977.

Eisemann, Moshe. *I Chronicles / A New Translation with a Commentary Anthologized from Talmudic, Midrashic and Rabbinic Sources.* Brooklyn, NY: Mesorah Publications, ltd., 1987.

Eisenberg, Azriel. *The Book of Books: The Story of the Bible Text.* New York: The Soncino Press Limited, 1976.

Exell, Joseph S., ed. *The Biblical Illustrator.* 23 vols. Grand Rapids: Baker, n. d.

Fairbairn, Patrick. *Commentary on Ezekiel.* Grand Rapids: Kregel Publications, 1989.

Fausset, A. R. *Fausset's Bible Dictionary* in *The Master Christian Library*, version 8 [CD-ROM]. Albany, OR: Ages Software, 1997.

Fenton, J. C. *The Gospel of St. Matthew* in *The Pelican Gospel Commentaries.* Edited by D. E. Nineham. Baltimore: Penguin Books, 1963.

Filson, Floyd V. *A Commentary on The Gospel According to St. Matthew* in *Harper's New Testament Commentaries.* Edited by Henry Chadwick. NY: Harper & Brothers, Publishers, 1960.

Fradersdorff, J. W. *A Copious Phraseological English-Lexicon*. Revised by Thomas Kerchever Arnold and Henry Browne. 2nd ed. London: Rivingtons, 1860.

Friberg, Timothy and Barbara Friberg. *Analytical Greek New Testament*. Grand Rapids: Baker, 1981.

Geisler, Norman and Thomas Howe. *When Critics Ask: A Popular Handbook on Bible Difficulties*. Wheaton: Victor Books, 1992.

Gill, John. *A Complete Body of Doctrinal and Practical Divinity: Or a System of Evangelical Truths Deduced from the Sacred Scriptures*. Paris, Arkansas: The Baptist Standard Bearer, 1989.

᠆᠆᠆᠆᠆᠆᠆᠆. *A Dissertation Concerning the Antiquity of the Hebrew Language, Letters, Vowel-Points, and Accents*. London: G. Keith, 1767.

᠆᠆᠆᠆᠆᠆᠆᠆. *Exposition of the Old Testament*, 6 vols. London: Matthews & Leigh, 1810. Reprinted Paris, Arkansas: The Baptist Standard Bearer, 1989.

᠆᠆᠆᠆᠆᠆᠆᠆. *John Gill's Expositor*. Edited and revised and updated for *Online Bible* by Larry Pierce [CD-ROM]. Winterbourne, Ontario: Timnath-serah, Inc., 2002.

᠆᠆᠆᠆᠆᠆᠆᠆. *The Collected Works of John Gill*, version 2.0 [CD-ROM]. Paris, Arkansas: The Baptist Standard Bearer, 2003.

Ginsburg, Christian D. *Jacob Ben Chajim Ibn Adonijah's Introduction to The Rabbinic Bible, Hebrew and English; with Explanatory Notes*, 2nd edition, in *The Library of Biblical Studies*. Edited by Harry M. Orlinsky. NY: KTAV Publishing House, Inc., 1968.

᠆᠆᠆᠆᠆᠆᠆᠆. *The Massoreth Ha-Massoreth of Elias Levita, Being an Exposition of the Massoretic Notes on the Hebrew Bible, or the Ancient Critical Apparatus of the Old Testament in Hebrew, with an English Translation, and Critical and Explanatory Notes, by Christian D. Ginsburg*. NY: KTAV Publishing House, Inc., 1968.

Girdlestone, Robert B. *Synonyms of the Old Testament: Their Bearing on Christian Doctrine*, 2d ed. Grand Rapids: Eerdmans, 1978.

Godet, Frederick Louis. *A Commentary on the Gospel of St. Luke*. New York: Funk & Wagnals, 1887.

Gouge, William. *Commentary on Hebrews.* Grand Rapids: Kregel Publications, 1980.

Gray, James M. *The Concise Bible Commentary* in *The Master Christian Library*, version 8 [CD-ROM]. Albany, OR: Ages Software, 1999.

Green, Joel B. *The Gospel of Luke* in *The New International Commentary on the New Testament.* Edited by Ned B. Stonehouse, F. F. Bruce, and Gordon D. Fee. Grand Rapids: Eerdmans, 1997.

Green, William Henry. *General Introduction to the Old Testament: the Text.* NY: Charles Scribner's Sons, 1899.

Greene, Oliver B. *The Epistle of Paul the Apostle to the Hebrews.* Greenville, SC: The Gospel Hour, Inc., 1976.

_____. *The Gospel According to John*, 3 vols. Greenville, SC: The Gospel Hour, Inc., 1966.

_____. *Thy Word Above All.* Greenville, SC: The Gospel Hour, Inc., 1971.

Grisanti, Michael A., ed. *The Bible Version Debate: The Perspective of Central Baptist Theological Seminary.* Plymouth, MN: Central Baptist Theological Seminary, 1997.

Gundry, Robert H. *Matthew: A Commentary on His Literary and Theological Art.* Grand Rapids: Eerdmans, 1982.

Haik-Vantoura, Suzanne. *The Music of the Bible Revealed.* Trans. by Dennis Weber. Edited by John Wheeler. Berkeley, CA: Bibal Press, 1991.

Haley, John W. *Alleged Discrepancies.* Springdale, PA: Whitaker House, n. d.

Hannah, Robert. *A Grammatical Aid to the Greek New Testament.* Grand Rapids: Baker, 1983.

Harrington, Daniel J. *The Gospel of Matthew*, vol. 1 in *Sacra Pagina Series.* Edited by Daniel J. Harrington. Collegeville, MN: The Liturgical Press, 1991.

Harris, R. Laird, ed. *Theological Wordbook of the Old Testament*, 2 vols. Chicago: Moody, 1981.

Harrison, Roland Kenneth. *Introduction to the Old Testament.* Grand Rapids: Eerdmans Publishing Co., 1969. Reprint, Peabody, MA: Prince Press, 1999.

Hastings, James, ed. *A Dictionary of the Bible Dealing with Its Language, Literature, and Contents,* 5 vols. Edinburgh: T & T Clark, 1904.

Hebrew Old Testament. London: Trinitarian Bible Society, 1998.

Hendriksen, William. *Exposition of the Gospel According to Luke.* Grand Rapids: Baker, 1981.

_____. *Exposition of the Gospel According to Matthew.* Grand Rapids: Baker, 1982.

Hengstenberg, E. W. *The Prophecies of the Prophet Ezekiel Elucidated.* Trans. by A. C. Murphy and J. G. Murphy. Edinburgh: T & T Clark, 1869. Reprinted Eugene, OR: Wipf and Stock Publishers, n. d.

Henry, Matthew. *Matthew Henry's Commentary on the Whole Bible.* 6 vols. Peabody: Hendrickson Publishers, Inc., 1991.

Heppe, Heinrich. *Reformed Dogmatics: Set Out and Illustrated from Sources.* Revised and edited by Ernst Bizer. Trans. by G. T. Thomson. London: George Allen & Unwin Ltd., 1950.

Hiebert, D. Edmond. *Second Peter and Jude: An Expositional Commentary.* Greenville, SC: Unusual Publications, 1989.

Hills, Edward F. *Believing Bible Study,* 2d ed. Des Moines: The Christian Research Press, 1977.

_____. *The King James Version Defended: A Space-Age Defense of the Historic Christian Faith,* 3d ed. Des Moines: The Christian Research Press, 1973.

Hindson, Edward E. and Woodrow Michael Kroll, eds. *The KJV Parallel Bible Commentary.* Nashville: Thomas Nelson Publishers, 1994.

Hiscox, Edward T. *The New Directory for Baptist Churches.* Grand Rapids: Kregel Publications, 1978.

Hodges, John C. and Mary E. Whitten. *Harbrace College Handbook 7th Edition.* New York: Harcourt Brace Jovanovich, Inc., 1972.

Hutcheson, George. *An Exposition of John's Gospel*. Grand Rapids: Sovereign Grace Publishers, 1971.

Jenkens, Charles A., editor. *Baptist Doctrines: Being an Exposition, in a Series of Essays by Representative Baptist Ministers, of the Distinctive Points of Baptist Faith and Practice*. St. Louis: C. R. Barns Publishing Co., 1890. Reprinted Watertown, WI: Baptist Heritage Press, 1989.

Johnson, Luke Timothy. *The Gospel of Luke*, vol. 3 in *Sacra Pagina Series*. Edited by Daniel J. Harrington. Collegeville, MN: The Liturgical Press, 1991.

Josephus, Flavius. *The Works of Josephus*. Translated by William Whitson. Peabody: Hendrickson Publishers, Inc., 1987.

Kaiser, Jr., Walter C., Peter H. Davids, F. F. Bruce, and Manfred T. Brauch. *Hard Sayings of the Bible*. Downers Grove, IL: InterVarsity Press, 1996.

Kautzsch, E., ed. *Gesenius' Hebrew Grammar*, 2d ed. Revised in accordance with the 29th ed. by A. E. Cowley. Oxford: Clarendon Press, 1982.

Keener, Craig S. *A Commentary on the Gospel of Matthew*. Grand Rapids: Eerdmans, 1999.

Keil, C. F. *Introduction to the Old Testament*, 2 vols. Translated by G. C. M. Douglas. Edinburgh: T & T Clark, 1869. Reprinted Peabody, MA: Hendrickson Publishers, Inc., 1991.

Keil, C. F. and F. Delitzsch. *Commentary on the Old Testament*, 10 vols. Edinburgh: T & T Clark, 1866-91. Reprinted Peabody: Hendrickson Publishers, Inc., 2001.

Kelley, Page H. *Biblical Hebrew: An Introductory Grammar*. Grand Rapids: Eerdmans, 1992.

Kelly, Balmer H. *The Layman's Bible Commentary*. Richmond, VA: John Knox Press, 1960.

Kent, Homer A. *The Epistle to the Hebrews: A Commentary*. Grand Rapids: Baker Book House, 1972.

Kittel, Gerhard, and Gerhard Friedrich, eds. *Theological Dictionary of the New Testament.* Translated and edited by Geoffrey W. Bromiley, 10 vols. Grand Rapids: Eerdmans, 1993.

Knight III, George W. *The Pastoral Epistles* in *The New International Greek Testament Commentary.* Edited by I. Howard Marshall and W. Ward Gasque. Grand Rapids: William B. Eerdmans Publishing Company, 1992.

Kulus, Chester. *Those So-Called Errors: Debunking the Liberal, New Evangelical, and Fundamentalist Myth that You Should Not Hear, Receive, and Believe All the Numbers of Scripture.* Newington, CT: Emmanuel Baptist Theological Press, 2003.

Lambdin, Thomas O. *Introduction to Biblical Hebrew.* New York: Charles Scribner's Sons, 1971.

Lampe, G. W. H., ed. *The Cambridge History of the Bible*, 3 vols. Cambridge: At the University Press, 1969.

Lange, John Peter. *The Gospel According to Matthew* in *A Commentary on the Holy Scriptures: Critical, Doctrinal, and Homiletical, with Special Reference to Ministers and Students.* Translated and edited by Philip Schaff. New York: Charles Scribner & Co., 1868.

_____. *The Life of the Lord Jesus Christ: A Complete Critical Examination of the Origin, Contents and Connection of the Gospels*, 4 vols. Edited by Marcus Dods. Grand Rapids: Zondervan, 1958.

Lenski, R. C. H. *The Interpretation of St. Luke's Gospel.* Minneapolis: Augsburg Publishing House, 1963.

_____. *The Interpretation of St. Matthew's Gospel.* Minneapolis: Augsburg Publishing House, 1963.

Levita, Elias. *The Massoreth Ha-Massoreth of Elias Levita, Being an Exposition of the Massoretic Notes on the Hebrew Bible, or the Ancient Critical Apparatus of the Old Testament in Hebrew, with an English Translation, and Critical and Explanatory Notes, by Christian D. Ginsburg.* NY: KTAV Publishing House, Inc., 1968.

Liddell, Henry George and Robert Scott. *A Greek-English Lexicon*, 9th ed., 2 volumes. Revised by Henry Stuart Jones. Oxford: The University Press, 1951.

Lightner, Robert. *The Saviour and The Scriptures*. Grand Rapids: Baker, 1978.

Lindsell, Harold. *The Battle for the Bible*. Grand Rapids: Zondervan, 1977.

Lightfoot, John. *The Whole Works of the Rev. John Lightfoot, D. D.* Edited by John Rogers Pitman. 10 vols. London: J. F. Dove, 1825.

Lockyer, Herbert. *All the Doctrines of the Bible*. Grand Rapids: Zondervan, 1964.

Lunemann, Gottlieb. *Critical and Exegetical Handbook to the Epistle to the Hebrews*. Translated by Maurice J. Evans. In *Critical and Exegetical Commentary of the New Testament* by Heinrich August Wilhelm Meyer. Edinburgh: T & T Clark, 1882.

Luz, Ulrich. *Matthew 1-7: A Commentary*. Translated by Wilhelm C. Linss. Augsburg, MN: Augsburg Fortress, 1985.

Marshall, I. Howard. *The Gospel of Luke: A Commentary on the Greek Text* in *The New International Greek Testament Commentary*. Edited by I. Howard Marshall and W. Ward Gasque. Grand Rapids: Eerdmans, 1978.

McClintock, John and James Strong, eds. *Cyclopedia of Biblical, Theological, and Ecclesiastical Literature*, 12 volumes. New York: Harper & Brothers, 1891.

McComiskey, Thomas Edward, ed. *The Minor Prophets*, 3 volumes. Grand Rapids: Baker, 2000.

M'Intosh, Hugh. *Is Christ Infallible and the Bible True?* Edinburgh: T & T Clark, 1902. Reprinted, Minneapolis: Klock & Klock, 1981.

Mead, Frank S. and Samuel S. Hill. *Handbook of Denominations in the United States*, 11th ed. Rev. by Craig D. Atwood. Nashville: Abingdon Press, 2001.

Meyer, Heinrich August Wilhelm. *Critical and Exegetical Handbook to the Gospels of Mark and Luke*, 2 volumes. Translated from the 5th German edition by Robert Ernest Wallis. Revised and edited by Frederick Crombie. Edinburgh: T & T Clark, 1880.

_____. *Critical and Exegetical Handbook to the Gospel of Matthew*, 2 volumes. Translated from the 6th German edition by Peter Christie. Revised and edited by Frederick Crombie. Edinburgh: T & T Clark, 1894.

Moncrieff, John. *An Essay on the Antiquity and Utility of the Hebrew Vowel-Points; with an Introduction Stating the Importance of the Question, and the Proper Manner of Discussing it – Likewise showing the Principal Advantages of Reading with the Points, and that the Difficulties have been Improperly Magnified. An Appendix is Added, Giving a Concise View of the Vowel-Points, Their Grammatical Changes, and Their Great use in Determining the Precise Meaning of Words.* London: Whittaker, Treacher, and Arnot, 1833.

Morgan, G. Campbell. *The Gospel According to John.* Old Tappan, NJ: Fleming H. Revell, n.d.

Morris, Henry M. *The Defender's Study Bible.* Iowa Falls: World Publishing, 1995.

Morris, Leon. *The Gospel According to John*, revised edition, in *The New International Commentary on the New Testament.* Edited by Ned B. Stonehouse, F. F. Bruce, and Gordon D. Fee. Grand Rapids: Eerdmans, 1995.

Morris, William, ed. *The American Heritage Dictionary of the English Language.* Boston: Houghton Mifflin, 1982.

Mounce, William D. *Basics of Biblical Greek Grammar.* Grand Rapids: Zondervan, 1993.

Muller, Richard A. *Dictionary of Latin and Greek Theological Terms Drawn Principally from Protestant Scholastic Theology.* Grand Rapids: Baker Book House, 1985.

Neilson, William Allan, ed. *Webster's New International Dictionary of the English Language.* 2nd ed. Springfield, MA: G & C Merriam Company, Publishers, 1961.

Nicoll, W. Robertson, ed. *The Expositor's Bible*, 6 vols. Grand Rapids: Wm. B. Eerdmans Publishing Co., 1947.

Online Bible Millennium Edition [CD-ROM]. Winterbourne, Ontario: Timnathserah Inc., 2002.

Orchard, Dom Bernard, ed. *A Catholic Commentary on Holy Scripture*. NY: Thomas Nelson and Sons Ltd., 1953.

Orchard, G. H. *A Concise History of Baptists*. Texarkana, Arkansas: Bogard Press, 1977.

Owen, John. *An Exposition of the Epistle to the Hebrews with Preliminary Exercitations*. 7 vols. Edited by W. H. Goold. Edinburgh: Johnstone and Hunter, 1855. Reprinted Carlisle: PA: Banner of Truth Trust, 1991.

_____. *The Works of John Owen*, 23 volumes. Edited by William H. Goold [CD-ROM]. Albany, OR: Ages Software, 2000.

Owen, John Joseph. *Analytical Key to the Old Testament*, 4 vols. Grand Rapids: Baker, 2000.

Pasor, George. *Lexicon Graeco-Latinum In novum domini nostri Iesu Christi testamentum, ubi omnium vocabulorum Graecorum themata indicantur, & utraque tam themata quam deriuata grammatice resoluuntur*. London: Apud Iohannem Billium, 1621.

Patte, Daniel. *The Gospel According to Matthew: A Structural Commentary on Matthew; Faith*. Philadelphia: Fortress, 1973.

Perowne, J. J. Stewart, ed. *Cambridge Bible for Schools and Colleges*. Cambridge: At the University Press, 1916.

Perschbacher, Wesley J. *The New Analytical Greek Lexicon*. Peabody, MA: Hendrickson Publishers, 1990.

Pickering, Wilbur N. *The Identity of the New Testament Text*, rev. ed. Nashville: Thomas Nelson Publishers, 1980.

Piscator, Johannes. *Analysis logica evangelii secundum Lucam Una cum scholis et observationibus locorum doctrinae*. London: Richardus Field, 1596.

_____. *Analysis logica evangelii secundum Matthaeum Una cum scholis et observationibus locorum doctrinae*. London: Richard Field, 1594.

Pink, Arthur. *The Divine Inspiration of the Bible* in *The Master Christian Library*, version 8 [CD-ROM]. Albany, OR: Ages Software, 1997.

Plummer, Alfred. *A Critical and Exegetical Commentary on the Gospel according to St. Luke.* Edinburgh: T & T Clark, 1913.

_____. *An Exegetical Commentary on the Gospel according to St. Matthew.* Grand Rapids: Eerdmans, 1956.

Poole, Matthew. *A Commentary on the Holy Bible*, 3 vols. McLean, VA: Macdonald Publishing Co., n. d.

Prideaux, John. *Viginti-duae lectiones de totidem relgionis captibus, praecipue hoc tempore controversis, prout publice habebantur oxoniae in vesperiis.* Oxoniae: Excedebat Hen. Hall, Impensis Hen. Cripps, Hen. Curteyn & Thom. Robinson, 1648.

Roberts, Alexander and James Donaldson, eds. *The Ante-Nicene Fathers: The Writings of the Fathers down to A. D. 325*, 10 vols. Edited by Alexander Roberts and James Donaldson. Revised by A. Cleveland Coxe. Peabody: Hendrickson Publishers, Inc., 1994.

Robertson, A. T. *A Grammar of the Greek New Testament in the Light of Historical Research.* Nashville: Broadman Press, 1934.

_____. *Word Pictures in the New Testament*, 6 vols. Nashville, TN: Broadman Press, 1930.

Robertson, Archibald and Alfred Plummer. *A Critical and Exegetical Commentary on the First Epistle of St. Paul to the Corinthians* in *The International Critical Commentary on the Holy Scriptures of the Old and New Testaments.* Edited by Samuel Rolles Driver, Alfred Plummer, and Charles Augustus Briggs. Edinburgh: T & T Clark, 1978.

Robertson, James. *Clavis Pentateuchi, sive Analysis omnium vocum hebraicarum suo ordine in Pentateucho Moseos occurrentium: una cum versione latina et anglica: notis criticus et philologicus adjectis; in quibus, ex lingua arabica, Judaeorum moribus, et doctorum iteneraiis, plurium locorum S. S. sensus eruitur, novaque versione illustratur. In usum juventutis academicae edinburgenae. Cui praemittuntur dissertationes duae; I. De antiquitate linguae arabicae, ejusque convenientia cum lingua hebraea, etc. II. De genuina punctorum vocalium antiquitate, contra clariss. Capellum,*

Waltonum, Masclefum, Hutchinsonium. Edinburg: R. Fleming and P. and A. Neill, 1770.

Ruckman, Peter S. *The "Errors" in the King James Bible.* Pensacola, FL: Bible Baptist Bookstore, 1999.

Ryle, J. C. *Expository Thoughts on John*, 3 volumes. Carlisle, PA: The Banner of Truth Trust, 1986.

_____. *Expository Thoughts on Luke*, 2 volumes. Carlisle, PA: The Banner of Truth Trust, 1986.

_____. *Expository Thoughts on Matthew.* Carlisle, PA: The Banner of Truth Trust, 1986.

Schaff, Philip, ed. *Nicene and Post-Nicene Fathers: First Series.* 14 vols. Peabody: Hendrickson Publishers, Inc., 1994.

Schaff, Philip and Henry Wace, eds. *Nicene and Post-Nicene Fathers: Second Series.* 14 vols. Peabody: Hendrickson Publishers, Inc., 1994.

Schrevelius. *The Greek Lexicon of Schrevelius Translated into English with Many Additions.* Boston: Cummings, Hilliard, and Company, 1826. In Dartmouth College Rauner Rare Book Collection.

Schurer, Emil. *A History of the Jewish People in the Time of Jesus Christ: Being a Second and Revised Editions of a "Manual of the History of New Testament Times,"* 3 vols. Trans. by Sophia Taylor and Peter Christie. Peabody, MA: Hendrickson Publishers, 1995.

Schweizer, Eduard. *The Good News According to Matthew.* Trans. by David E. Green. Atlanta: John Knox Press, 1975.

Scofield, C. I., ed. *The Scofield Study Bible.* New York: Oxford University Press, 1945.

_____. *The New Scofield Reference Bible.* New York: Oxford University Press, 1967.

Scott, Thomas. *The Holy Bible Containing the Old and New Testaments, with Original Notes, Practical Observations and Copious References*, 6 volumes. New York: Whiting and Watson, 1812.

Scrivener, Frederick H. A. *Scrivener's Annotated Greek New Testament: Being the Exact Greek Textus Receptus the Underlies the King James Bible*. Collingswood, NJ: Dean Burgon Society Press, 1999.

Senior, Donald. *Matthew* in *Abingdon New Testament Commentaries*. Edited by Victor Paul Furnish. Nashville: Abingdon Press, 1998.

Shedd, William G. T. *Dogmatic Theology*. 3 vols. Minneapolis: Klock & Klock, 1979.

Simpson, J. A. and E. S. C. Weiner, eds. *The Oxford English Dictionary*, 20 vols. Oxford: Clarendon Press, 1989.

Singer, Isidore, ed. *The Jewish Encyclopedia: a Descriptive Record of the History, Religion, Literature, and Customs of the Jewish People from the Earliest Times to the Present Day*. 12 volumes. New York: Funk and Wagnalls Company, 1907.

Smith, Henry Preserved. *A Critical and Exegetical Commentary on the Books of Samuel*. Edinburgh: T & T Clark, 1899.

Smith, John C. P. *Every Joy & Tittle—A Study of Matthew 5$^{17-20}$* available on http:\www.jotandtittle.co.uk. Internet.

Sorenson, David H. *Touch Not The Unclean Thing: The Text Issue and Separation*. Duluth, MN: Northstar Baptist Ministries, 2001.

Spence, H. D. M. and Joseph S. Exell, eds. *The Pulpit Commentary*. 23 vols. Peabody: Hendrickson Publishers, Inc., n. d.

Strong, Augustus H. *Systematic Theology*. Valley Forge: Judson Press, 1976.

Strouse, Thomas M. *"But My Words Shall Not Pass Away": The Biblical Defense of the Doctrine of the Preservation of Scripture*. Newington, CT: Emmanuel Baptist Theological Press, 2001.

_____. *I Will Build My Church: The Doctrine and History of Baptists*. Newington, CT: Emmanuel Baptist Theological Press, 2001.

_____. *Sound Doctrine: The Theology of I and II Timothy*. Newington, CT: Emmanuel Baptist Theological Press, 2001.

_____. *The Lord God Hath Spoken: A Guide to Bibliology*. Newington: Emmanuel Theological Press, 2001.

Strouse, Thomas M. and Jeffrey Khoo. *Reviews of the book From the Mind of God to the Mind of Man*. Pensacola: Pensacola Theological Seminary, 2001.

Tenney, Merrill C., ed. *The Bible – The Living Word of Revelation*. Grand Rapids: Zondervan, 1968.

_____, ed. *The Zondervan Pictorial Encyclopedia of the Bible*, 5 vols. Grand Rapids: Zondervan, 1976.

Thayer, Joseph H. *A Greek-English Lexicon of the New Testament*. Grand Rapids: Baker, 1977.

The Holy Bible Containing the Old and New Testaments: Revised Standard Version. NY: Thomas Nelson & Sons, 1952.

The Holy Bible, English Standard Version. Wheaton, IL: Good News Publishers, 2001.

The Holy Scriptures of the Old Testament Hebrew and English. London: The British & Foreign Bible Society, n. d.

Theissen, Henry Clarence. *Introductory Lectures in Systematic Theology*. Grand Rapids: Eerdmans, 1976.

Thomas, David. *The Genius of the Fourth Gospel: The Gospel of John, Exegetically and Practically Considered, Containing One Hundred and Two Homiletic Sketches and Fifty-One Germs of Thought*. London: R. D. Dickinson, 1885.

Thompson, Frank Charles. *The Thompson Chain-Reference Bible*, fifth ed. Indianapolis: B. B. Kirkbride Bible Co., 2000.

Torbet, Robert G. *A History of the Baptists*. Third ed. Valley Forge: Judson Press, 1980.

Torrey, R. A., A. C. Dixon, et al., eds. *The Fundamentals – A Testimony to the Truth*, 4 vols. in *The Master Christian Library*, version 8 [CD-ROM]. Rio, WI: Ages Software, 2000.

Trench, Richard C. *Synonyms of the New Testament*, 9th ed. Grand Rapids: Eerdmans, 1980.

Turretin, Francis. *Institutes of Elentic Theology*. 3 vols. Trans. by George Musgrave Giger. Edited by James T. Dennison, Jr. Phillipsburg, NJ: P & R Publishing, 1992.

Unger, Merrill F. *Introductory Guide to the Old Testament*. Grand Rapids: Zondervan, 1979.

Vance, Laurence M. *Archaic Words and the Authorized Version*. Pensacola: Vance Publications, 1999.

Van Doren, W. H. *A Suggestive Commentary on St. Luke: with Critical and Homiletical Notes*. NY: I . K. Funk & Co., Publishers, 1867.

_____. *Gospel of John*. Grand Rapids: Kregel, 1981.

VanGemeren, Willem A., ed. *New International Dictionary of Old Testament Theology and Exegesis*, version 2.8 [CD-ROM]. Grand Rapids: Zondervan Reference Software, 2001.

Vanhetloo, Warren. "Hebrew Syntax 202 Syllabus." Lansdale, PA: Calvary Baptist School of Theology, 1980.

Van Oosterzee, J. J. *The Gospel According to Luke* in *A Commentary on the Holy Scriptures: Critical, Doctrinal, and Homiletical, with Special Reference to Ministers and Students*. Edited by John Peter Lange. Translated by Philip Schaff. Grand Rapids: Zondervan, n.d.

Vedder, Henry C. *A Short History of the Baptists*. Valley Forge: Judson Press, 1974.

Vine, W. E., Merrill F. Unger, and William White, Jr., eds. *Vine's Expository Dictionary of Biblical Words*. Nashville: Nelson, 1985.

Waite, D. A. *Defending the King James Version*. Collingswood, NJ: The Bible for Today Press, 1992.

_____. *Dr. Stewart Custer Answered on the T. R. & K. J. V.* Collingswood, NJ: The Bible for Today, 1985.

Wallace, Daniel B. *The Basics of New Testament Syntax*. Grand Rapids: Zondervan, 2000.

Waltke, Bruce K. and M. O'Connor. *An Introduction to Biblical Hebrew Syntax.* Winona Lake, IN: Eisenbraus, 1990.

Walton, Brian. *The Considerator Considered: or, A brief view of certain Considerations upon the Biblia Polyglotta, the Prolegomena and Appendix thereof.* London: Roycroft, 1659.

Warfield, Benjamin Breckinridge. *Revelation and Inspiration,* vol. 1 of *The Works of B. B. Warfield.* NY: Oxford University Press, 1932. Reprint, Grand Rapids: Baker Book House Company, 2003.

Weemes, John. *The Christian Synagogue: Wherein is contained the diverse Reading, The right Pointing, Translation, and Collation of Scripture with Scripture.* London: T. and B. Gates, 1630.

Wenham, John W. *Christ and the Bible.* London: Tyndale Press, 1972.

Whitaker, William. *A Disputation on Holy Scripture Against the Papists Especially Bellarmine and Stapleton.* Trans. and edited by William Fitzgerald. Cambridge: Parker Society, 1849. Reprint, Morgan, PA: Soli Deo Gloria Publications, 2000.

White, James R. *The King James Only Controversy: Can You Trust the Modern Versions?* Minneapolis: Bethany House Publishers, 1995.

Whitfield, Peter. *A dissertation on the Hebrew vowel-points. Shewing that they are an original and essential part of the language.* Liverpoole: Peter Whitfield, 1748.

Williams, James B., ed. *From the Mind of God to the Mind of Man: A Layman's Guide to How We Got Out Bible,* 3d ed. Greenville, SC: Ambassador-Emerald International, 1999.

Willoughby, C. Allen. *A Critical and Exegetical Commentary on The Gospel According to Saint Matthew,* 3rd ed., in *The International Critical Commentary on the Holy Scriptures of the Old and New Testaments.* Edited by Samuel Rolles Driver, Alfred Plummer, and Charles Augustus Briggs. Edinburgh: T & T Clark, 1985.

Wilson, Robert Dick. *A Scientific Investigation of the Old Testament.* Revised by Edward J. Young. Chicago: Moody Press, 1959.

Wilson, William. *Wilson's Old Testament Word Studies.* Peabody, MA: Hendrickson Publishers, n.d.

Wright, G. Ernest, John Bright, James Barr, and Peter Ackroyd, eds. *The Old Testament Library.* London: SCM Press Ltd., 1964.

Wuest, Kenneth S. *Wuest's Word Studies from the Greek New Testament*, 3 vols. Grand Rapids: Eerdmans, 1975.

Yates, Kyle M. *The Essentials of Biblical Hebrew.* Revised by John Joseph Owen. New York: Harper & Row, 1954.

Yeager, Randolph O. *Matthew 1-7* in *The Renaissance New Testament.* Gretna, LA: Pelican Publishing Co., 1986.

Zilberman, Shimon. *The Compact Up-to-Date English-Hebrew Hebrew-English Dictionary.* Jerusalem: Zilberman, 2001.

Zockler, Otto. *The First and Second Book of Chronicles* in *A Commentary on the Holy Scriptures: Critical, Doctrinal, and Homiletical, with Special Reference to Ministers and Students.* Edited by John Peter Lange. Translated by Philip Schaff. Grand Rapids: Zondervan, n. d.

Zodhiates, Spiros. *The Complete Word Study Bible & Reference CD* [CD-ROM]. Chattanooga, TN: AMG Publishers, 1997.

ARTICLES, SERMONS, AND VIDEOS

Anderson, Debra E. "A Brief History of the Hebrew Bible" available on http:\www.trinitarianbiblesociety.org. Internet.

Anderson, Robert. "Christ and Criticism" in *The Fundamentals – A Testimony to the Truth*, vol. 1. Edited by R. A. Torrey, A. C. Dixon, et. al. In *The Master Christian Library*, version 8 [CD-ROM]. Rio, WI: Ages Software, 2000.

Armitage, Thomas. "Baptist Faith and Practice," in *Baptist Doctrines: Being an Exposition, in a Series of Essays by Representative Baptist Ministers, of the Distinctive Points of Baptist Faith and Practice.* Edited by Charles Jenkins. St. Louis: C. R. Barns Publishing Co., 1890. Reprint, Watertown, WI: Baptist Heritage Press, 1989.

Barrick, William D. "Ancient Manuscripts and Biblical Exposition." *Master's Seminary Journal* 9 (Spring 1998): 25-38.

Beacham, Roy E. "The Old Testament Text and English Versions" in *The Bible Version Debate: The Perspective of Central Baptist Theological Seminary*. Edited by Michael A. Grisanti. Plymouth, MN: Central Baptist Theological Seminary, 1997.

Bennetch, John Henry. "The New Testament as Literature Part 1." *Bibliotheca Sacra* 107 (April 1950): 175-180.

Bettex, F. "The Bible and Modern Criticism" in *The Fundamentals – A Testimony to the Truth*, vol. 1. Edited by R. A. Torrey, A. C. Dixon, et. al. In *The Master Christian Library*, version 8 [CD-ROM]. Rio, WI: Ages Software, 2000.

Bishop, George Sayles. "The Inspiration of the Hebrew Letters and Vowel-Points." *Plains Baptist Challenger* L (July 1991): 47-52.

Borland, James A. "The Preservation of the New Testament Text: A Common Sense Approach." *Master's Seminary Journal* 10 (Spring 1999):41-51.

Brandenburg, Kent. "It Is Not Hidden, Neither Is It Far Off Deuteronomy 30:11-14," in *Thou Shalt Keep Them: A Biblical Theology of the Perfect Preservation of Scripture*. Edited by Kent Brandenburg. El Sobrante, CA: Pillar & Ground Publishing, 2003.

Brown, Harold O. J. "The Inerrancy and Infallibility of the Bible" in *The Origin of the Bible*. Edited by Philip Wesley Comfort. Wheaton, IL: Tyndale House Publishers, Inc., 1992.

Bruce, F. F. "The Bible" in *The Origin of the Bible*. Edited by Philip Wesley Comfort. Wheaton, IL: Tyndale House Publishers, Inc., 1992.

Caven, William. "The Testimony of Christ to the Old Testament" in *The Fundamentals – A Testimony to the Truth*, vol. 1. Edited by R. A. Torrey, A. C. Dixon, et. al. In *The Master Christian Library*, version 8 [CD-ROM]. Rio, WI: Ages Software, 2000.

Charles, J. Daryl. "The Greatest or the Least in the Kingdom?: The Disciple's Relationship to the Law (Matt 5:17-20)." *Trinity Journal* 13 (Fall 1992): 139-162.

Combs, William. "The Preservation of Scripture." *Detroit Baptist Seminary Journal* 5 (Fall 2000): 3-44.

Eichhorst, William R. "The Issue of Biblical Inerrancy in Definition and Defense." *Grace Theological Journal* 10 (Winter 1969): 3-17.

Fausset, A. R. "Old Testament" in *Fausset's Bible Dictionary*, vol. 3 in *The Master Christian Library*, version 8 [CD-ROM]. Albany, OR: Ages Software, 2000.

Frank, Harry Thomas. "Discovering the Scrolls" in *Understanding the Dead Sea Scrolls*. Edited by Hershel Shanks. NY: Random House, 1992.

Franklin, Carl D. "In Defense of Jehovah: An Analysis of the Article 'FACTS and *MYTHS* about the Sacred Name'." August 9, 1998. Available online at: http://www.biblestudy.org.

Fundamentalism and the Word of God. Allen Park, MI: Coalition for the Defense of the Scriptures, 1998. Videocassette.

Gaebelein, Frank E. "Towards a Christian Philosophy of Education." *Grace Theological Journal* 3 (Fall 1962): 3-11.

Glenny, W. Edward. "The Preservation of Scripture" in *The Bible Version Debate: The Perspective of Central Baptist Theological Seminary*. Edited by Michael A. Grisanti. Plymouth, MN: Central Baptist Theological Seminary, 1997.

Gray, James M. "The Inspiration of the Bible – Definition, Extent and Proof" in *The Fundamentals – A Testimony to the Truth*, vol. 2. Edited by R. A. Torrey, A. C. Dixon, et. al. In *The Master Christian Library*, version 8 [CD-ROM]. Rio, WI: Ages Software, 2000.

Hague, Dyson. "The History of the Higher Criticism" in *The Fundamentals – A Testimony to the Truth*, vol. 1. Edited by R. A. Torrey, A. C. Dixon, et. al. In *The Master Christian Library*, version 8 [CD-ROM]. Rio, WI: Ages Software, 2000.

Harris, R. Laird. "The Basis for Our Belief in Inerrancy." *Journal of the Evangelical Theological Society* 9 (Winter 1966): 13-18.

_____. "The Problem of Communication" in *The Bible – The Living Word of Revelation*. Edited by Merrill C. Tenney. Grand Rapids: Zondervan, 1968.

Henry, Carl F. H. "The Authority of the Bible" in *The Origin of the Bible*. Edited by Philip Wesley Comfort. Wheaton, IL: Tyndale House Publishers, Inc., 1992.

Holmes, Michael W. "Origen and The Inerrancy of Scripture." *Journal of the Evangelical Theological Society* 24 (September 1981): 221-231.

Johnson, Dell. *PCC's Response to Coalition Critics*. Pensacola: Pensacola Christian College, 1999. Videocassette.

_____. *Preservation of the Bible: A Bible Foundational Doctrine*. Pensacola: Pensacola Christian College, March 7, 2002. Cassette.

_____. *The Bible . . . Preserved from Satan's Attack*. Pensacola: Pensacola Christian College, 1996. Videocassette.

Johnson, Dell, J. Michael Bates, and Theodore Letis. *The Bible . . . The Text Is the Issue*. Pensacola: Pensacola Christian College, 1997. Videocassette.

Johnson, Dell and Theodore Letis. *The Leaven in Fundamentalism*. Pensacola: Pensacola Christian College, 1998. Videocassette.

Johnson, Franklin. "Fallacies of the Higher Criticism" in *The Fundamentals – A Testimony to the Truth*, vol. 1. Edited by R. A. Torrey, A. C. Dixon, et. al. In *The Master Christian Library*, version 8 [CD-ROM]. Rio, WI: Ages Software, 2000.

Levias, Casper. "Vocalization" in volume 12 of *The Jewish Encyclopedia: a Descriptive Record of the History, Religion, Literature, and Customs of the Jewish People from the Earliest Times to the Present Day.* Edited by Isidore Singer. New York: Funk and Wagnalls Company, 1907.

Lloyd-Jones, Martin. "Christ and the Old Testament" in *Studies in the Sermon on the Mount*, volume 1. Grand Rapids: Eerdmans, 1989.

_____. "Christ Fulfilling the Law and the Prophets" in *Studies in the Sermon on the Mount*, volume 1. Grand Rapids: Eerdmans, 1989.

Margolis, Max L. "Accents in Hebrew" in volume 1 of *The Jewish Encyclopedia: a Descriptive Record of the History, Religion, Literature, and Customs of the Jewish People from the Earliest Times to the Present Day.* Edited by Isidore Singer. New York: Funk and Wagnalls Company, 1907.

McClain, Alva J. "What Is 'The Law'?" *Bibliotheca Sacra* 110 (October 1953): 333-341.

McClintock, John and James Strong, eds.. "Criticism, Biblical" in *Cyclopedia of Biblical, Theological, and Ecclesiastical Literature*, vol. 2. New York: Harper & Brothers, 1883.

_____. "Unbelief" in *Cyclopedia of Biblical, Theological, and Ecclesiastical Literature*, vol. 10. New York: Harper & Brothers, 1891.

_____. "Vowel Points" in *Cyclopedia of Biblical, Theological, and Ecclesiastical Literature*, vol. 10. New York: Harper & Brothers, 1891.

Muller, Richard A. "The debate over the vowel points and the crisis in orthodox hermeneutics." *The Journal of Medieval and Renaissance Studies* 10 (Spring 1980): 53-72.

Mutsch, Greg. *Approaches to the Text Issue: Faith, Scientific, or Extremist* in *PCC's Response to Coalition Critics*. Pensacola: Pensacola Christian College, 1999. Videocassette.

Murphy, James G. "Introduction to the Bible" in *Barnes' Notes on the Bible, Volume 1 – Genesis* in *The Master Christian Library*, version 8 [CD-ROM]. Rio, WI: Ages Software, 2000.

Noordtzy, A. "The Old Testament Problem: Part 1." Trans. by Miner B. Stearm. *Bibliotheca Sacra* 97 (Oct. 1940): 456-475.

Oats, Larry. *Thou Shalt Keep Them: A Review by Larry Oats*. Watertown, WI: Maranatha Baptist Bible College, n. d.

Owen, John. "Of the Divine Original, Authority, Self-Evidencing Light, and Power of the Scriptures" in *The Works of John Owen*, vol. 16 in *The Works of John Owen*. Edited by William H. Goold. London: Johnstone & Hunter, 1850-53. Reprinted Carlisle, PA: The Banner of Truth Trust, 1968.

_____. "Of the Integrity and Purity of the Hebrew and Greek Text of the Scripture" in *The Works of John Owen*, vol. 16 in *The Works of John Owen*. Edited by William H. Goold. London: Johnstone & Hunter, 1850-53. Reprinted Carlisle, PA: The Banner of Truth Trust, 1968.

_____. "The Causes, Ways, and Means of Understanding the Mind of God as Revealed in His Word, with Assurance Therein" in A Discourse Concerning the Holy Spirit, Continued in *The Works of John Owen*, vol. 4 in *The Works of John Owen*. Edited by William H. Goold. London: Johnstone & Hunter, 1850-53. Reprinted Carlisle, PA: The Banner of Truth Trust, 1967.

Peterson, Roger. "Baptist Distinctives among other denominations." Minneapolis: Central Baptist Theological Seminary, n.d.

Pick, B. "The Vowel-Points Controversy in the XVI, XVII, and XVIII Centuries." *The Princeton Review* 6 (January 1877): 163-168.

Pinnock, Clark H. "Our Source of Authority: The Bible." *Bibliotheca Sacra* 124 (April 1967): 150-156.

Porcher, Jr., Joel P. "Psalm 12:6-7 Grammatical Study of the Hebrew Text and the Rendering of the Authorized Version in English." Pensacola, FL: Pensacola Theological Seminary, 2001.

Reeve, J. J. "My Personal Experience with the Higher Criticism" in *The Fundamentals – A Testimony to the Truth*, vol. 1. Edited by R. A. Torrey, A. C. Dixon, et. al. In *The Master Christian Library*, version 8 [CD-ROM]. Rio, WI: Ages Software, 2000.

Rippon, John. "A Brief Memoir of the Life and Writings of the Reverend and Learned John Gill, D.D." in vol. 1 of *An Exposition of the Old Testament*. London: Mathews and Leigh, 1810, reprinted, Paris, Arkansas: The Baptist Standard Bearer, 1989.

Ryken, Leland. "The Bible as Literature" in *The Origin of the Bible*. Edited by Philip Wesley Comfort. Wheaton, IL: Tyndale House Publishers, Inc., 1992.

Shaylor, Randolph. "Our Final Authority" in *From the Mind of God to the Mind of Man: A Layman's Guide to How We Got Out Bible*, 3d ed. Edited by James B. Williams. Greenville, SC: Ambassador-Emerald International, 1999.

Stigers, Harold G. "Preservation: The Corollary of Inspiration." *Journal of the Evangelical Theological Society* 22 (1979): 217-222.

Strouse, Thomas M. "Article Review: A review of Combs, William W. 'The Preservation of Scripture.' " Newington, CT: Emmanuel Baptist Theological Seminary, 2001.

_____. "Luke 16:17 – One Tittle." *Emmanuel Baptist Theological Journal* 2 (Spring 2006): 7-23.

_____. "Psalm 12:6-7 and the Permanent Preservation of God's Words." Newington, CT: Emmanuel Baptist Theological Seminary, 2001.

_____. "Scholarly Myths Perpetuated on Rejecting the Masoretic Text of the OT." *Emmanuel Baptist Theological Journal* 1 (Spring 2005): 37-64.

_____. "The Lord Jesus Christ and 'Scribal Errors'." Newington, CT: Emmanuel Baptist Theological Seminary, 2002.

_____. "The Lord Jesus Christ and the Received Bible John 17:8." Newington, CT: Emmanuel Baptist Theological Seminary, 2002.

_____. "The Permanent Preservation of God's Words." *Emmanuel Baptist Theological Journal* 2 (Fall/Winter 2006): 27-36.

_____. "Who is this Deity names Yahweh?" *The Biblical Astronomer* 15 (Winter 2005): 15-23.

Thomas, W. H. Griffith. "Old Testament Criticism and New Testament Christianity" in *The Fundamentals – A Testimony to the Truth*, vol. 1. Edited by R. A. Torrey, A. C. Dixon, et. al. In *The Master Christian Library*, version 8 [CD-ROM]. Rio, WI: Ages Software, 2000.

Turretin, Francis. "The Holy Scriptures" in vol. 1 of *Institutes of Elenctic Theology*. Trans. by George Musgrave Giger. Edited by James T. Dennison, Jr. Phillipsburg, NJ: P & R Publishing, 1992.

Voetius, Gisbert. "Selectae Disputationes Theologicae" in *Reformed Dogmatics*. Edited and Trans. by John W. Beardslee III. NY: Oxford University Press, 1965.

Walvoord, John F. "The Pragmatic Confirmation of Scriptural Authority" in *The Bible – The Living Word of Revelation*. Edited by Merrill C. Tenney. Grand Rapids: Zondervan, 1968.

Watts, Malcolm H. "The Lord Gave the Word: A Study in the History of the Biblical Text" available from http:\www.triniarianbiblesociety.org. Internet.

Webb, Gary. "Not One Jot or One Tittle Matthew 5:17,18" in *Thou Shalt Keep Them: A Biblical Theology of the Perfect Preservation of Scripture*. Edited by Kent Brandenburg. El Sobrante, CA: Pillar & Ground Publishing, 2003.

Wheeler, John. "Music of the Temple." *Bible and Spade* 2 (Winter 1989): 12-19.

_____. "The Origin of the Music of the Temple." *Bible and Spade* 2 (Autumn 1989): 113-122.

Wilson, Robert Dick. "Is the Higher Criticism Scholarly?" in *Which Bible?* Edited by David Otis Fuller. Grand Rapids: Grand Rapids International Publications, 1978.

Woudstra, Marten H. "The Inspiration of the Old Testament" in *The Bible – The Living Word of Revelation*. Edited by Merrill C. Tenney. Grand Rapids: Zondervan, 1968.

Wright, George Frederick. "The Testimony of the Monuments to the Truth of the Scriptures" in *The Fundamentals – A Testimony to the Truth*, vol. 1. Edited by R. A. Torrey, A. C. Dixon, et. al. In *The Master Christian Library*, version 8 [CD-ROM]. Rio, WI: Ages Software, 2000.

Young, Edward J. "Are the Scriptures Inerrant?" in *The Bible – The Living Word of Revelation*. Edited by Merrill C. Tenney. Grand Rapids: Zondervan, 1968.

BIOGRAPHICAL SKETCH

Dr. Chester W. Kulus received Christ in 1975 after graduating from Tilton School in Tilton, New Hampshire. In response to an invitation from one of the school's janitors, he attended "The Burning Hell," a film put on by Calvary Independent Baptist Church, which was renting the school's chapel. At the invitation, Dr. Kulus responded and received Jesus Christ as his personal Savior. The following year he attended Worcester Polytechnic Institute and, while being an active witness for Christ, answered the call to enter the ministry. In the fall of 1976, he transferred to Bob Jones University and graduated in 1979 with a B. A. in Pastoral Studies. During his time at college, he married Miss Nancy Dowie who had also received Christ through the same ministry in Tilton.

After college, Dr. Kulus desired more training and, at that time, made an unpopular decision with his alma mater to attend Calvary Baptist Theological Seminary in Lansdale, PA. He received his M. Div. in 1982 and started work on a Th. M. the following year. In 1983, through God's leading, and under the direction of Pastor G. Richard Anderson, Dr. Kulus started Calvary Independent Baptist Church in a storefront on Main Street in Enfield, NH, an area where there was no Independent Baptist Church. In 1998, through God's grace, the church purchased a piece of land in Lebanon and built a new building just off exit 17 of Interstate-89 and is still there today.

In 2001, Dr. Kulus started taking video-courses with Emmanuel Baptist Theological Seminary in Newington, CT. By 2003, he had finished his D. Min. work and graduated in May of the same year. In the summer of 2003, he published his first book, *Those So-Called Errors: Debunking the Liberal, New Evangelical, and Fundamentalist Myth that You Should Not Hear, Receive, and Believe All the Numbers of Scripture*. After publishing his first book, Dr. Kulus began study toward a Th. D. degree with Emmanuel Baptist Theological Seminary, which he finished in 2006.

In April of 2007 with the passing of Dr. Anderson, the pastor of Calvary Independent Baptist Churches of Plymouth and Tilton, NH, Dr. Kulus became the interim-pastor of those churches as well as the principal of Calvary Christian School, a ministry of the church in Plymouth. In January of 2008, Dr. Kulus, in addition to pastoring the Calvary Independent Baptist Church of Lebanon, became the pastor of the Calvary Independent Baptist Churches of Plymouth and Tilton. The Lord has blessed in great ways and Dr. Kulus thanks the Lord for His strength and wisdom and the opportunity to serve such a wonderful Saviour.

www.ingramcontent.com/pod-product-compliance
Lightning Source LLC
Chambersburg PA
CBHW071940220426
43662CB00009B/931